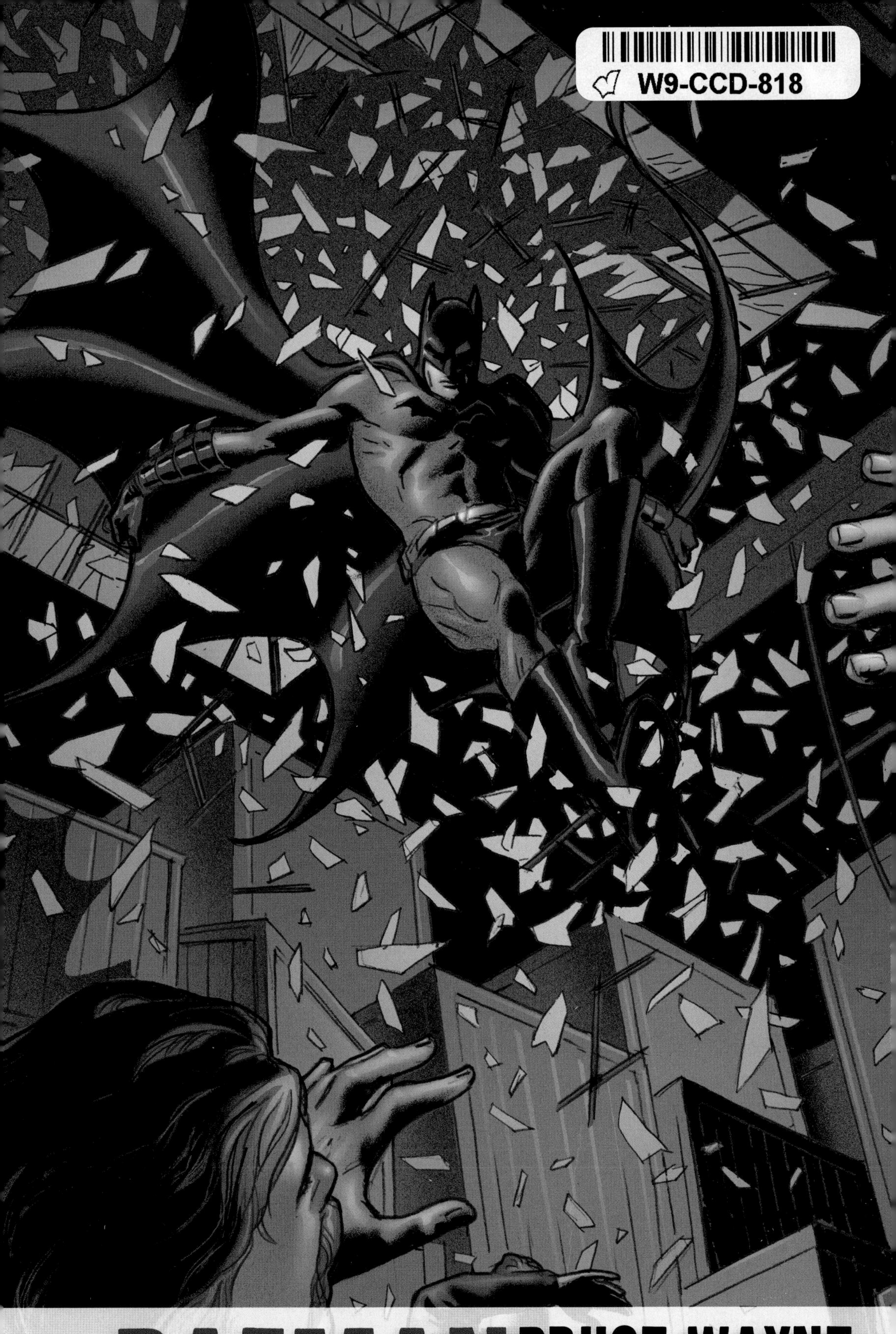

BATMAN BRUCE WAYNE THE ROAD HOME

Written by
Fabian Nicieza
Mike W. Barr
Bryan Q. Miller
Derek Fridolfs
Adam Beechen
Marc Andreyko

Art by
Cliff Richards
Ramon Bachs
John Lucas
Javier Saltares
Rebecca Buchman
Walden Wong
Pere Perez
Peter Nguyen
Ryan Winn
Szymon Kudranski
Agustin Padilla
Scott McDaniel
Andy Owens

Colors by
Ian Hannin
Guy Major
Pete Pantazis
John Kalisz
Brian Buccellato

Letters by
Dave Sharpe

Cover Art and Original Series Covers by
Shane Davis and Barbara Ciardo

Publication Design by
Louis Prandi

Batman created by Bob Kane

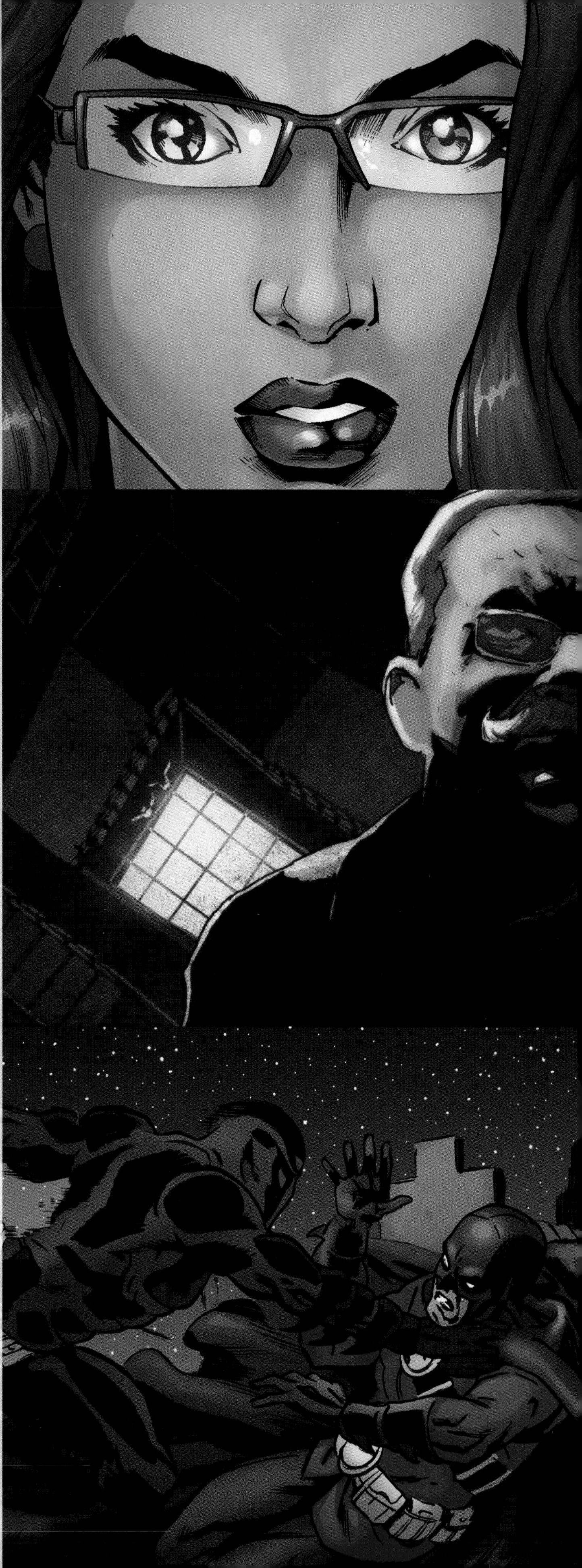

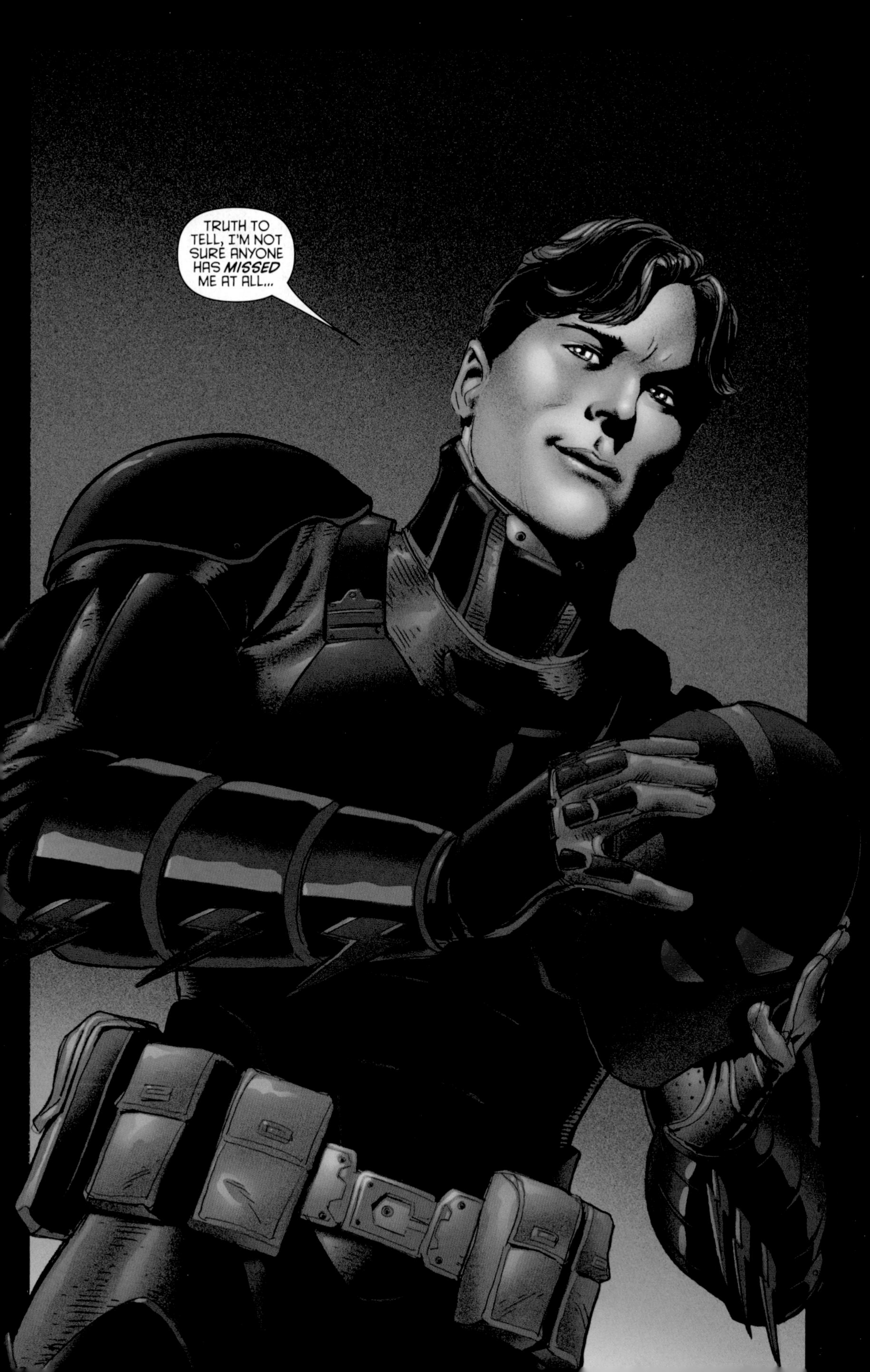
TRUTH TO TELL, I'M NOT SURE ANYONE HAS *MISSED* ME AT ALL...

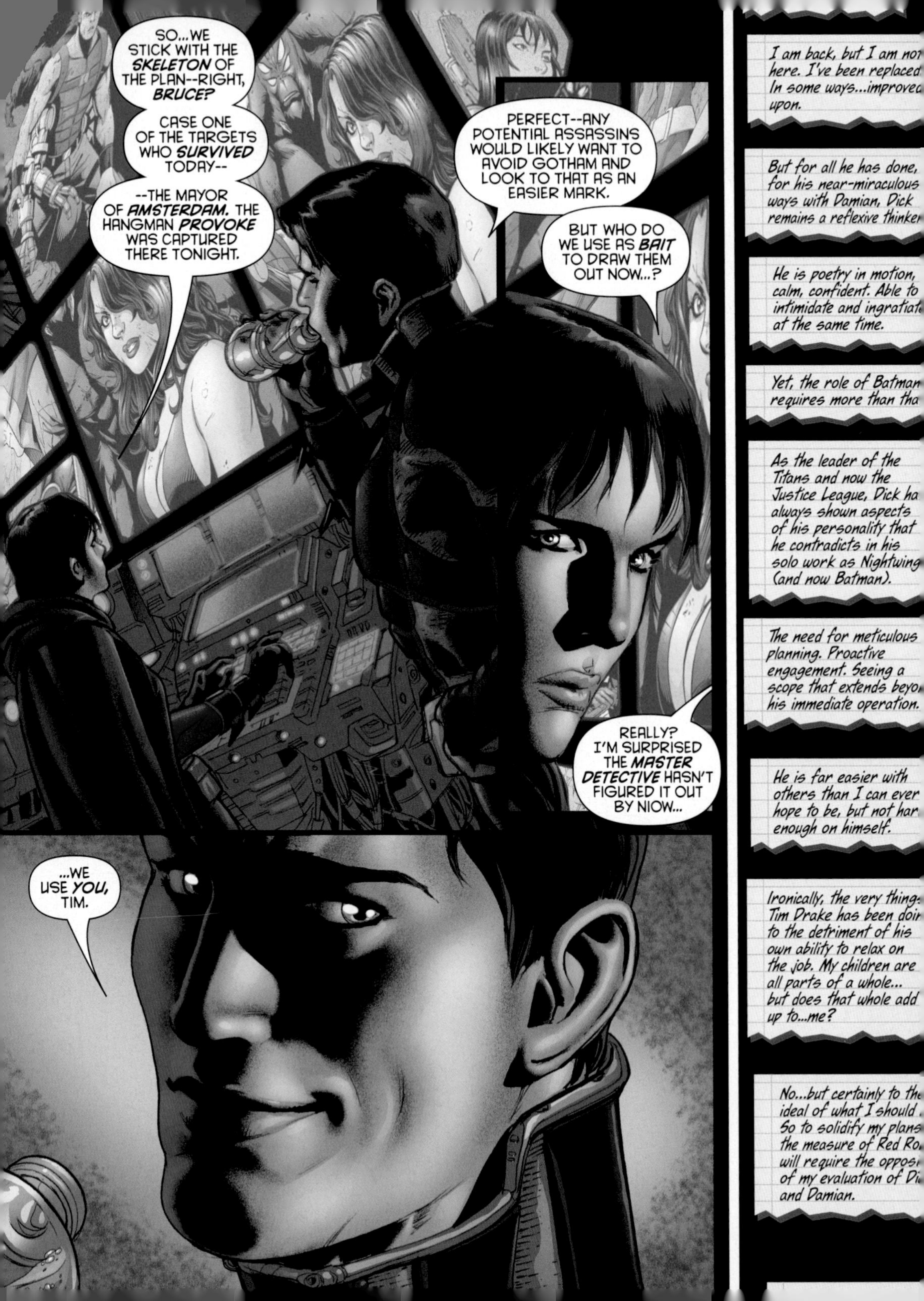
SO...WE STICK WITH THE SKELETON OF THE PLAN--RIGHT, BRUCE?
CASE ONE OF THE TARGETS WHO SURVIVED TODAY--
--THE MAYOR OF AMSTERDAM. THE HANGMAN PROVOKE WAS CAPTURED THERE TONIGHT.
PERFECT--ANY POTENTIAL ASSASSINS WOULD LIKELY WANT TO AVOID GOTHAM AND LOOK TO THAT AS AN EASIER MARK.
BUT WHO DO WE USE AS BAIT TO DRAW THEM OUT NOW...?
REALLY? I'M SURPRISED THE MASTER DETECTIVE HASN'T FIGURED IT OUT BY NIOW...
...WE USE YOU, TIM.
I am back, but I am no here. I've been replace In some ways...improve upon.
But for all he has done, for his near-miraculous ways with Damian, Dick remains a reflexive thinke
He is poetry in motion, calm, confident. Able to intimidate and ingratia at the same time.
Yet, the role of Batma requires more than th
As the leader of the Titans and now the Justice League, Dick ha always shown aspects of his personality that he contradicts in his solo work as Nightwing (and now Batman).
The need for meticulous planning. Proactive engagement. Seeing a scope that extends beyo his immediate operation.
He is far easier with others than I can ever hope to be, but not har enough on himself.
Ironically, the very thing Tim Drake has been doi to the detriment of his own ability to relax on the job. My children are all parts of a whole... but does that whole add up to...me?
No...but certainly to th ideal of what I should So to solidify my plan the measure of Red Ro will require the oppos of my evaluation of D and Damian.

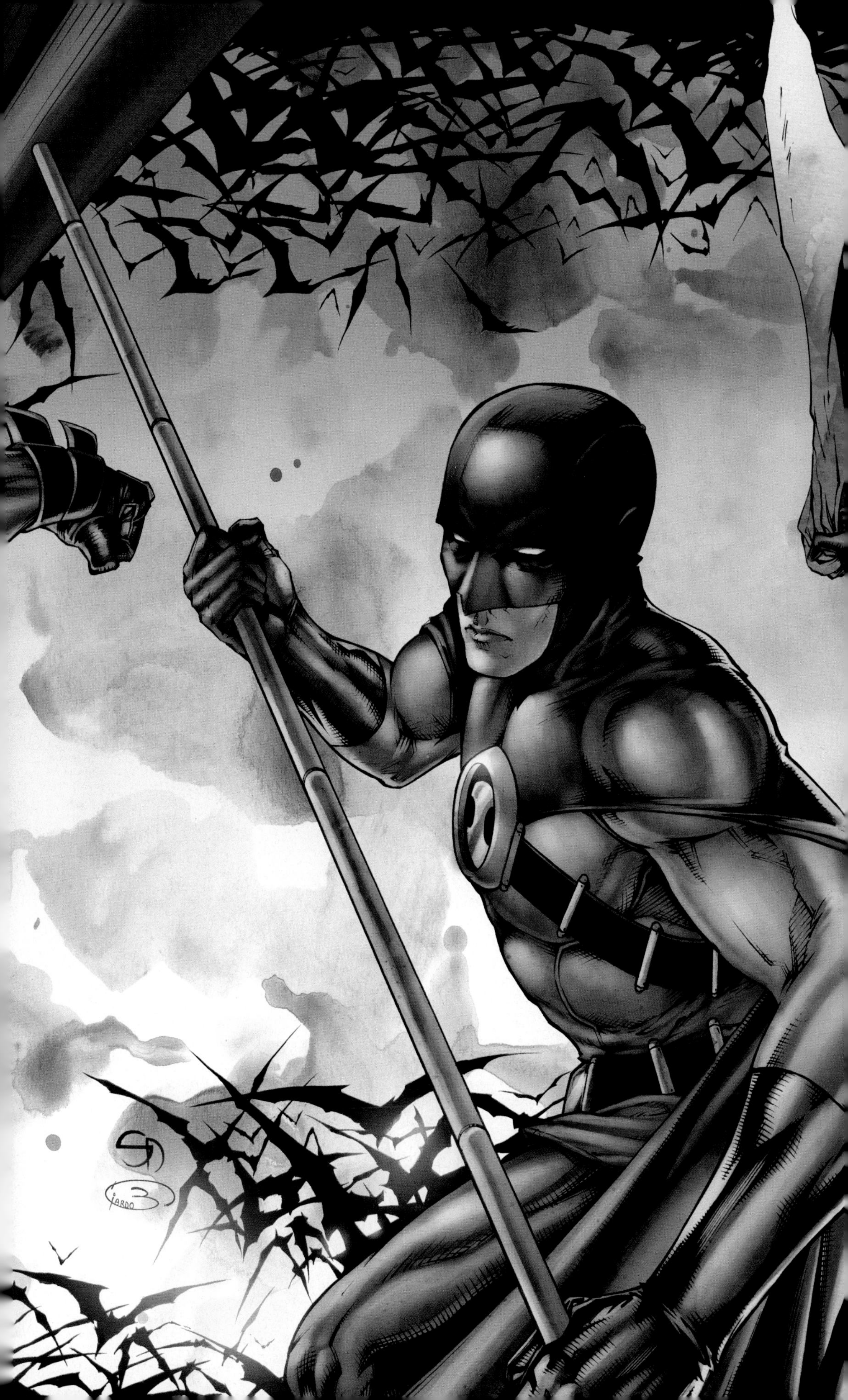

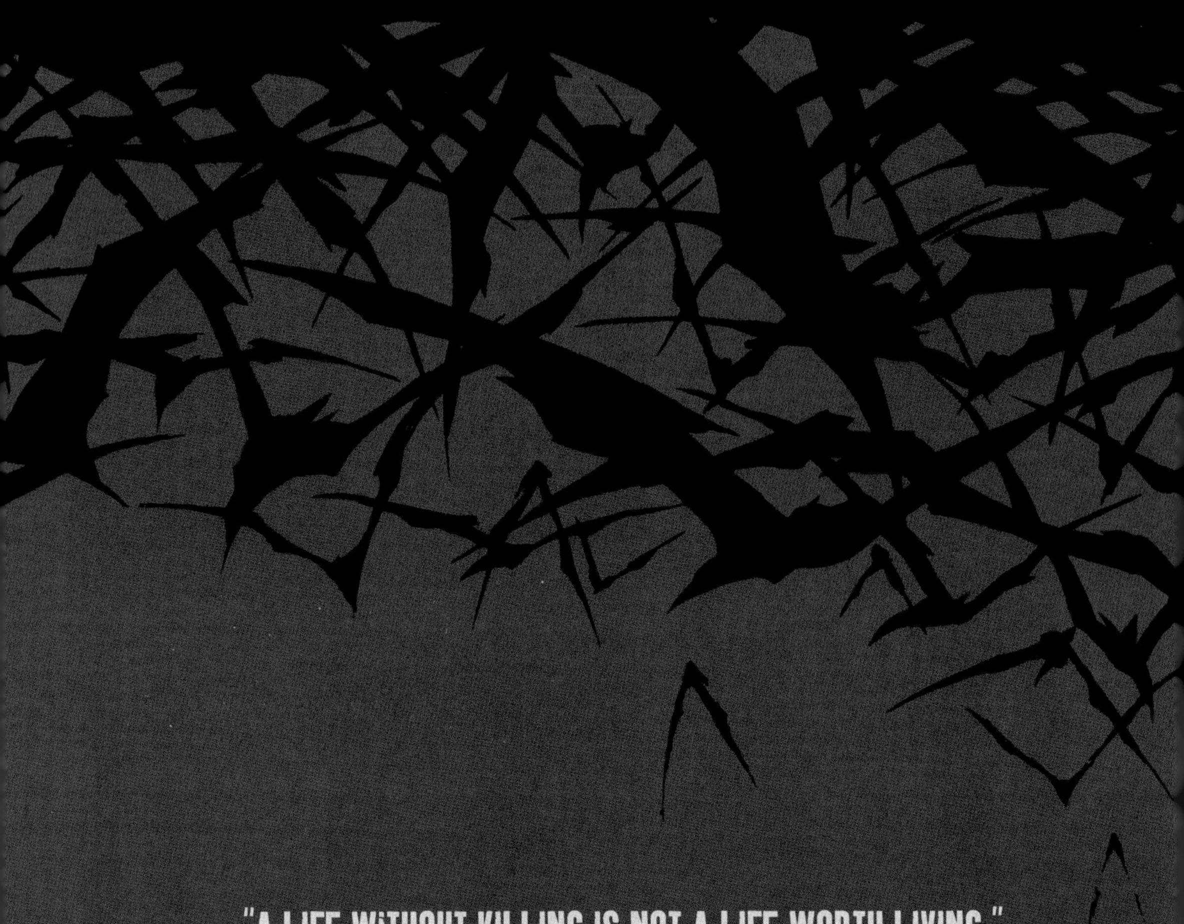

"A LIFE WITHOUT KILLING IS NOT A LIFE WORTH LIVING."

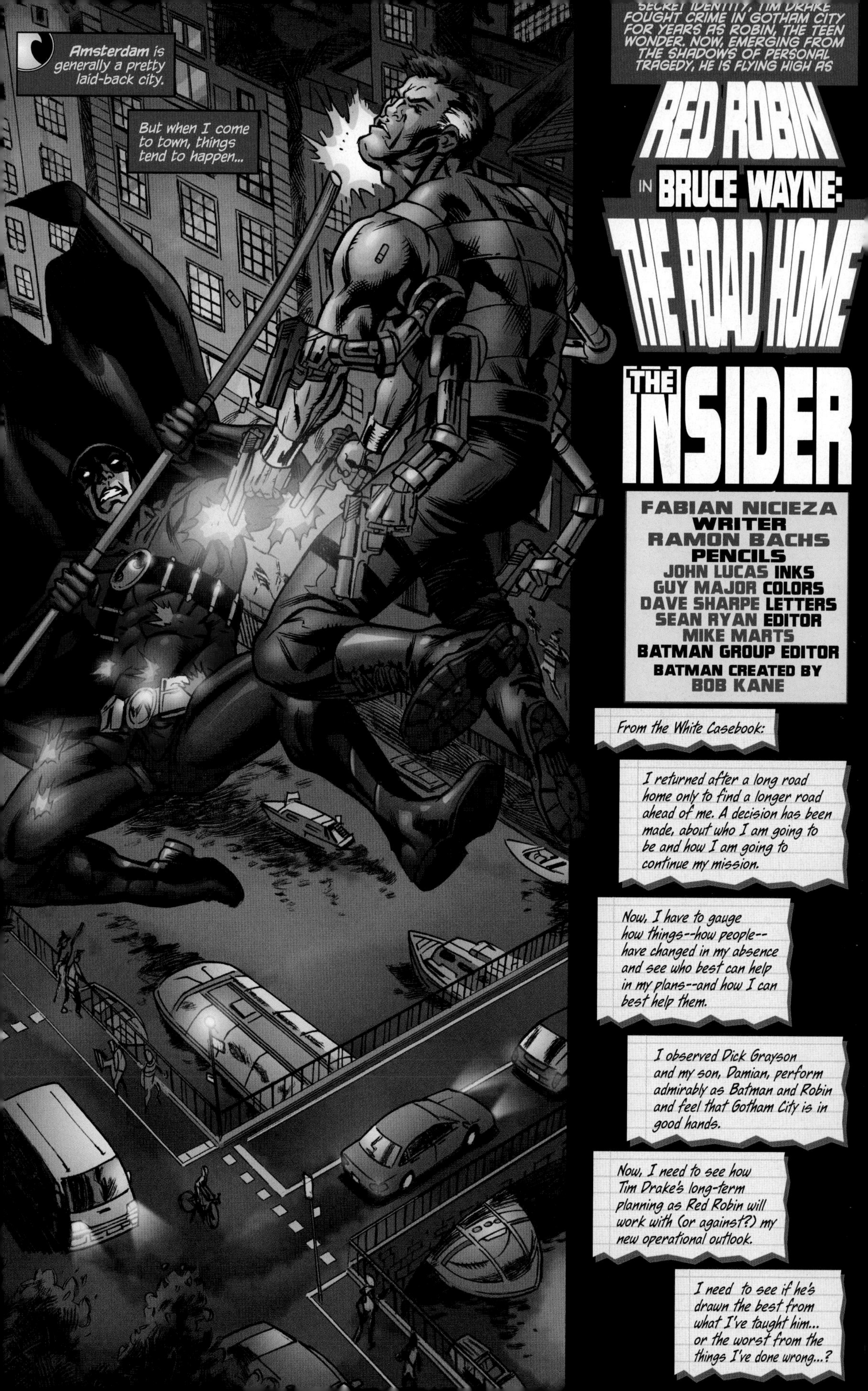

Amsterdam is generally a pretty laid-back city.
But when I come to town, things tend to happen...
SECRET IDENTITY, TIM DRAKE FOUGHT CRIME IN GOTHAM CITY FOR YEARS AS ROBIN, THE TEEN WONDER. NOW, EMERGING FROM THE SHADOWS OF PERSONAL TRAGEDY, HE IS FLYING HIGH AS
RED ROBIN
IN BRUCE WAYNE: THE ROAD HOME
THE INSIDER
FABIAN NICIEZA WRITER
RAMON BACHS PENCILS
JOHN LUCAS INKS
GUY MAJOR COLORS
DAVE SHARPE LETTERS
SEAN RYAN EDITOR
MIKE MARTS BATMAN GROUP EDITOR
BATMAN CREATED BY BOB KANE
From the White Casebook:
I returned after a long road home only to find a longer road ahead of me. A decision has been made, about who I am going to be and how I am going to continue my mission.
Now, I have to gauge how things--how people--have changed in my absence and see who best can help in my plans--and how I can best help them.
I observed Dick Grayson and my son, Damian, perform admirably as Batman and Robin and feel that Gotham City is in good hands.
Now, I need to see how Tim Drake's long-term planning as Red Robin will work with (or against?) my new operational outlook.
I need to see if he's drawn the best from what I've taught him... or the worst from the things I've done wrong...?

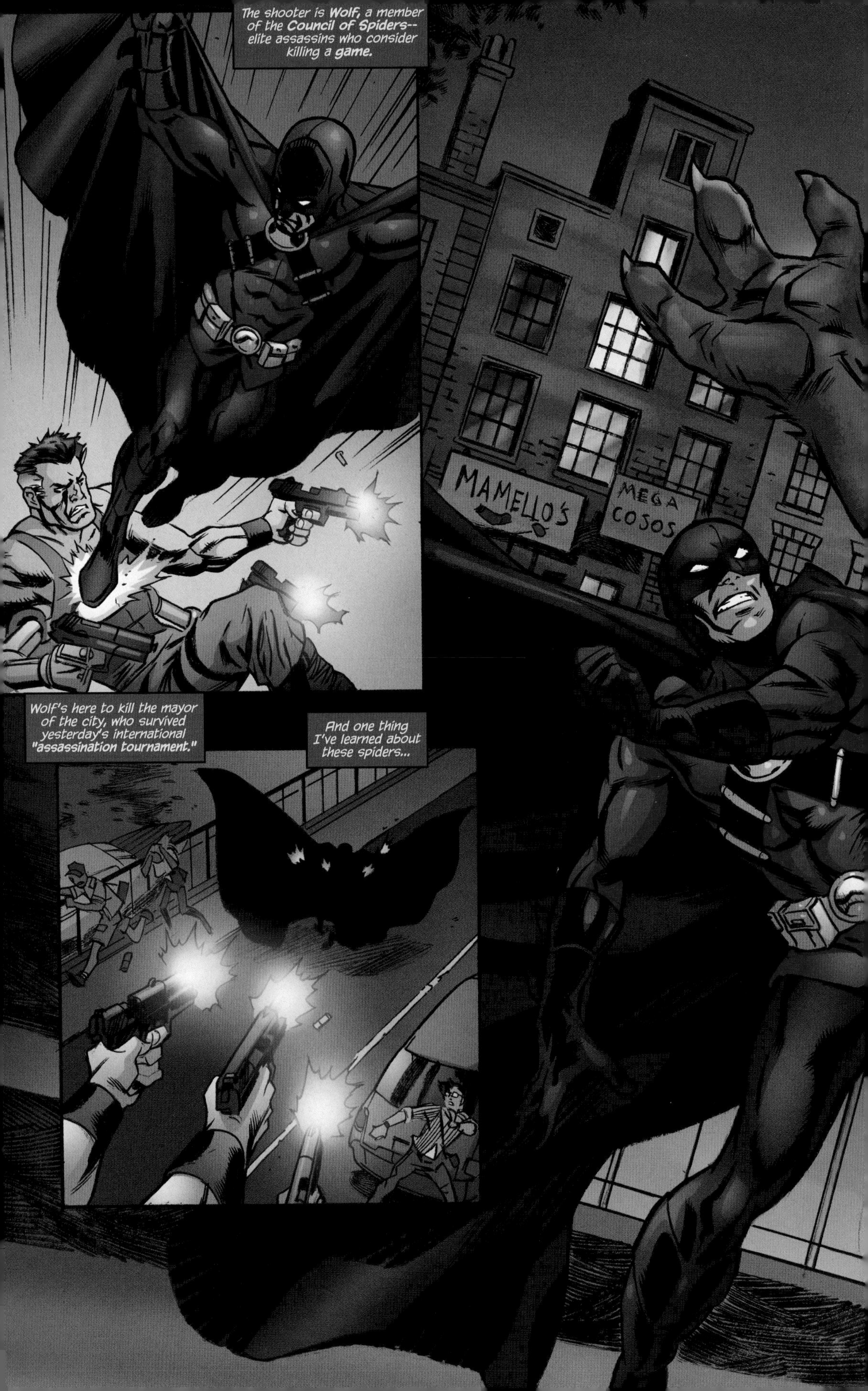
The shooter is Wolf, a member of the Council of Spiders-- elite assassins who consider killing a game.
MAMELLO'S
MEGA COSOS
Wolf's here to kill the mayor of the city, who survived yesterday's international "assassination tournament."
And one thing I've learned about these spiders...

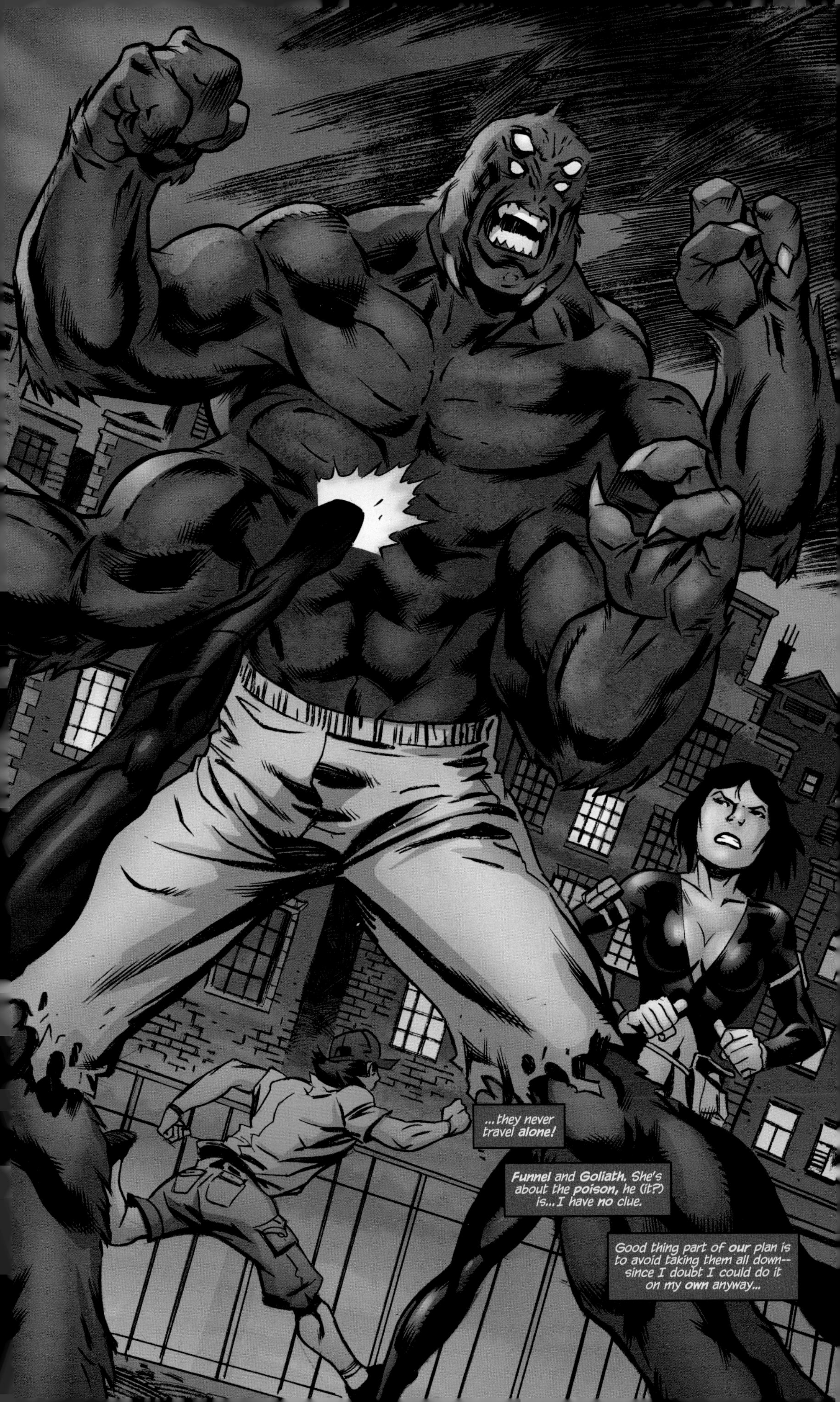
...they never travel alone!
Funnel and Goliath. She's about the poison, he (it?) is...I have no clue.
Good thing part of our plan is to avoid taking them all down--since I doubt I could do it on my own anyway...

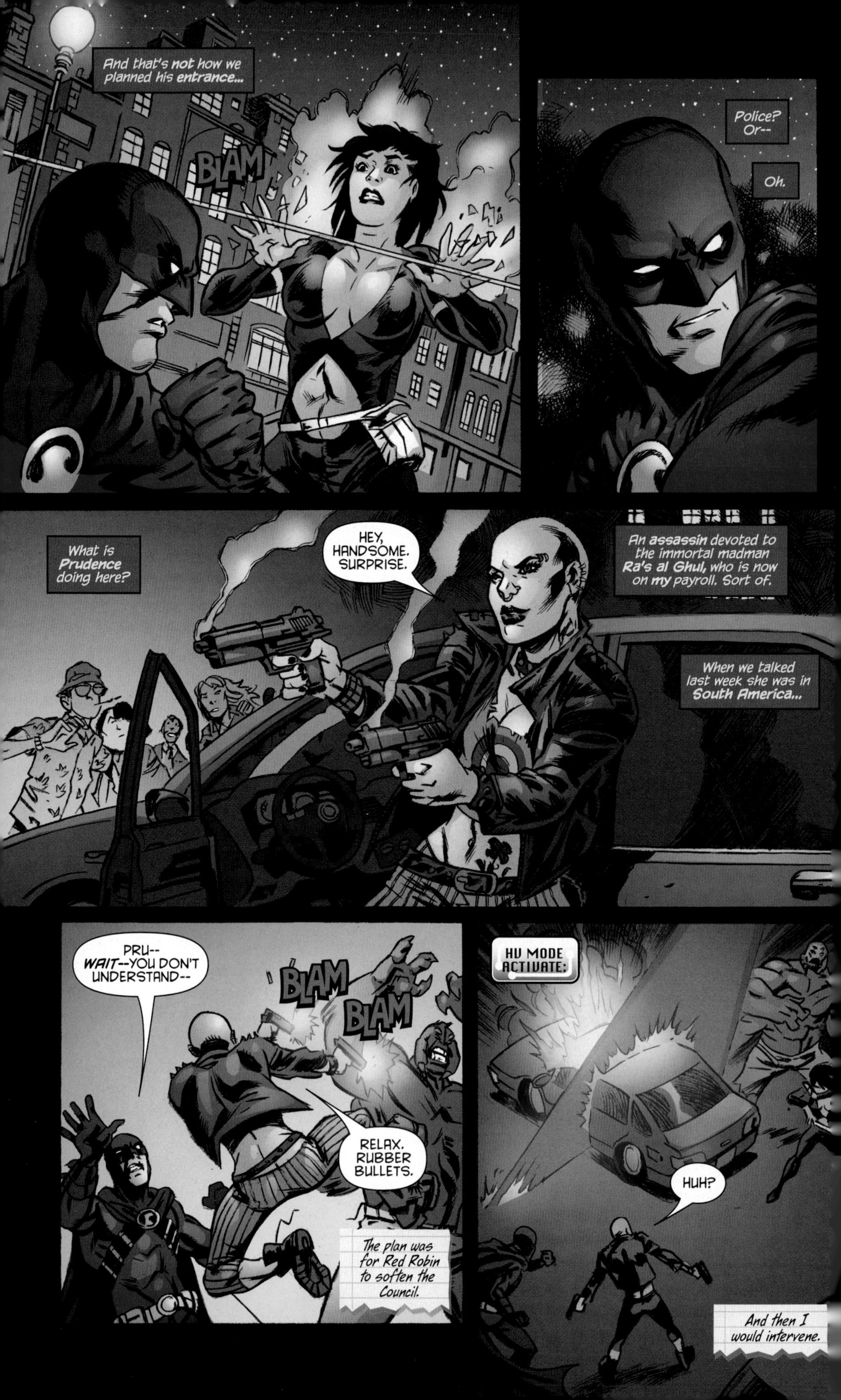

And that's not how we planned his entrance...
BLAM
Police? Or--
Oh.
What is Prudence doing here?
HEY, HANDSOME. SURPRISE.
An assassin devoted to the immortal madman Ra's al Ghul, who is now on my payroll. Sort of.
When we talked last week she was in South America...
PRU-- WAIT--YOU DON'T UNDERSTAND--
BLAM
BLAM
RELAX. RUBBER BULLETS.
The plan was for Red Robin to soften the Council.
HV MODE ACTIVATE:
HUH?
And then I would intervene.

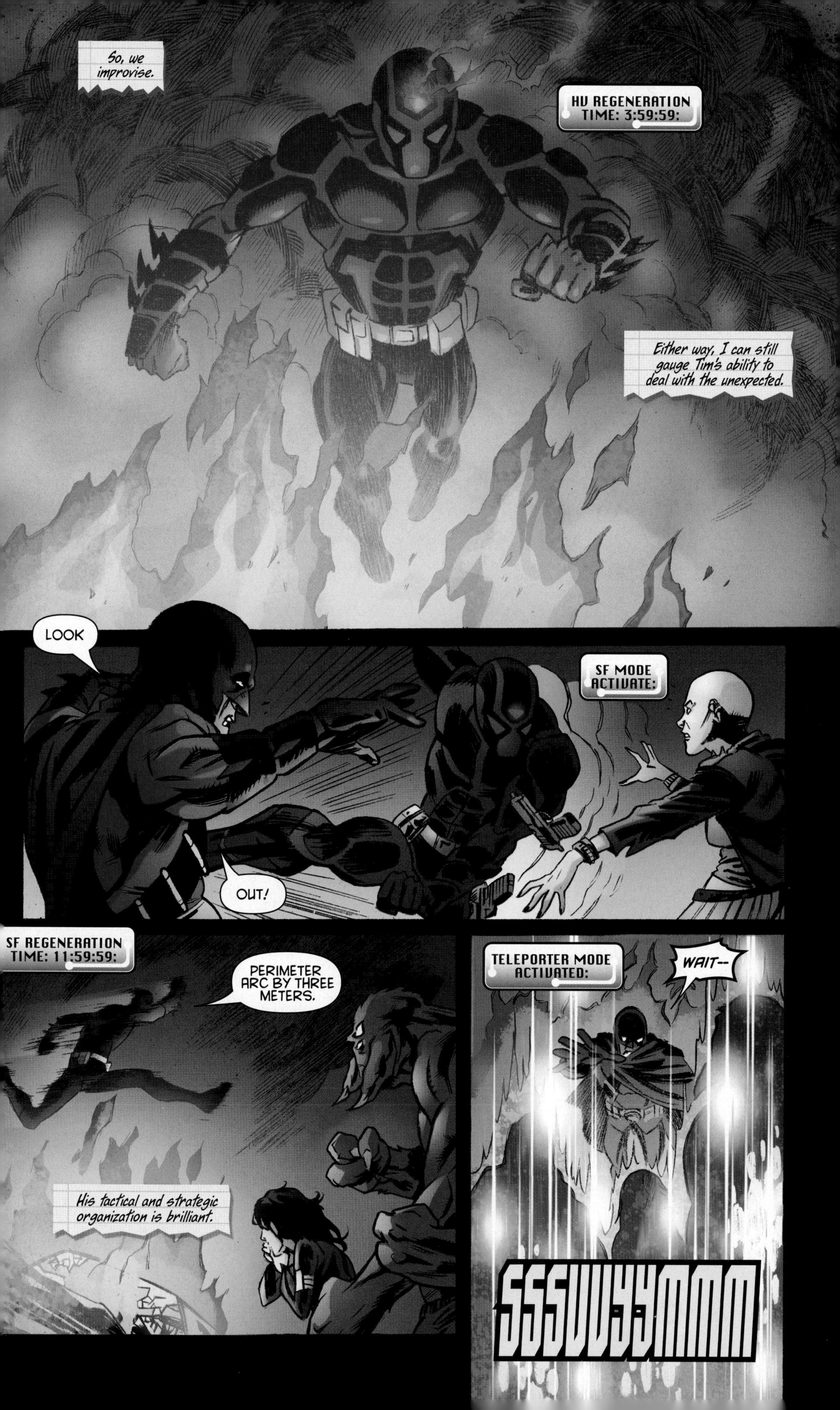

So, we improvise.
HV REGENERATION TIME: 3:59:59:
Either way, I can still gauge Tim's ability to deal with the unexpected.
LOOK
SF MODE ACTIVATE:
OUT!
SF REGENERATION TIME: 11:59:59:
PERIMETER ARC BY THREE METERS.
His tactical and strategic organization is brilliant.
TELEPORTER MODE ACTIVATED:
WAIT--
SSSVVYSMMMM

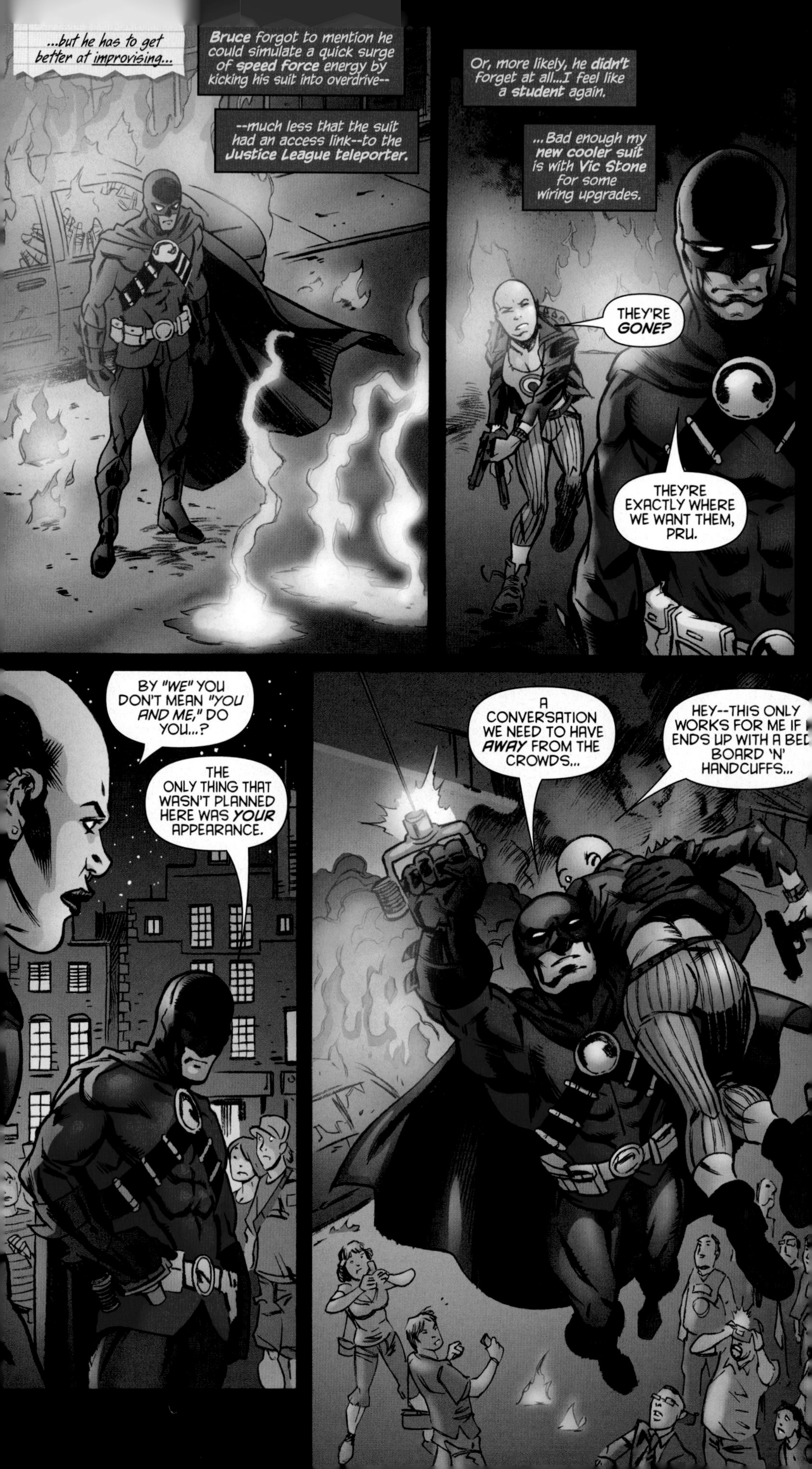
...but he has to get better at improvising...
Bruce forgot to mention he could simulate a quick surge of speed force energy by kicking his suit into overdrive--
--much less that the suit had an access link--to the Justice League teleporter.
Or, more likely, he didn't forget at all...I feel like a student again.
...Bad enough my new cooler suit is with Vic Stone for some wiring upgrades.
THEY'RE GONE?
THEY'RE EXACTLY WHERE WE WANT THEM, PRU.
BY "WE" YOU DON'T MEAN "YOU AND ME," DO YOU...?
THE ONLY THING THAT WASN'T PLANNED HERE WAS YOUR APPEARANCE.
A CONVERSATION WE NEED TO HAVE AWAY FROM THE CROWDS...
HEY--THIS ONLY WORKS FOR ME IF ENDS UP WITH A BED BOARD 'N' HANDCUFFS...

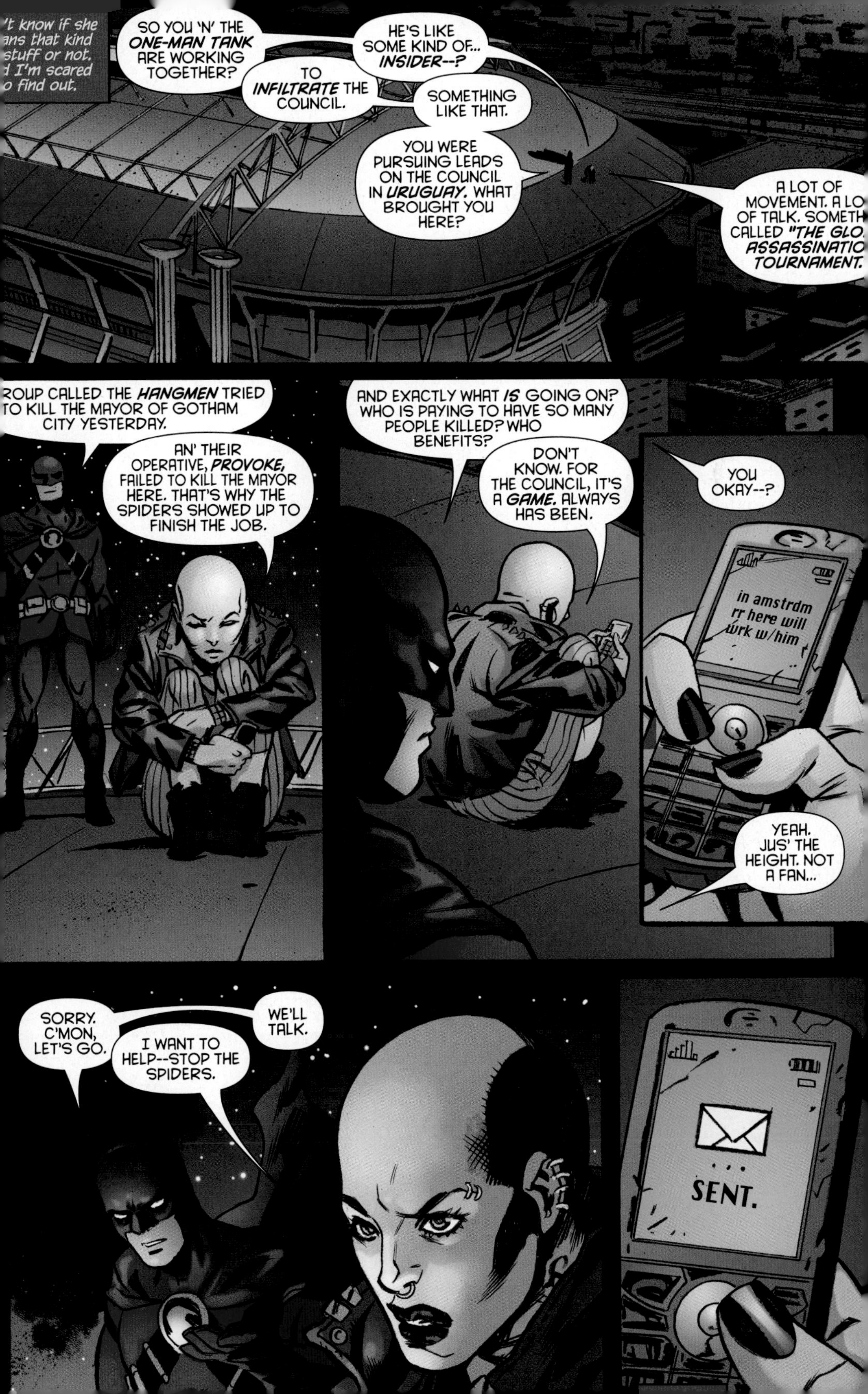
't know if she
ans that kind
stuff or not.
d I'm scared
o find out.
SO YOU 'N' THE ONE-MAN TANK ARE WORKING TOGETHER?
HE'S LIKE SOME KIND OF... INSIDER--?
TO INFILTRATE THE COUNCIL.
SOMETHING LIKE THAT.
YOU WERE PURSUING LEADS ON THE COUNCIL IN URUGUAY. WHAT BROUGHT YOU HERE?
A LOT OF MOVEMENT. A LO OF TALK. SOMETH CALLED "THE GLO ASSASSINATIO TOURNAMENT.
ROUP CALLED THE HANGMEN TRIED TO KILL THE MAYOR OF GOTHAM CITY YESTERDAY.
AN' THEIR OPERATIVE, PROVOKE, FAILED TO KILL THE MAYOR HERE. THAT'S WHY THE SPIDERS SHOWED UP TO FINISH THE JOB.
AND EXACTLY WHAT IS GOING ON? WHO IS PAYING TO HAVE SO MANY PEOPLE KILLED? WHO BENEFITS?
DON'T KNOW. FOR THE COUNCIL, IT'S A GAME. ALWAYS HAS BEEN.
YOU OKAY--?
in amstrdm
rr here will
wrk w/him
YEAH. JUS' THE HEIGHT. NOT A FAN...
SORRY. C'MON, LET'S GO.
I WANT TO HELP--STOP THE SPIDERS.
WE'LL TALK.
SENT.

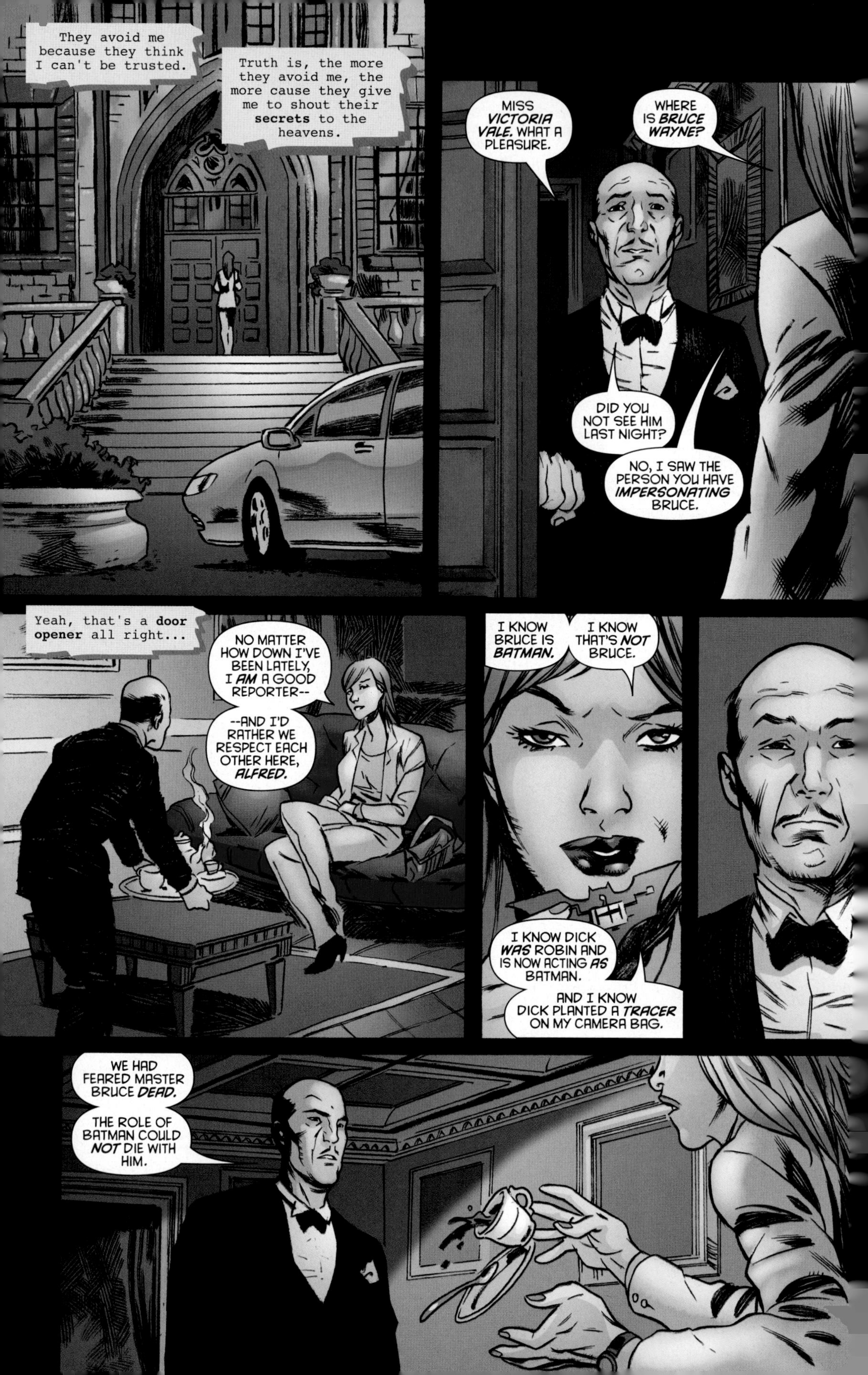
They avoid me because they think I can't be trusted.
Truth is, the more they avoid me, the more cause they give me to shout their **secrets** to the heavens.
MISS *VICTORIA VALE.* WHAT A PLEASURE.
WHERE IS *BRUCE WAYNE?*
DID YOU NOT SEE HIM LAST NIGHT?
NO, I SAW THE PERSON YOU HAVE *IMPERSONATING* BRUCE.
Yeah, that's a **door opener** all right...
NO MATTER HOW DOWN I'VE BEEN LATELY, I *AM* A GOOD REPORTER--
--AND I'D RATHER WE RESPECT EACH OTHER HERE, *ALFRED.*
I KNOW BRUCE IS *BATMAN.*
I KNOW THAT'S *NOT* BRUCE.
I KNOW DICK *WAS* ROBIN AND IS NOW ACTING *AS* BATMAN.
AND I KNOW DICK PLANTED A *TRACER* ON MY CAMERA BAG.
WE HAD FEARED MASTER BRUCE *DEAD.*
THE ROLE OF BATMAN COULD *NOT* DIE WITH HIM.

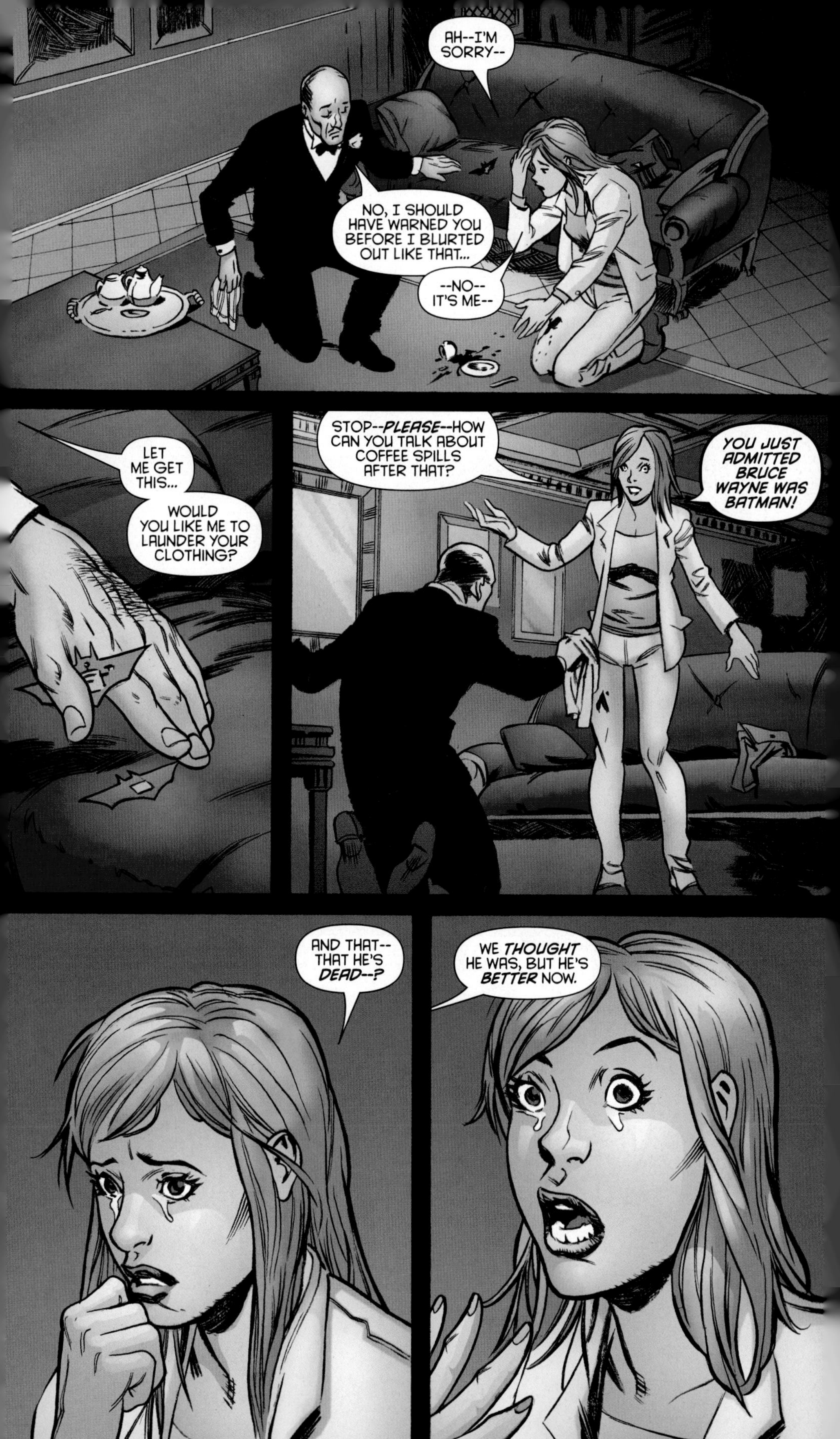
AH--I'M SORRY--
NO, I SHOULD HAVE WARNED YOU BEFORE I BLURTED OUT LIKE THAT...
--NO-- IT'S ME--
LET ME GET THIS...
WOULD YOU LIKE ME TO LAUNDER YOUR CLOTHING?
STOP--PLEASE--HOW CAN YOU TALK ABOUT COFFEE SPILLS AFTER THAT?
YOU JUST ADMITTED BRUCE WAYNE WAS BATMAN!
AND THAT--THAT HE'S DEAD--?
WE THOUGHT HE WAS, BUT HE'S BETTER NOW.

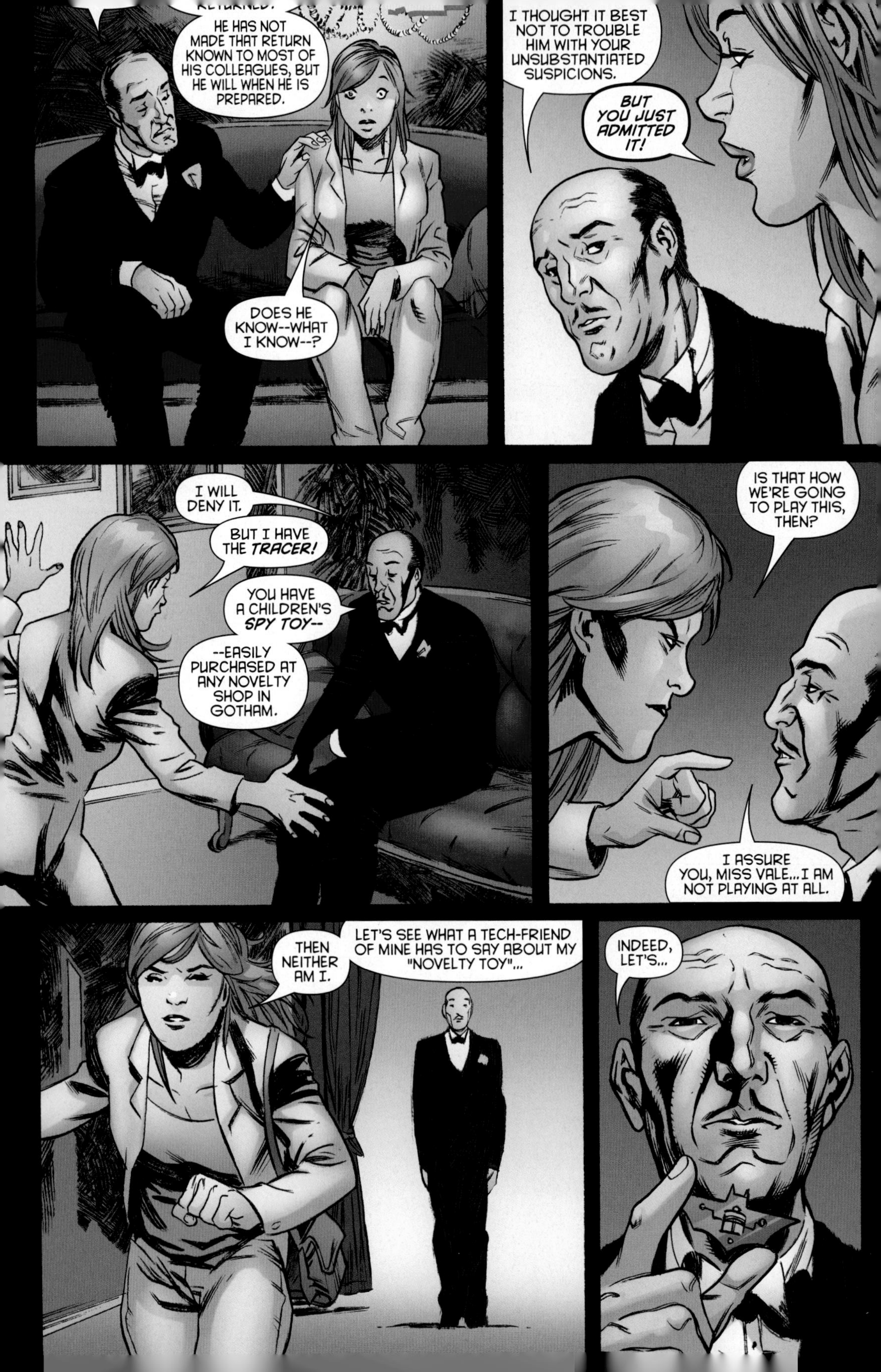
HE HAS NOT MADE THAT RETURN KNOWN TO MOST OF HIS COLLEAGUES, BUT HE WILL WHEN HE IS PREPARED.
DOES HE KNOW--WHAT I KNOW--?
I THOUGHT IT BEST NOT TO TROUBLE HIM WITH YOUR UNSUBSTANTIATED SUSPICIONS.
BUT YOU JUST ADMITTED IT!
I WILL DENY IT.
BUT I HAVE THE TRACER!
YOU HAVE A CHILDREN'S SPY TOY--
--EASILY PURCHASED AT ANY NOVELTY SHOP IN GOTHAM.
IS THAT HOW WE'RE GOING TO PLAY THIS, THEN?
I ASSURE YOU, MISS VALE...I AM NOT PLAYING AT ALL.
THEN NEITHER AM I.
LET'S SEE WHAT A TECH-FRIEND OF MINE HAS TO SAY ABOUT MY "NOVELTY TOY"...
INDEED, LET'S...

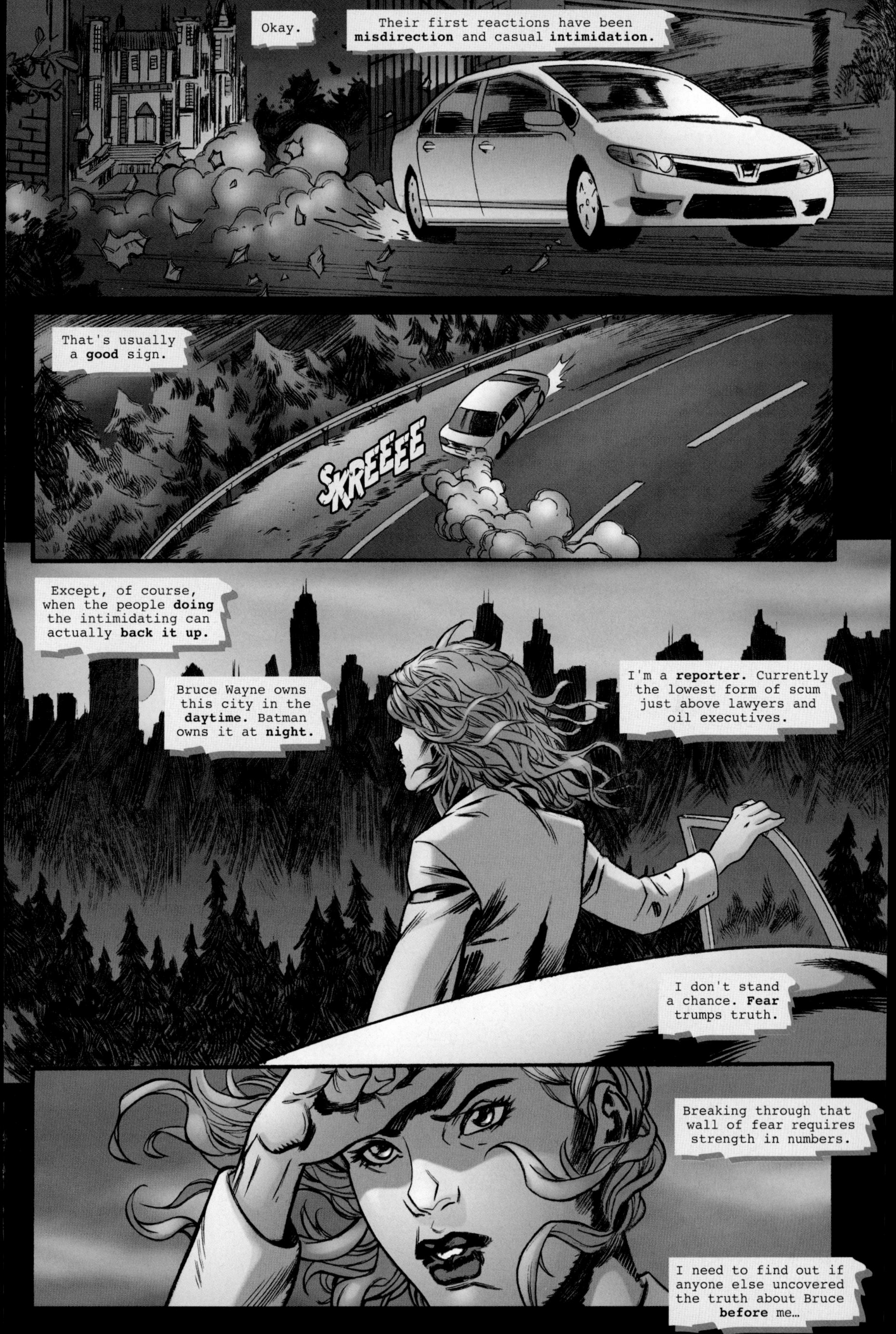
Okay.
Their first reactions have been misdirection and casual intimidation.
That's usually a good sign.
SKREEEE
Except, of course, when the people doing the intimidating can actually back it up.
Bruce Wayne owns this city in the daytime. Batman owns it at night.
I'm a reporter. Currently the lowest form of scum just above lawyers and oil executives.
I don't stand a chance. Fear trumps truth.
Breaking through that wall of fear requires strength in numbers.
I need to find out if anyone else uncovered the truth about Bruce before me…

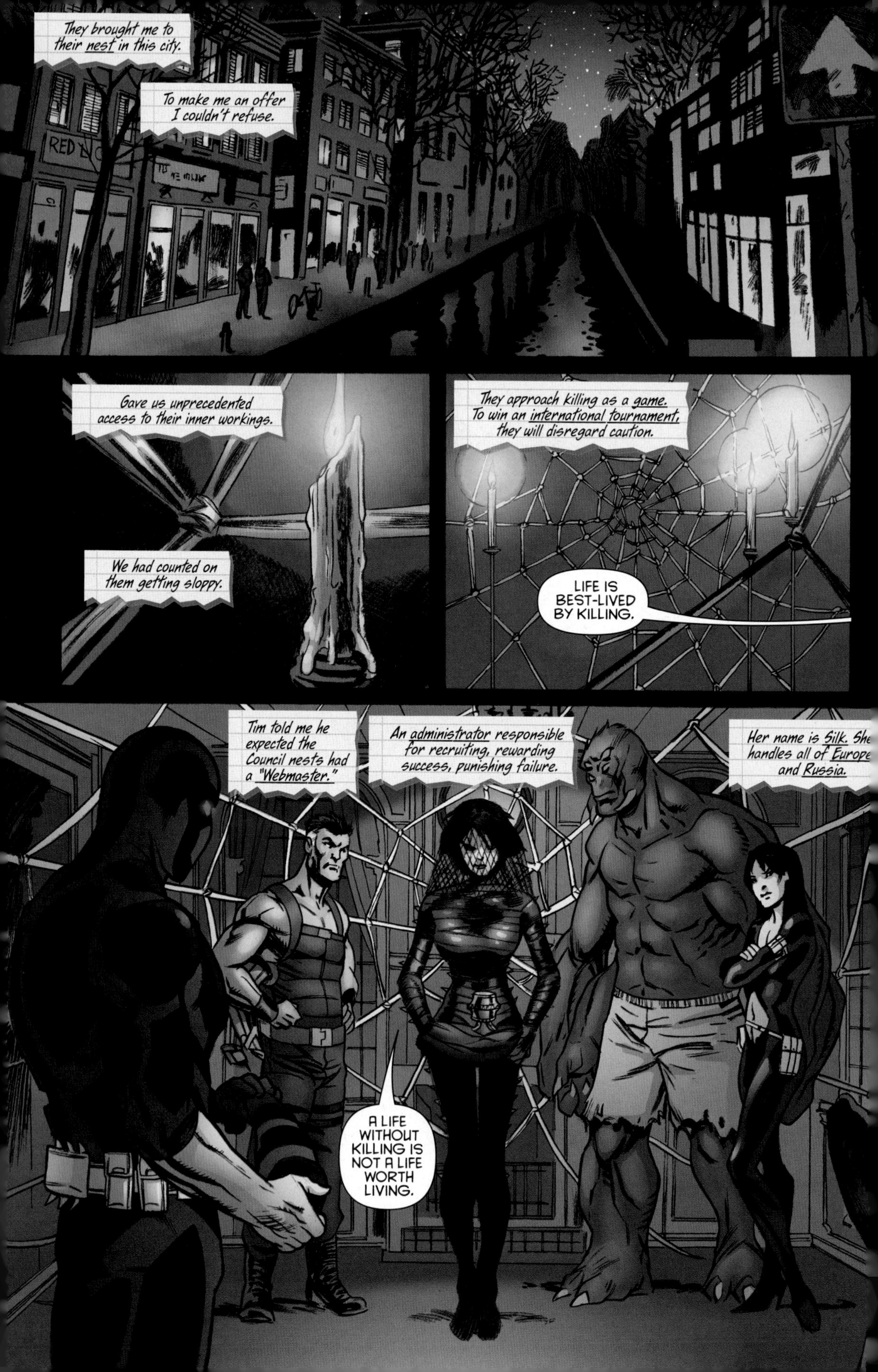
They brought me to their nest in this city.
To make me an offer I couldn't refuse.
Gave us unprecedented access to their inner workings.
We had counted on them getting sloppy.
They approach killing as a game. To win an international tournament, they will disregard caution.
LIFE IS BEST-LIVED BY KILLING.
Tim told me he expected the Council nests had a "Webmaster."
An administrator responsible for recruiting, rewarding success, punishing failure.
Her name is Silk. She handles all of Europe and Russia.
A LIFE WITHOUT KILLING IS NOT A LIFE WORTH LIVING.

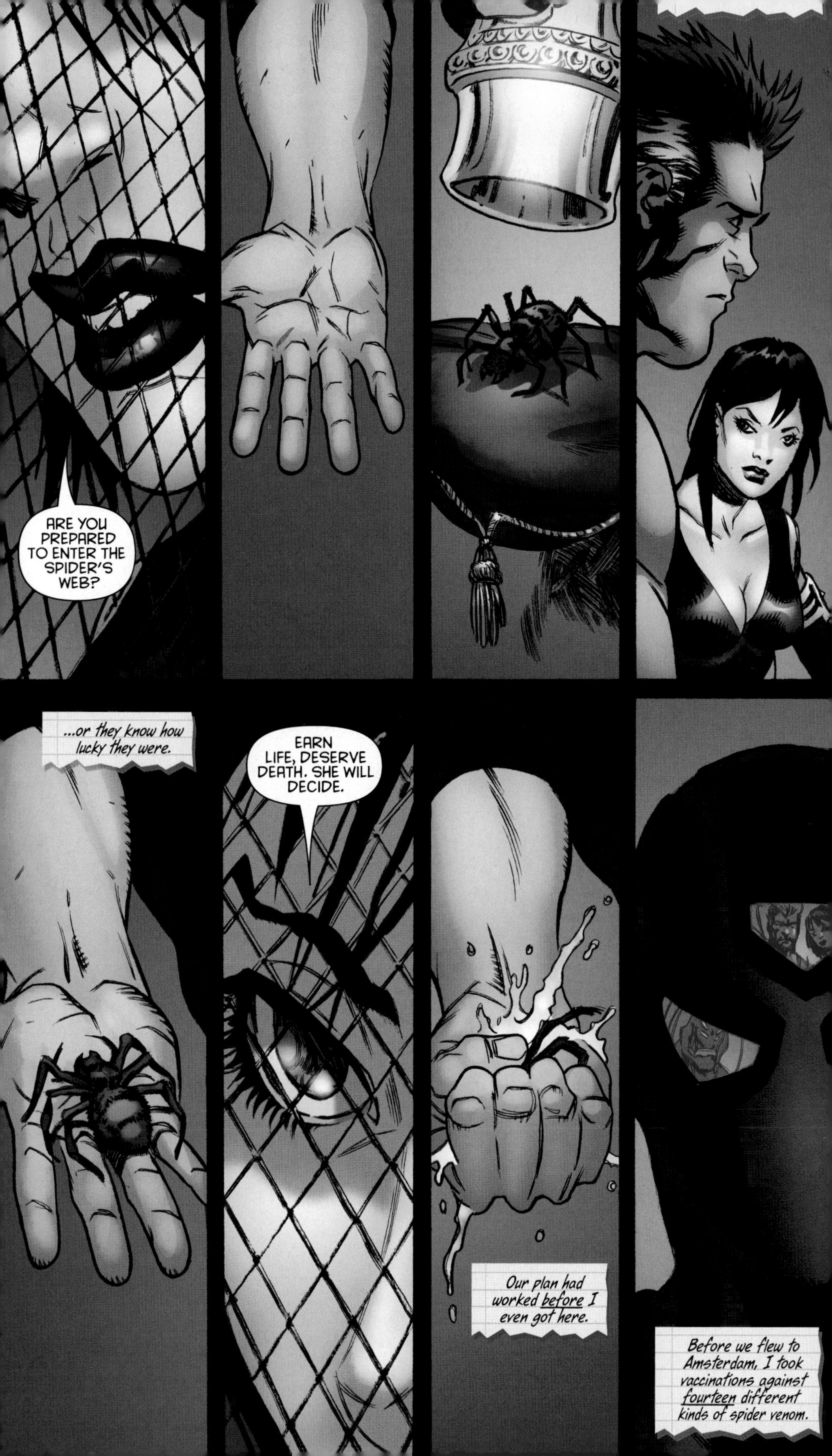

ARE YOU PREPARED TO ENTER THE SPIDER'S WEB?
...or they know how lucky they were.
EARN LIFE, DESERVE DEATH. SHE WILL DECIDE.
Our plan had worked before I even got here.
Before we flew to Amsterdam, I took vaccinations against fourteen different kinds of spider venom.

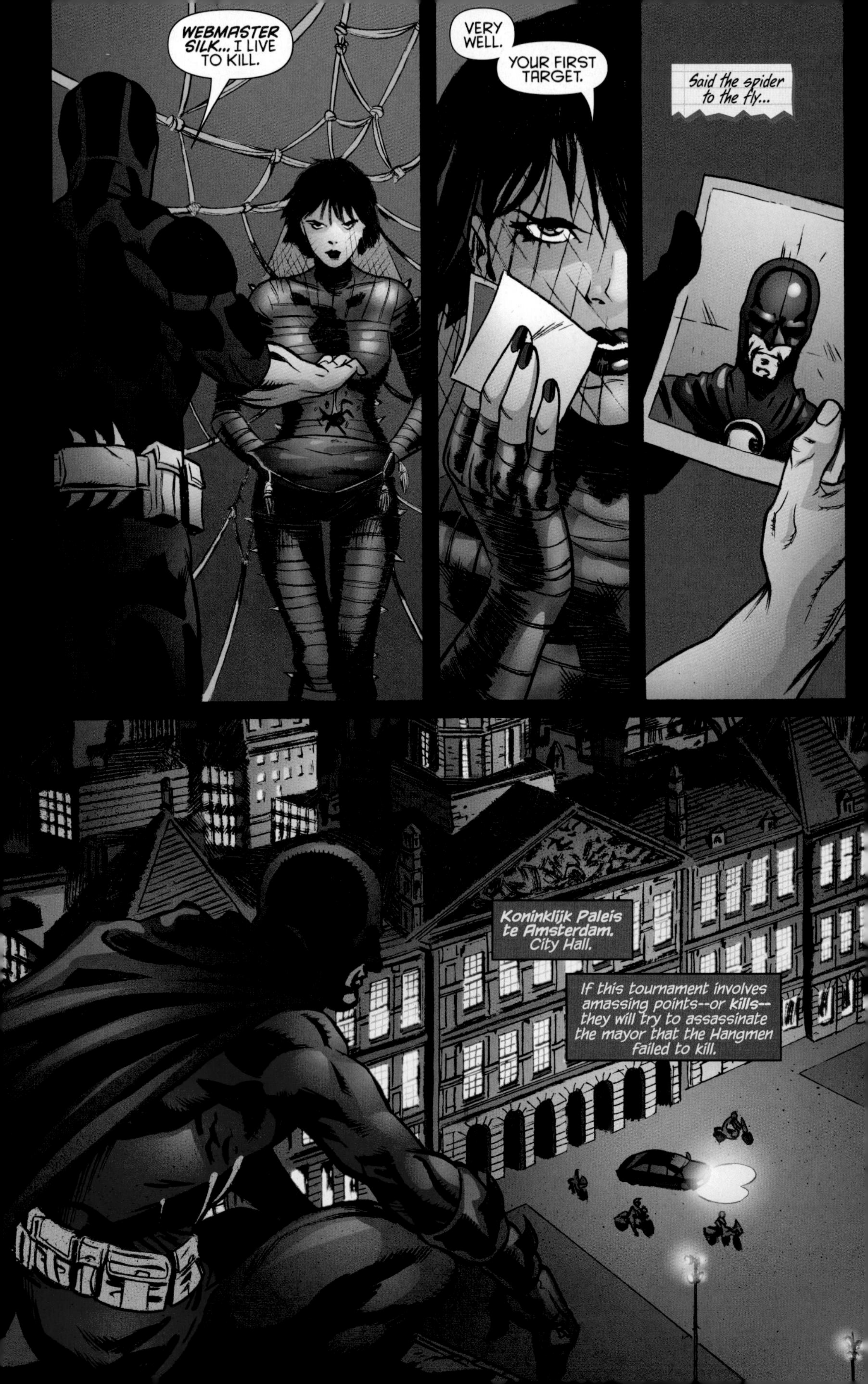
WEBMASTER SILK... I LIVE TO KILL.
VERY WELL.
YOUR FIRST TARGET.
Said the spider to the fly...
Koninklijk Paleis te Amsterdam. City Hall.
If this tournament involves amassing points--or kills--they will try to assassinate the mayor that the Hangmen failed to kill.

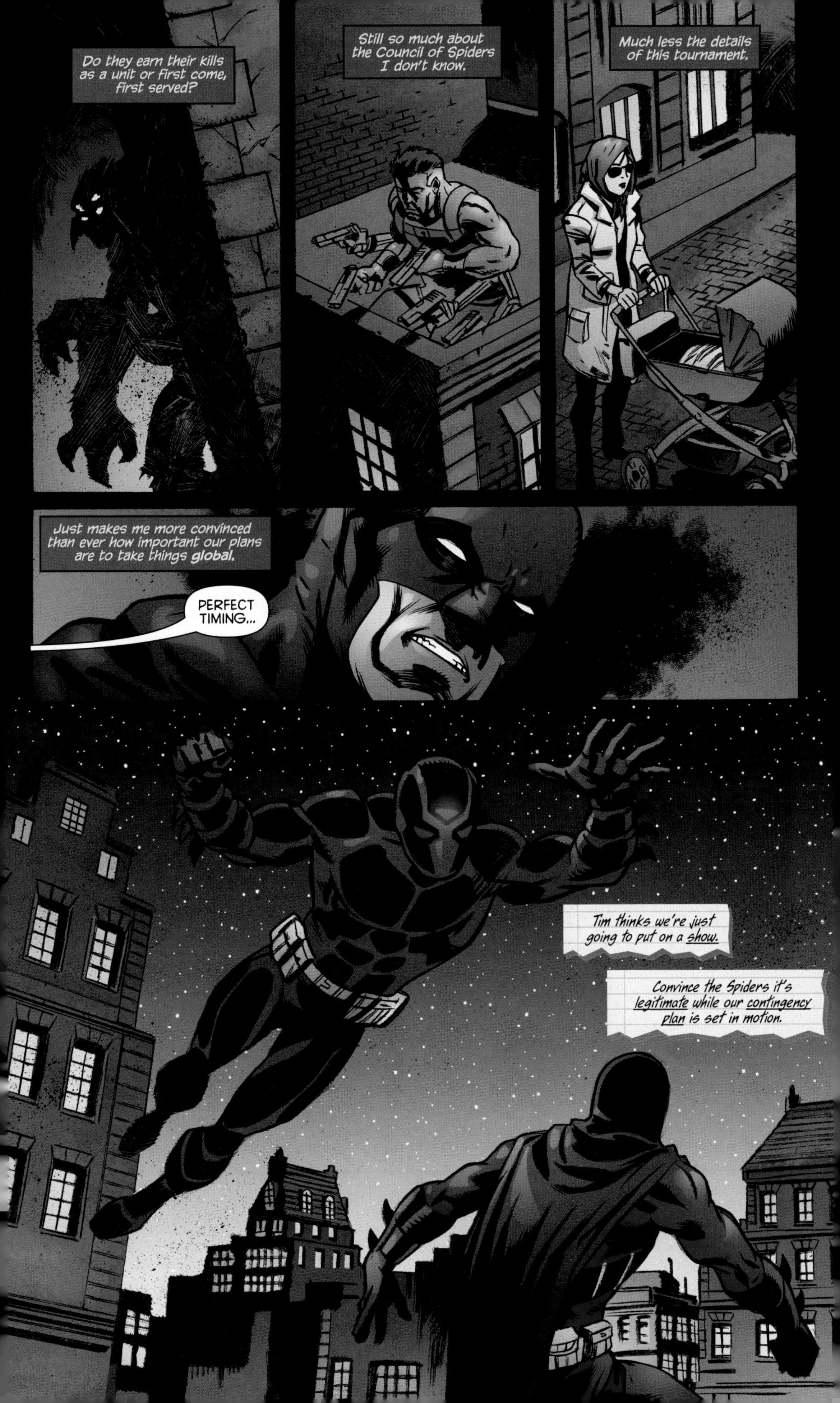
Do they earn their kills as a unit or first come, first served?
Still so much about the Council of Spiders I don't know.
Much less the details of this tournament.
Just makes me more convinced than ever how important our plans are to take things global.
PERFECT TIMING...
Tim thinks we're just going to put on a show.
Convince the Spiders it's legitimate while our contingency plan is set in motion.

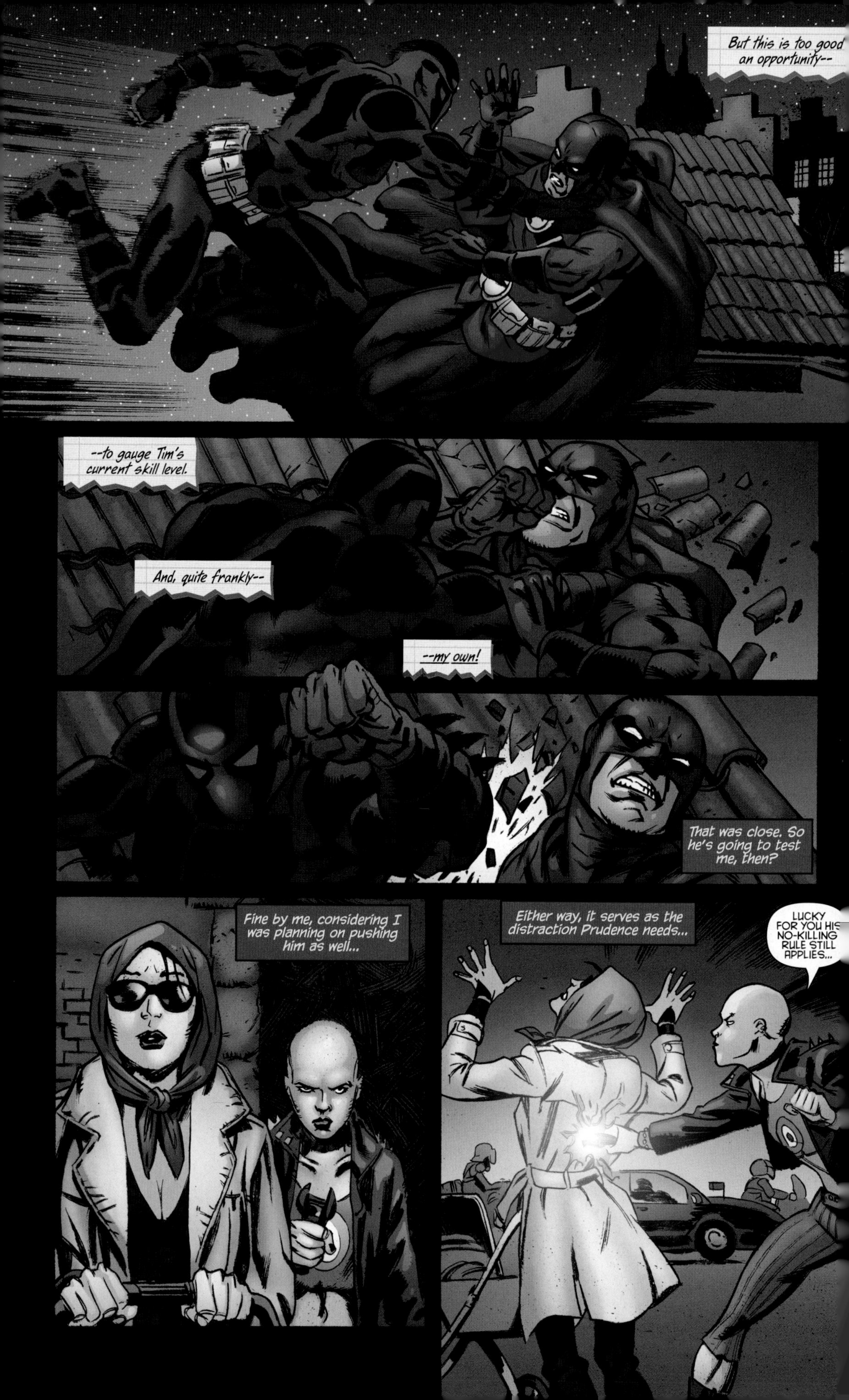
But this is too good an opportunity--
--to gauge Tim's current skill level.
And, quite frankly--
--my own!
That was close. So he's going to test me, then?
Fine by me, considering I was planning on pushing him as well...
Either way, it serves as the distraction Prudence needs...
LUCKY FOR YOU HIS NO-KILLING RULE STILL APPLIES...

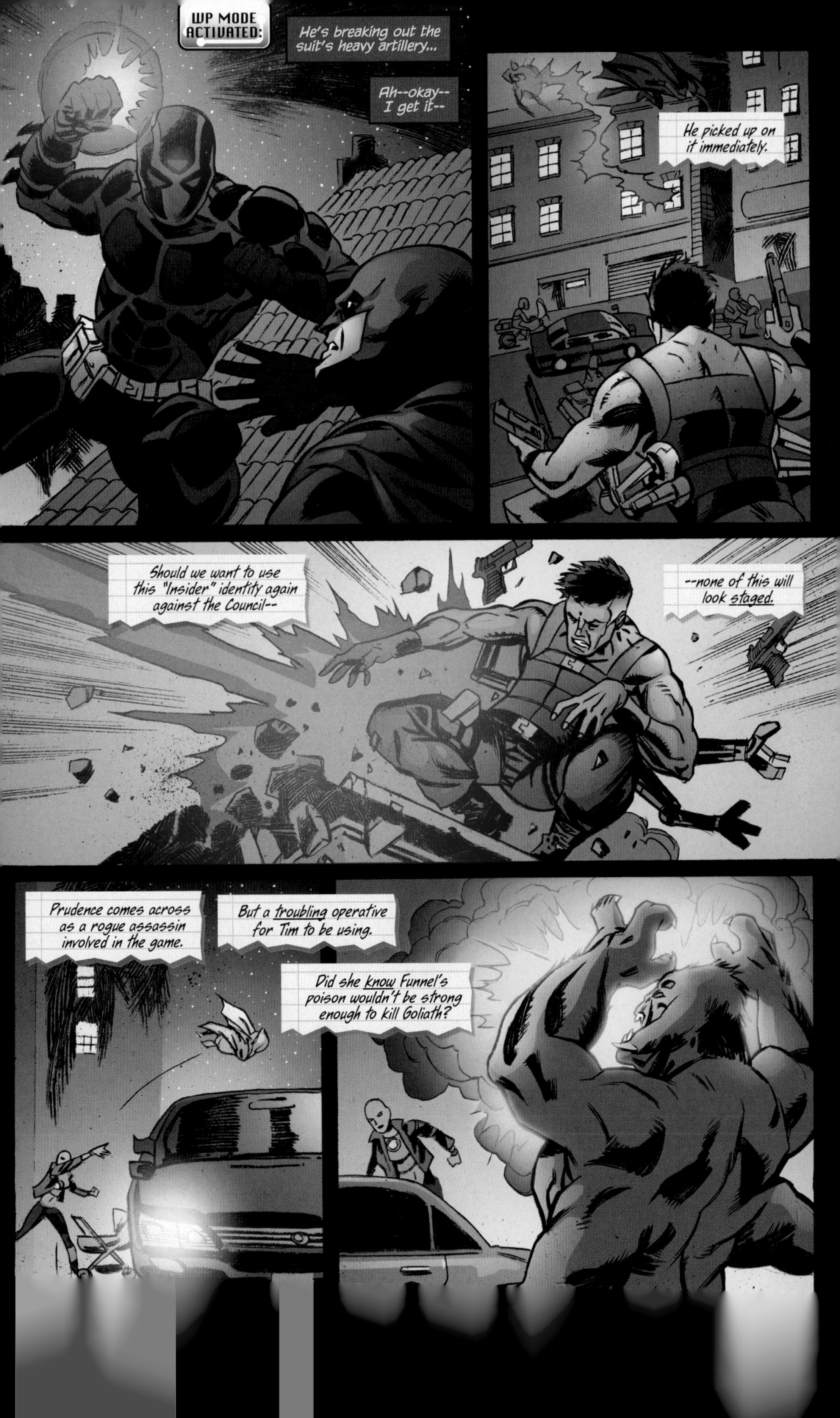
WP MODE ACTIVATED:
He's breaking out the suit's heavy artillery...
Ah--okay-- I get it--
He picked up on it immediately.
Should we want to use this "Insider" identity again against the Council--
--none of this will look staged.
Prudence comes across as a rogue assassin involved in the game.
But a troubling operative for Tim to be using.
Did she know Funnel's poison wouldn't be strong enough to kill Goliath?

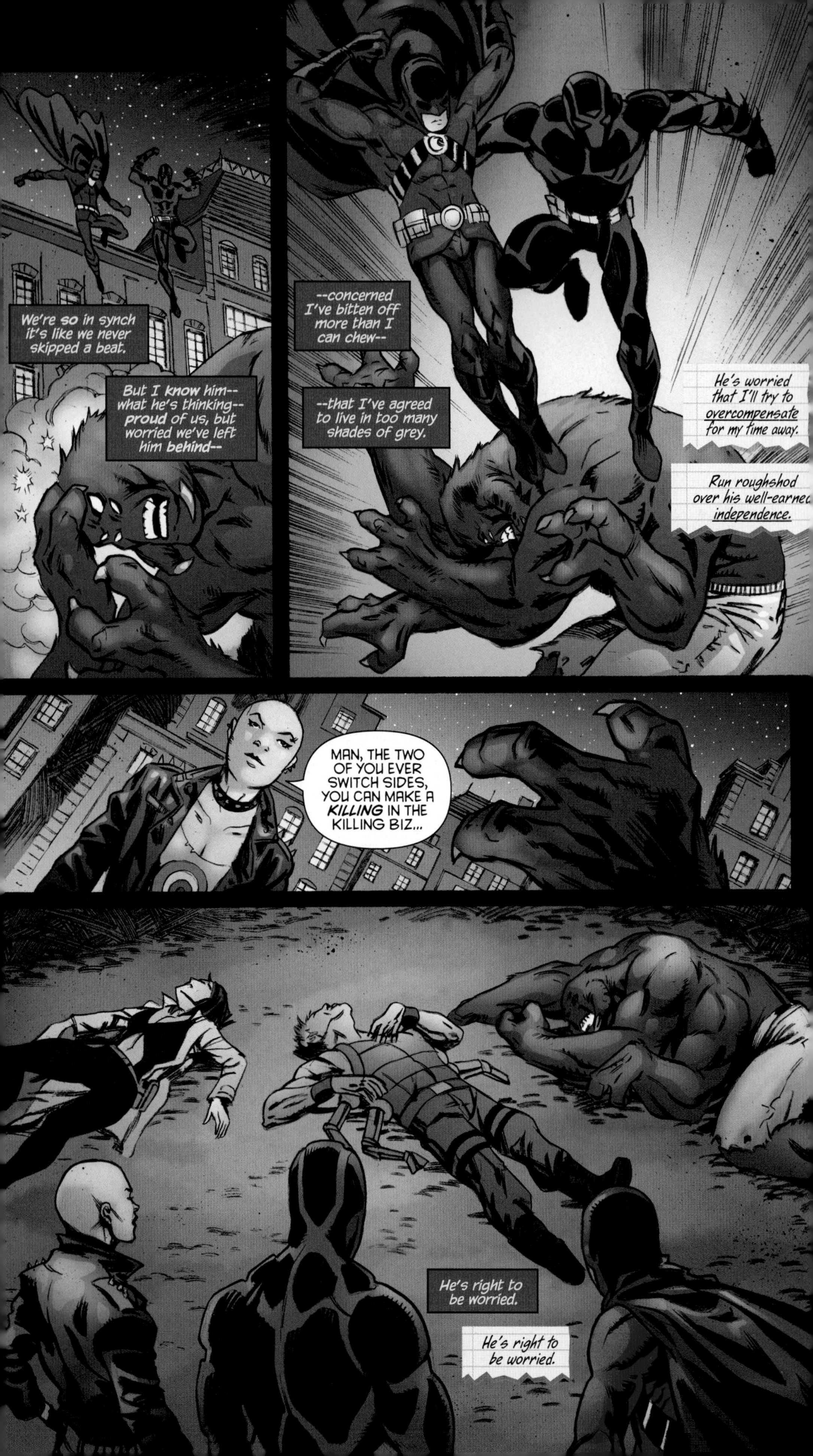

We're so in synch it's like we never skipped a beat.
But I know him--what he's thinking--proud of us, but worried we've left him behind--
--concerned I've bitten off more than I can chew--
--that I've agreed to live in too many shades of grey.
He's worried that I'll try to overcompensate for my time away.
Run roughshod over his well-earned independence.
MAN, THE TWO OF YOU EVER SWITCH SIDES, YOU CAN MAKE A KILLING IN THE KILLING BIZ...
He's right to be worried.
He's right to be worried.

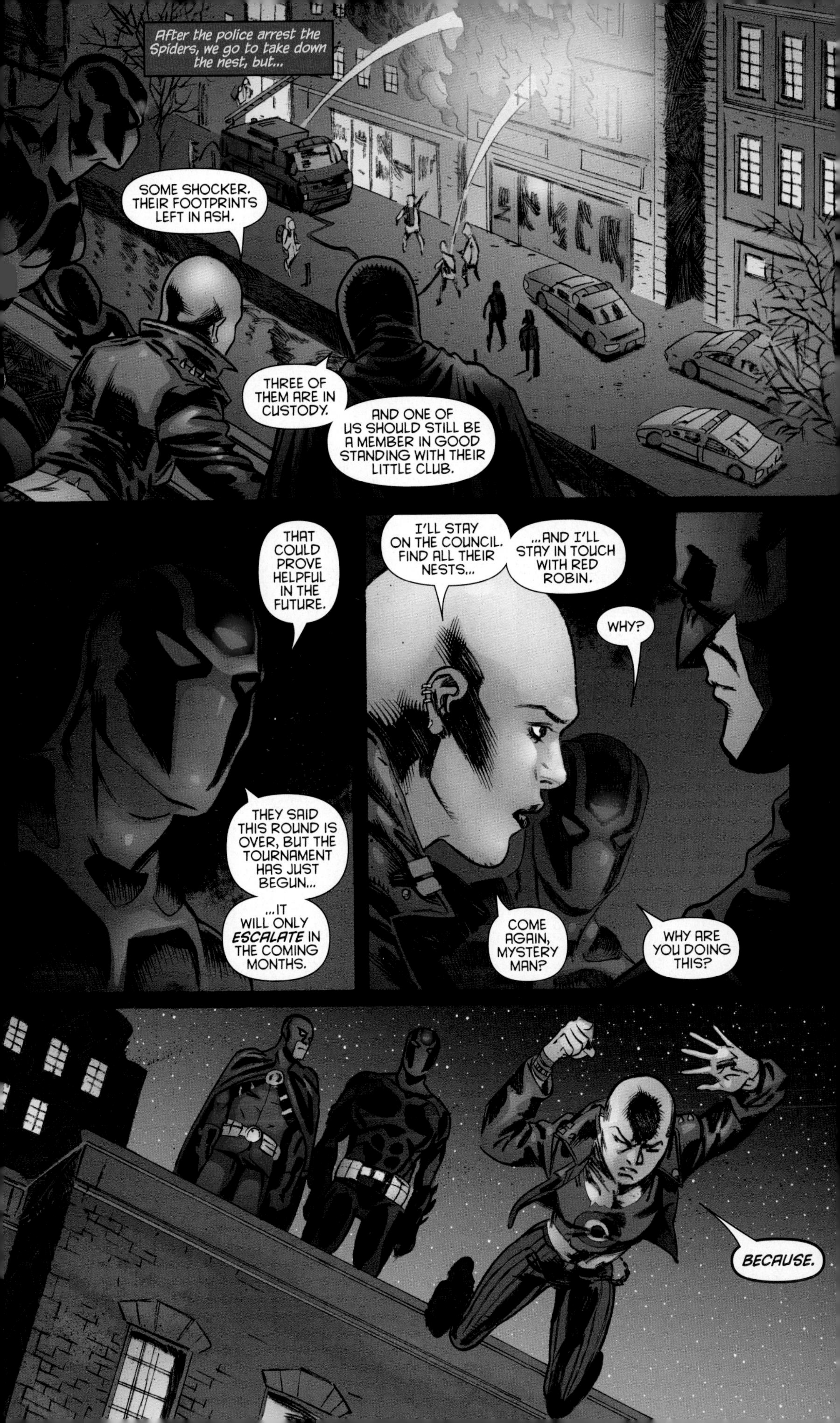
After the police arrest the Spiders, we go to take down the nest, but...
SOME SHOCKER. THEIR FOOTPRINTS LEFT IN ASH.
THREE OF THEM ARE IN CUSTODY.
AND ONE OF US SHOULD STILL BE A MEMBER IN GOOD STANDING WITH THEIR LITTLE CLUB.
THAT COULD PROVE HELPFUL IN THE FUTURE.
THEY SAID THIS ROUND IS OVER, BUT THE TOURNAMENT HAS JUST BEGUN...
...IT WILL ONLY *ESCALATE* IN THE COMING MONTHS.
I'LL STAY ON THE COUNCIL. FIND ALL THEIR NESTS...
...AND I'LL STAY IN TOUCH WITH RED ROBIN.
WHY?
COME AGAIN, MYSTERY MAN?
WHY ARE YOU DOING THIS?
BECAUSE.

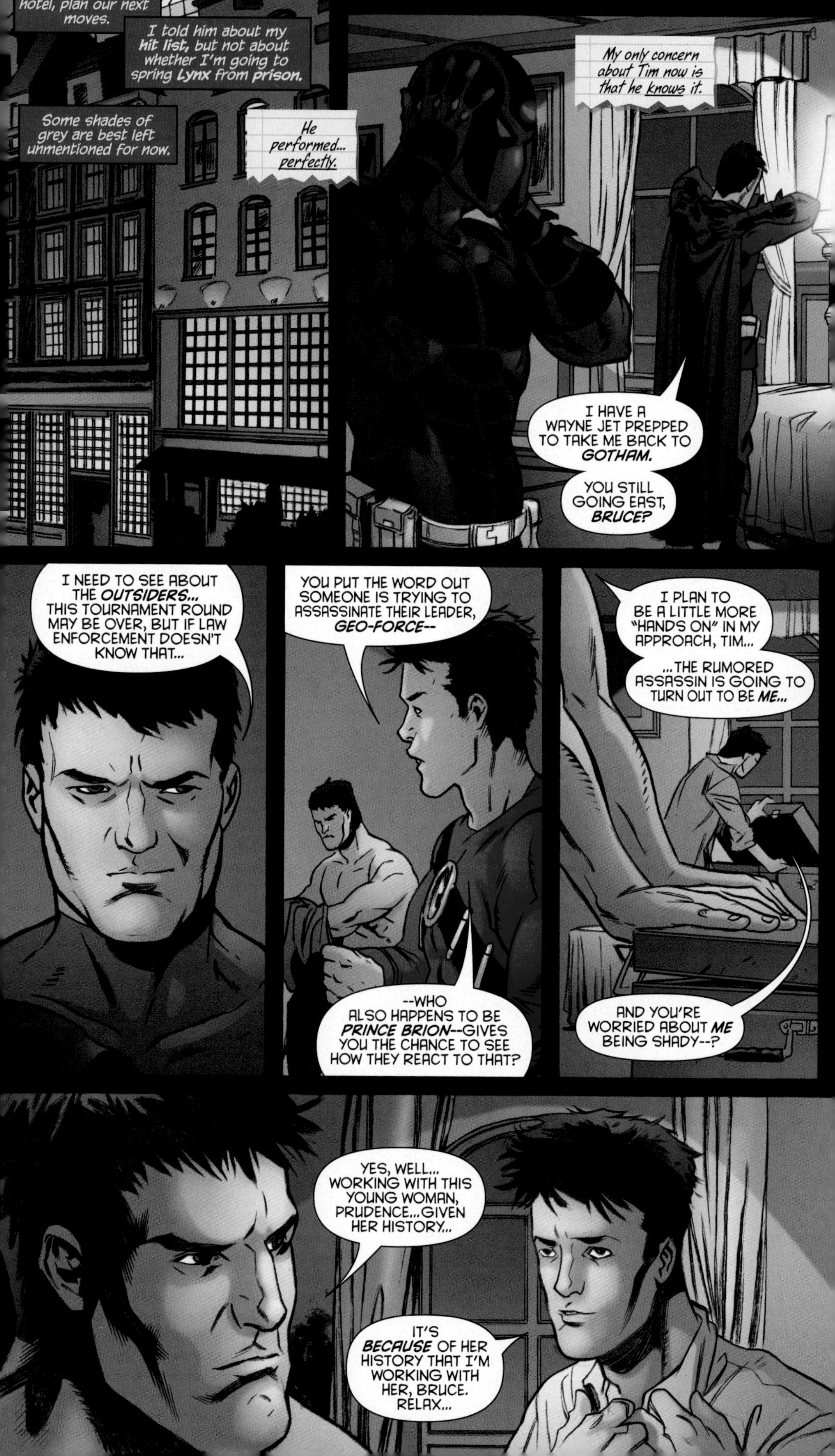

We go back to our hotel, plan our next moves.
I told him about my hit list, but not about whether I'm going to spring Lynx from prison.
Some shades of grey are best left unmentioned for now.
He performed... perfectly.
My only concern about Tim now is that he knows it.
I HAVE A WAYNE JET PREPPED TO TAKE ME BACK TO GOTHAM.
YOU STILL GOING EAST, BRUCE?
I NEED TO SEE ABOUT THE OUTSIDERS... THIS TOURNAMENT ROUND MAY BE OVER, BUT IF LAW ENFORCEMENT DOESN'T KNOW THAT...
YOU PUT THE WORD OUT SOMEONE IS TRYING TO ASSASSINATE THEIR LEADER, GEO-FORCE--
--WHO ALSO HAPPENS TO BE PRINCE BRION--GIVES YOU THE CHANCE TO SEE HOW THEY REACT TO THAT?
I PLAN TO BE A LITTLE MORE "HANDS ON" IN MY APPROACH, TIM...
...THE RUMORED ASSASSIN IS GOING TO TURN OUT TO BE ME...
AND YOU'RE WORRIED ABOUT ME BEING SHADY--?
YES, WELL... WORKING WITH THIS YOUNG WOMAN, PRUDENCE...GIVEN HER HISTORY...
IT'S BECAUSE OF HER HISTORY THAT I'M WORKING WITH HER, BRUCE. RELAX...

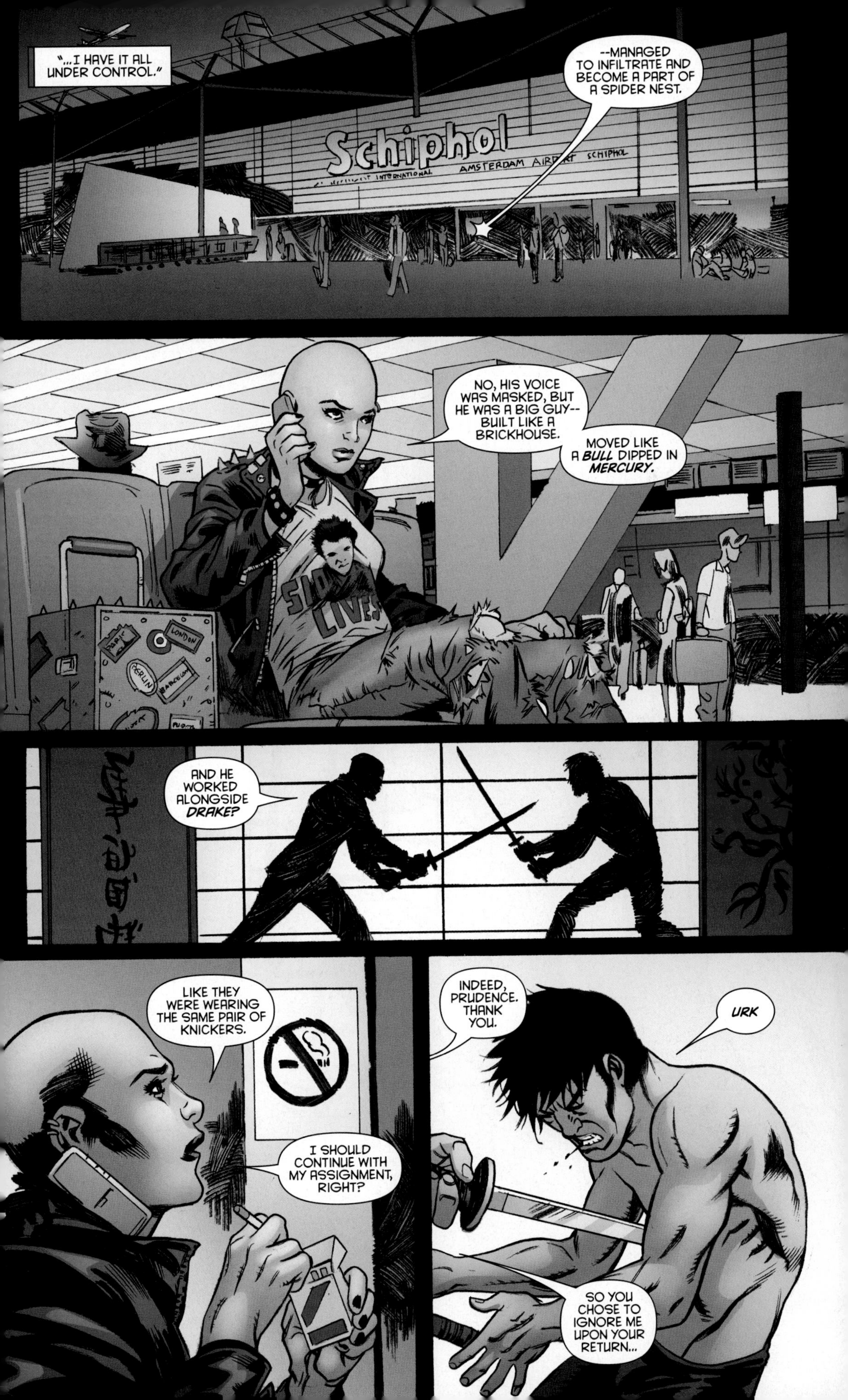

"...I HAVE IT ALL UNDER CONTROL."
--MANAGED TO INFILTRATE AND BECOME A PART OF A SPIDER NEST.
Schiphol
AMSTERDAM AIRPORT SCHIPHOL
NO, HIS VOICE WAS MASKED, BUT HE WAS A BIG GUY-- BUILT LIKE A BRICKHOUSE.
MOVED LIKE A BULL DIPPED IN MERCURY.
AND HE WORKED ALONGSIDE DRAKE?
LIKE THEY WERE WEARING THE SAME PAIR OF KNICKERS.
I SHOULD CONTINUE WITH MY ASSIGNMENT, RIGHT?
INDEED, PRUDENCE. THANK YOU.
URK
SO YOU CHOSE TO IGNORE ME UPON YOUR RETURN...

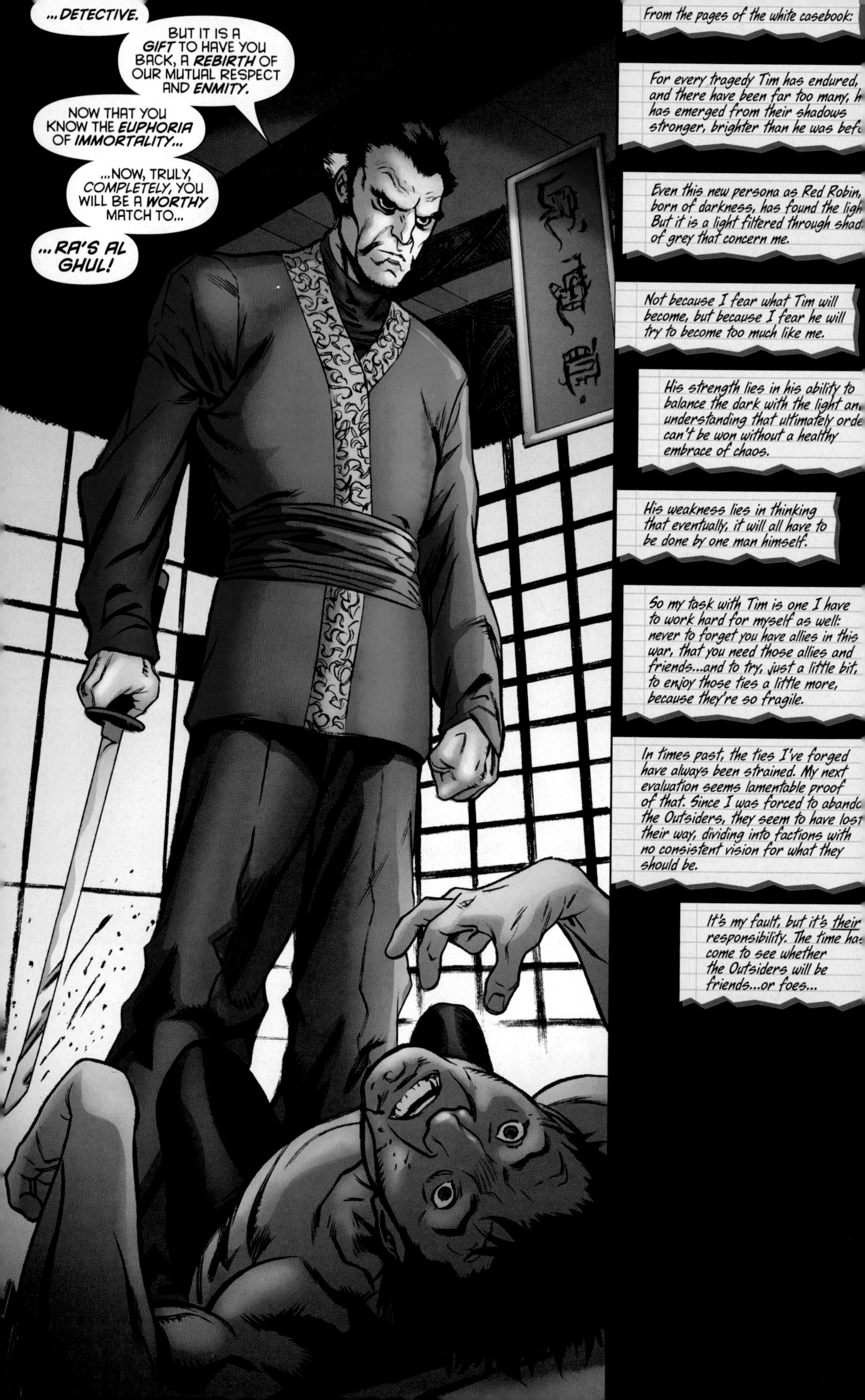

...DETECTIVE.
BUT IT IS A GIFT TO HAVE YOU BACK, A REBIRTH OF OUR MUTUAL RESPECT AND ENMITY.
NOW THAT YOU KNOW THE EUPHORIA OF IMMORTALITY...
...NOW, TRULY, COMPLETELY, YOU WILL BE A WORTHY MATCH TO...
...RA'S AL GHUL!
From the pages of the white casebook:
For every tragedy Tim has endured, and there have been far too many, h has emerged from their shadows stronger, brighter than he was bef
Even this new persona as Red Robin, born of darkness, has found the ligh But it is a light filtered through shad of grey that concern me.
Not because I fear what Tim will become, but because I fear he will try to become too much like me.
His strength lies in his ability to balance the dark with the light an understanding that ultimately orde can't be won without a healthy embrace of chaos.
His weakness lies in thinking that eventually, it will all have to be done by one man himself.
So my task with Tim is one I have to work hard for myself as well: never to forget you have allies in this war, that you need those allies and friends...and to try, just a little bit, to enjoy those ties a little more, because they're so fragile.
In times past, the ties I've forged have always been strained. My next evaluation seems lamentable proof of that. Since I was forced to abando the Outsiders, they seem to have lost their way, dividing into factions with no consistent vision for what they should be.
It's my fault, but it's their responsibility. The time ha come to see whether the Outsiders will be friends...or foes...

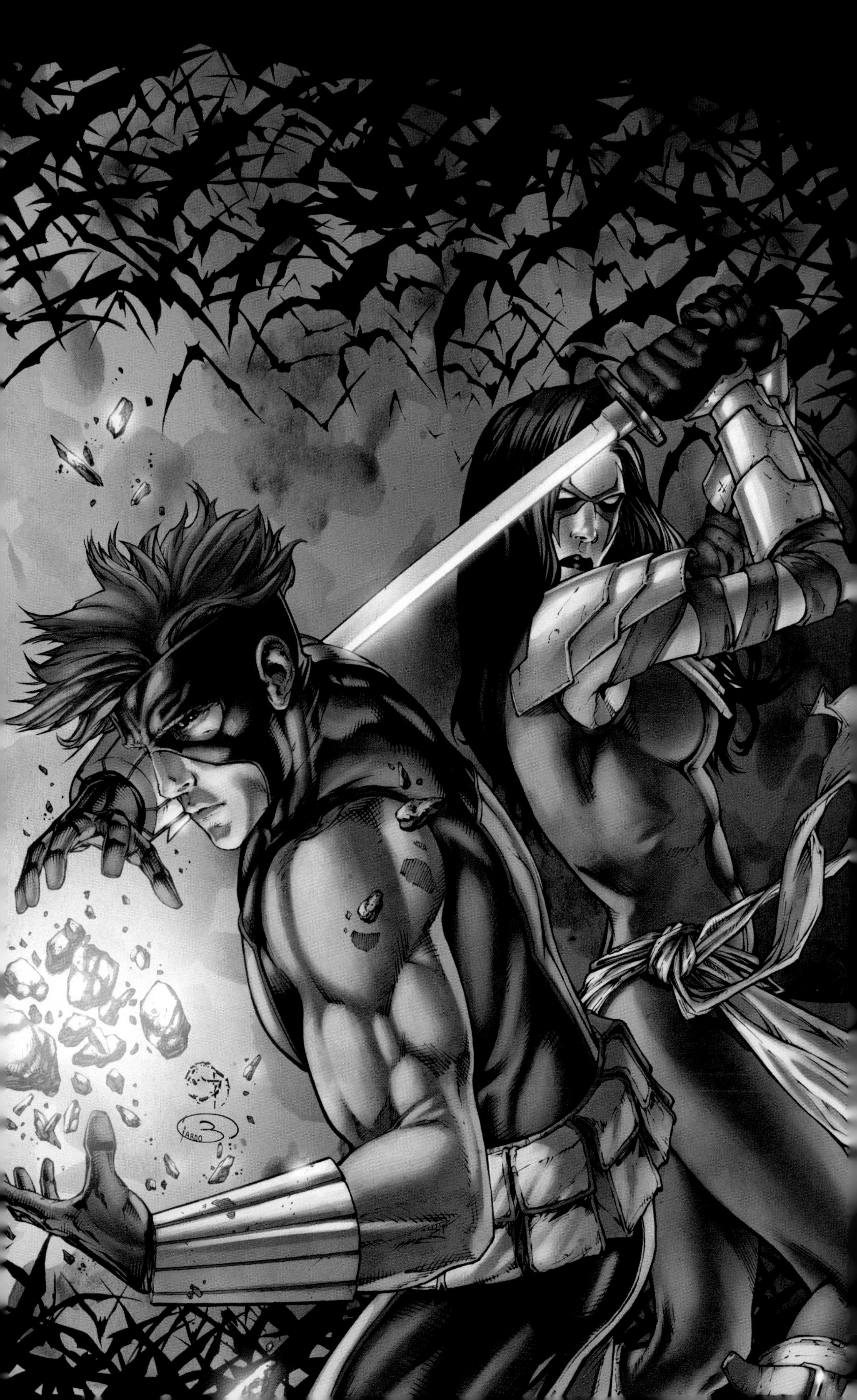

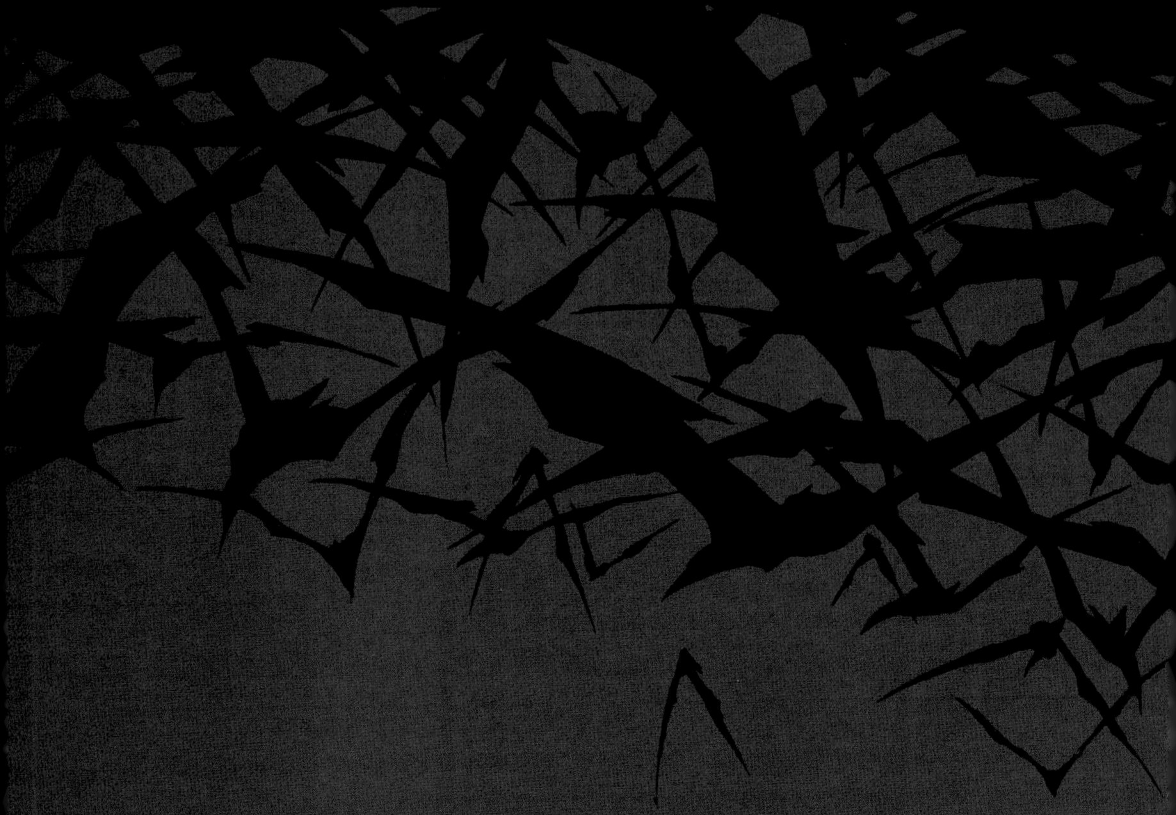

"NOTHING GROWS FASTER THAN A RUMOR."

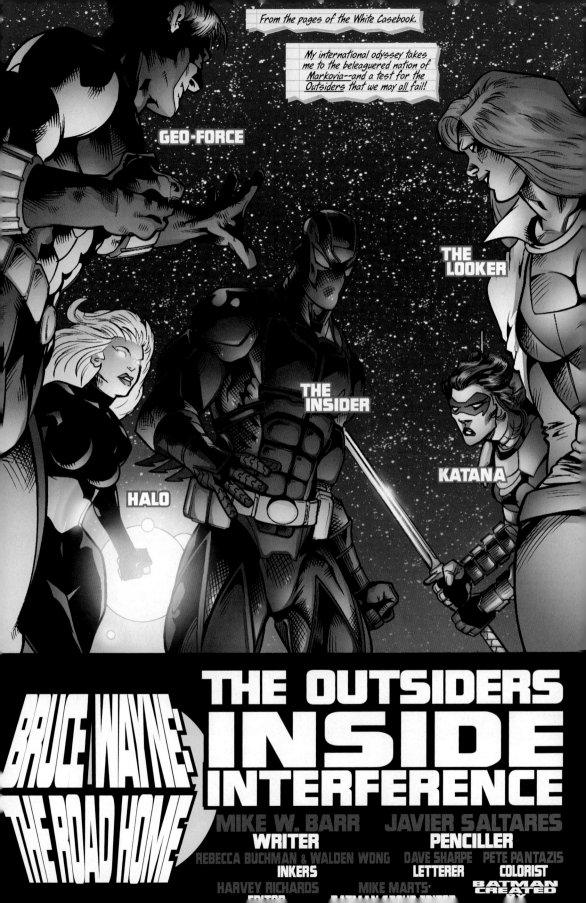

From the pages of the White Casebook.

My international odyssey takes me to the beleaguered nation of *Markovia*--and a test for the Outsiders that we may all fail!

GEO-FORCE

THE LOOKER

THE INSIDER

HALO

KATANA

THE OUTSIDERS INSIDE INTERFERENCE

BRUCE WAYNE: THE ROAD HOME

MIKE W. BARR
WRITER

JAVIER SALTARES
PENCILLER

REBECCA BUCHMAN & WALDEN WONG
INKERS

DAVE SHARPE
LETTERER

PETE PANTAZIS
COLORIST

HARVEY RICHARDS
EDITOR

MIKE MARTS

BATMAN CREATED

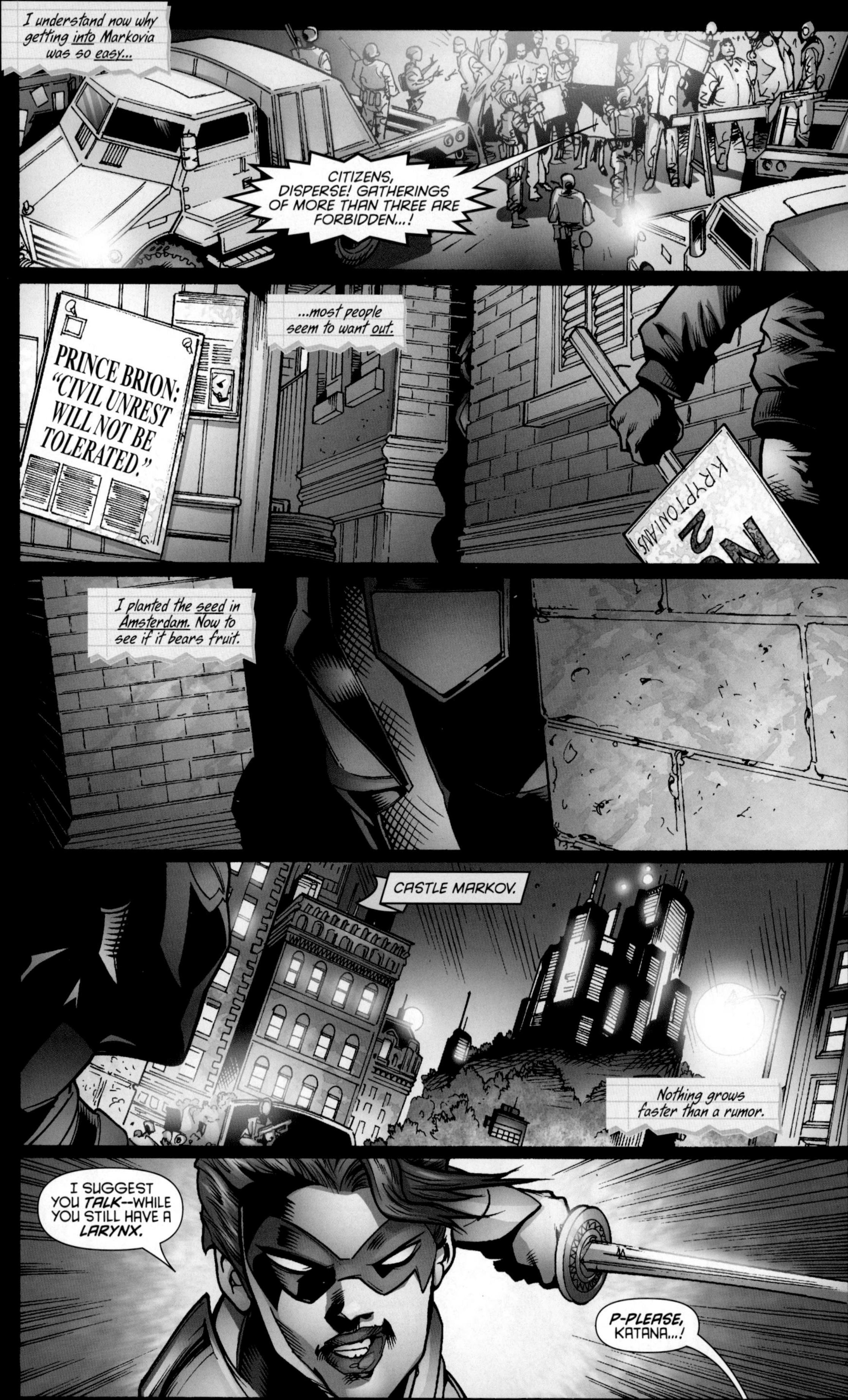
I understand now why getting into Markovia was so easy...
CITIZENS, DISPERSE! GATHERINGS OF MORE THAN THREE ARE FORBIDDEN...!
PRINCE BRION: "CIVIL UNREST WILL NOT BE TOLERATED."
...most people seem to want out.
KRYPTONIANS
I planted the seed in Amsterdam. Now to see if it bears fruit.
CASTLE MARKOV.
Nothing grows faster than a rumor.
I SUGGEST YOU TALK--WHILE YOU STILL HAVE A LARYNX.
P-PLEASE, KATANA...!

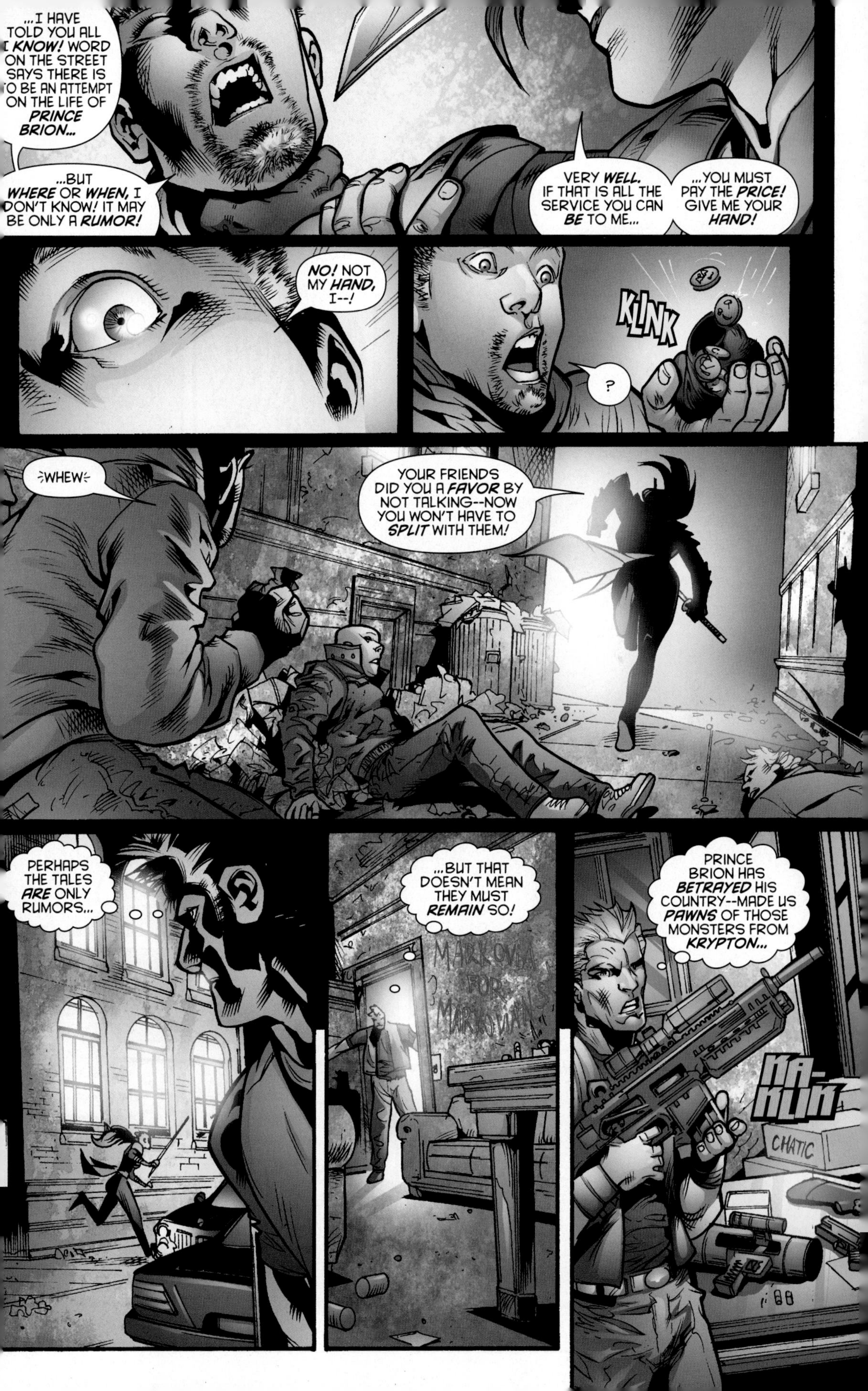
...I HAVE TOLD YOU ALL I KNOW! WORD ON THE STREET SAYS THERE IS TO BE AN ATTEMPT ON THE LIFE OF PRINCE BRION...
...BUT WHERE OR WHEN, I DON'T KNOW! IT MAY BE ONLY A RUMOR!
VERY WELL. IF THAT IS ALL THE SERVICE YOU CAN BE TO ME...
...YOU MUST PAY THE PRICE! GIVE ME YOUR HAND!
NO! NOT MY HAND, I--!
KLINK
?
WHEW
YOUR FRIENDS DID YOU A FAVOR BY NOT TALKING--NOW YOU WON'T HAVE TO SPLIT WITH THEM!
PERHAPS THE TALES ARE ONLY RUMORS...
...BUT THAT DOESN'T MEAN THEY MUST REMAIN SO!
MARKOVIA FOR MARKOVIAN
PRINCE BRION HAS BETRAYED HIS COUNTRY--MADE US PAWNS OF THOSE MONSTERS FROM KRYPTON...
KA-KLIK
CHATIC

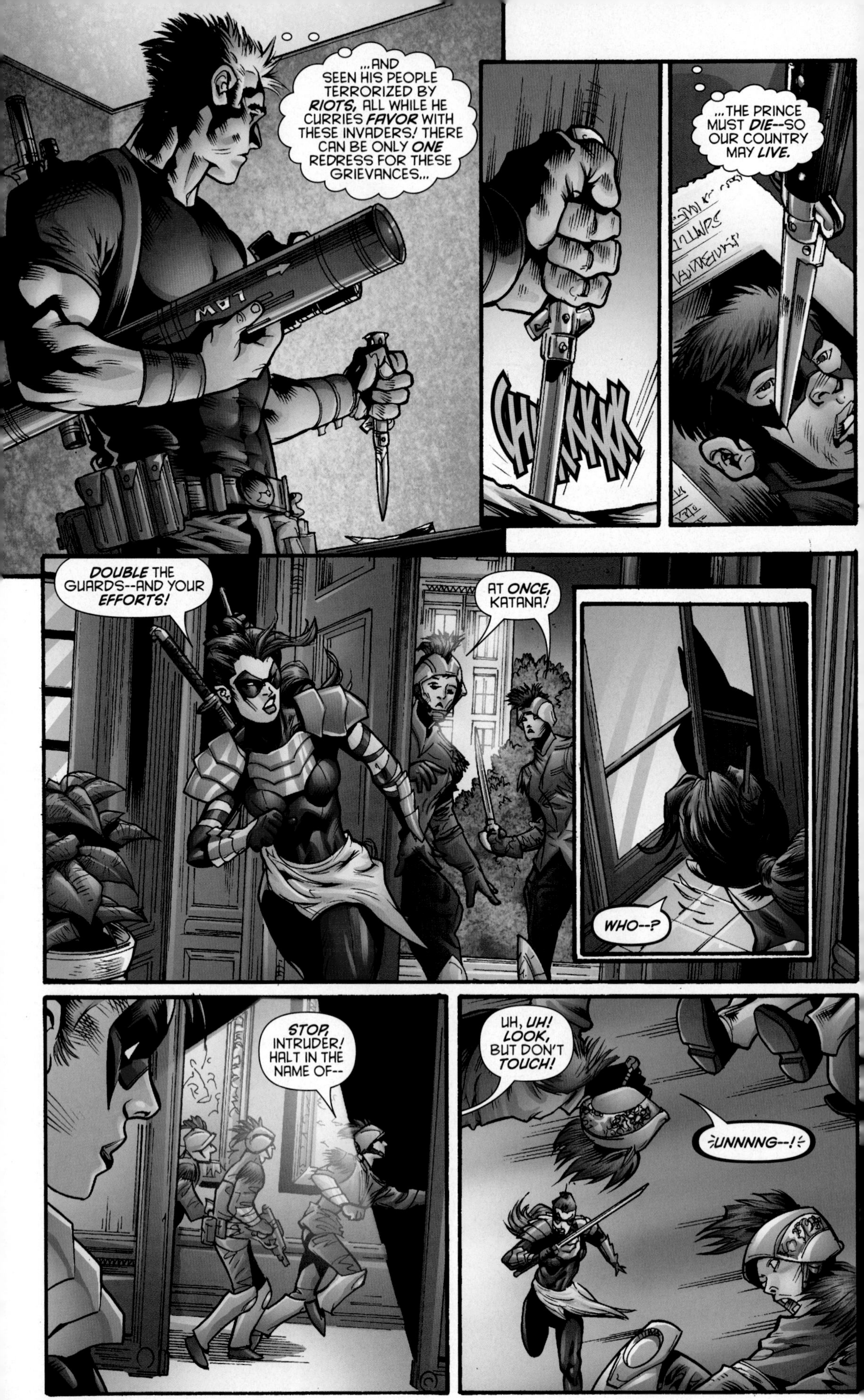
...AND SEEN HIS PEOPLE TERRORIZED BY RIOTS, ALL WHILE HE CURRIES FAVOR WITH THESE INVADERS! THERE CAN BE ONLY ONE REDRESS FOR THESE GRIEVANCES...
LAW
CHUKKKK
...THE PRINCE MUST DIE--SO OUR COUNTRY MAY LIVE.
DOUBLE THE GUARDS--AND YOUR EFFORTS!
AT ONCE, KATANA!
WHO--?
STOP, INTRUDER! HALT IN THE NAME OF--
UH, UH! LOOK, BUT DON'T TOUCH!
UNNNNG--!

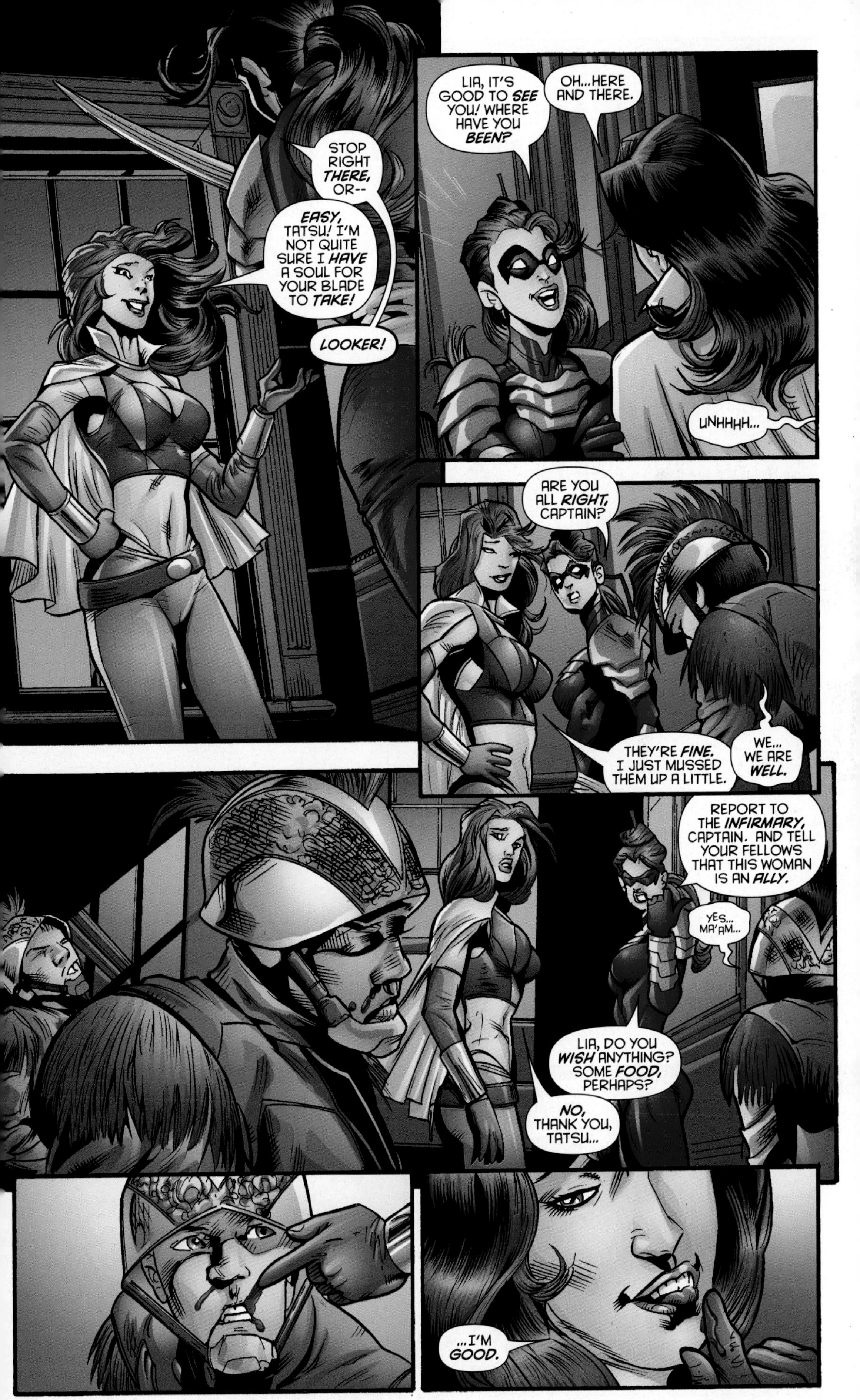

STOP RIGHT THERE, OR--
EASY, TATSU! I'M NOT QUITE SURE I HAVE A SOUL FOR YOUR BLADE TO TAKE!
LOOKER!
LIA, IT'S GOOD TO SEE YOU! WHERE HAVE YOU BEEN?
OH...HERE AND THERE.
UNHHHH...
ARE YOU ALL RIGHT, CAPTAIN?
THEY'RE FINE. I JUST MUSSED THEM UP A LITTLE.
WE... WE ARE WELL.
REPORT TO THE INFIRMARY, CAPTAIN. AND TELL YOUR FELLOWS THAT THIS WOMAN IS AN ALLY.
YES... MA'AM...
LIA, DO YOU WISH ANYTHING? SOME FOOD, PERHAPS?
NO, THANK YOU, TATSU...
...I'M GOOD.

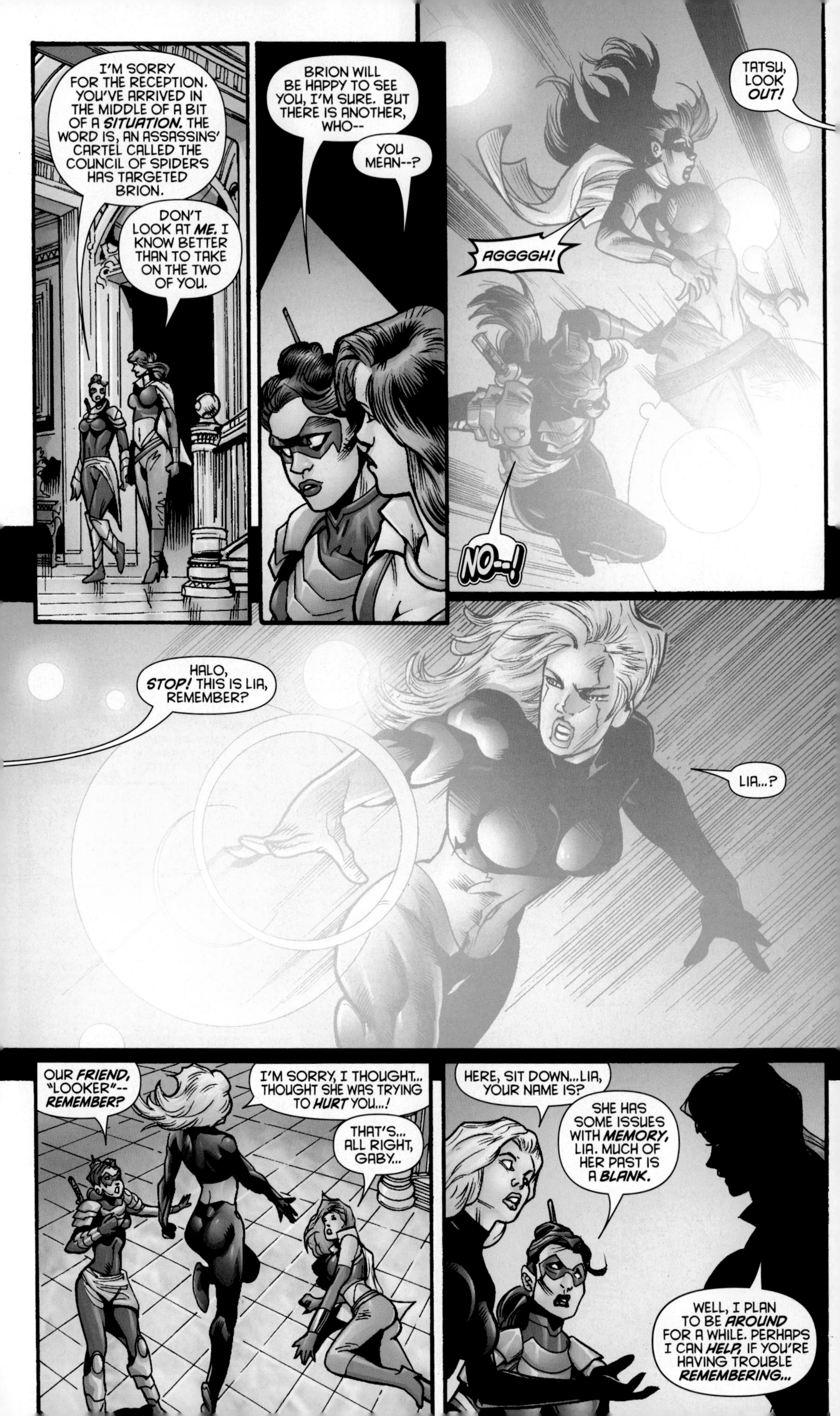
I'M SORRY FOR THE RECEPTION. YOU'VE ARRIVED IN THE MIDDLE OF A BIT OF A SITUATION. THE WORD IS, AN ASSASSINS' CARTEL CALLED THE COUNCIL OF SPIDERS HAS TARGETED BRION.
DON'T LOOK AT ME. I KNOW BETTER THAN TO TAKE ON THE TWO OF YOU.
BRION WILL BE HAPPY TO SEE YOU, I'M SURE. BUT THERE IS ANOTHER, WHO--
YOU MEAN--?
TATSU, LOOK OUT!
AGGGGH!
NO--!
HALO, STOP! THIS IS LIA, REMEMBER?
LIA...?
OUR FRIEND, "LOOKER"-- REMEMBER?
I'M SORRY, I THOUGHT... THOUGHT SHE WAS TRYING TO HURT YOU...!
THAT'S... ALL RIGHT, GABY...
HERE, SIT DOWN...LIA, YOUR NAME IS?
SHE HAS SOME ISSUES WITH MEMORY, LIA. MUCH OF HER PAST IS A BLANK.
WELL, I PLAN TO BE AROUND FOR A WHILE. PERHAPS I CAN HELP, IF YOU'RE HAVING TROUBLE REMEMBERING...

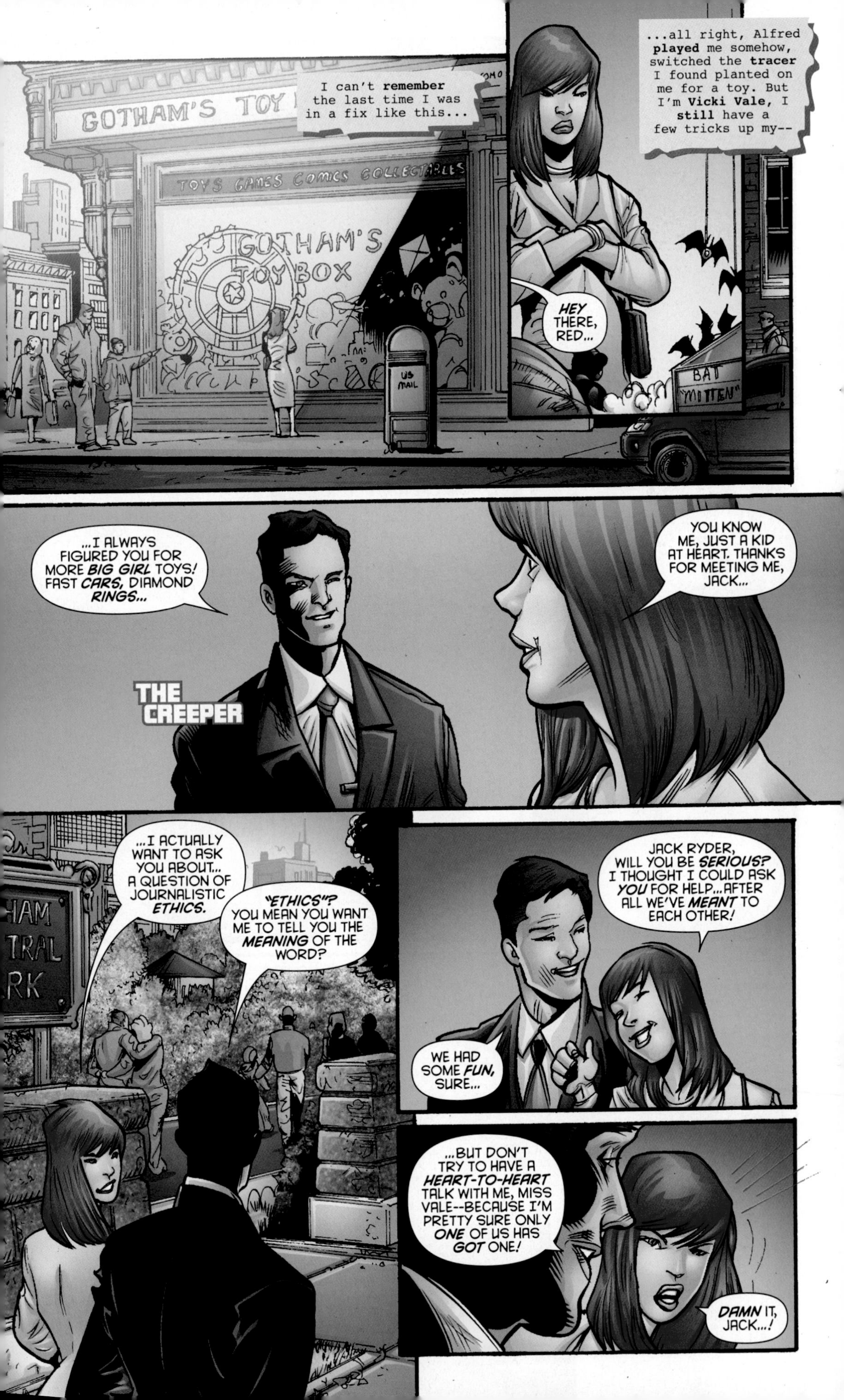

GOTHAM'S TOY
I can't **remember** the last time I was in a fix like this...
...all right, Alfred **played** me somehow, switched the **tracer** I found planted on me for a toy. But I'm **Vicki Vale**, I **still** have a few tricks up my--
TOYS GAMES COMICS COLLECTABLES
GOTHAM'S TOY BOX
US MAIL
HEY THERE, RED...
BAT "MITTEN"
...I ALWAYS FIGURED YOU FOR MORE *BIG GIRL* TOYS! FAST *CARS*, DIAMOND *RINGS*...
YOU KNOW ME, JUST A KID AT HEART. THANKS FOR MEETING ME, JACK...
THE CREEPER
...I ACTUALLY WANT TO ASK YOU ABOUT... A QUESTION OF JOURNALISTIC *ETHICS*.
"ETHICS"? YOU MEAN YOU WANT ME TO TELL YOU THE *MEANING* OF THE WORD?
JACK RYDER, WILL YOU BE *SERIOUS?* I THOUGHT I COULD ASK *YOU* FOR HELP...AFTER ALL WE'VE *MEANT* TO EACH OTHER!
WE HAD SOME *FUN*, SURE...
...BUT DON'T TRY TO HAVE A *HEART-TO-HEART* TALK WITH ME, MISS VALE--BECAUSE I'M PRETTY SURE ONLY *ONE* OF US HAS *GOT* ONE!
DAMN IT, JACK...!

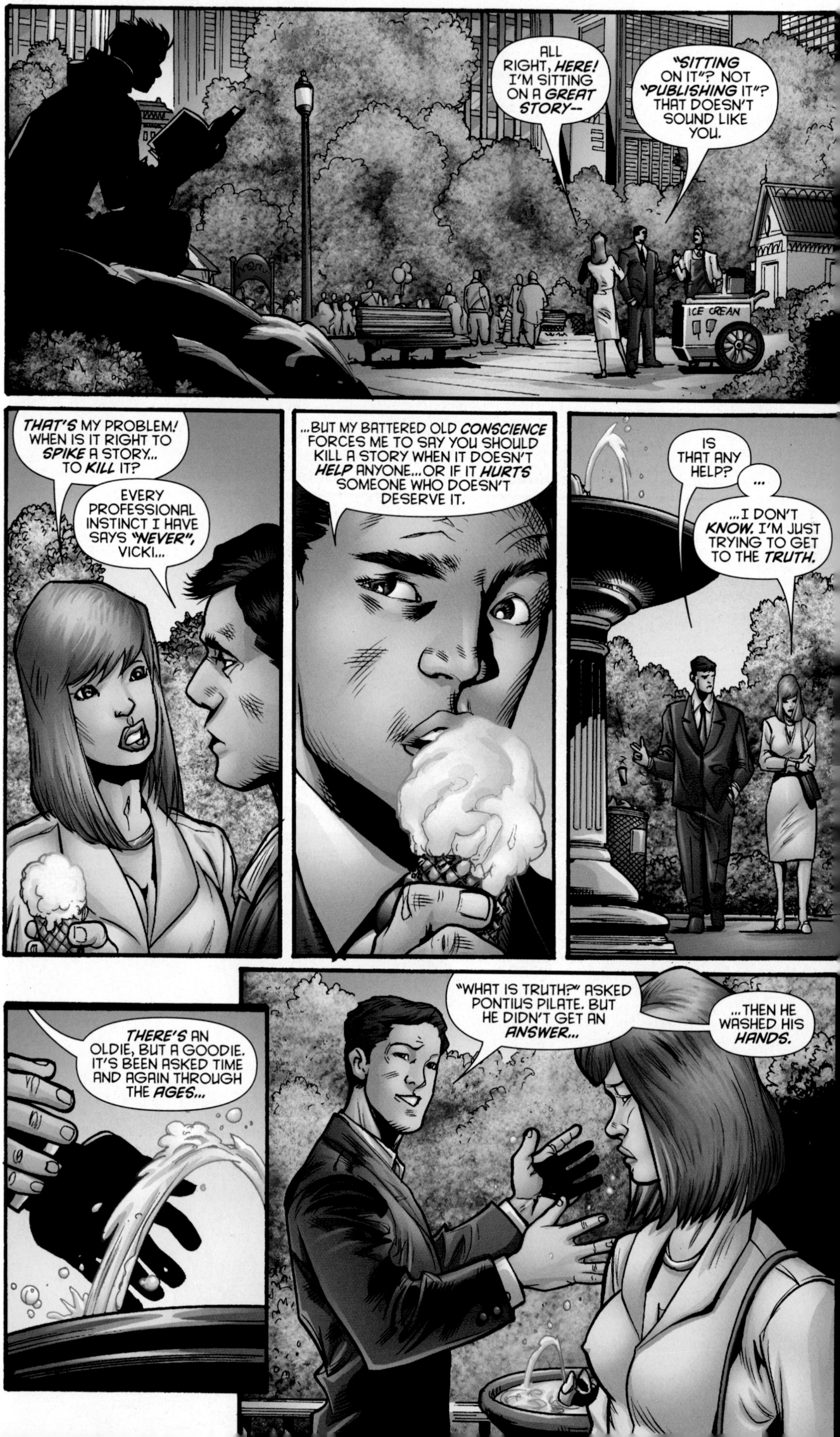
ALL RIGHT, HERE! I'M SITTING ON A GREAT STORY--
"SITTING ON IT"? NOT "PUBLISHING IT"? THAT DOESN'T SOUND LIKE YOU.
ICE CREAM
THAT'S MY PROBLEM! WHEN IS IT RIGHT TO SPIKE A STORY... TO KILL IT?
EVERY PROFESSIONAL INSTINCT I HAVE SAYS "NEVER", VICKI...
...BUT MY BATTERED OLD CONSCIENCE FORCES ME TO SAY YOU SHOULD KILL A STORY WHEN IT DOESN'T HELP ANYONE...OR IF IT HURTS SOMEONE WHO DOESN'T DESERVE IT.
IS THAT ANY HELP?
...
...I DON'T KNOW. I'M JUST TRYING TO GET TO THE TRUTH.
THERE'S AN OLDIE, BUT A GOODIE. IT'S BEEN ASKED TIME AND AGAIN THROUGH THE AGES...
"WHAT IS TRUTH?" ASKED PONTIUS PILATE. BUT HE DIDN'T GET AN ANSWER...
...THEN HE WASHED HIS HANDS.

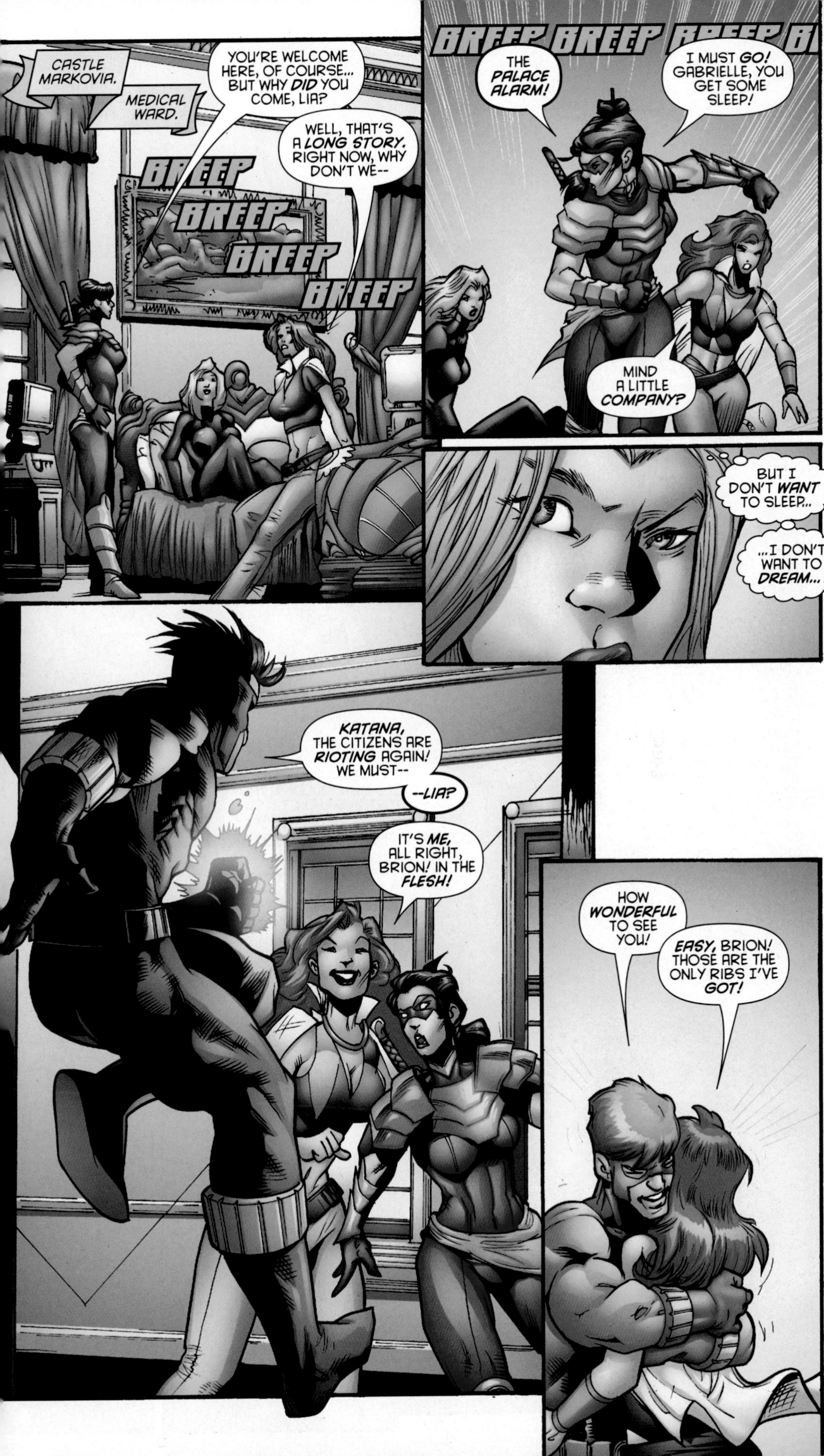

CASTLE MARKOVIA.
MEDICAL WARD.
YOU'RE WELCOME HERE, OF COURSE... BUT WHY DID YOU COME, LIA?
WELL, THAT'S A LONG STORY. RIGHT NOW, WHY DON'T WE--
BREEP BREEP BREEP BREEP
BREEP BREEP BREEP
THE PALACE ALARM!
I MUST GO! GABRIELLE, YOU GET SOME SLEEP!
MIND A LITTLE COMPANY?
BUT I DON'T WANT TO SLEEP...
...I DON'T WANT TO DREAM...!
KATANA, THE CITIZENS ARE RIOTING AGAIN! WE MUST--
--LIA?
IT'S ME, ALL RIGHT, BRION! IN THE FLESH!
HOW WONDERFUL TO SEE YOU!
EASY, BRION! THOSE ARE THE ONLY RIBS I'VE GOT!

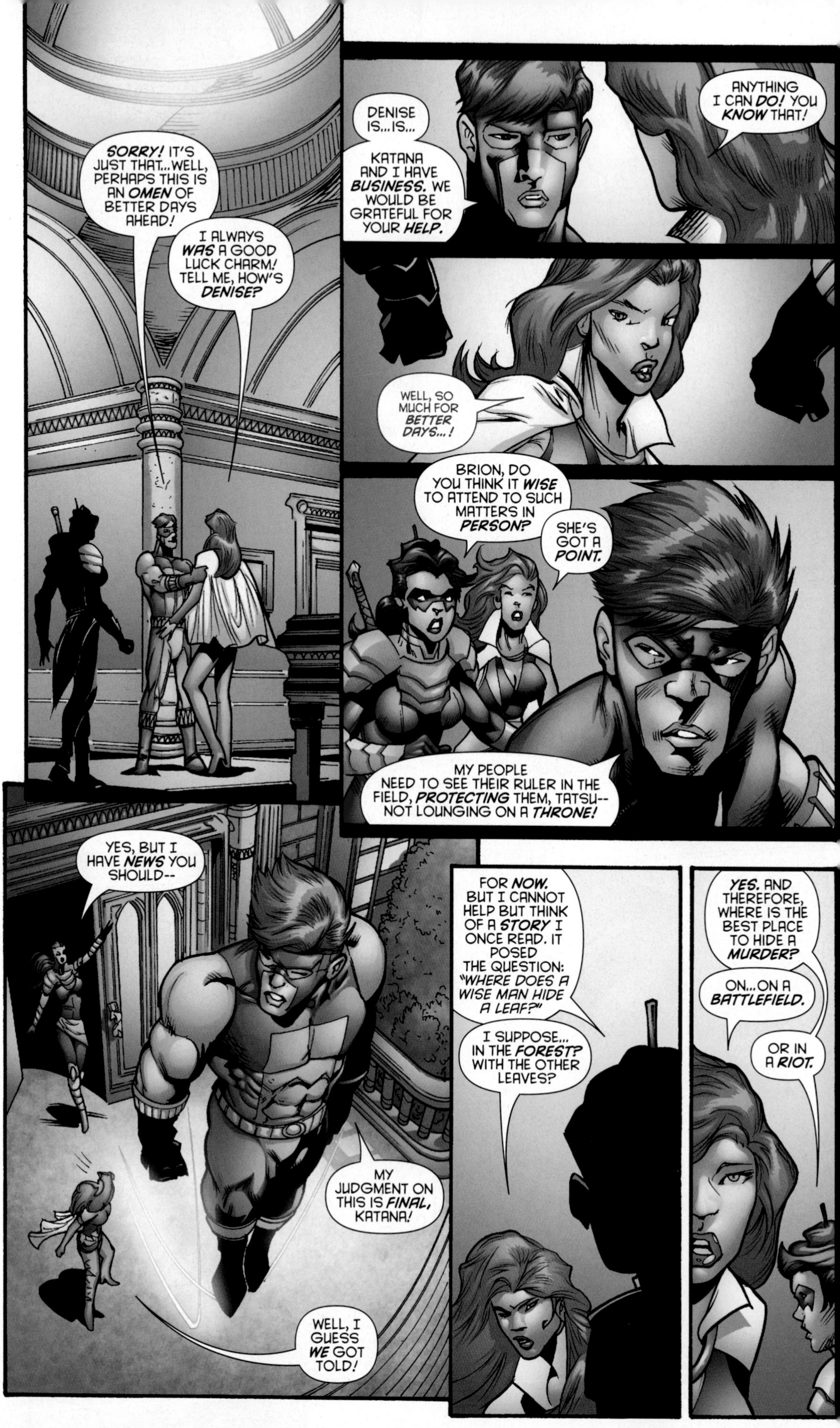

SORRY! IT'S JUST THAT...WELL, PERHAPS THIS IS AN OMEN OF BETTER DAYS AHEAD!
I ALWAYS WAS A GOOD LUCK CHARM! TELL ME, HOW'S DENISE?
DENISE IS...IS...
KATANA AND I HAVE BUSINESS. WE WOULD BE GRATEFUL FOR YOUR HELP.
ANYTHING I CAN DO! YOU KNOW THAT!
WELL, SO MUCH FOR BETTER DAYS...!
BRION, DO YOU THINK IT WISE TO ATTEND TO SUCH MATTERS IN PERSON?
SHE'S GOT A POINT.
MY PEOPLE NEED TO SEE THEIR RULER IN THE FIELD, PROTECTING THEM, TATSU-- NOT LOUNGING ON A THRONE!
YES, BUT I HAVE NEWS YOU SHOULD--
MY JUDGMENT ON THIS IS FINAL, KATANA!
WELL, I GUESS WE GOT TOLD!
FOR NOW. BUT I CANNOT HELP BUT THINK OF A STORY I ONCE READ. IT POSED THE QUESTION: "WHERE DOES A WISE MAN HIDE A LEAF?"
I SUPPOSE... IN THE FOREST? WITH THE OTHER LEAVES?
YES. AND THEREFORE, WHERE IS THE BEST PLACE TO HIDE A MURDER?
ON...ON A BATTLEFIELD.
OR IN A RIOT.

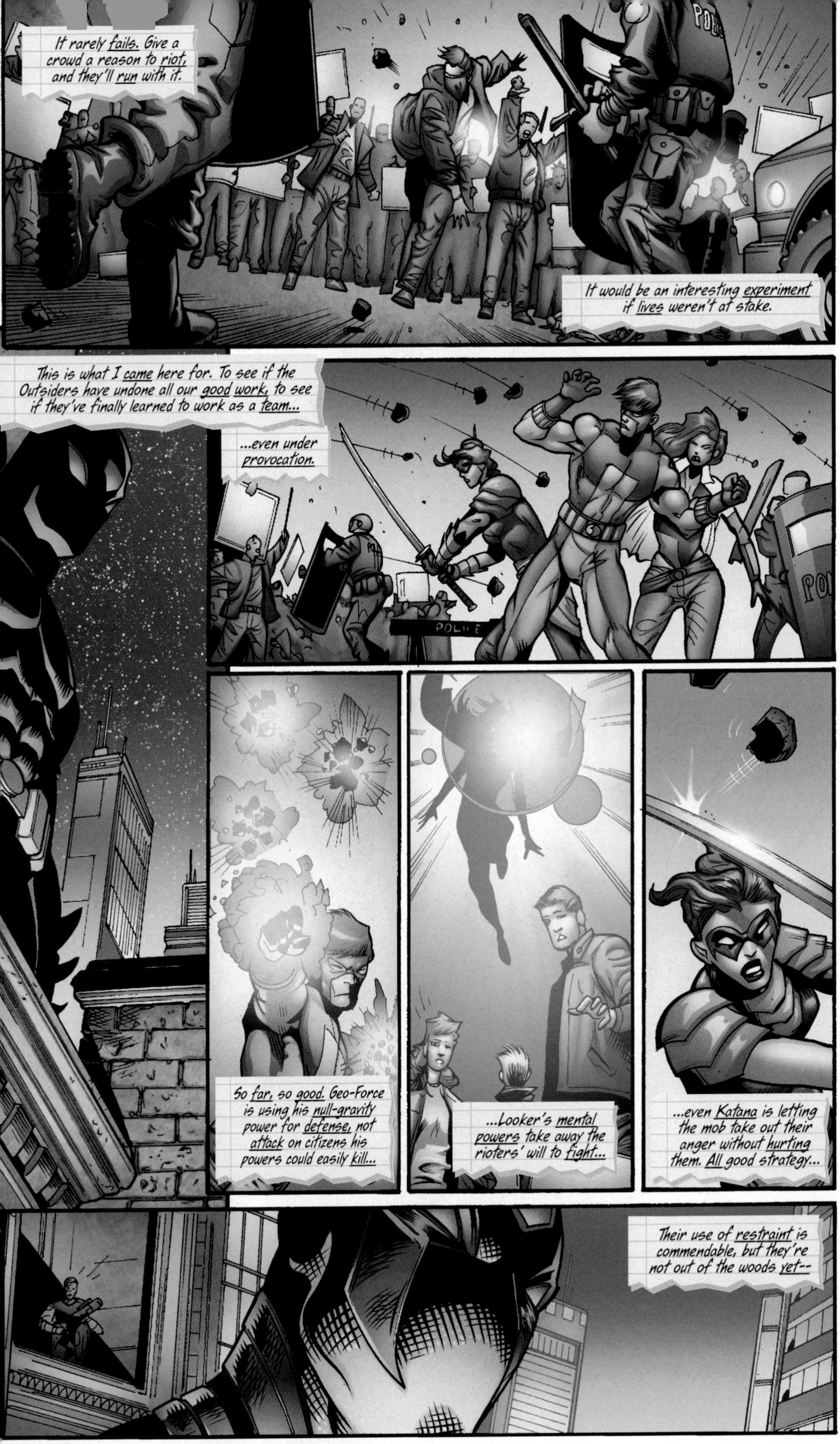
It rarely fails. Give a crowd a reason to riot, and they'll run with it.
POLICE
It would be an interesting experiment if lives weren't at stake.
This is what I came here for. To see if the Outsiders have undone all our good work, to see if they've finally learned to work as a team...
...even under provocation.
POLICE
So far, so good. Geo-Force is using his null-gravity power for defense, not attack on citizens his powers could easily kill...
...Looker's mental powers take away the rioters' will to fight...
...even Katana is letting the mob take out their anger without hurting them. All good strategy...
Their use of restraint is commendable, but they're not out of the woods yet--

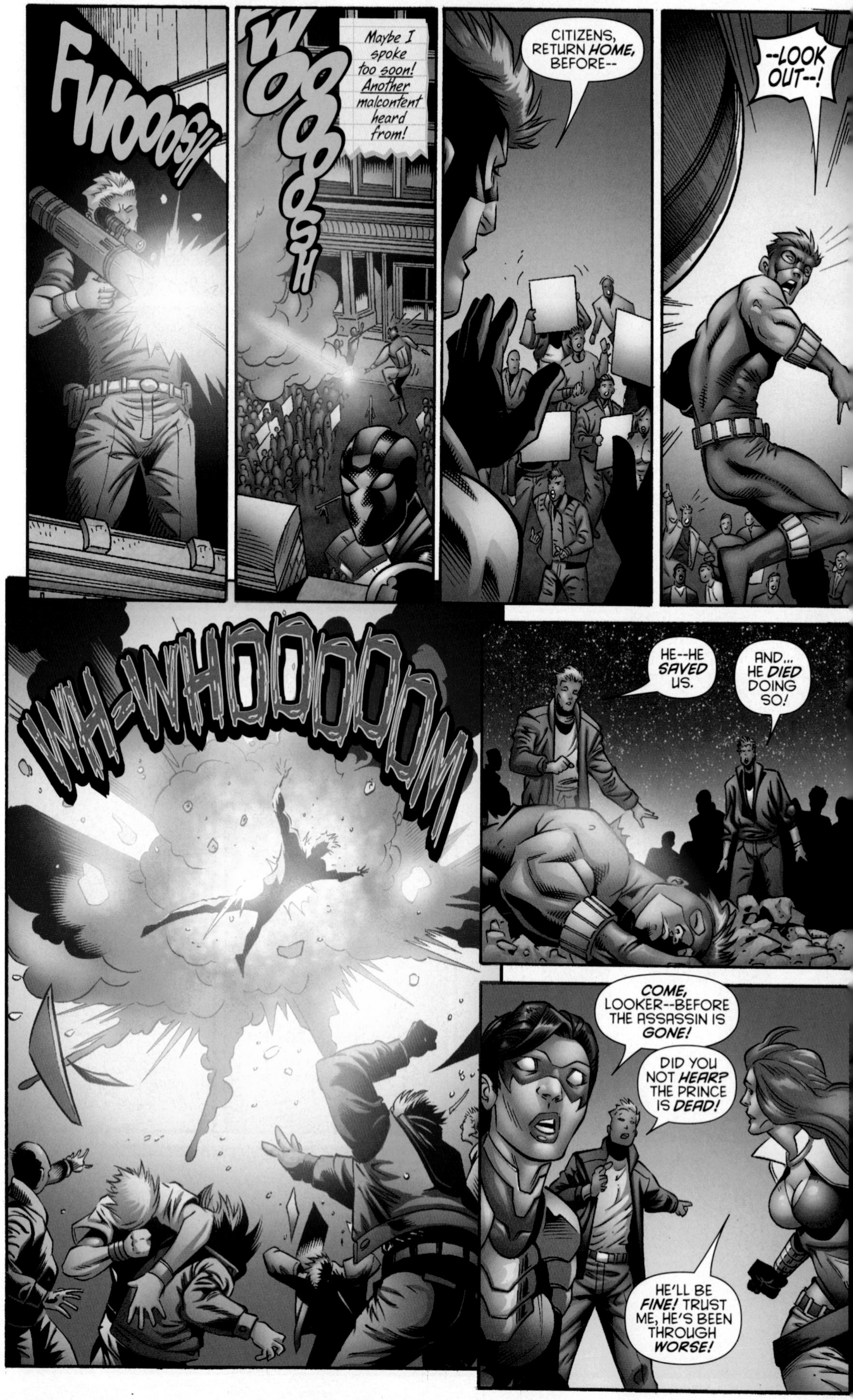
FWOOOSH
WOOOOOOSH
Maybe I spoke too soon! Another malcontent heard from!
CITIZENS, RETURN HOME, BEFORE--
--LOOK OUT--!
WH-WHOOOOOM
HE--HE SAVED US.
AND... HE DIED DOING SO!
COME, LOOKER--BEFORE THE ASSASSIN IS GONE!
DID YOU NOT HEAR? THE PRINCE IS DEAD!
HE'LL BE FINE! TRUST ME, HE'S BEEN THROUGH WORSE!

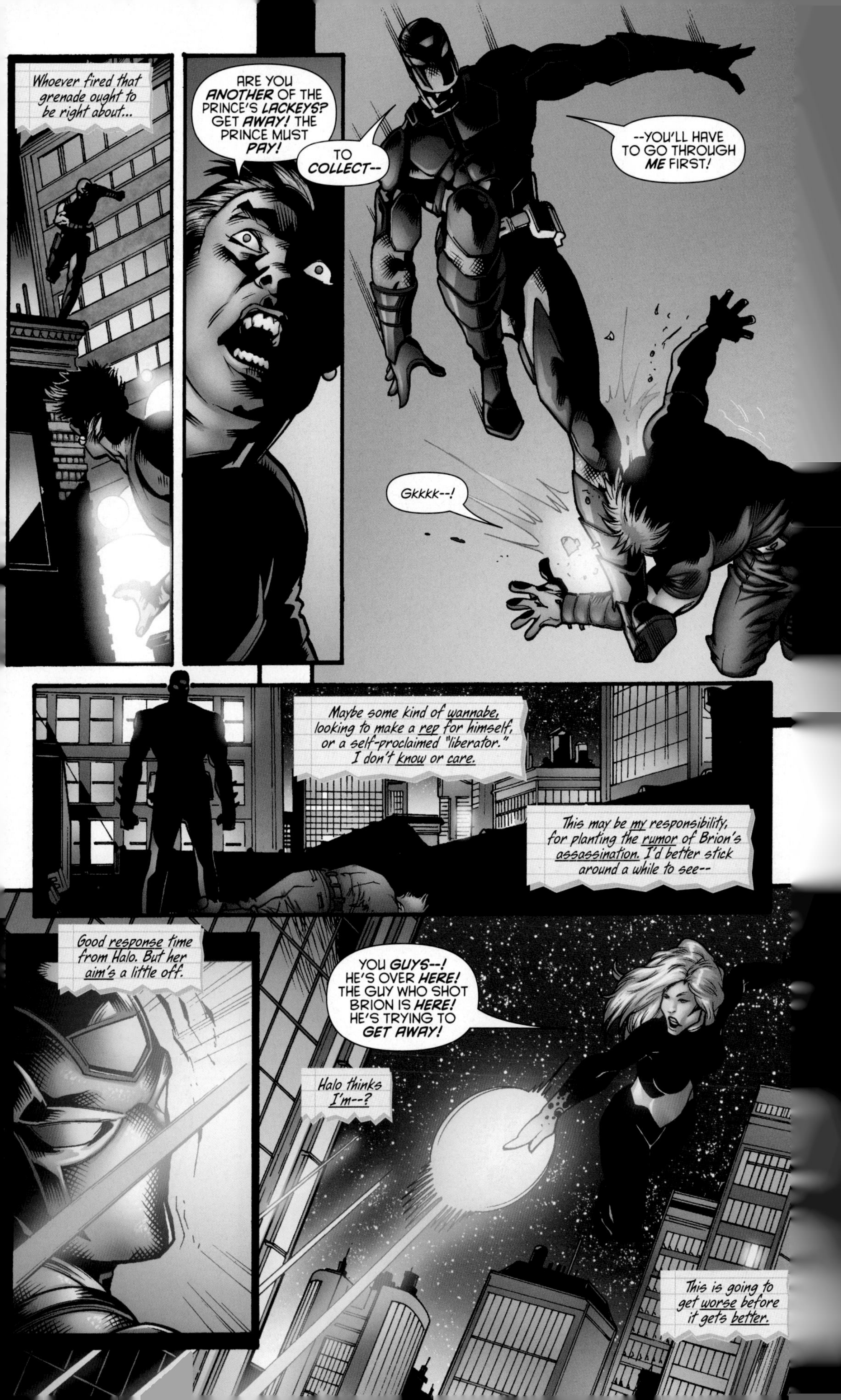

Whoever fired that grenade ought to be right about...
ARE YOU ANOTHER OF THE PRINCE'S LACKEYS? GET AWAY! THE PRINCE MUST PAY!
TO COLLECT--
--YOU'LL HAVE TO GO THROUGH ME FIRST!
Gkkkk--!
Maybe some kind of wannabe, looking to make a rep for himself, or a self-proclaimed "liberator." I don't know or care.
This may be my responsibility, for planting the rumor of Brion's assassination. I'd better stick around a while to see--
Good response time from Halo. But her aim's a little off.
YOU GUYS--! HE'S OVER HERE! THE GUY WHO SHOT BRION IS HERE! HE'S TRYING TO GET AWAY!
Halo thinks I'm--?
This is going to get worse before it gets better.

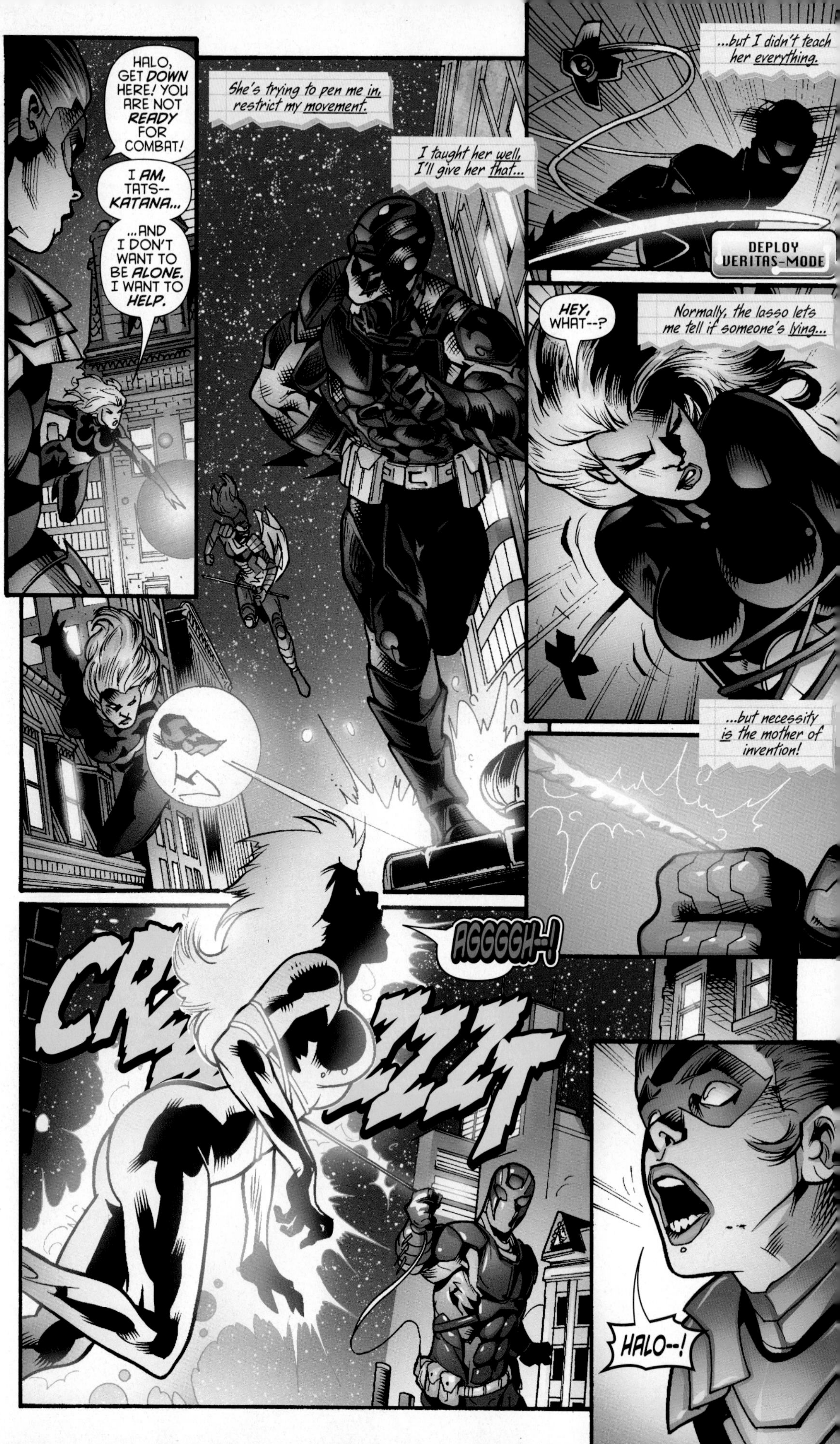
HALO, GET DOWN HERE! YOU ARE NOT READY FOR COMBAT!
I AM, TATS-- KATANA...
...AND I DON'T WANT TO BE ALONE. I WANT TO HELP.
She's trying to pen me in, restrict my movement.
I taught her well, I'll give her that...
...but I didn't teach her everything.
DEPLOY VERITAS-MODE
HEY, WHAT--?
Normally, the lasso lets me tell if someone's lying...
...but necessity is the mother of invention!
AGGGGH--!
CRZZZT
HALO--!

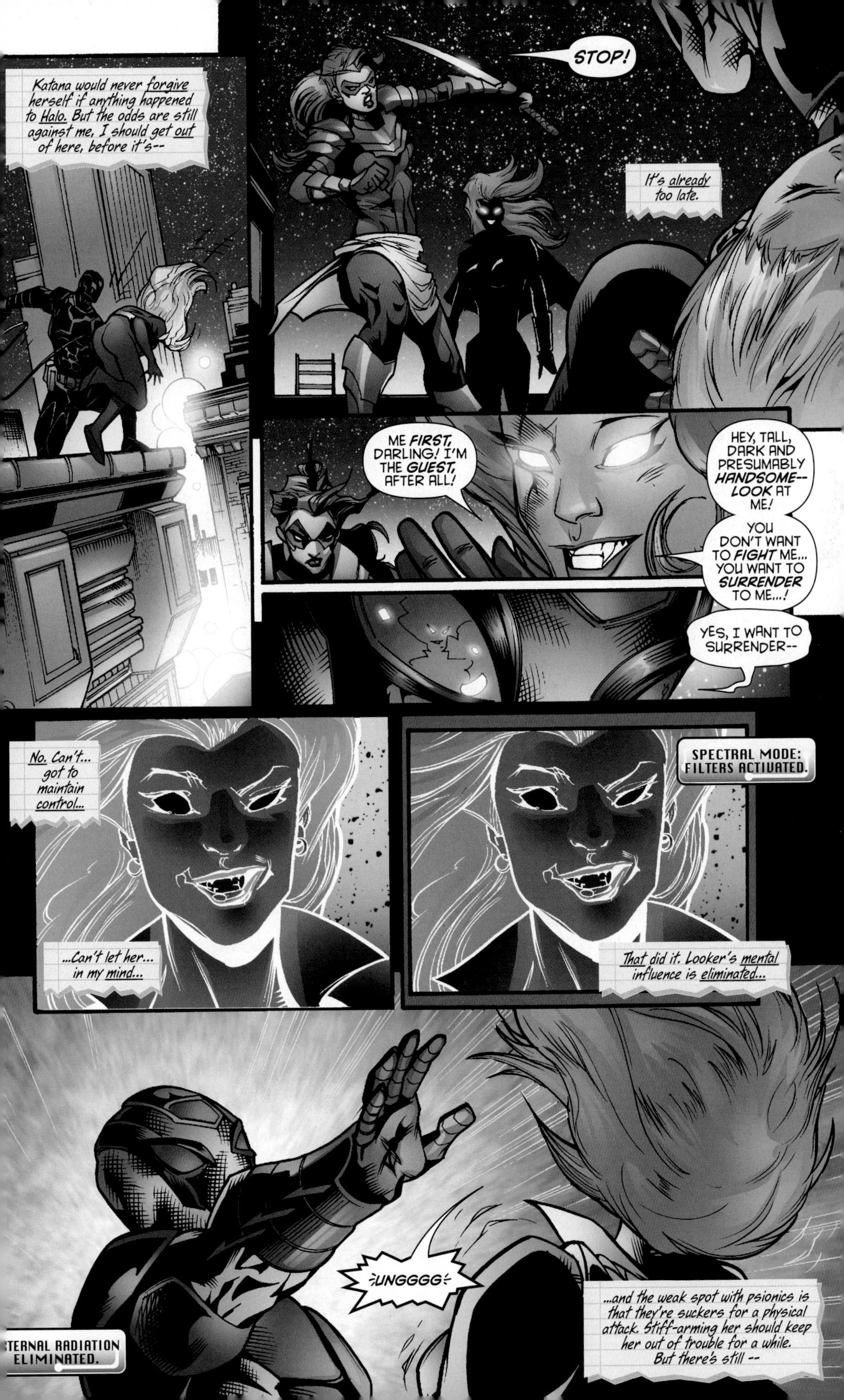
Katana would never forgive herself if anything happened to Halo. But the odds are still against me, I should get out of here, before it's--
STOP!
It's already too late.
ME FIRST, DARLING! I'M THE GUEST, AFTER ALL!
HEY, TALL, DARK AND PRESUMABLY HANDSOME-- LOOK AT ME!
YOU DON'T WANT TO FIGHT ME... YOU WANT TO SURRENDER TO ME...!
YES, I WANT TO SURRENDER--
No. Can't... got to maintain control...
...Can't let her... in my mind...
SPECTRAL MODE: FILTERS ACTIVATED.
That did it. Looker's mental influence is eliminated...
UNGGGG
TERNAL RADIATION ELIMINATED.
...and the weak spot with psionics is that they're suckers for a physical attack. Stiff-arming her should keep her out of trouble for a while. But there's still --

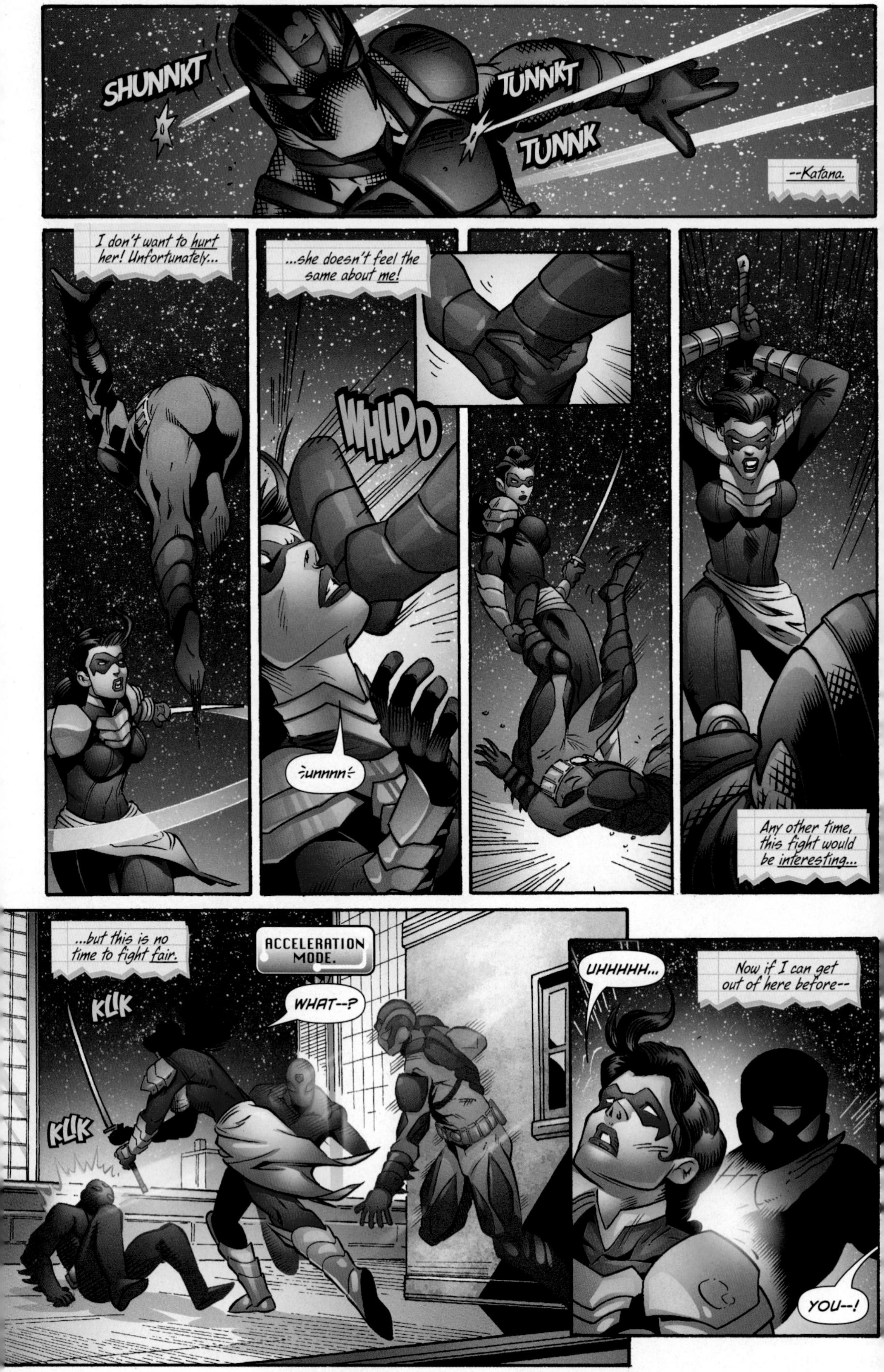
SHUNNKT
TUNNKT
TUNNK
--Katana.
I don't want to hurt her! Unfortunately...
...she doesn't feel the same about me!
WHUDD
unnnn
Any other time, this fight would be interesting...
...but this is no time to fight fair.
ACCELERATION MODE.
KLIK
KLIK
WHAT--?
UHHHHH...
Now if I can get out of here before--
YOU--!

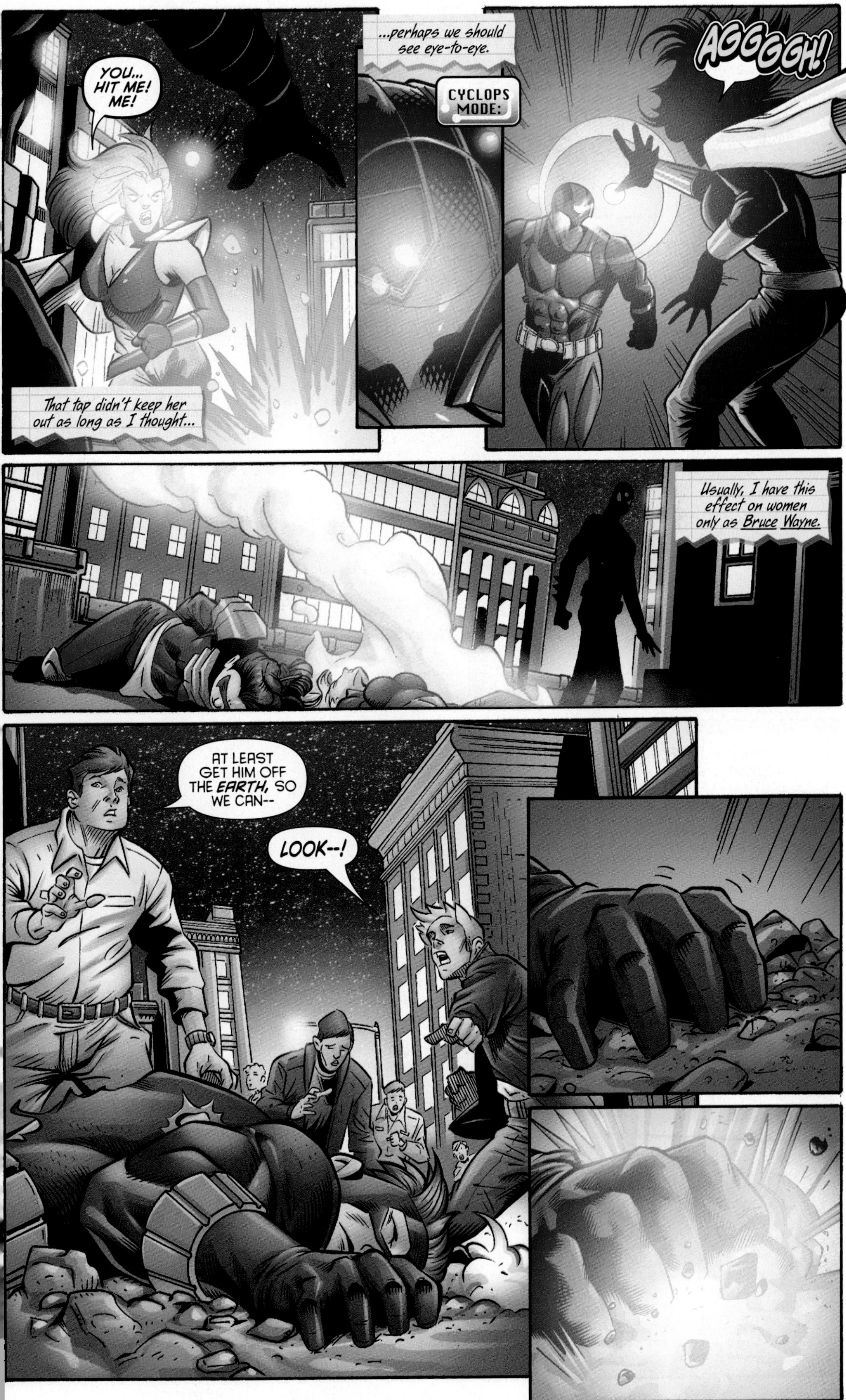
YOU... HIT ME! ME!
That tap didn't keep her out as long as I thought...
...perhaps we should see eye-to-eye.
CYCLOPS MODE:
AGGGGH!
Usually, I have this effect on women only as Bruce Wayne.
AT LEAST GET HIM OFF THE EARTH, SO WE CAN--
LOOK--!

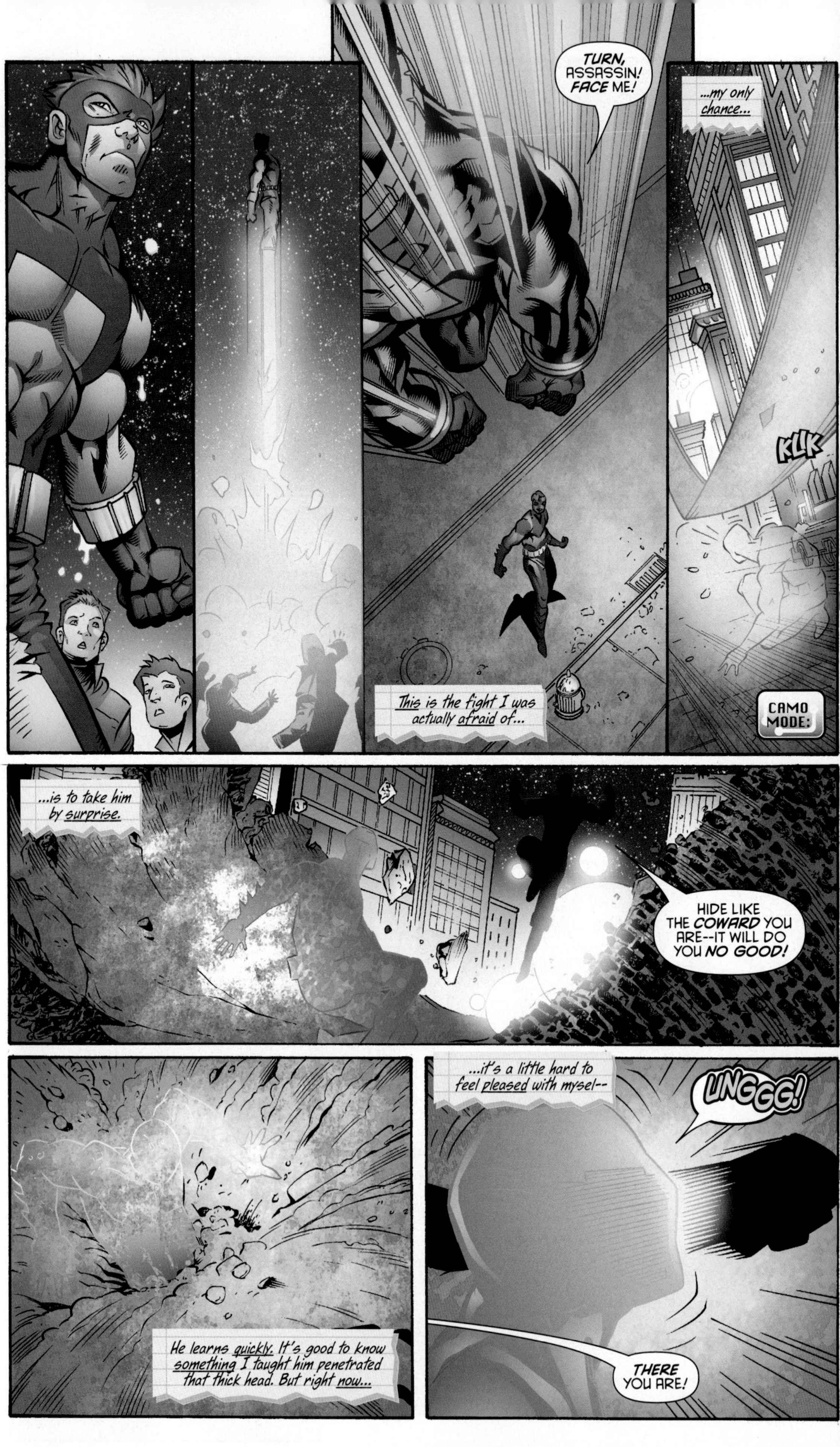
TURN, ASSASSIN! FACE ME!
...my only chance...
This is the fight I was actually afraid of...
KLIK
CAMO MODE:
...is to take him by surprise.
HIDE LIKE THE COWARD YOU ARE--IT WILL DO YOU NO GOOD!
He learns quickly. It's good to know something I taught him penetrated that thick head. But right now...
...it's a little hard to feel pleased with mysel--
UNGGG!
THERE YOU ARE!

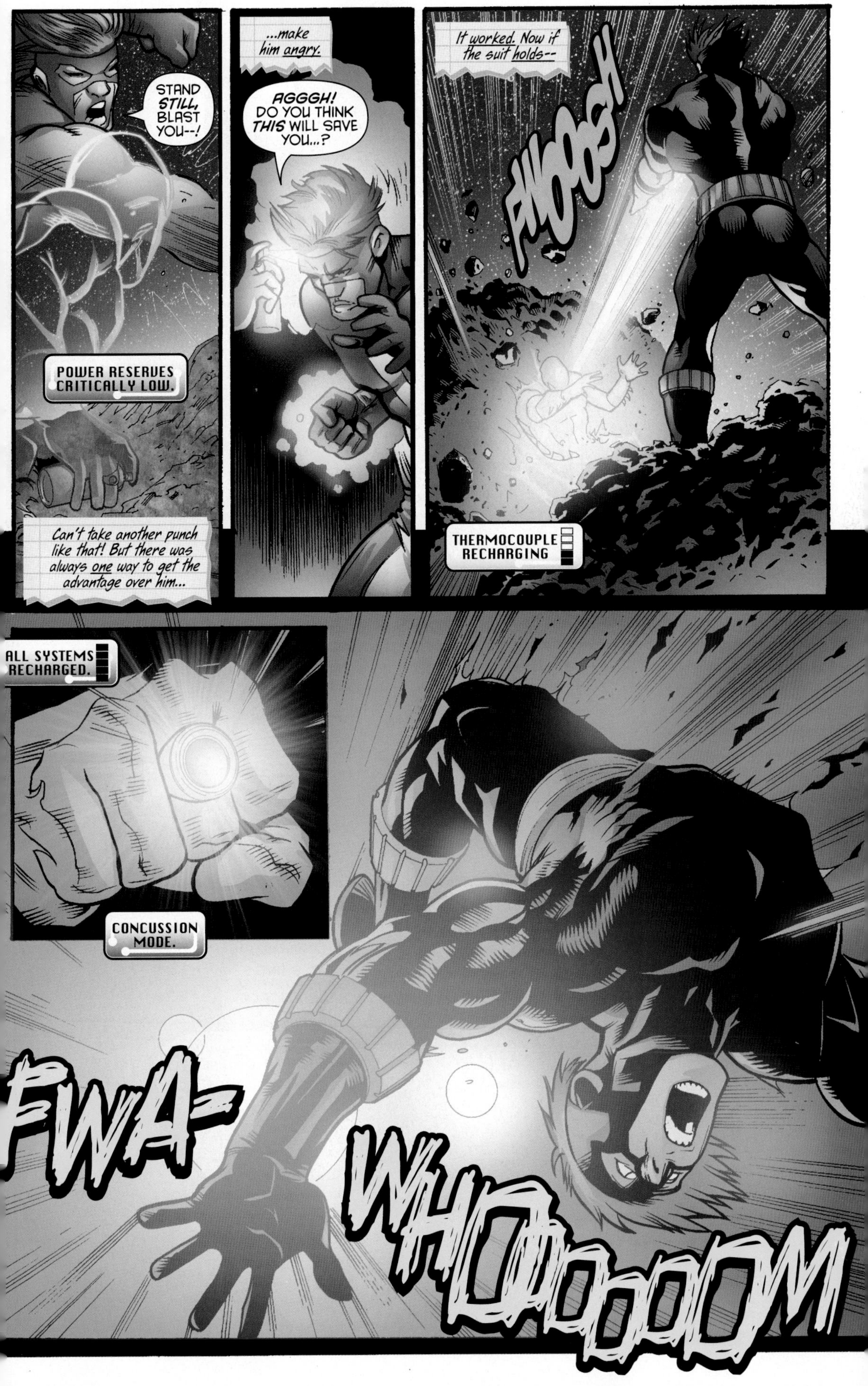
STAND STILL, BLAST YOU--!
POWER RESERVES CRITICALLY LOW.
Can't take another punch like that! But there was always one way to get the advantage over him...
...make him angry.
AGGGH! DO YOU THINK THIS WILL SAVE YOU...?
It worked. Now if the suit holds--
FWOOOSH
THERMOCOUPLE RECHARGING
ALL SYSTEMS RECHARGED.
CONCUSSION MODE.
FWA-
WHOOOOOOM

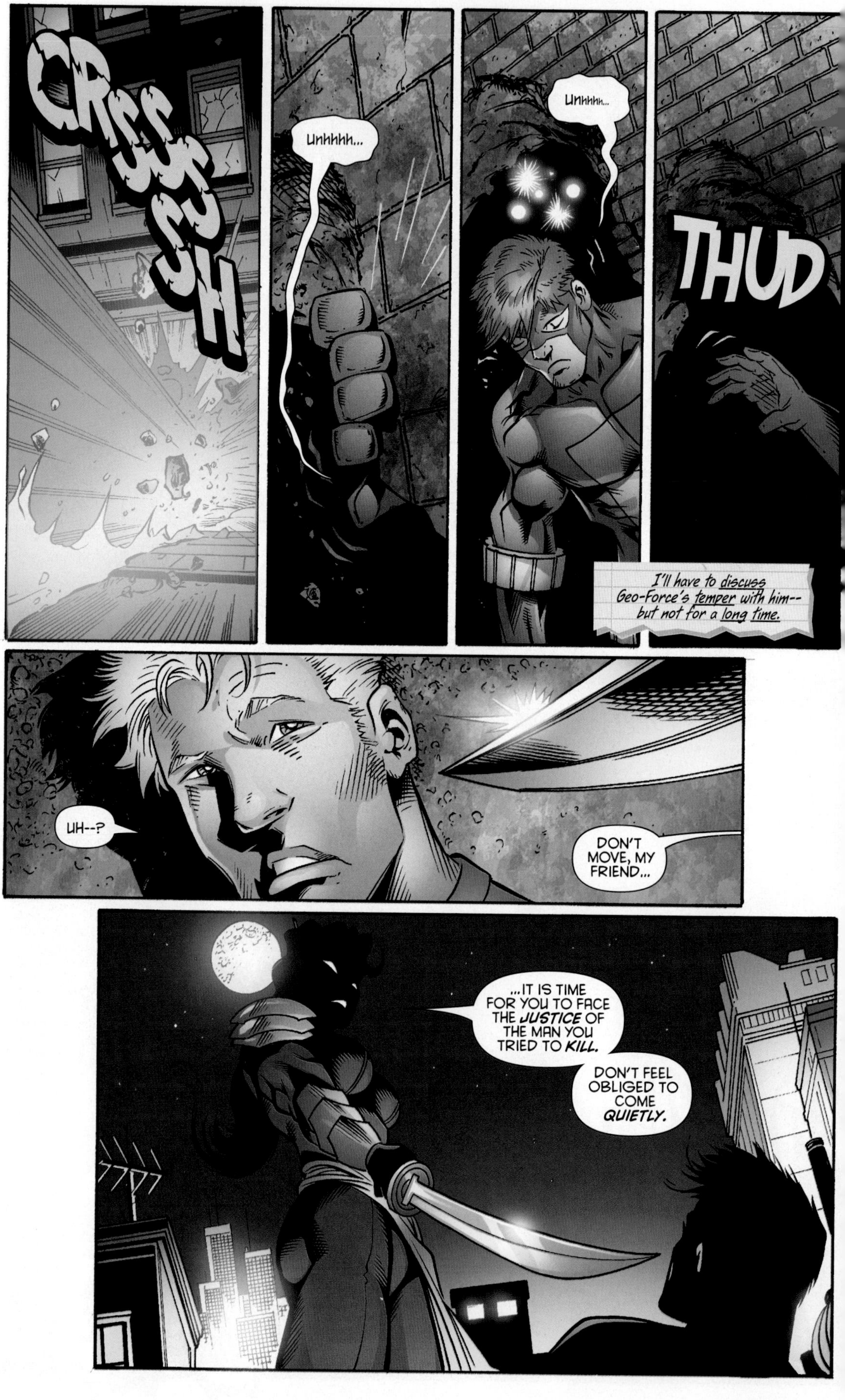
CRSSSSH
Unhhhh...
Unhhhh...
THUD
I'll have to discuss Geo-Force's temper with him-- but not for a long time.
UH--?
DON'T MOVE, MY FRIEND...
...IT IS TIME FOR YOU TO FACE THE JUSTICE OF THE MAN YOU TRIED TO KILL.
DON'T FEEL OBLIGED TO COME QUIETLY.

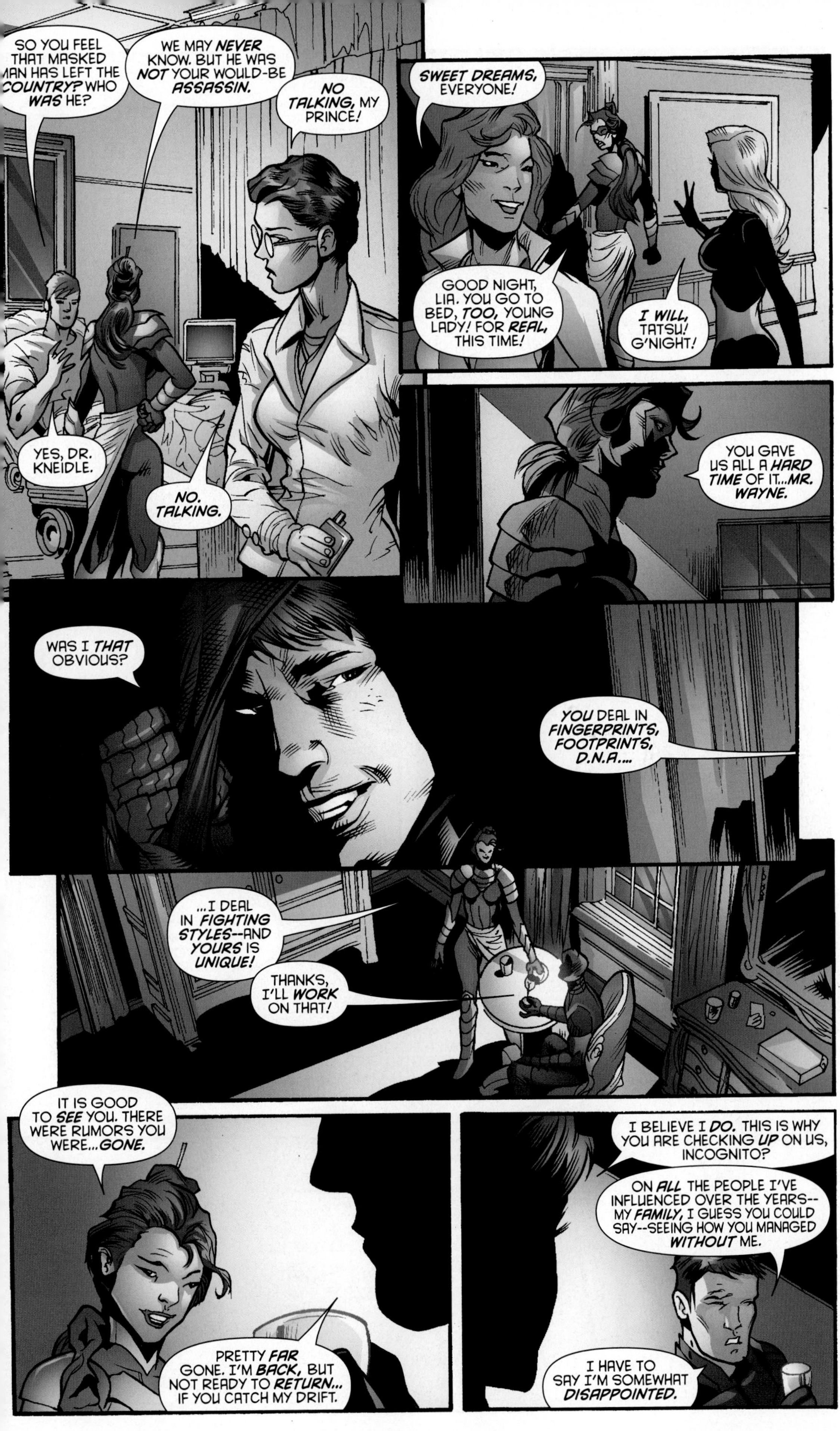
SO YOU FEEL THAT MASKED MAN HAS LEFT THE COUNTRY? WHO WAS HE?
WE MAY NEVER KNOW. BUT HE WAS NOT YOUR WOULD-BE ASSASSIN.
NO TALKING, MY PRINCE!
YES, DR. KNEIDLE.
NO. TALKING.
SWEET DREAMS, EVERYONE!
GOOD NIGHT, LIA. YOU GO TO BED, TOO, YOUNG LADY! FOR REAL, THIS TIME!
I WILL, TATSU! G'NIGHT!
YOU GAVE US ALL A HARD TIME OF IT...MR. WAYNE.
WAS I THAT OBVIOUS?
YOU DEAL IN FINGERPRINTS, FOOTPRINTS, D.N.A....
...I DEAL IN FIGHTING STYLES--AND YOURS IS UNIQUE!
THANKS, I'LL WORK ON THAT!
IT IS GOOD TO SEE YOU. THERE WERE RUMORS YOU WERE...GONE.
PRETTY FAR GONE. I'M BACK, BUT NOT READY TO RETURN... IF YOU CATCH MY DRIFT.
I BELIEVE I DO. THIS IS WHY YOU ARE CHECKING UP ON US, INCOGNITO?
ON ALL THE PEOPLE I'VE INFLUENCED OVER THE YEARS-- MY FAMILY, I GUESS YOU COULD SAY--SEEING HOW YOU MANAGED WITHOUT ME.
I HAVE TO SAY I'M SOMEWHAT DISAPPOINTED.

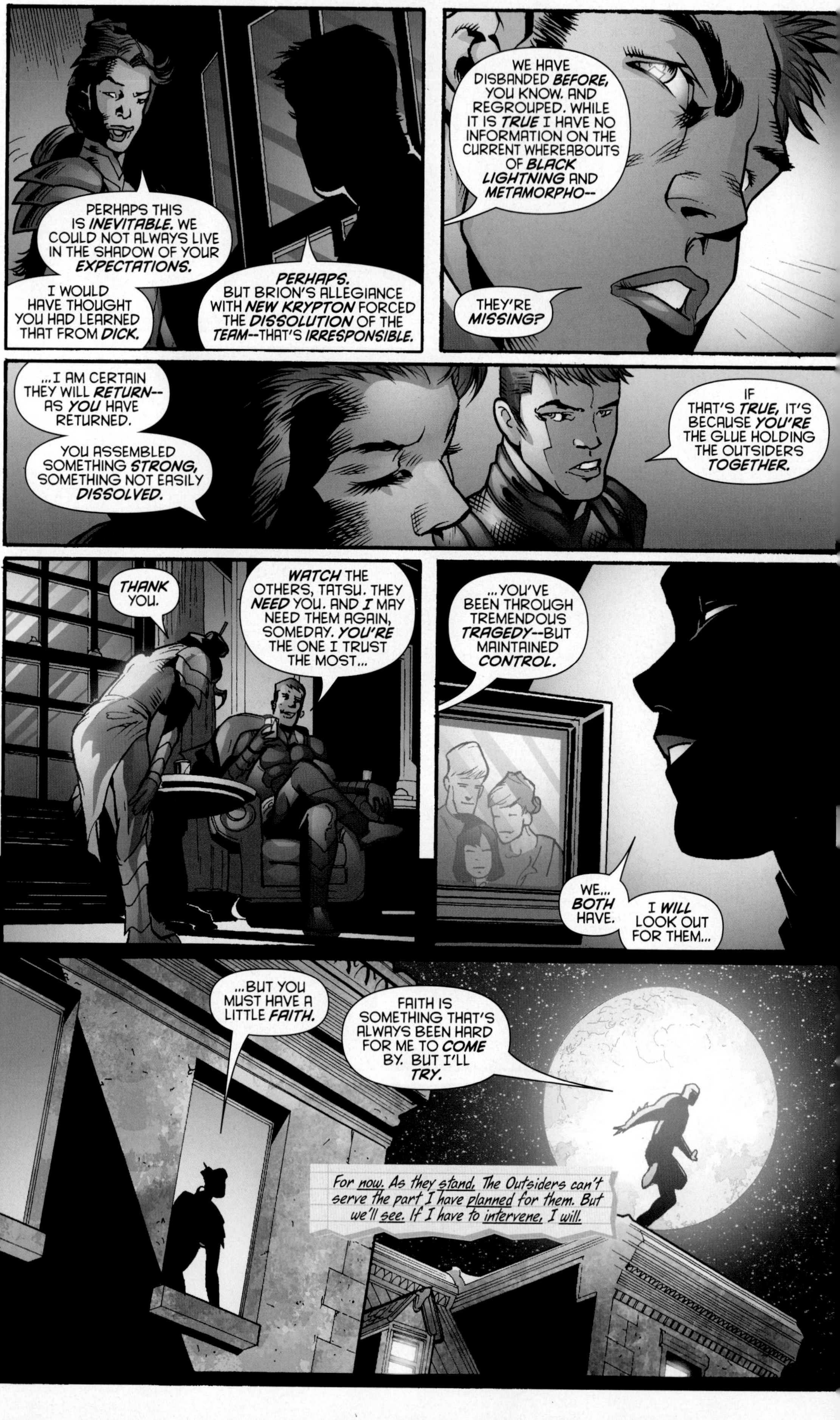
PERHAPS THIS IS INEVITABLE. WE COULD NOT ALWAYS LIVE IN THE SHADOW OF YOUR EXPECTATIONS.
I WOULD HAVE THOUGHT YOU HAD LEARNED THAT FROM DICK.
PERHAPS. BUT BRION'S ALLEGIANCE WITH NEW KRYPTON FORCED THE DISSOLUTION OF THE TEAM--THAT'S IRRESPONSIBLE.
WE HAVE DISBANDED BEFORE, YOU KNOW. AND REGROUPED. WHILE IT IS TRUE I HAVE NO INFORMATION ON THE CURRENT WHEREABOUTS OF BLACK LIGHTNING AND METAMORPHO--
THEY'RE MISSING?
...I AM CERTAIN THEY WILL RETURN-- AS YOU HAVE RETURNED.
YOU ASSEMBLED SOMETHING STRONG, SOMETHING NOT EASILY DISSOLVED.
IF THAT'S TRUE, IT'S BECAUSE YOU'RE THE GLUE HOLDING THE OUTSIDERS TOGETHER.
THANK YOU.
WATCH THE OTHERS, TATSU. THEY NEED YOU. AND I MAY NEED THEM AGAIN, SOMEDAY. YOU'RE THE ONE I TRUST THE MOST...
...YOU'VE BEEN THROUGH TREMENDOUS TRAGEDY--BUT MAINTAINED CONTROL.
WE... BOTH HAVE.
I WILL LOOK OUT FOR THEM...
...BUT YOU MUST HAVE A LITTLE FAITH.
FAITH IS SOMETHING THAT'S ALWAYS BEEN HARD FOR ME TO COME BY. BUT I'LL TRY.
For now. As they stand, The Outsiders can't serve the part I have planned for them. But we'll see. If I have to intervene, I will.

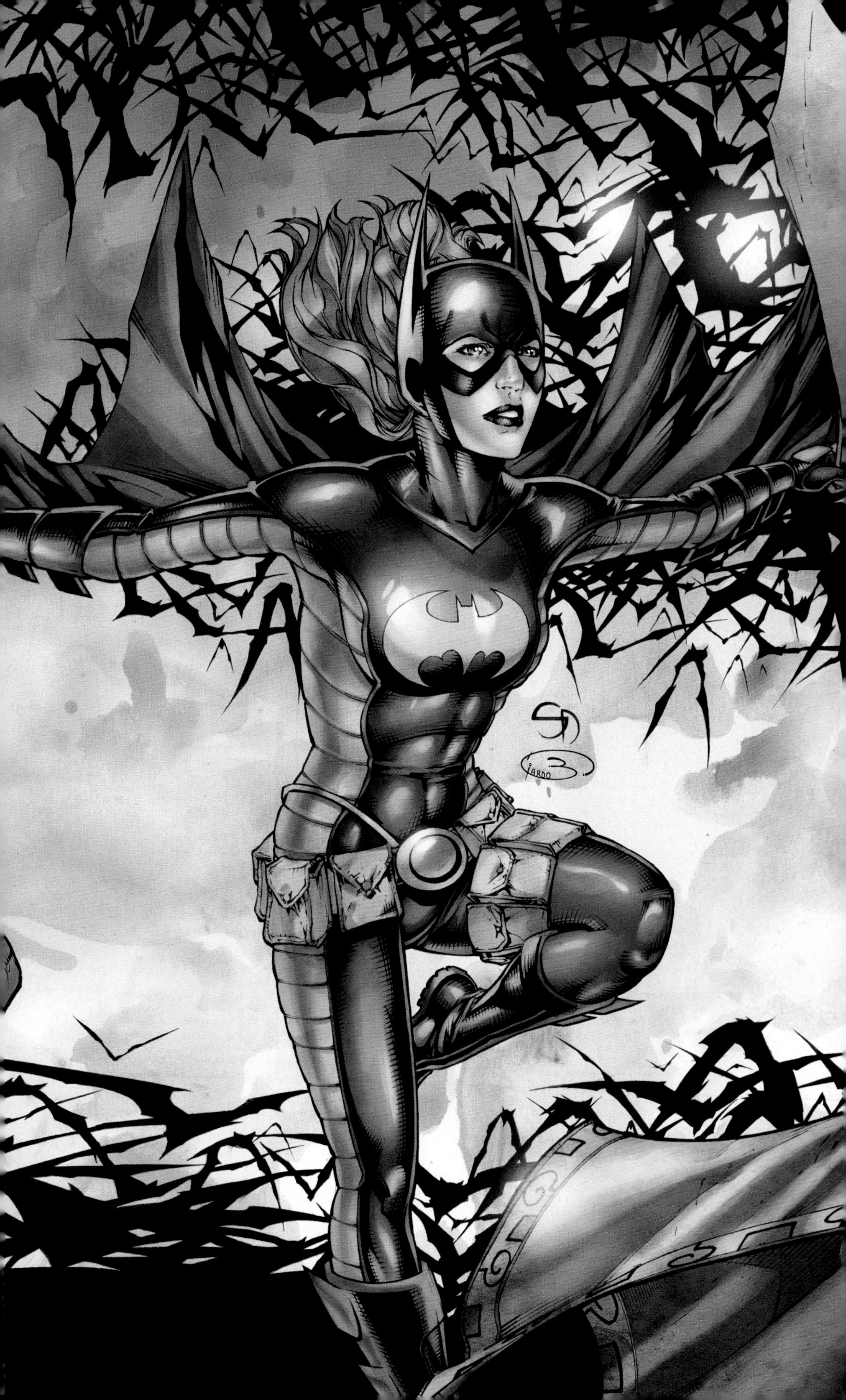

"BRUCE NEVER GAVE ME A FAIR SHOT."

BRUCE WAYNE: THE ROAD HOME

BATGIRL

BRYAN Q. MILLER WRITER

PERE PEREZ ARTIST

GUY MAJOR COLORIST

DAVE SHARPE LETTERER

SHANE DAVIS AND BARBARA CIARDO COVER

SEAN RYAN EDITOR

MIKE MARTS BATMAN GROUP EDITOR

BATMAN CREATED BY BOB KANE

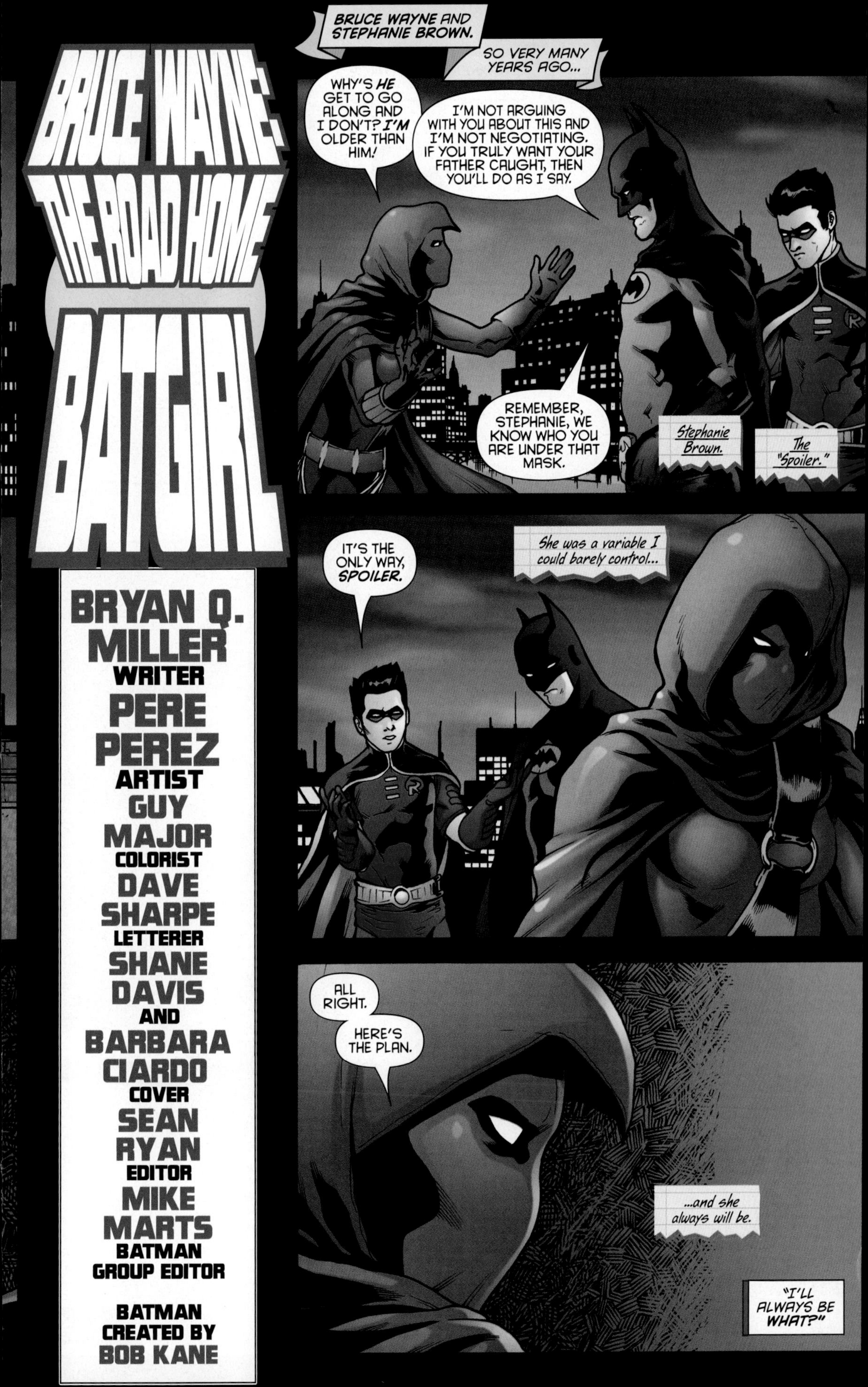

BRUCE WAYNE AND STEPHANIE BROWN.
SO VERY MANY YEARS AGO...
WHY'S HE GET TO GO ALONG AND I DON'T? I'M OLDER THAN HIM!
I'M NOT ARGUING WITH YOU ABOUT THIS AND I'M NOT NEGOTIATING. IF YOU TRULY WANT YOUR FATHER CAUGHT, THEN YOU'LL DO AS I SAY.
REMEMBER, STEPHANIE, WE KNOW WHO YOU ARE UNDER THAT MASK.
Stephanie Brown.
The "Spoiler."
IT'S THE ONLY WAY, SPOILER.
She was a variable I could barely control...
ALL RIGHT.
HERE'S THE PLAN.
...and she always will be.
"I'LL ALWAYS BE WHAT?"

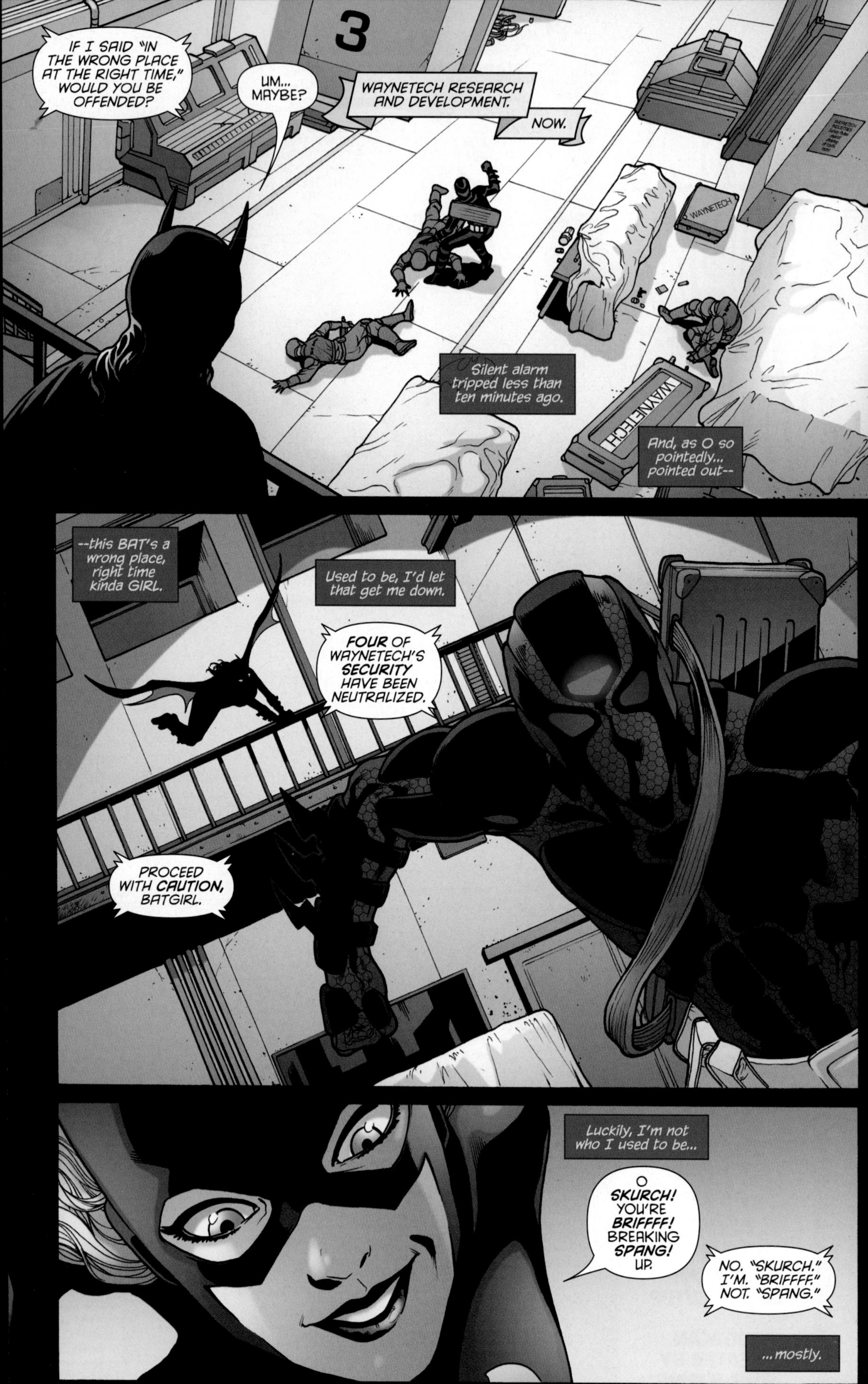
3
IF I SAID "IN THE WRONG PLACE AT THE RIGHT TIME," WOULD YOU BE OFFENDED?
UM... MAYBE?
WAYNETECH RESEARCH AND DEVELOPMENT.
NOW.
WAYNETECH
Silent alarm tripped less than ten minutes ago.
WAYNETECH
And, as O so pointedly... pointed out--
--this BAT's a wrong place, right time kinda GIRL.
Used to be, I'd let that get me down.
FOUR OF WAYNETECH'S SECURITY HAVE BEEN NEUTRALIZED.
PROCEED WITH CAUTION, BATGIRL.
Luckily, I'm not who I used to be...
O SKURCH! YOU'RE BRIFFFF! BREAKING SPANG! UP.
NO. "SKURCH." I'M. "BRIFFFF." NOT. "SPANG."
...mostly.

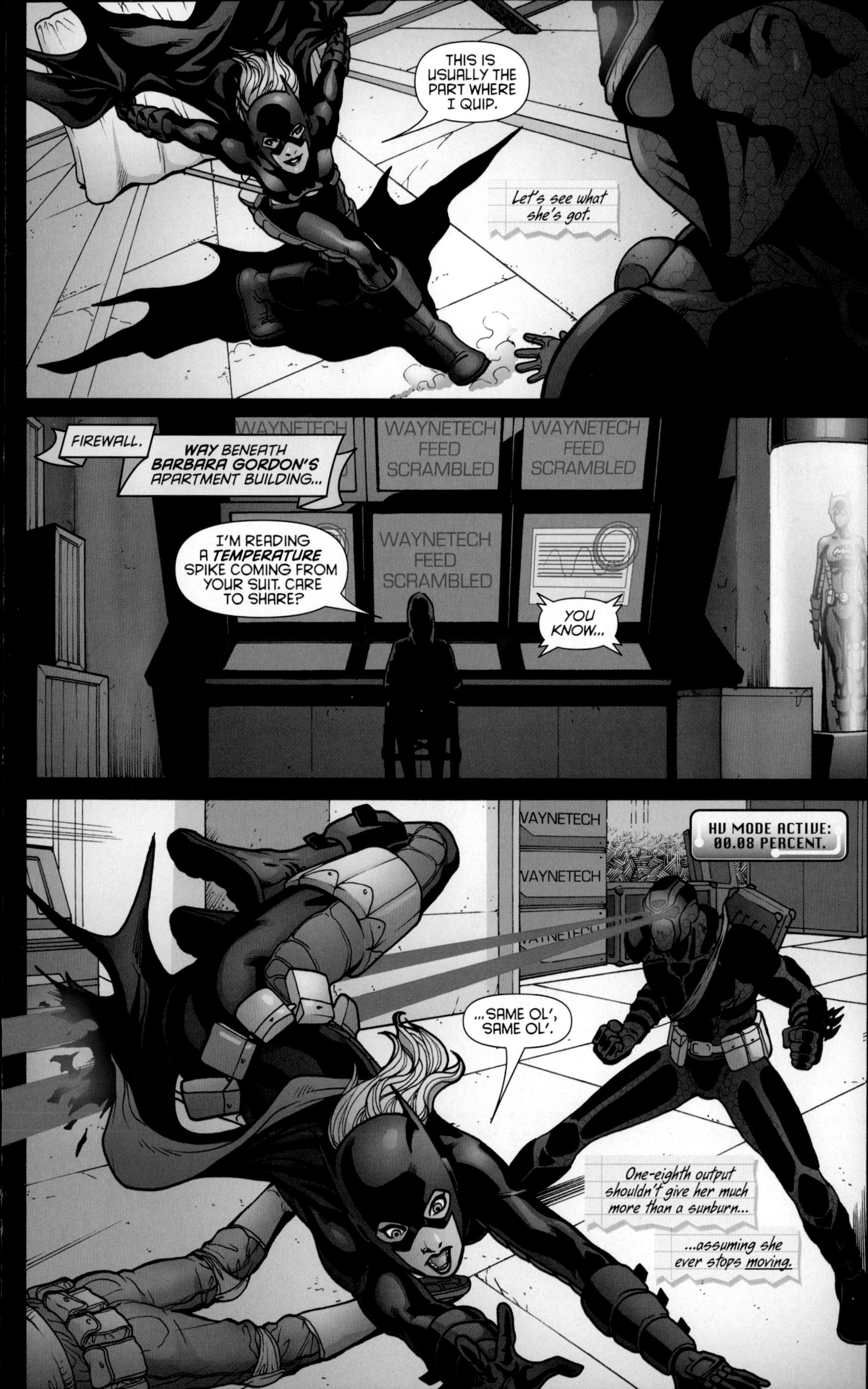
THIS IS USUALLY THE PART WHERE I QUIP.
Let's see what she's got.
FIREWALL.
WAY BENEATH BARBARA GORDON'S APARTMENT BUILDING...
WAYNETECH
WAYNETECH FEED SCRAMBLED
WAYNETECH FEED SCRAMBLED
I'M READING A TEMPERATURE SPIKE COMING FROM YOUR SUIT. CARE TO SHARE?
WAYNETECH FEED SCRAMBLED
YOU KNOW...
WAYNETECH
WAYNETECH
HV MODE ACTIVE: 00.08 PERCENT.
...SAME OL', SAME OL'.
One-eighth output shouldn't give her much more than a sunburn...
...assuming she ever stops moving.

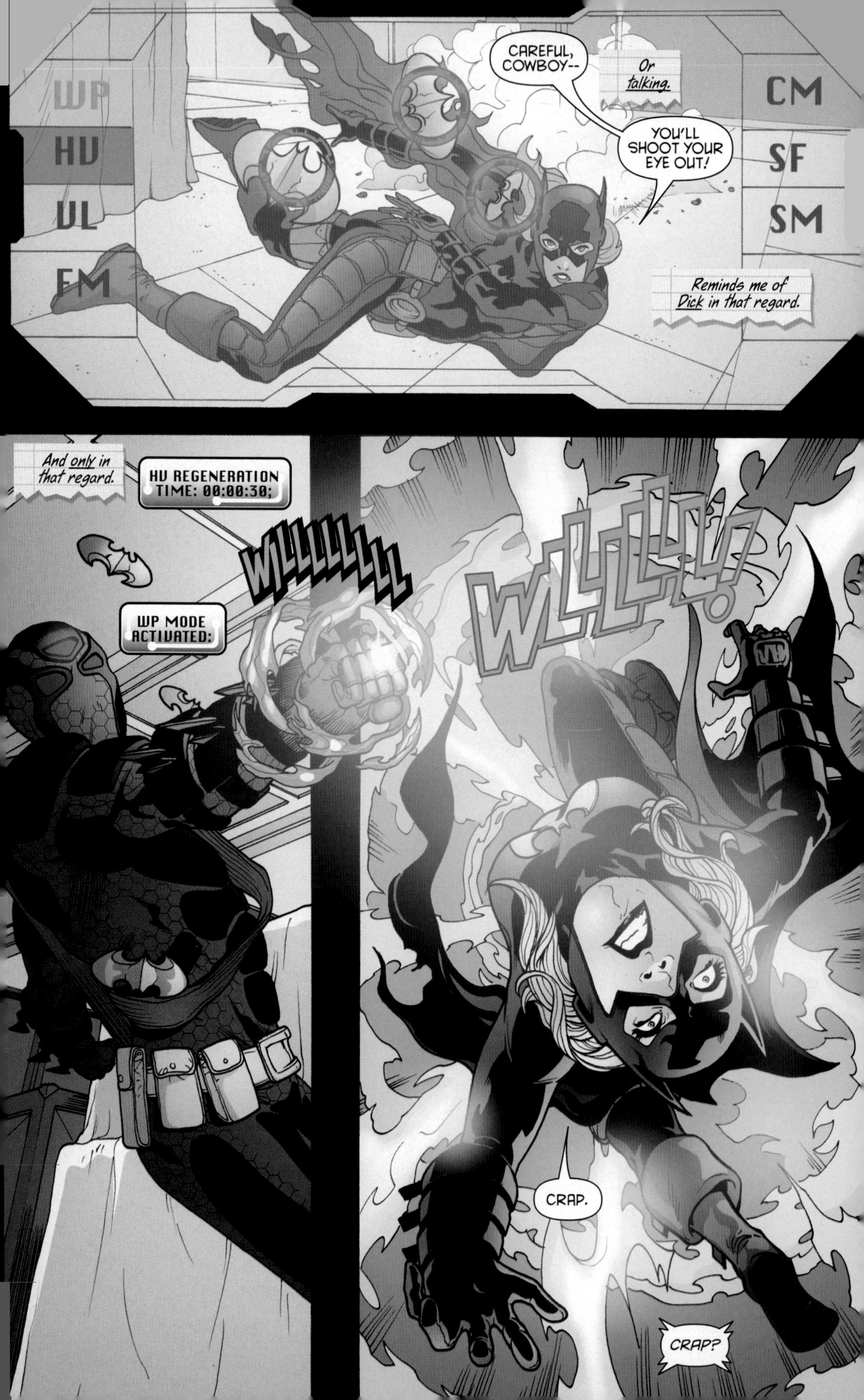
WP
HV
VL
FM
CAREFUL, COWBOY--
Or talking.
YOU'LL SHOOT YOUR EYE OUT!
CM
SF
SM
Reminds me of Dick in that regard.
And only in that regard.
HV REGENERATION TIME: 00:00:30;
WLLLLLLLL
WP MODE ACTIVATED:
WLLLLL!
CRAP.
CRAP?

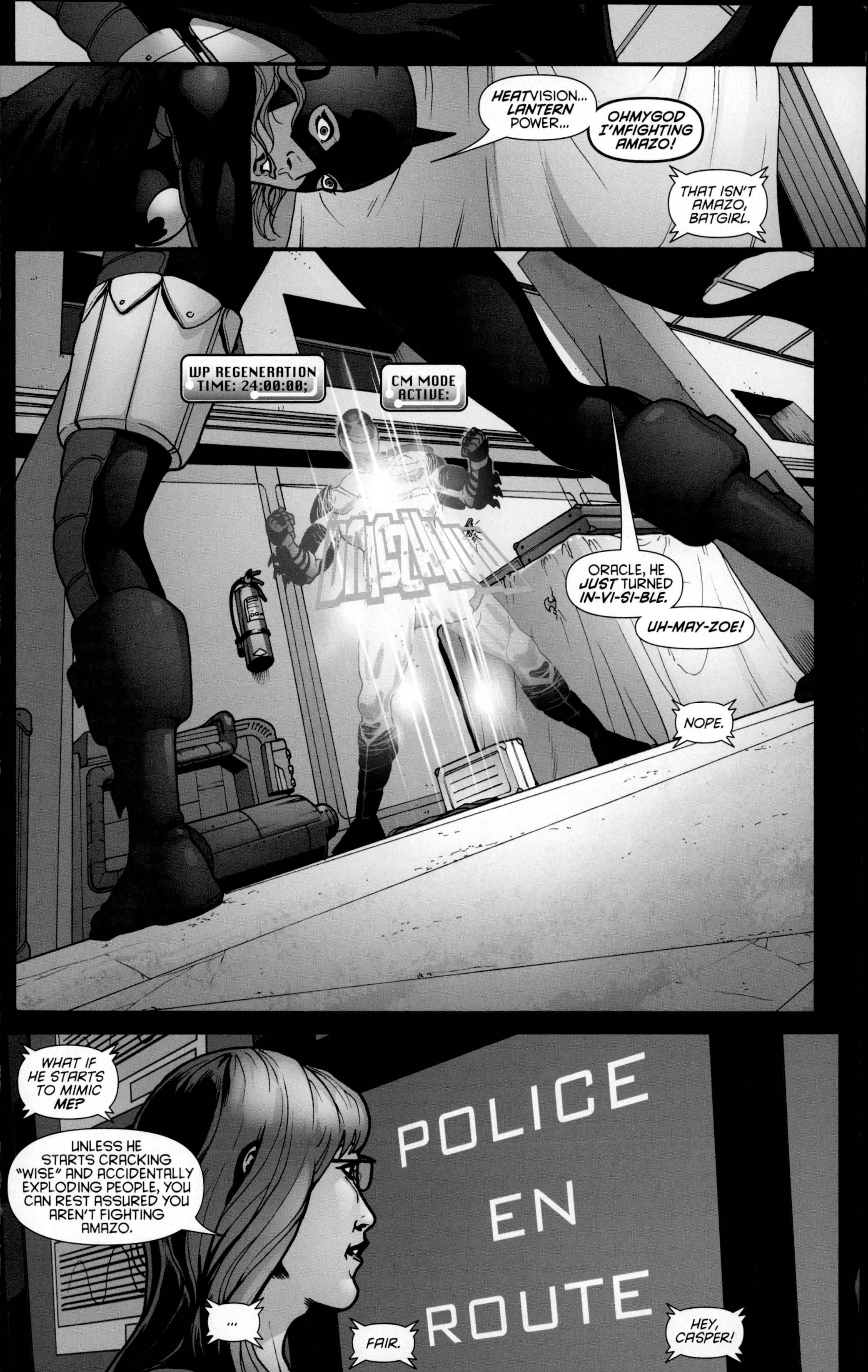
HEATVISION... LANTERN POWER...
OHMYGOD I'MFIGHTING AMAZO!
THAT ISN'T AMAZO, BATGIRL.
WP REGENERATION TIME: 24:00:00;
CM MODE ACTIVE:
ORACLE, HE JUST TURNED IN-VI-SI-BLE.
UH-MAY-ZOE!
NOPE.
WHAT IF HE STARTS TO MIMIC ME?
UNLESS HE STARTS CRACKING "WISE" AND ACCIDENTALLY EXPLODING PEOPLE, YOU CAN REST ASSURED YOU AREN'T FIGHTING AMAZO.
POLICE EN ROUTE
...
FAIR.
HEY, CASPER!

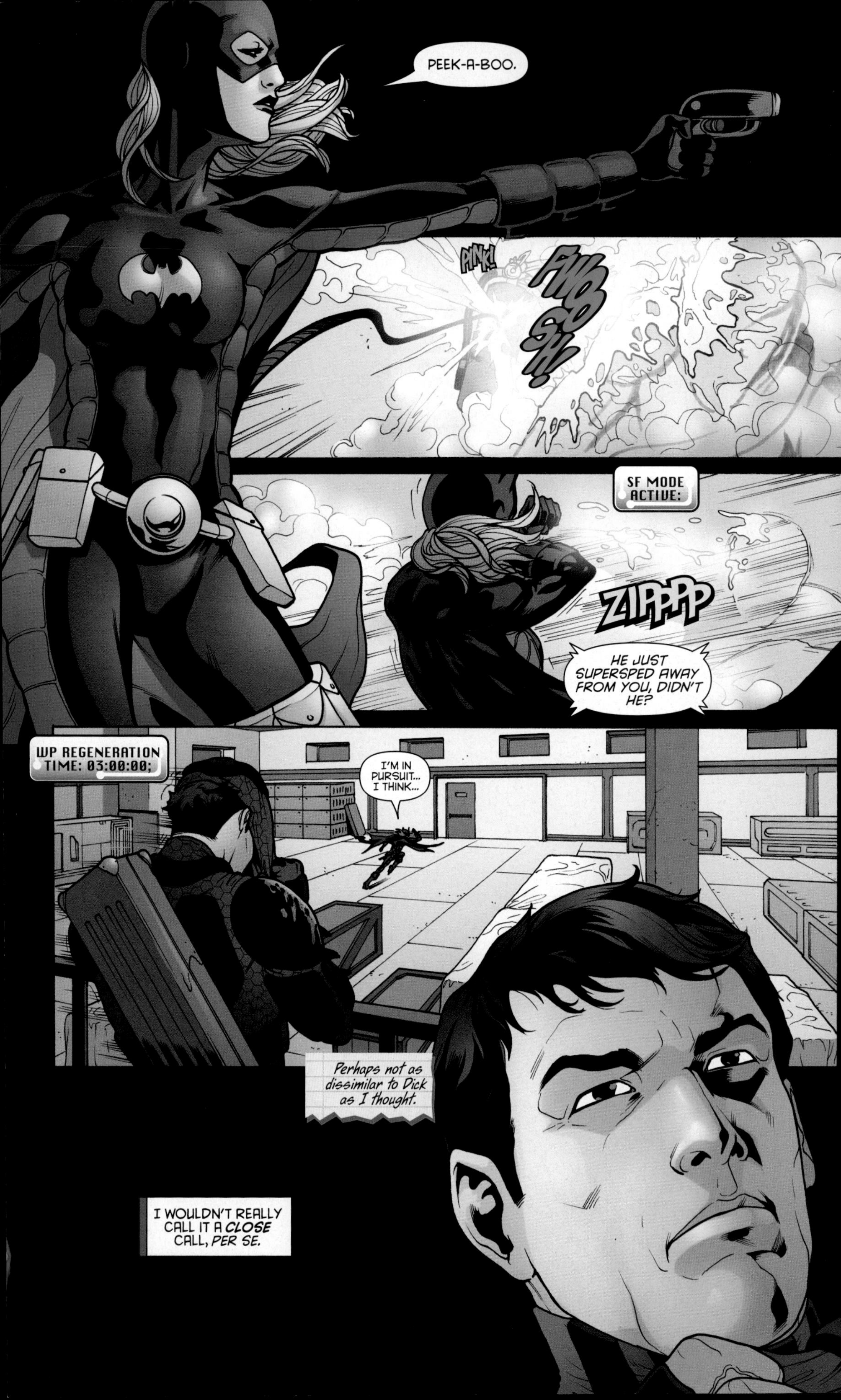

PEEK-A-BOO.
PINK!
FWOOSH!
SF MODE ACTIVE:
ZIPPPP
HE JUST SUPERSPED AWAY FROM YOU, DIDN'T HE?
WP REGENERATION TIME: 03:00:00;
I'M IN PURSUIT... I THINK...
Perhaps not as dissimilar to Dick as I thought.
I WOULDN'T REALLY CALL IT A CLOSE CALL, PER SE.

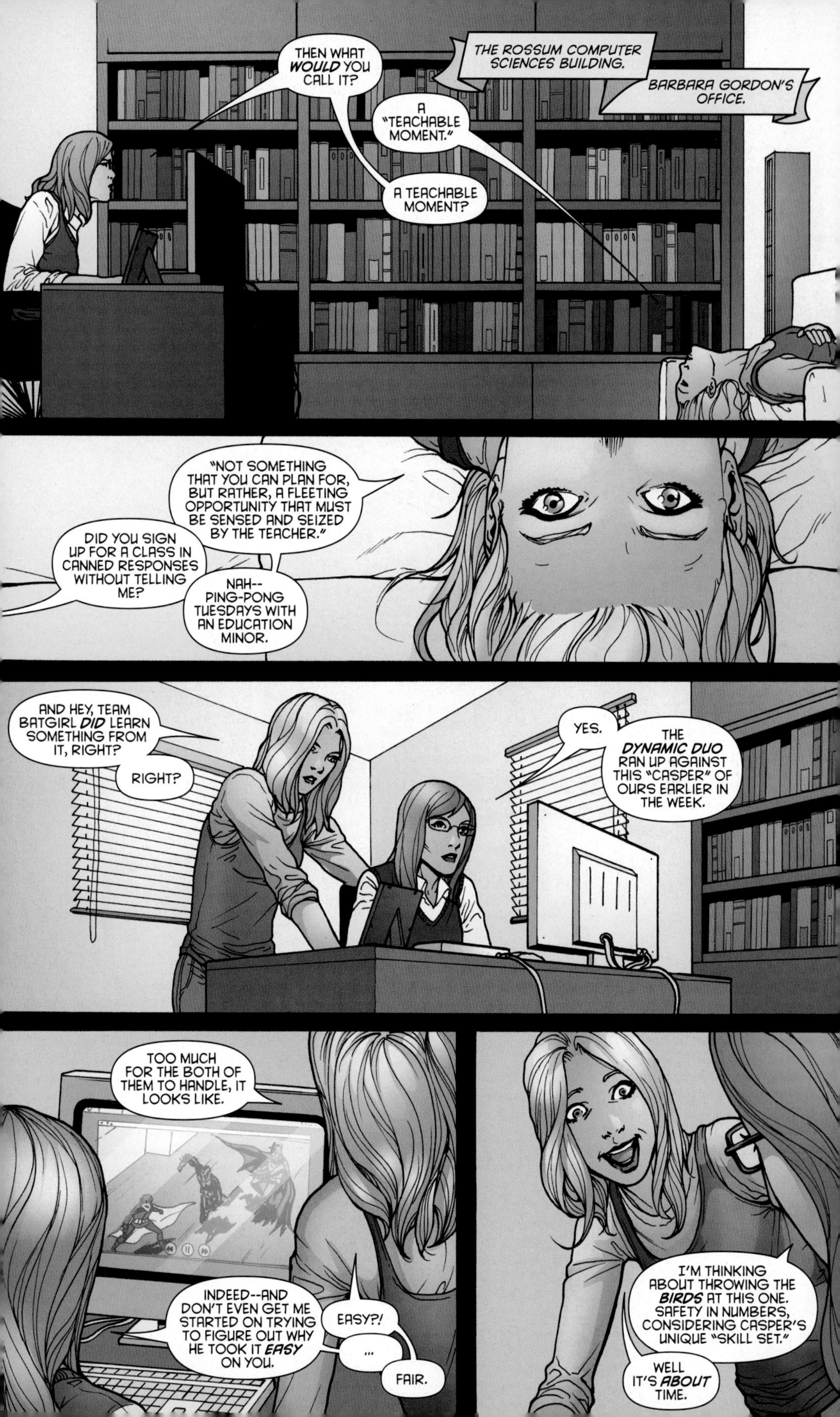
THE ROSSUM COMPUTER SCIENCES BUILDING.
BARBARA GORDON'S OFFICE.
THEN WHAT WOULD YOU CALL IT?
A "TEACHABLE MOMENT."
A TEACHABLE MOMENT?
"NOT SOMETHING THAT YOU CAN PLAN FOR, BUT RATHER, A FLEETING OPPORTUNITY THAT MUST BE SENSED AND SEIZED BY THE TEACHER."
DID YOU SIGN UP FOR A CLASS IN CANNED RESPONSES WITHOUT TELLING ME?
NAH-- PING-PONG TUESDAYS WITH AN EDUCATION MINOR.
AND HEY, TEAM BATGIRL DID LEARN SOMETHING FROM IT, RIGHT?
RIGHT?
YES.
THE DYNAMIC DUO RAN UP AGAINST THIS "CASPER" OF OURS EARLIER IN THE WEEK.
TOO MUCH FOR THE BOTH OF THEM TO HANDLE, IT LOOKS LIKE.
INDEED--AND DON'T EVEN GET ME STARTED ON TRYING TO FIGURE OUT WHY HE TOOK IT EASY ON YOU.
EASY?!
...
FAIR.
I'M THINKING ABOUT THROWING THE BIRDS AT THIS ONE. SAFETY IN NUMBERS, CONSIDERING CASPER'S UNIQUE "SKILL SET."
WELL IT'S ABOUT TIME.

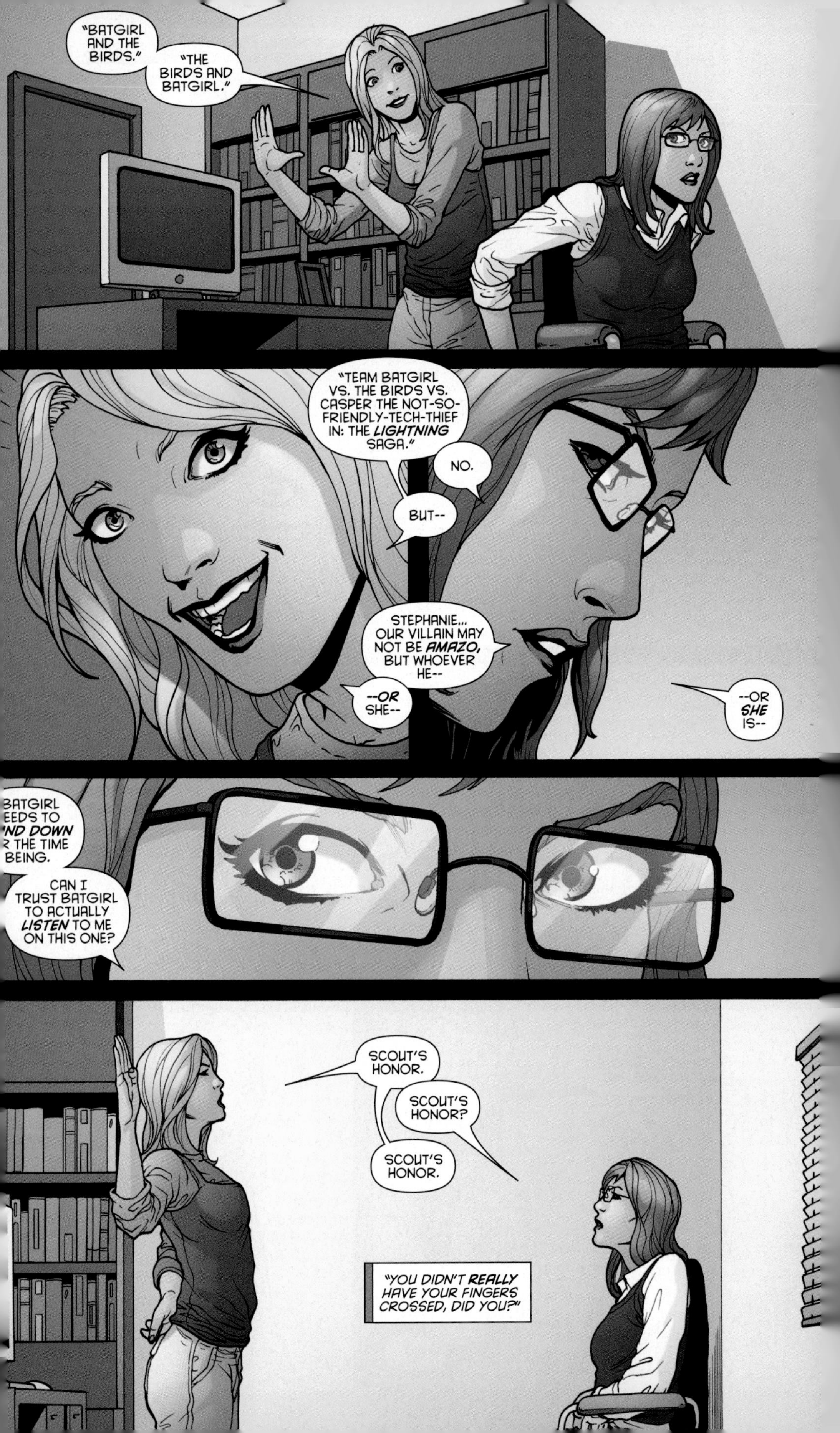
"BATGIRL AND THE BIRDS."
"THE BIRDS AND BATGIRL."
"TEAM BATGIRL VS. THE BIRDS VS. CASPER THE NOT-SO-FRIENDLY-TECH-THIEF IN: THE *LIGHTNING* SAGA."
NO.
BUT--
STEPHANIE... OUR VILLAIN MAY NOT BE *AMAZO,* BUT WHOEVER HE--
--OR SHE--
--OR *SHE* IS--
BATGIRL EEDS TO *ND DOWN* R THE TIME BEING.
CAN I TRUST BATGIRL TO ACTUALLY *LISTEN* TO ME ON THIS ONE?
SCOUT'S HONOR.
SCOUT'S HONOR?
SCOUT'S HONOR.
*"YOU DIDN'T **REALLY** HAVE YOUR FINGERS CROSSED, DID YOU?"*

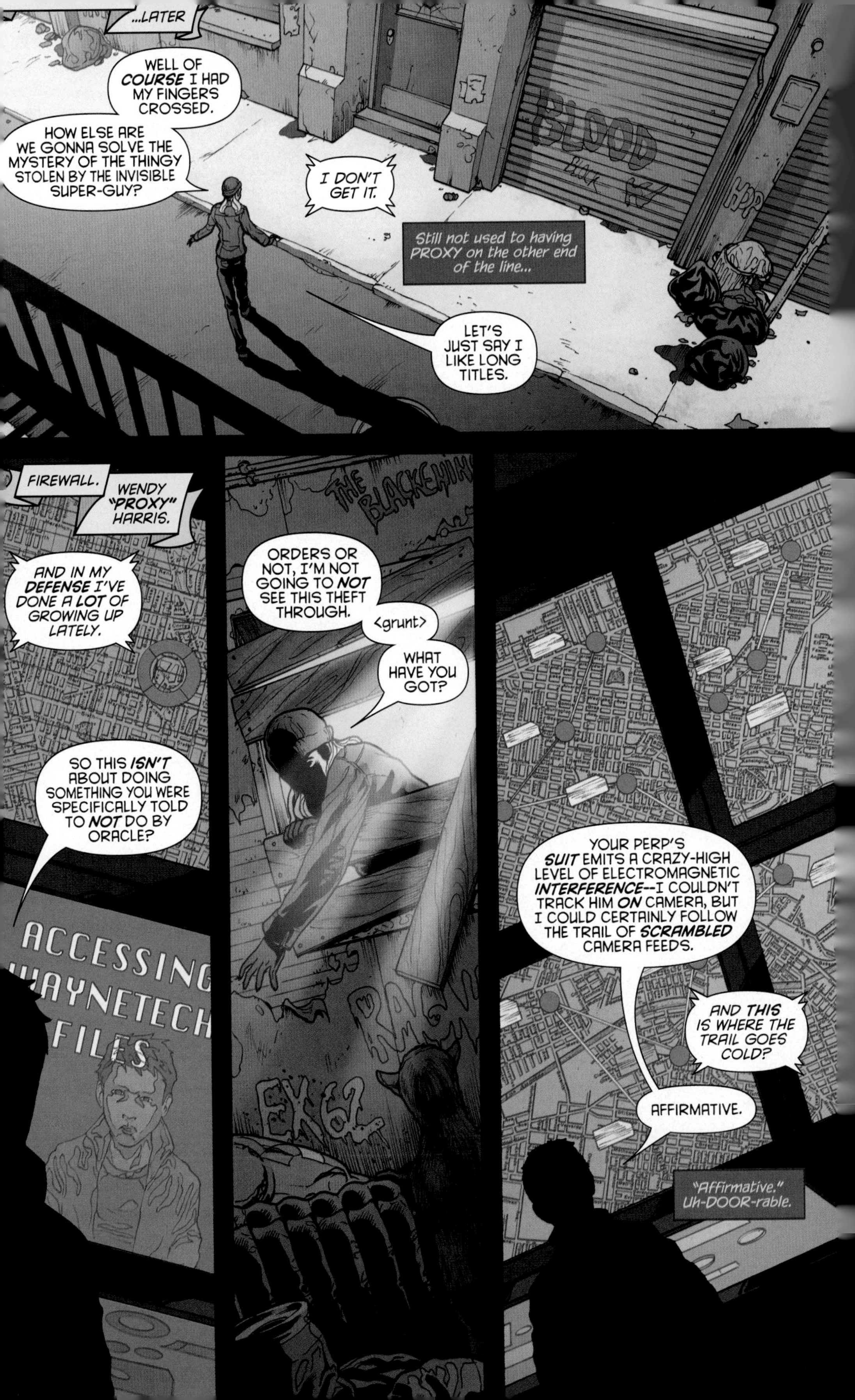
...LATER
WELL OF COURSE I HAD MY FINGERS CROSSED.
HOW ELSE ARE WE GONNA SOLVE THE MYSTERY OF THE THINGY STOLEN BY THE INVISIBLE SUPER-GUY?
I DON'T GET IT.
BLOOD
Still not used to having PROXY on the other end of the line...
LET'S JUST SAY I LIKE LONG TITLES.
FIREWALL.
WENDY "PROXY" HARRIS.
AND IN MY DEFENSE I'VE DONE A LOT OF GROWING UP LATELY.
SO THIS ISN'T ABOUT DOING SOMETHING YOU WERE SPECIFICALLY TOLD TO NOT DO BY ORACLE?
ACCESSING
FILES
ORDERS OR NOT, I'M NOT GOING TO NOT SEE THIS THEFT THROUGH.
<grunt>
WHAT HAVE YOU GOT?
YOUR PERP'S SUIT EMITS A CRAZY-HIGH LEVEL OF ELECTROMAGNETIC INTERFERENCE--I COULDN'T TRACK HIM ON CAMERA, BUT I COULD CERTAINLY FOLLOW THE TRAIL OF SCRAMBLED CAMERA FEEDS.
AND THIS IS WHERE THE TRAIL GOES COLD?
AFFIRMATIVE.
"Affirmative." Uh-DOOR-rable.

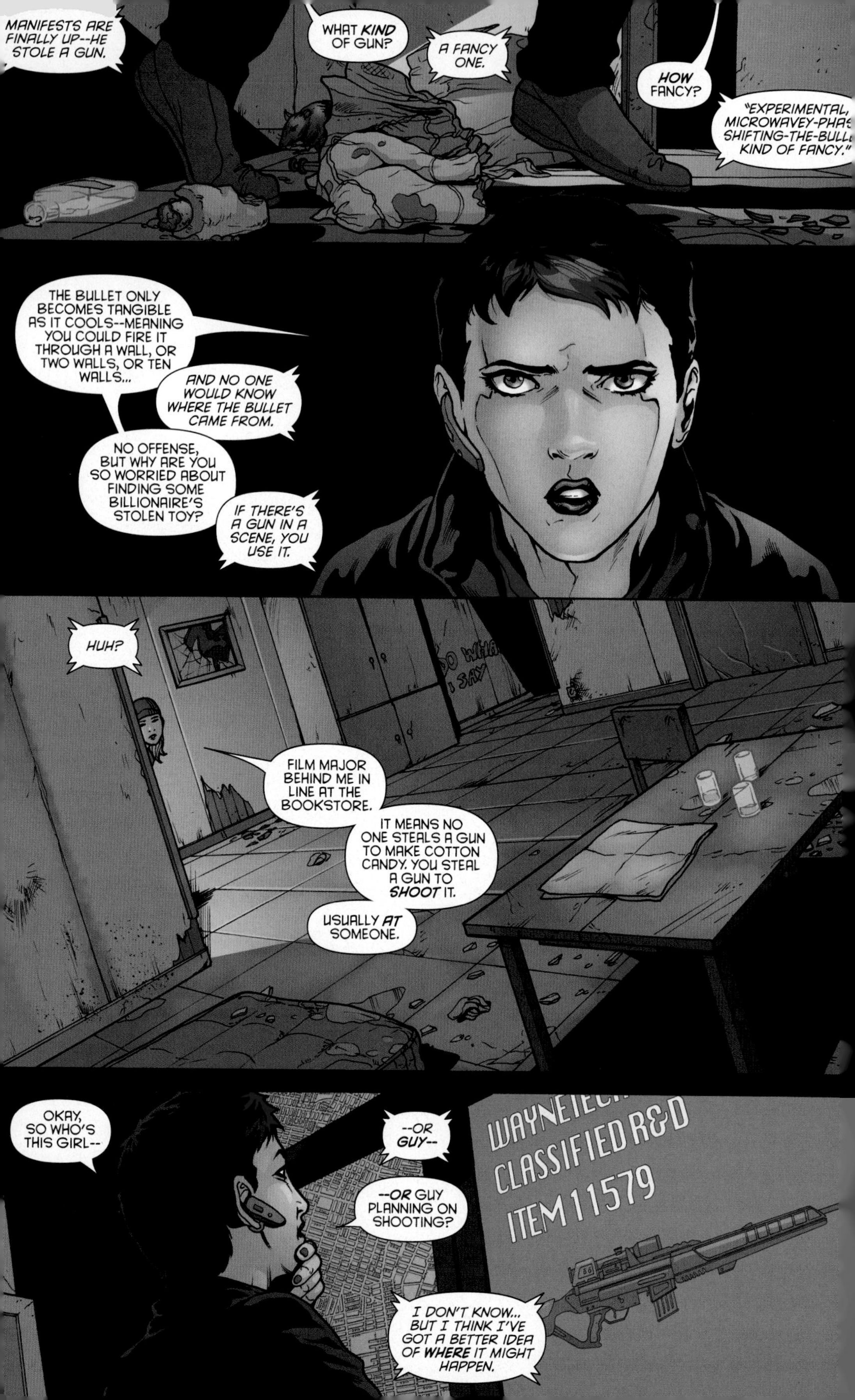

MANIFESTS ARE FINALLY UP--HE STOLE A GUN.
WHAT KIND OF GUN?
A FANCY ONE.
HOW FANCY?
"EXPERIMENTAL, MICROWAVEY-PHAS SHIFTING-THE-BULL KIND OF FANCY."
THE BULLET ONLY BECOMES TANGIBLE AS IT COOLS--MEANING YOU COULD FIRE IT THROUGH A WALL, OR TWO WALLS, OR TEN WALLS...
AND NO ONE WOULD KNOW WHERE THE BULLET CAME FROM.
NO OFFENSE, BUT WHY ARE YOU SO WORRIED ABOUT FINDING SOME BILLIONAIRE'S STOLEN TOY?
IF THERE'S A GUN IN A SCENE, YOU USE IT.
HUH?
FILM MAJOR BEHIND ME IN LINE AT THE BOOKSTORE.
IT MEANS NO ONE STEALS A GUN TO MAKE COTTON CANDY. YOU STEAL A GUN TO SHOOT IT.
USUALLY AT SOMEONE.
OKAY, SO WHO'S THIS GIRL--
--OR GUY--
--OR GUY PLANNING ON SHOOTING?
WAYNETEC
CLASSIFIED R&D
ITEM 11579
I DON'T KNOW... BUT I THINK I'VE GOT A BETTER IDEA OF WHERE IT MIGHT HAPPEN.

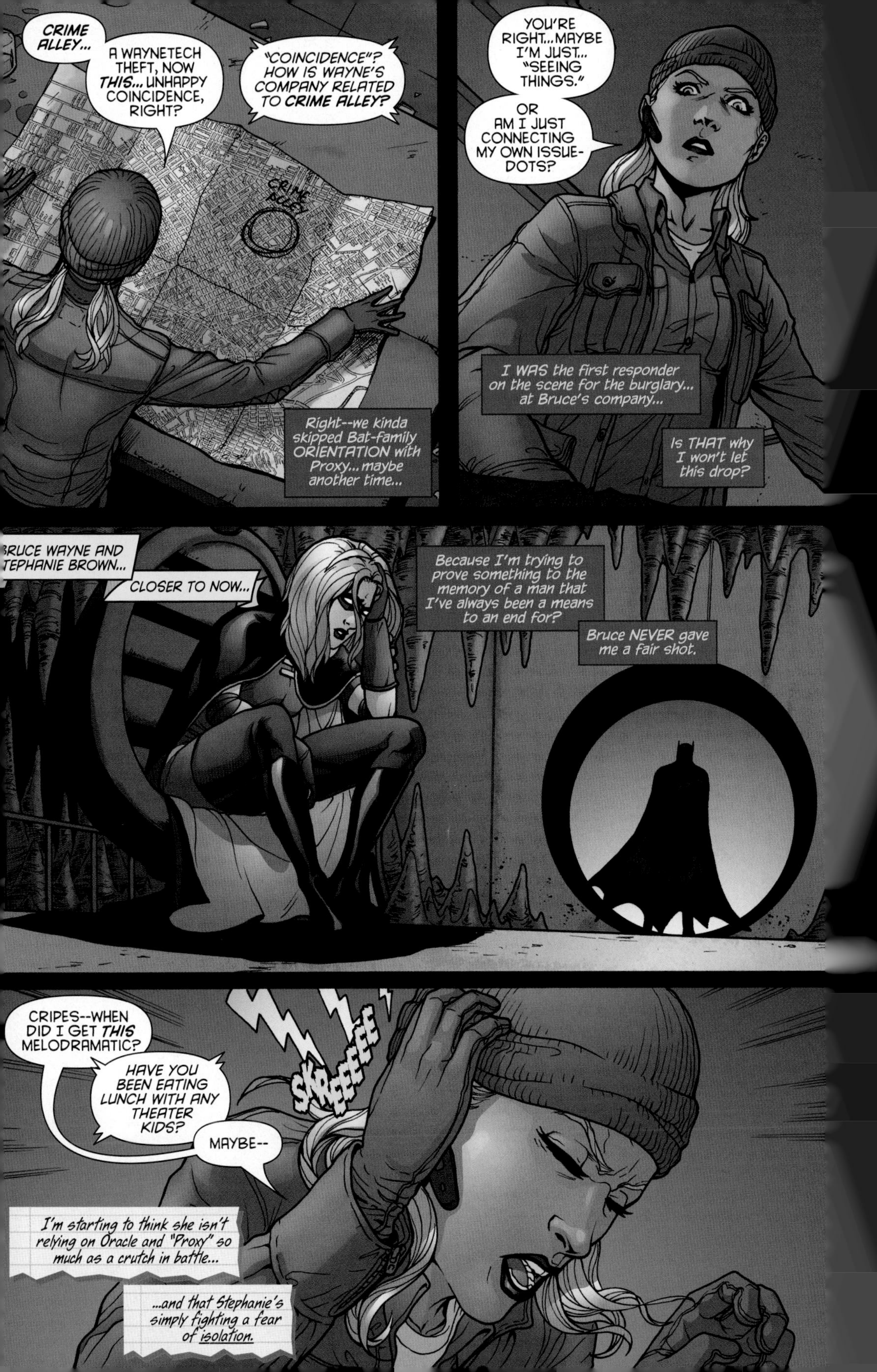

CRIME ALLEY...
A WAYNETECH THEFT, NOW THIS... UNHAPPY COINCIDENCE, RIGHT?
"COINCIDENCE"? HOW IS WAYNE'S COMPANY RELATED TO CRIME ALLEY?
CRIME ALLEY
Right--we kinda skipped Bat-family ORIENTATION with Proxy... maybe another time...
YOU'RE RIGHT... MAYBE I'M JUST... "SEEING THINGS."
OR AM I JUST CONNECTING MY OWN ISSUE-DOTS?
I WAS the first responder on the scene for the burglary... at Bruce's company...
Is THAT why I won't let this drop?
BRUCE WAYNE AND STEPHANIE BROWN...
CLOSER TO NOW...
Because I'm trying to prove something to the memory of a man that I've always been a means to an end for?
Bruce NEVER gave me a fair shot.
CRIPES--WHEN DID I GET THIS MELODRAMATIC?
HAVE YOU BEEN EATING LUNCH WITH ANY THEATER KIDS?
MAYBE--
SKREEEEEE
I'm starting to think she isn't relying on Oracle and "Proxy" so much as a crutch in battle...
...and that Stephanie's simply fighting a fear of isolation.

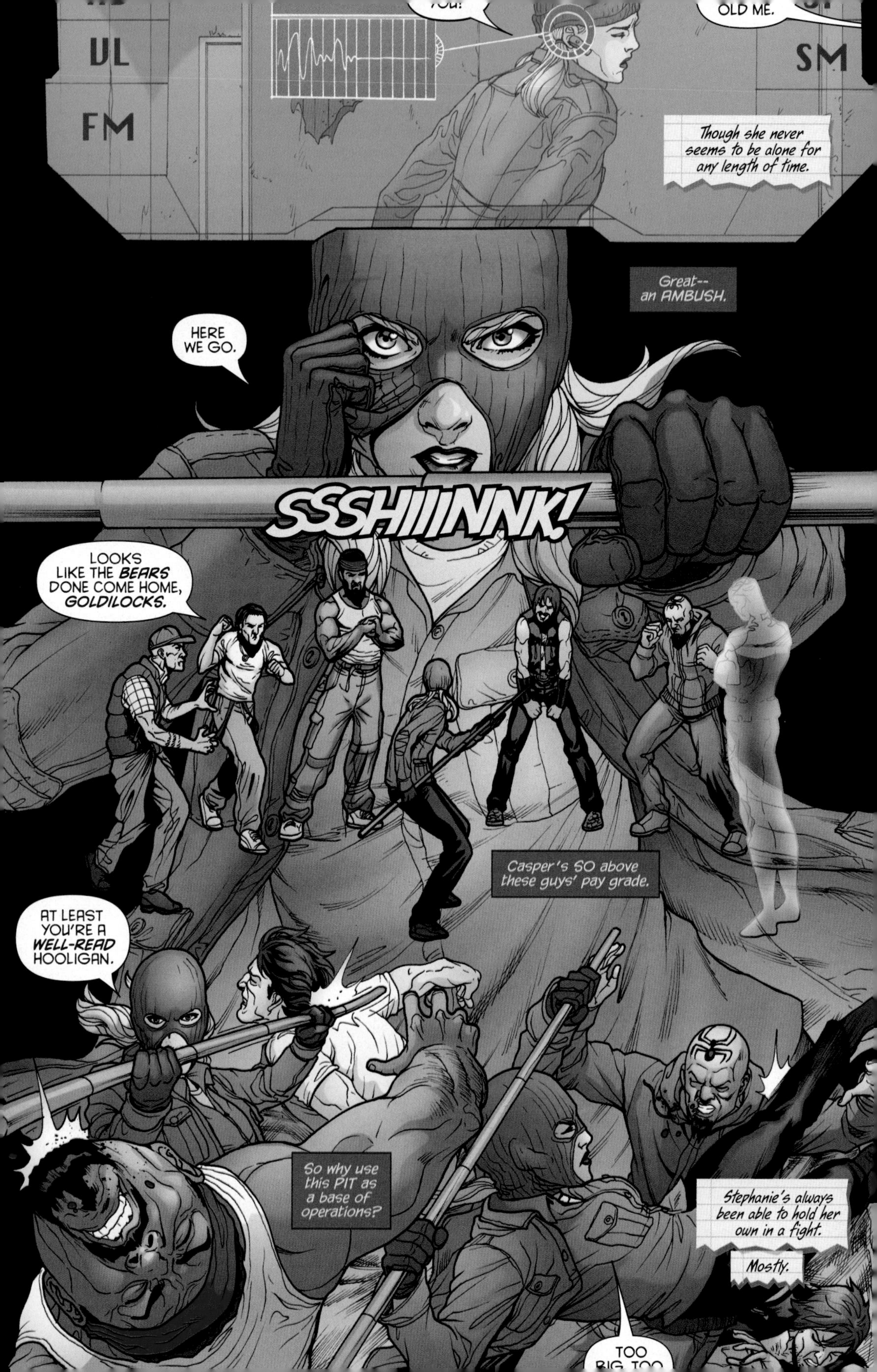

YOU!
OLD ME.
UL
FM
SM
Though she never seems to be alone for any length of time.
Great-- an AMBUSH.
HERE WE GO.
SSSHIIINNK!
LOOKS LIKE THE BEARS DONE COME HOME, GOLDILOCKS.
Casper's SO above these guys' pay grade.
AT LEAST YOU'RE A WELL-READ HOOLIGAN.
So why use this PIT as a base of operations?
Stephanie's always been able to hold her own in a fight.
Mostly.
TOO

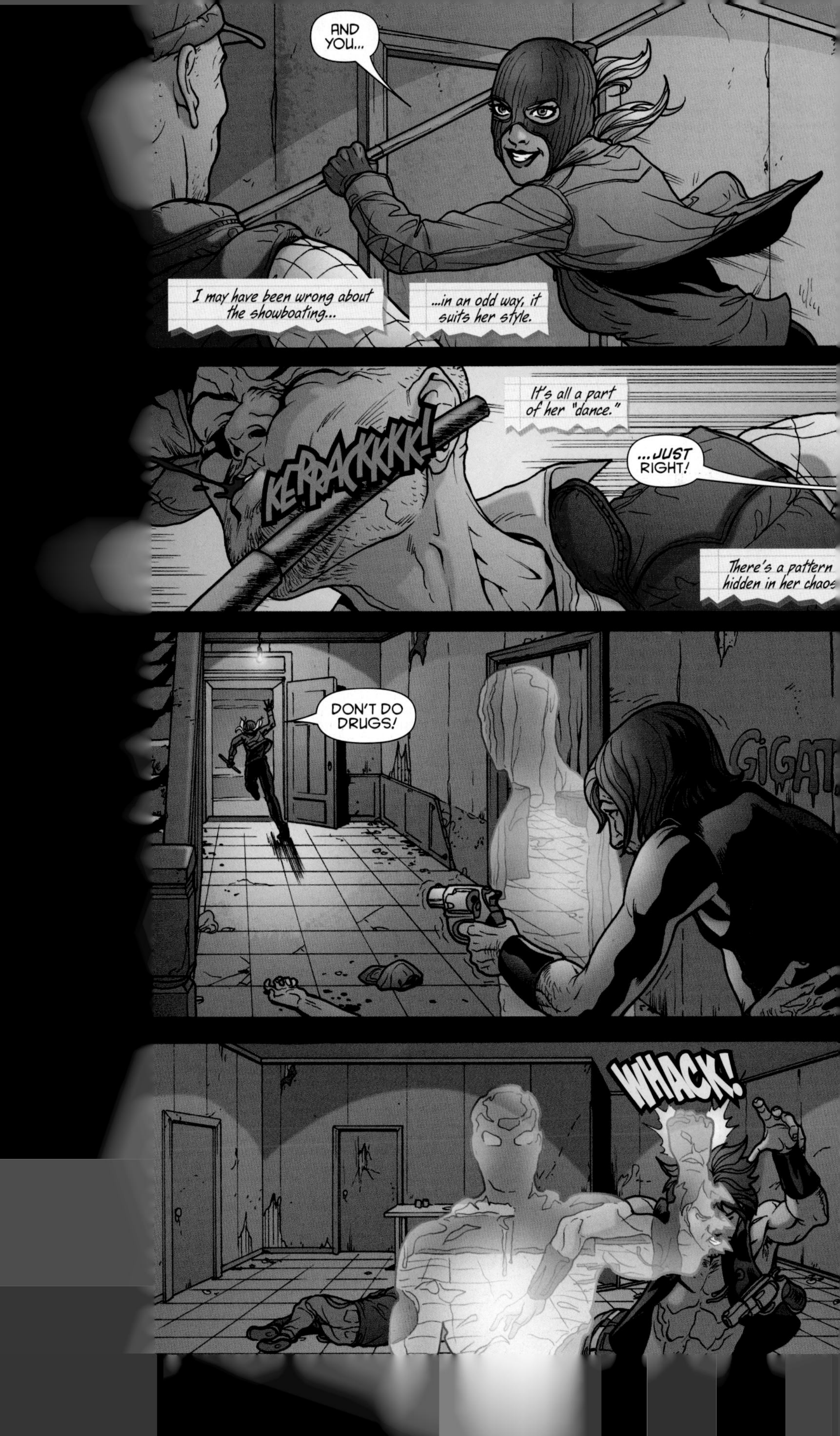
AND YOU...
I may have been wrong about the showboating...
...in an odd way, it suits her style.
It's all a part of her "dance."
KERRACKKKK!
...JUST RIGHT!
There's a pattern hidden in her chaos
DON'T DO DRUGS!
WHACK!

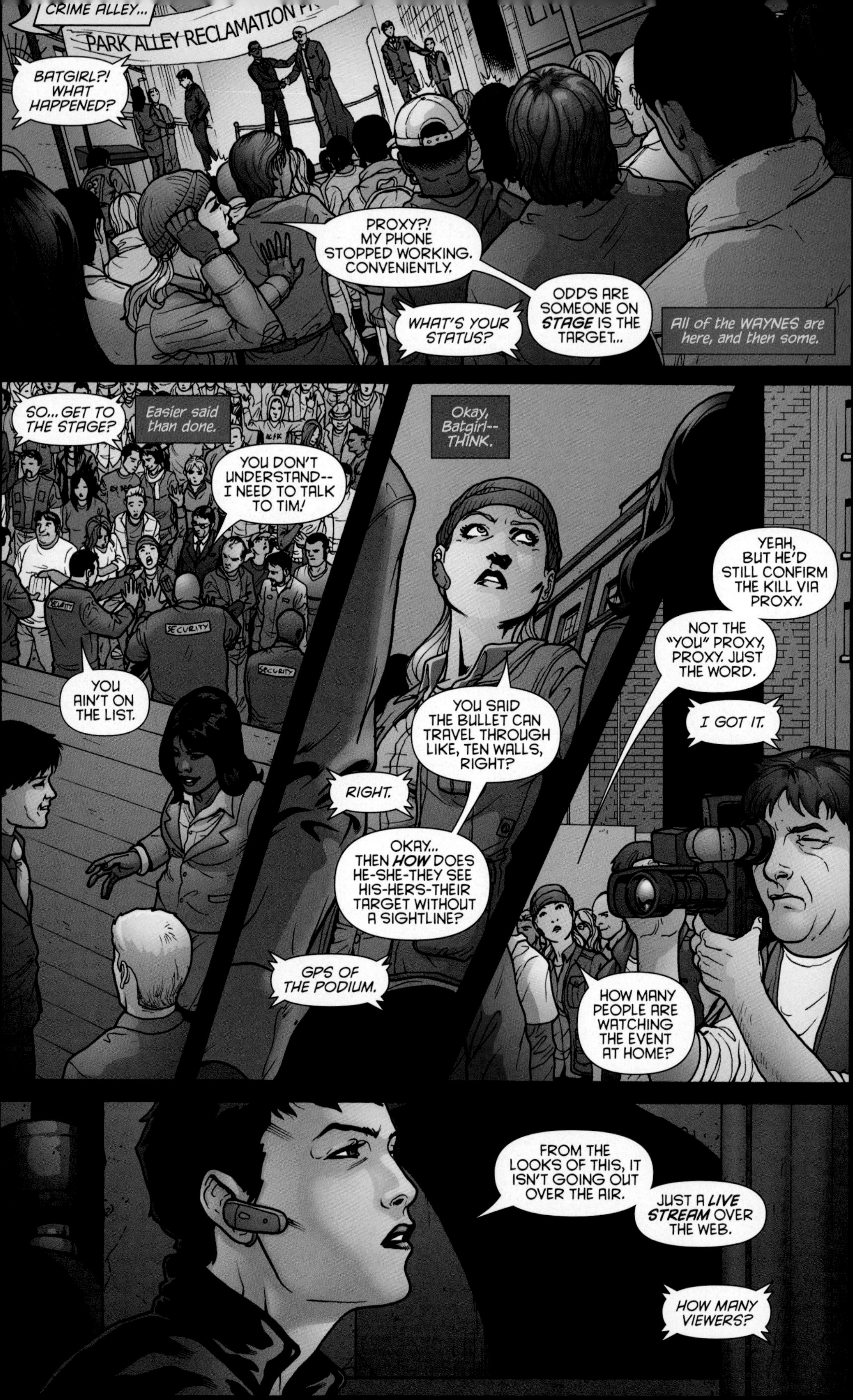
CRIME ALLEY...
PARK ALLEY RECLAMATION
BATGIRL?! WHAT HAPPENED?
PROXY?! MY PHONE STOPPED WORKING. CONVENIENTLY.
ODDS ARE SOMEONE ON STAGE IS THE TARGET...
WHAT'S YOUR STATUS?
All of the WAYNES are here, and then some.
SO... GET TO THE STAGE?
Easier said than done.
YOU DON'T UNDERSTAND-- I NEED TO TALK TO TIM!
SECURITY
YOU AIN'T ON THE LIST.
Okay, Batgirl-- THINK.
YOU SAID THE BULLET CAN TRAVEL THROUGH LIKE, TEN WALLS, RIGHT?
RIGHT.
OKAY... THEN HOW DOES HE-SHE-THEY SEE HIS-HERS-THEIR TARGET WITHOUT A SIGHTLINE?
GPS OF THE PODIUM.
YEAH, BUT HE'D STILL CONFIRM THE KILL VIA PROXY.
NOT THE "YOU" PROXY, PROXY. JUST THE WORD.
I GOT IT.
HOW MANY PEOPLE ARE WATCHING THE EVENT AT HOME?
FROM THE LOOKS OF THIS, IT ISN'T GOING OUT OVER THE AIR.
JUST A LIVE STREAM OVER THE WEB.
HOW MANY VIEWERS?

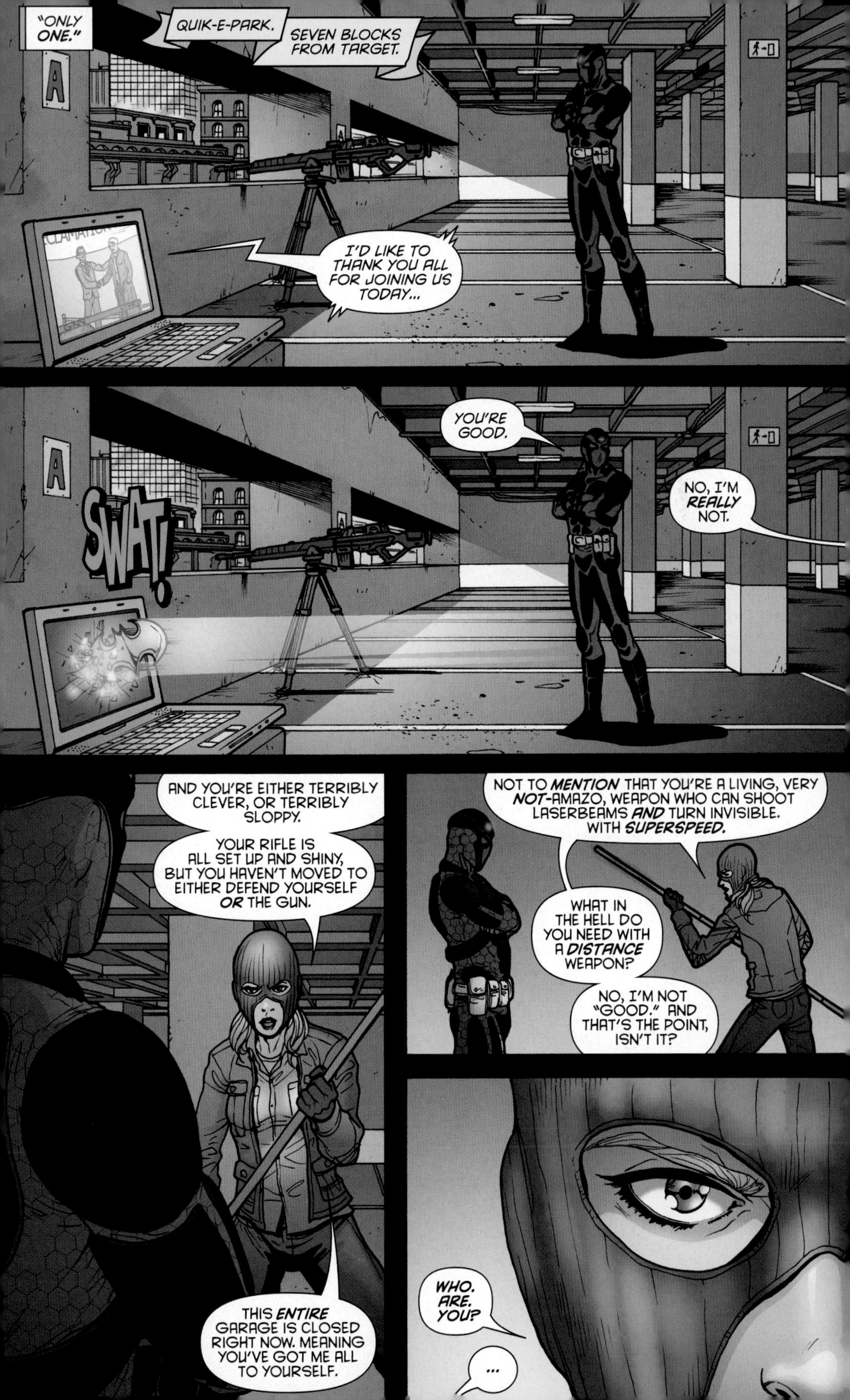
"ONLY ONE."
QUIK-E-PARK.
SEVEN BLOCKS FROM TARGET.
I'D LIKE TO THANK YOU ALL FOR JOINING US TODAY...
SWAT!
YOU'RE GOOD.
NO, I'M REALLY NOT.
AND YOU'RE EITHER TERRIBLY CLEVER, OR TERRIBLY SLOPPY.
YOUR RIFLE IS ALL SET UP AND SHINY, BUT YOU HAVEN'T MOVED TO EITHER DEFEND YOURSELF OR THE GUN.
THIS ENTIRE GARAGE IS CLOSED RIGHT NOW. MEANING YOU'VE GOT ME ALL TO YOURSELF.
NOT TO MENTION THAT YOU'RE A LIVING, VERY NOT-AMAZO, WEAPON WHO CAN SHOOT LASERBEAMS AND TURN INVISIBLE. WITH SUPERSPEED.
WHAT IN THE HELL DO YOU NEED WITH A DISTANCE WEAPON?
NO, I'M NOT "GOOD." AND THAT'S THE POINT, ISN'T IT?
WHO. ARE. YOU?
...

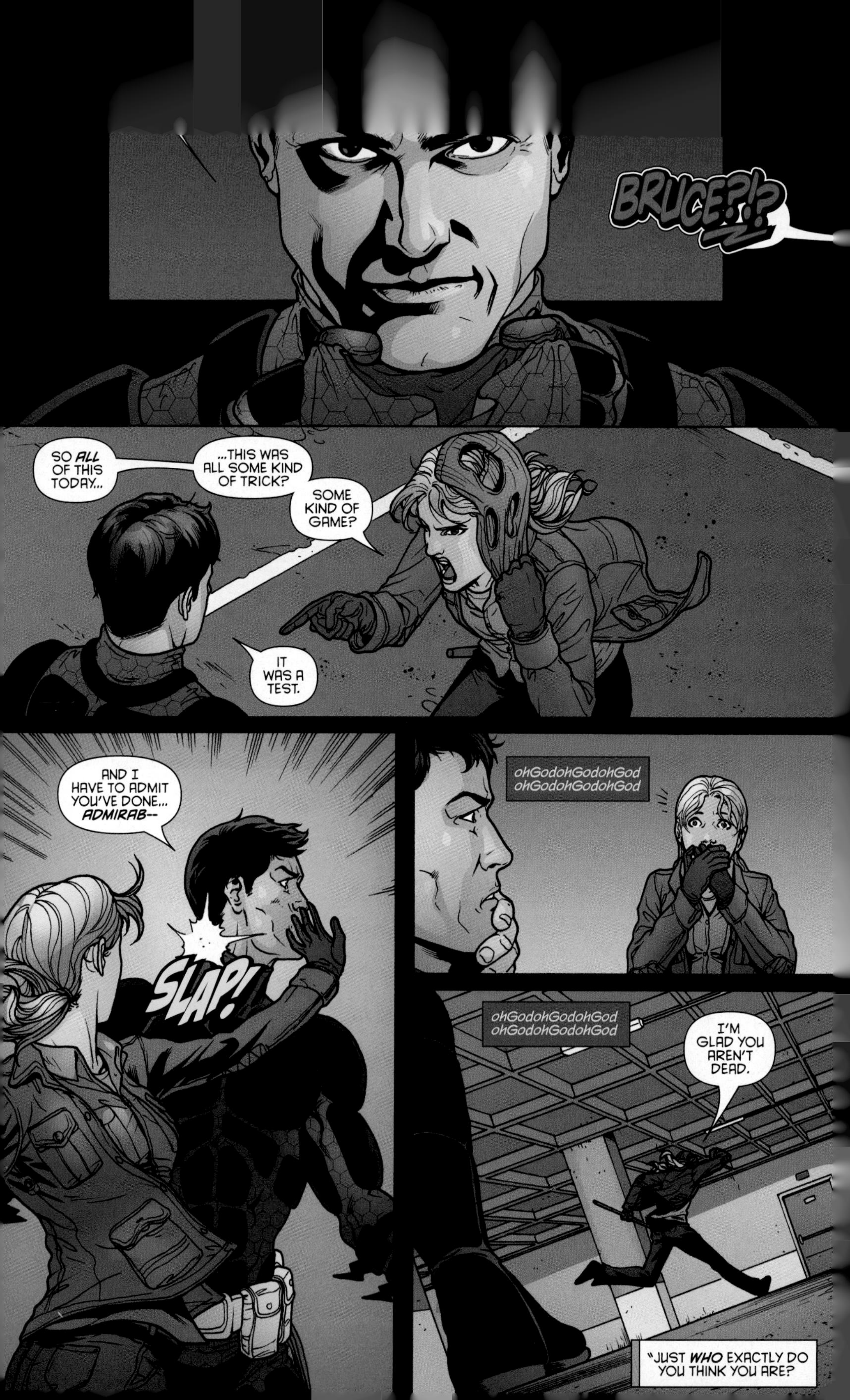
BRUCE?!?
SO ALL OF THIS TODAY...
...THIS WAS ALL SOME KIND OF TRICK?
SOME KIND OF GAME?
IT WAS A TEST.
AND I HAVE TO ADMIT YOU'VE DONE... ADMIRAB--
SLAP!
ohGodohGodohGod ohGodohGodohGod
ohGodohGodohGod ohGodohGodohGod
I'M GLAD YOU AREN'T DEAD.
"JUST WHO EXACTLY DO YOU THINK YOU ARE?

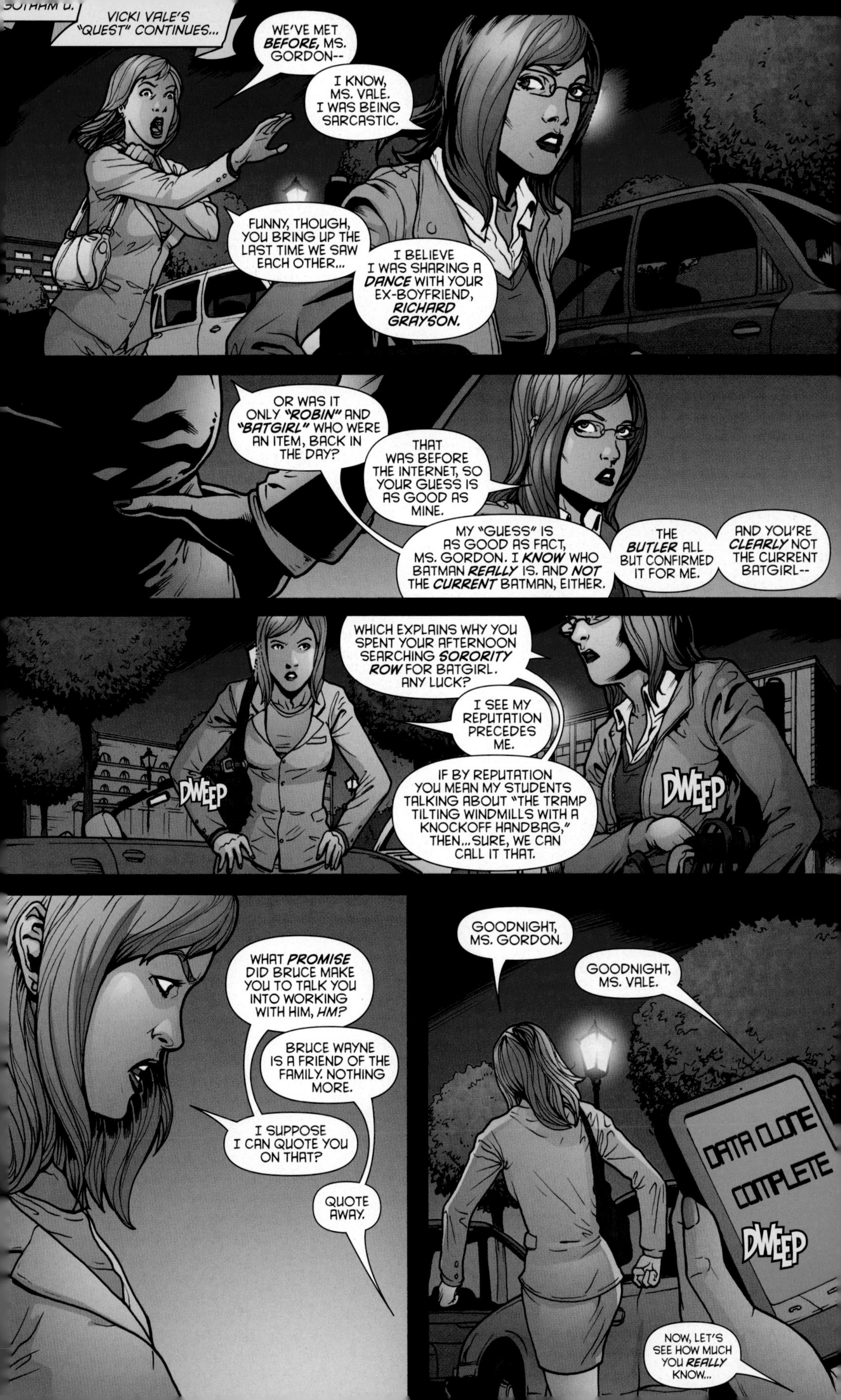

GOTHAM U.
VICKI VALE'S "QUEST" CONTINUES...
WE'VE MET *BEFORE*, MS. GORDON--
I KNOW, MS. VALE. I WAS BEING SARCASTIC.
FUNNY, THOUGH, YOU BRING UP THE LAST TIME WE SAW EACH OTHER...
I BELIEVE I WAS SHARING A *DANCE* WITH YOUR EX-BOYFRIEND, *RICHARD GRAYSON.*
OR WAS IT ONLY *"ROBIN"* AND *"BATGIRL"* WHO WERE AN ITEM, BACK IN THE DAY?
THAT WAS BEFORE THE INTERNET, SO YOUR GUESS IS AS GOOD AS MINE.
MY "GUESS" IS AS GOOD AS FACT, MS. GORDON. I *KNOW* WHO BATMAN *REALLY* IS. AND *NOT* THE *CURRENT* BATMAN, EITHER.
THE *BUTLER* ALL BUT CONFIRMED IT FOR ME.
AND YOU'RE *CLEARLY* NOT THE CURRENT BATGIRL--
WHICH EXPLAINS WHY YOU SPENT YOUR AFTERNOON SEARCHING *SORORITY ROW* FOR BATGIRL. ANY LUCK?
I SEE MY REPUTATION PRECEDES ME.
DWEEP
IF BY REPUTATION YOU MEAN MY STUDENTS TALKING ABOUT "THE TRAMP TILTING WINDMILLS WITH A KNOCKOFF HANDBAG," THEN... SURE, WE CAN CALL IT THAT.
DWEEP
WHAT *PROMISE* DID BRUCE MAKE YOU TO TALK YOU INTO WORKING WITH HIM, *HM?*
BRUCE WAYNE IS A FRIEND OF THE FAMILY. NOTHING MORE.
I SUPPOSE I CAN QUOTE YOU ON THAT?
QUOTE AWAY.
GOODNIGHT, MS. GORDON.
GOODNIGHT, MS. VALE.
DATA CLONE COMPLETE
DWEEP
NOW, LET'S SEE HOW MUCH YOU *REALLY* KNOW...

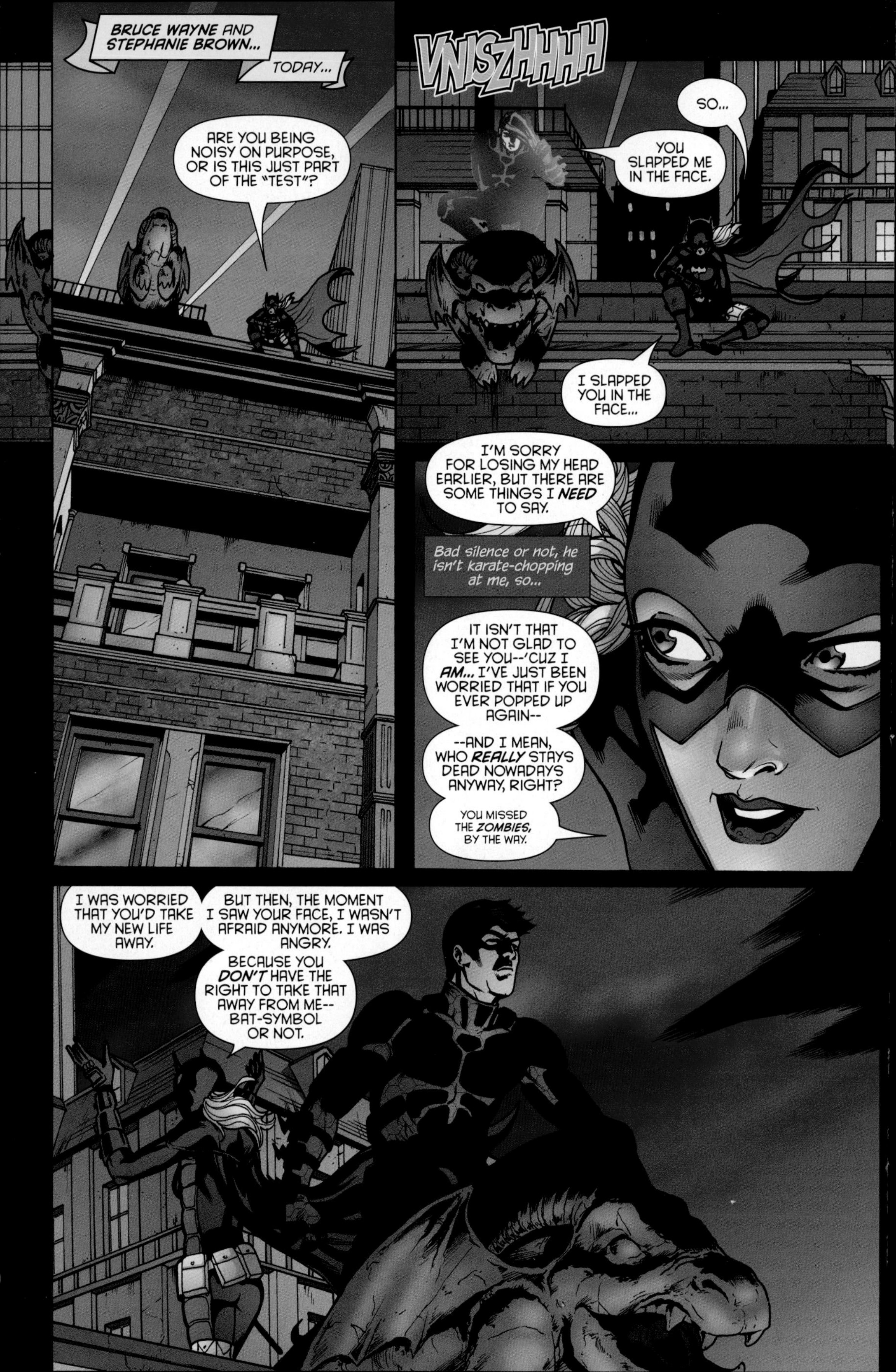
BRUCE WAYNE AND STEPHANIE BROWN...
TODAY...
ARE YOU BEING NOISY ON PURPOSE, OR IS THIS JUST PART OF THE "TEST"?
VNISZHHHH
SO...
YOU SLAPPED ME IN THE FACE.
I SLAPPED YOU IN THE FACE...
I'M SORRY FOR LOSING MY HEAD EARLIER, BUT THERE ARE SOME THINGS I NEED TO SAY.
Bad silence or not, he isn't karate-chopping at me, so...
IT ISN'T THAT I'M NOT GLAD TO SEE YOU--'CUZ I AM... I'VE JUST BEEN WORRIED THAT IF YOU EVER POPPED UP AGAIN--
--AND I MEAN, WHO REALLY STAYS DEAD NOWADAYS ANYWAY, RIGHT?
YOU MISSED THE ZOMBIES, BY THE WAY.
I WAS WORRIED THAT YOU'D TAKE MY NEW LIFE AWAY.
BUT THEN, THE MOMENT I SAW YOUR FACE, I WASN'T AFRAID ANYMORE. I WAS ANGRY.
BECAUSE YOU DON'T HAVE THE RIGHT TO TAKE THAT AWAY FROM ME-- BAT-SYMBOL OR NOT.

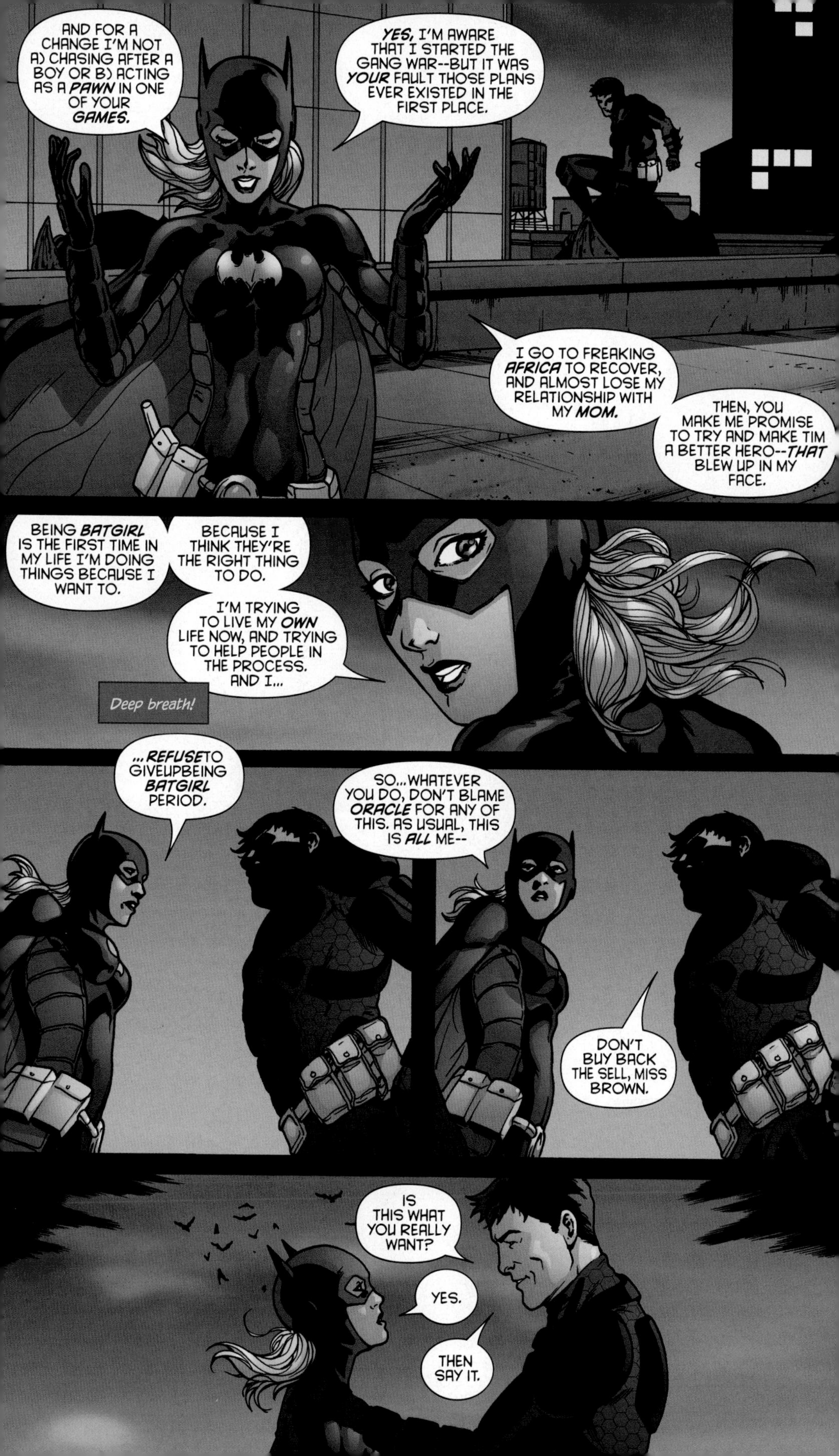

AND FOR A CHANGE I'M NOT A) CHASING AFTER A BOY OR B) ACTING AS A PAWN IN ONE OF YOUR GAMES.
YES, I'M AWARE THAT I STARTED THE GANG WAR--BUT IT WAS YOUR FAULT THOSE PLANS EVER EXISTED IN THE FIRST PLACE.
I GO TO FREAKING AFRICA TO RECOVER, AND ALMOST LOSE MY RELATIONSHIP WITH MY MOM.
THEN, YOU MAKE ME PROMISE TO TRY AND MAKE TIM A BETTER HERO--THAT BLEW UP IN MY FACE.
BEING BATGIRL IS THE FIRST TIME IN MY LIFE I'M DOING THINGS BECAUSE I WANT TO.
BECAUSE I THINK THEY'RE THE RIGHT THING TO DO.
I'M TRYING TO LIVE MY OWN LIFE NOW, AND TRYING TO HELP PEOPLE IN THE PROCESS. AND I...
Deep breath!
...REFUSETO GIVEUPBEING BATGIRL PERIOD.
SO...WHATEVER YOU DO, DON'T BLAME ORACLE FOR ANY OF THIS. AS USUAL, THIS IS ALL ME--
DON'T BUY BACK THE SELL, MISS BROWN.
IS THIS WHAT YOU REALLY WANT?
YES.
THEN SAY IT.

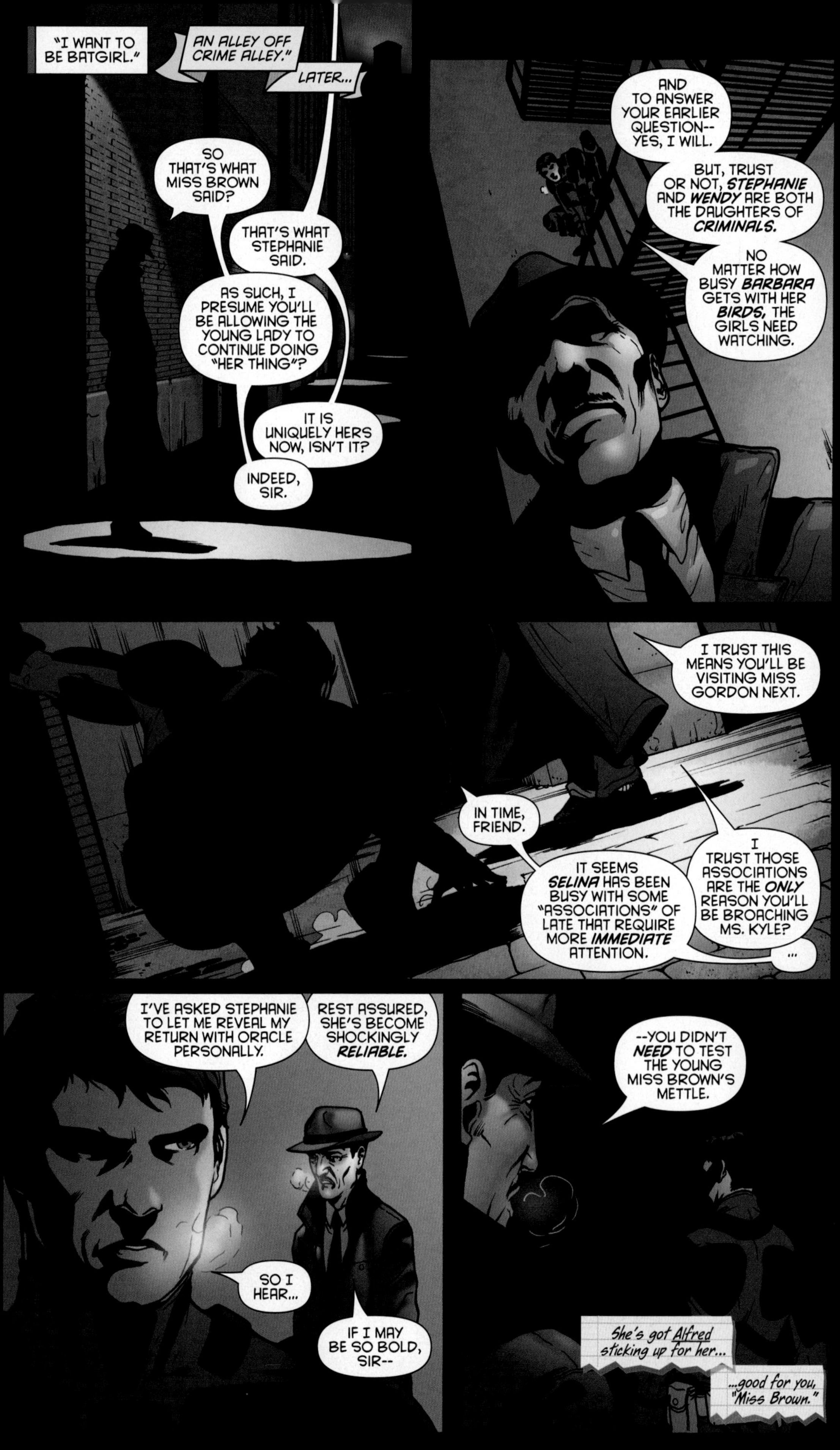

"I WANT TO BE BATGIRL."
AN ALLEY OFF CRIME ALLEY."
LATER...
SO THAT'S WHAT MISS BROWN SAID?
THAT'S WHAT STEPHANIE SAID.
AS SUCH, I PRESUME YOU'LL BE ALLOWING THE YOUNG LADY TO CONTINUE DOING "HER THING"?
IT IS UNIQUELY HERS NOW, ISN'T IT?
INDEED, SIR.
AND TO ANSWER YOUR EARLIER QUESTION-- YES, I WILL.
BUT, TRUST OR NOT, STEPHANIE AND WENDY ARE BOTH THE DAUGHTERS OF CRIMINALS.
NO MATTER HOW BUSY BARBARA GETS WITH HER BIRDS, THE GIRLS NEED WATCHING.
I TRUST THIS MEANS YOU'LL BE VISITING MISS GORDON NEXT.
IN TIME, FRIEND.
IT SEEMS SELINA HAS BEEN BUSY WITH SOME "ASSOCIATIONS" OF LATE THAT REQUIRE MORE IMMEDIATE ATTENTION.
I TRUST THOSE ASSOCIATIONS ARE THE ONLY REASON YOU'LL BE BROACHING MS. KYLE?
...
I'VE ASKED STEPHANIE TO LET ME REVEAL MY RETURN WITH ORACLE PERSONALLY.
REST ASSURED, SHE'S BECOME SHOCKINGLY RELIABLE.
SO I HEAR...
IF I MAY BE SO BOLD, SIR--
--YOU DIDN'T NEED TO TEST THE YOUNG MISS BROWN'S METTLE.
She's got Alfred sticking up for her...
...good for you, "Miss Brown."

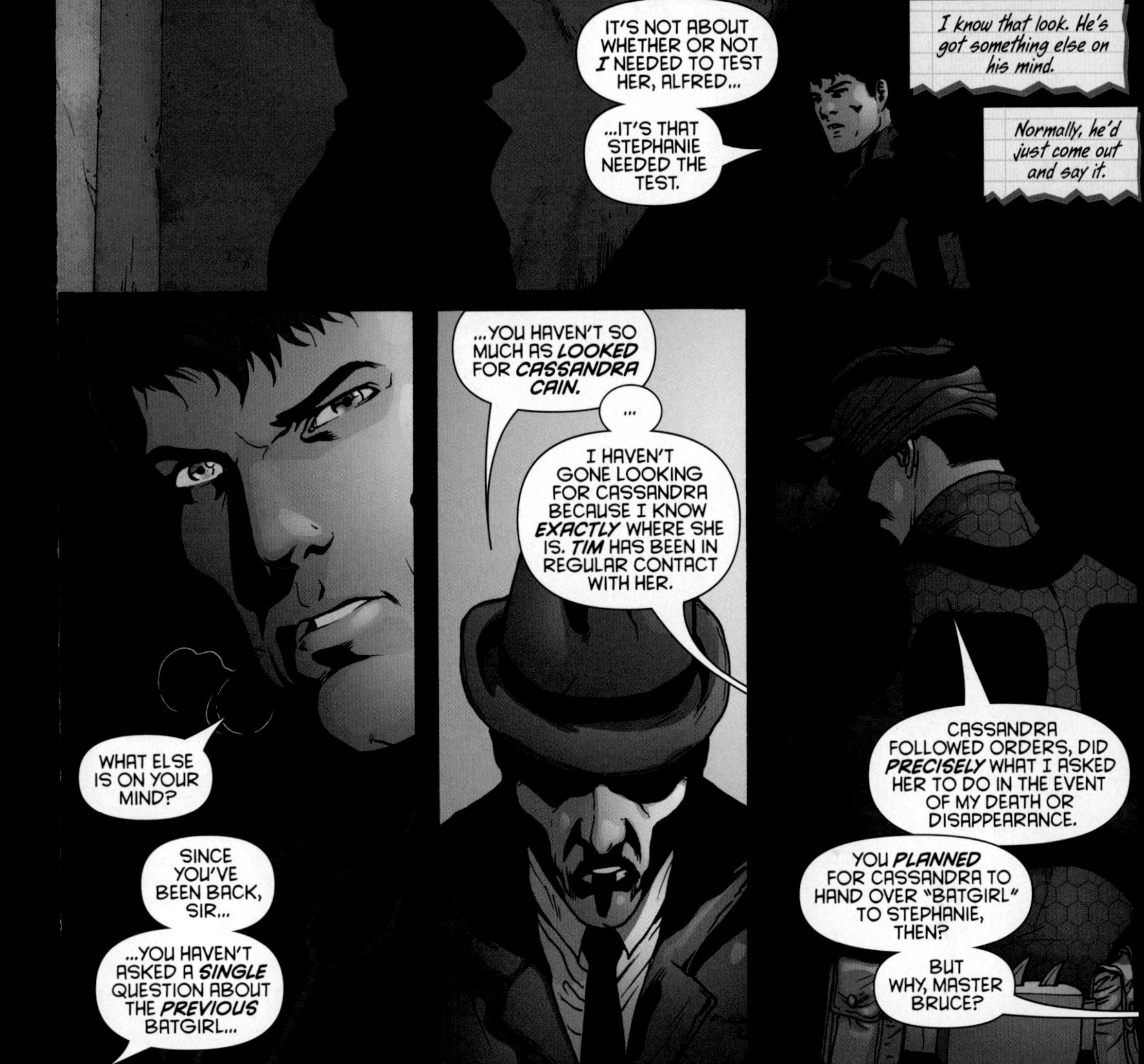
IT'S NOT ABOUT WHETHER OR NOT *I* NEEDED TO TEST HER, ALFRED...
...IT'S THAT STEPHANIE NEEDED THE TEST.
I know that look. He's got something else on his mind.
Normally, he'd just come out and say it.
WHAT ELSE IS ON YOUR MIND?
SINCE YOU'VE BEEN BACK, SIR...
...YOU HAVEN'T ASKED A *SINGLE* QUESTION ABOUT THE *PREVIOUS* BATGIRL...
...YOU HAVEN'T SO MUCH AS *LOOKED* FOR *CASSANDRA CAIN.*
...
I HAVEN'T GONE LOOKING FOR CASSANDRA BECAUSE I KNOW *EXACTLY* WHERE SHE IS. *TIM* HAS BEEN IN REGULAR CONTACT WITH HER.
CASSANDRA FOLLOWED ORDERS, DID *PRECISELY* WHAT I ASKED HER TO DO IN THE EVENT OF MY DEATH OR DISAPPEARANCE.
YOU *PLANNED* FOR CASSANDRA TO HAND OVER "BATGIRL" TO STEPHANIE, THEN?
BUT WHY, MASTER BRUCE?

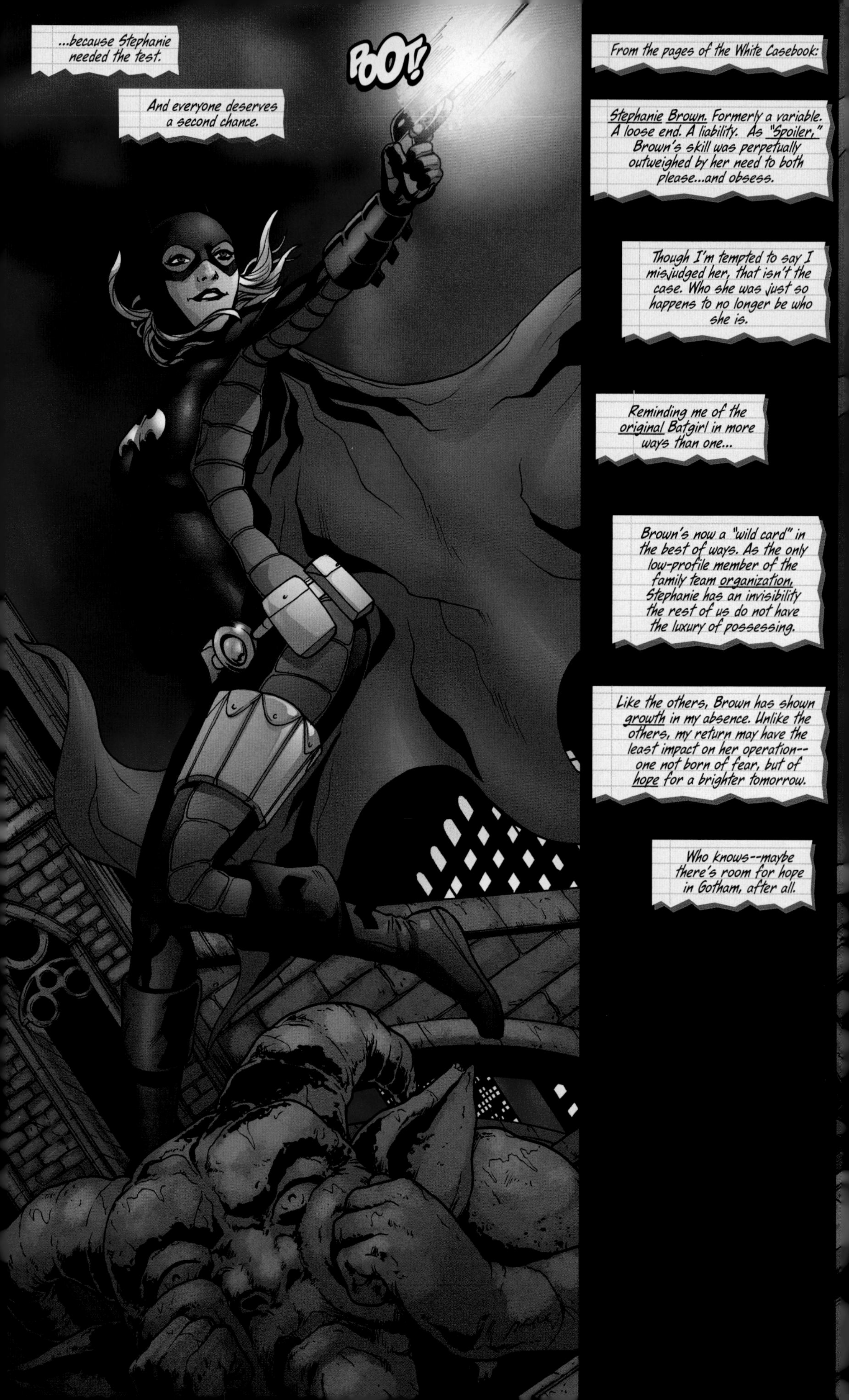
...because Stephanie needed the test.
And everyone deserves a second chance.
POOT!
From the pages of the White Casebook:
Stephanie Brown. Formerly a variable. A loose end. A liability. As "Spoiler," Brown's skill was perpetually outweighed by her need to both please...and obsess.
Though I'm tempted to say I misjudged her, that isn't the case. Who she was just so happens to no longer be who she is.
Reminding me of the original Batgirl in more ways than one...
Brown's now a "wild card" in the best of ways. As the only low-profile member of the family team organization, Stephanie has an invisibility the rest of us do not have the luxury of possessing.
Like the others, Brown has shown growth in my absence. Unlike the others, my return may have the least impact on her operation--one not born of fear, but of hope for a brighter tomorrow.
Who knows--maybe there's room for hope in Gotham, after all.

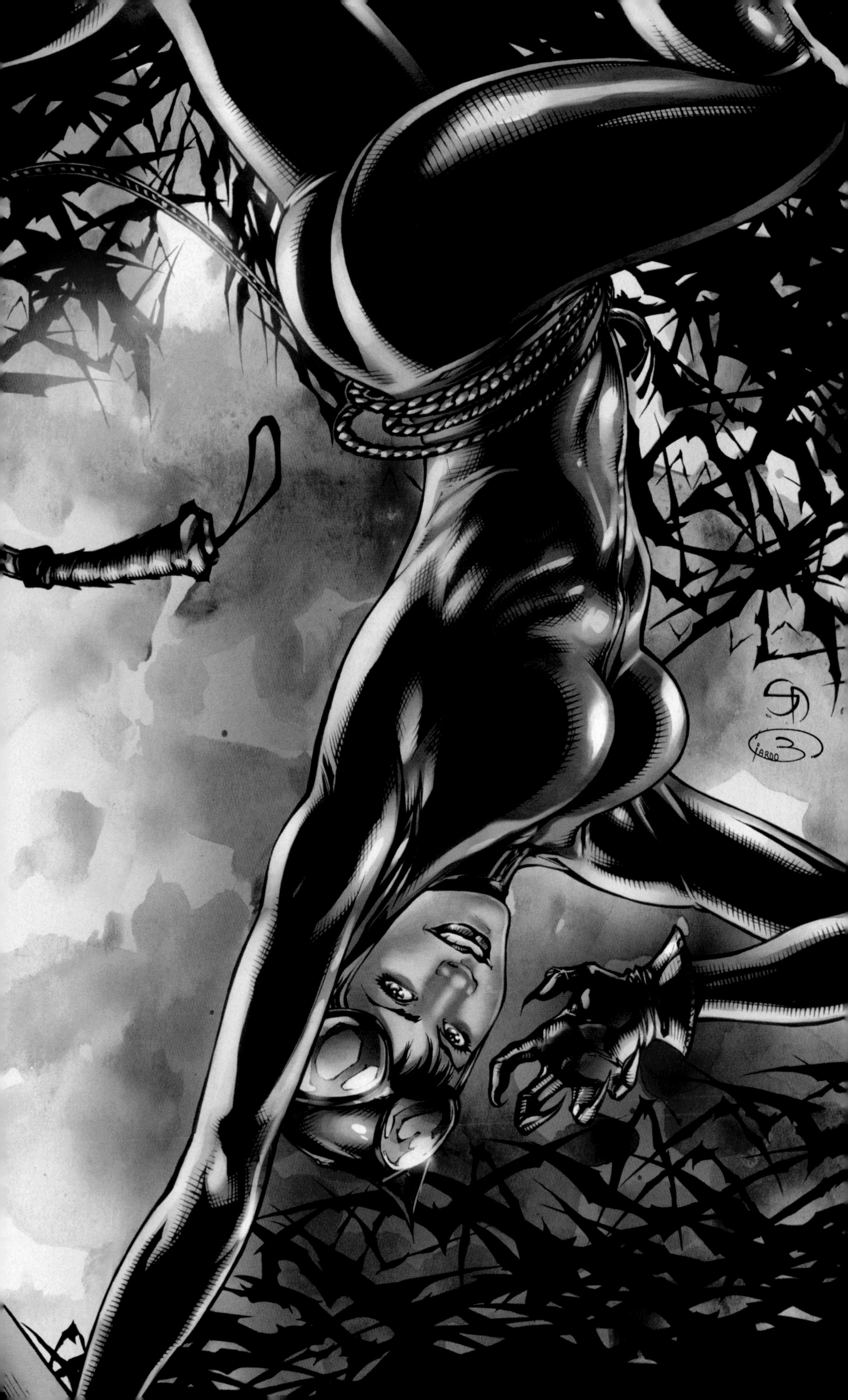

"WITH HER, I'LL ALWAYS REMAIN GUARDED."

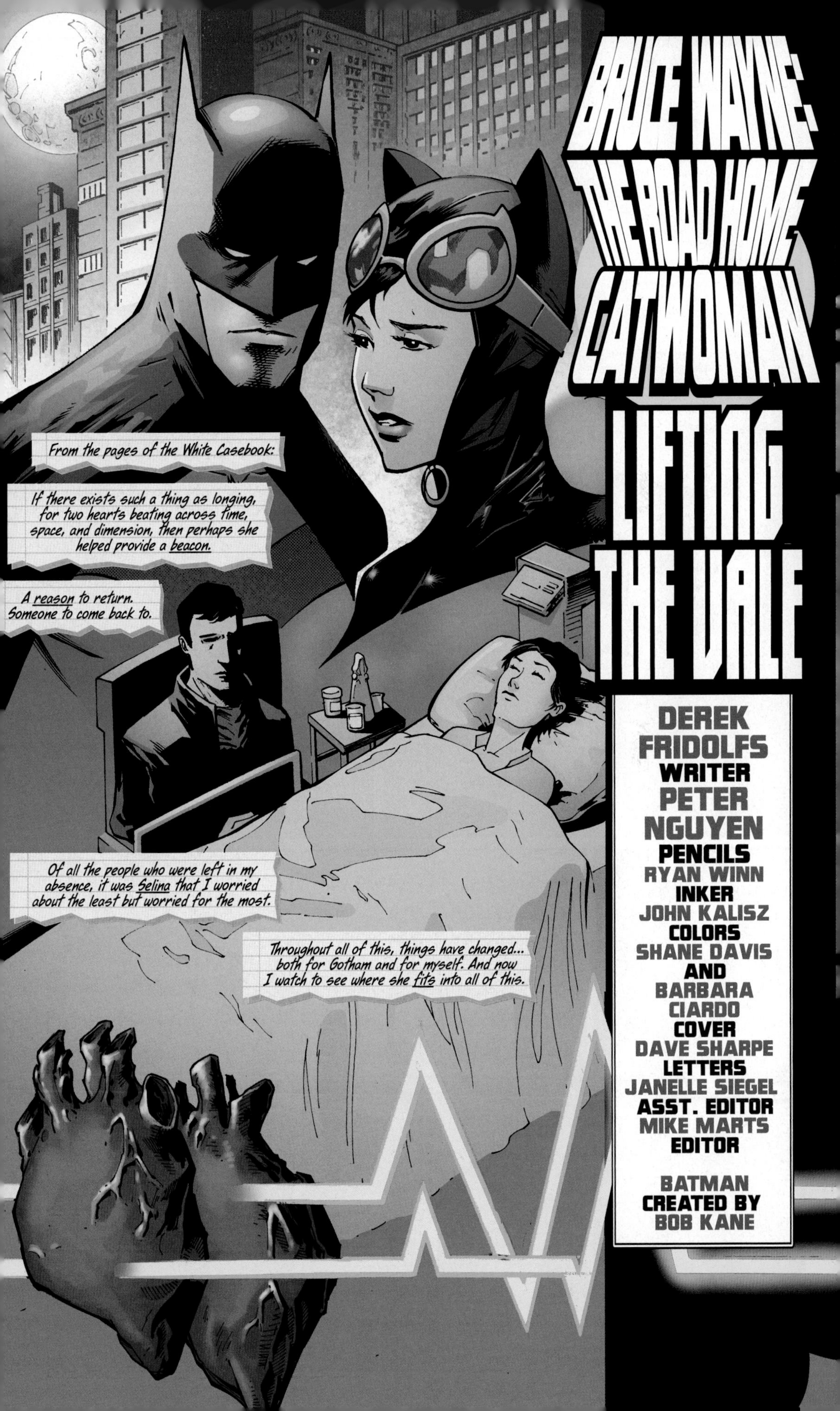
BRUCE WAYNE: THE ROAD HOME
CATWOMAN
LIFTING THE VALE
From the pages of the White Casebook:
If there exists such a thing as longing, for two hearts beating across time, space, and dimension, then perhaps she helped provide a beacon.
A reason to return. Someone to come back to.
Of all the people who were left in my absence, it was Selina that I worried about the least but worried for the most.
Throughout all of this, things have changed... both for Gotham and for myself. And now I watch to see where she fits into all of this.
DEREK FRIDOLFS WRITER
PETER NGUYEN PENCILS
RYAN WINN INKER
JOHN KALISZ COLORS
SHANE DAVIS AND BARBARA CIARDO COVER
DAVE SHARPE LETTERS
JANELLE SIEGEL ASST. EDITOR
MIKE MARTS EDITOR
BATMAN CREATED BY BOB KANE

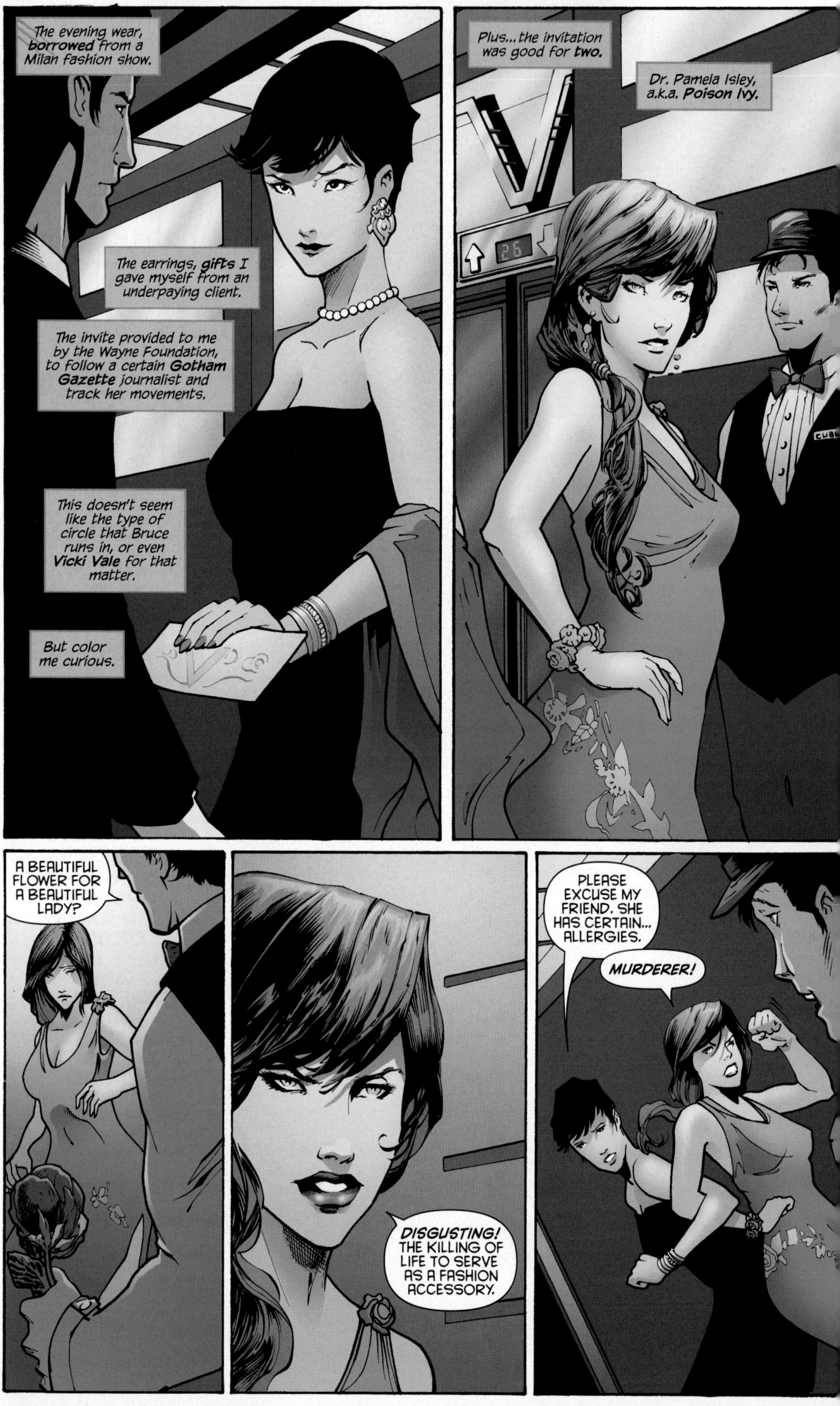
The evening wear, borrowed from a Milan fashion show.
The earrings, gifts I gave myself from an underpaying client.
The invite provided to me by the Wayne Foundation, to follow a certain Gotham Gazette journalist and track her movements.
This doesn't seem like the type of circle that Bruce runs in, or even Vicki Vale for that matter.
But color me curious.
Plus... the invitation was good for two.
Dr. Pamela Isley, a.k.a. Poison Ivy.
A BEAUTIFUL FLOWER FOR A BEAUTIFUL LADY?
DISGUSTING! THE KILLING OF LIFE TO SERVE AS A FASHION ACCESSORY.
PLEASE EXCUSE MY FRIEND. SHE HAS CERTAIN... ALLERGIES.
MURDERER!

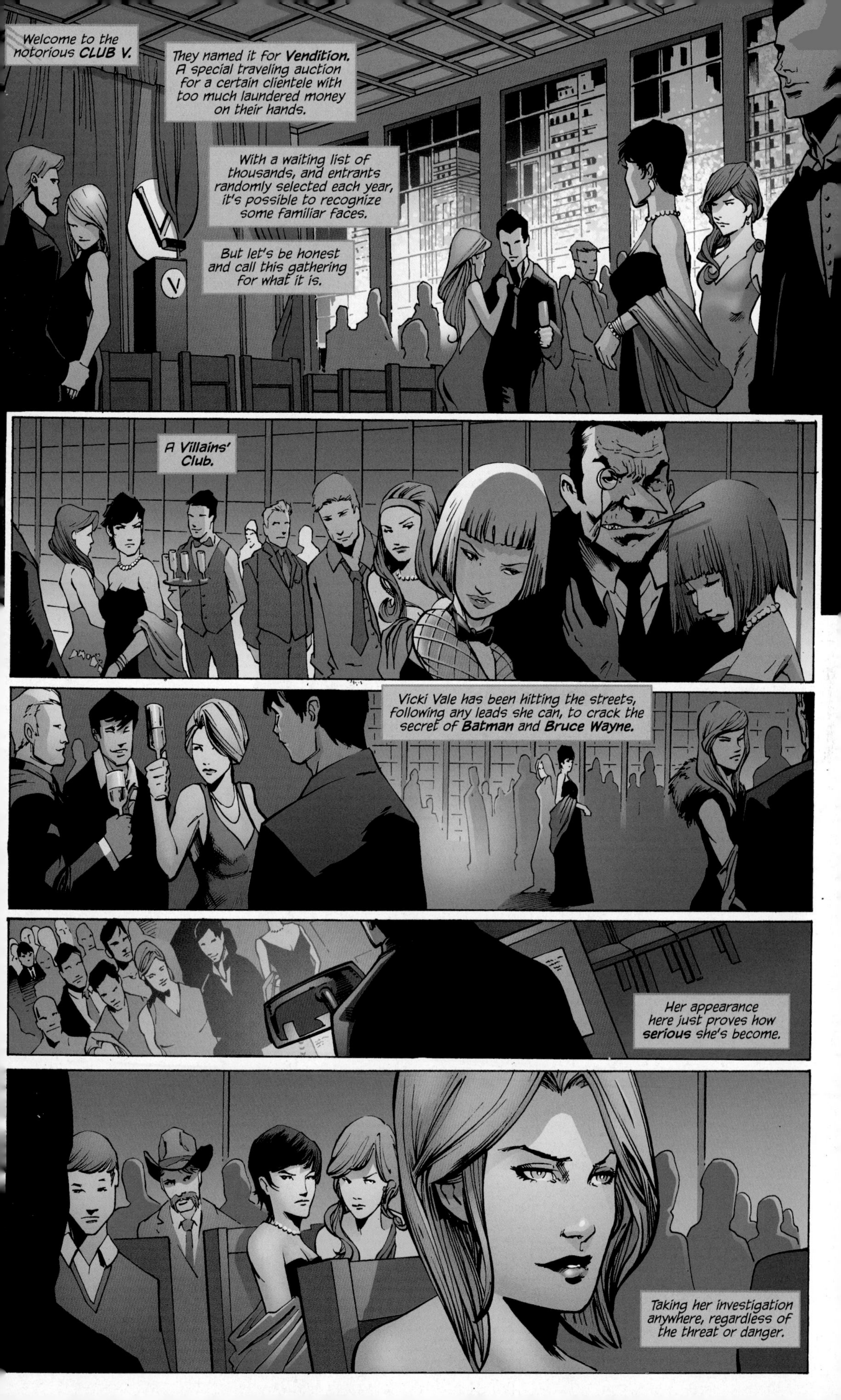

Welcome to the notorious CLUB V.
They named it for Vendition. A special traveling auction for a certain clientele with too much laundered money on their hands.
With a waiting list of thousands, and entrants randomly selected each year, it's possible to recognize some familiar faces.
But let's be honest and call this gathering for what it is.
A Villains' Club.
Vicki Vale has been hitting the streets, following any leads she can, to crack the secret of Batman and Bruce Wayne.
Her appearance here just proves how serious she's become.
Taking her investigation anywhere, regardless of the threat or danger.

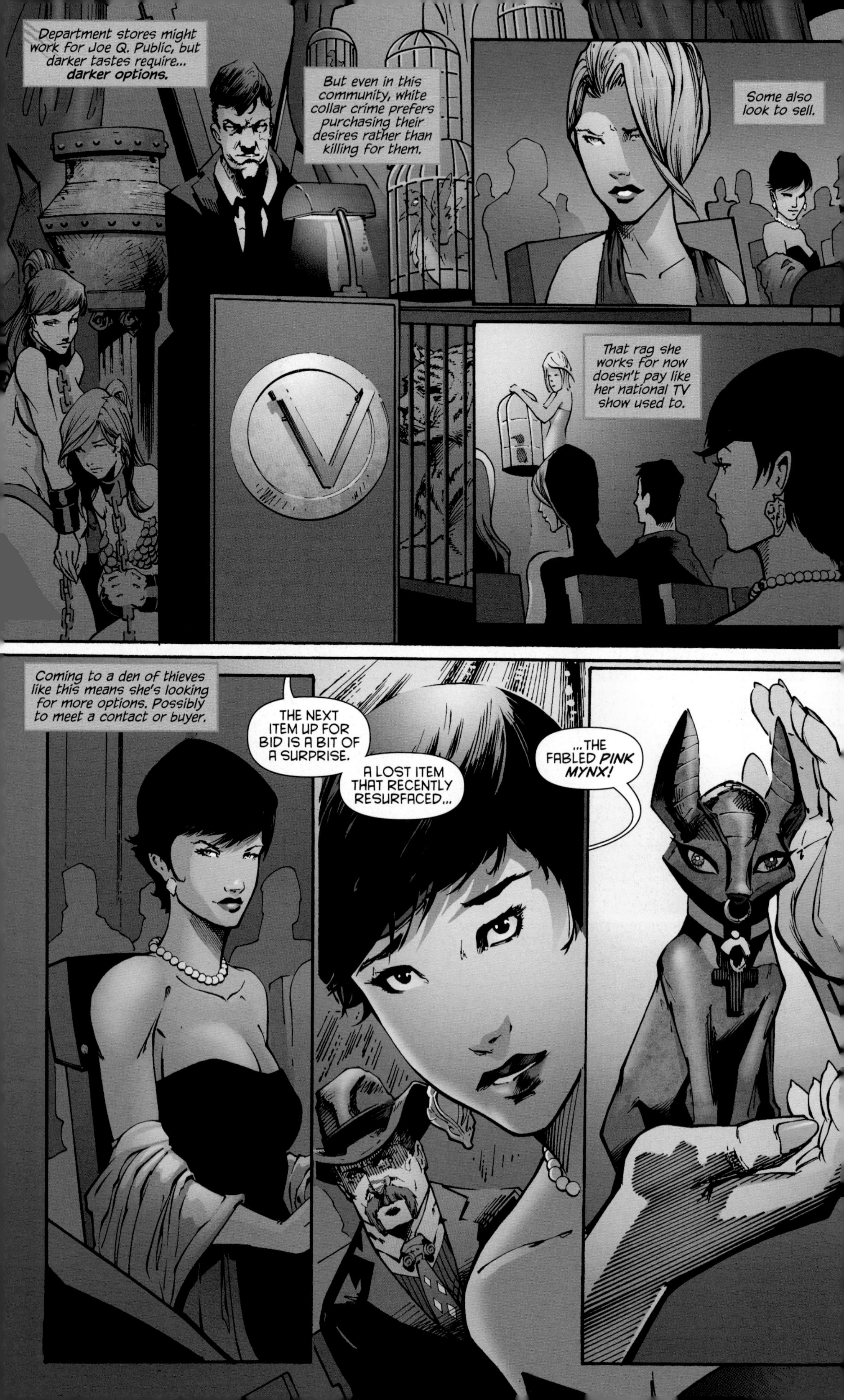
Department stores might work for Joe Q. Public, but darker tastes require... **darker options.**
But even in this community, white collar crime prefers purchasing their desires rather than killing for them.
Some also look to sell.
That rag she works for now doesn't pay like her national TV show used to.
Coming to a den of thieves like this means she's looking for more options. Possibly to meet a contact or buyer.
THE NEXT ITEM UP FOR BID IS A BIT OF A SURPRISE.
A LOST ITEM THAT RECENTLY RESURFACED...
...THE FABLED ***PINK MYNX!***

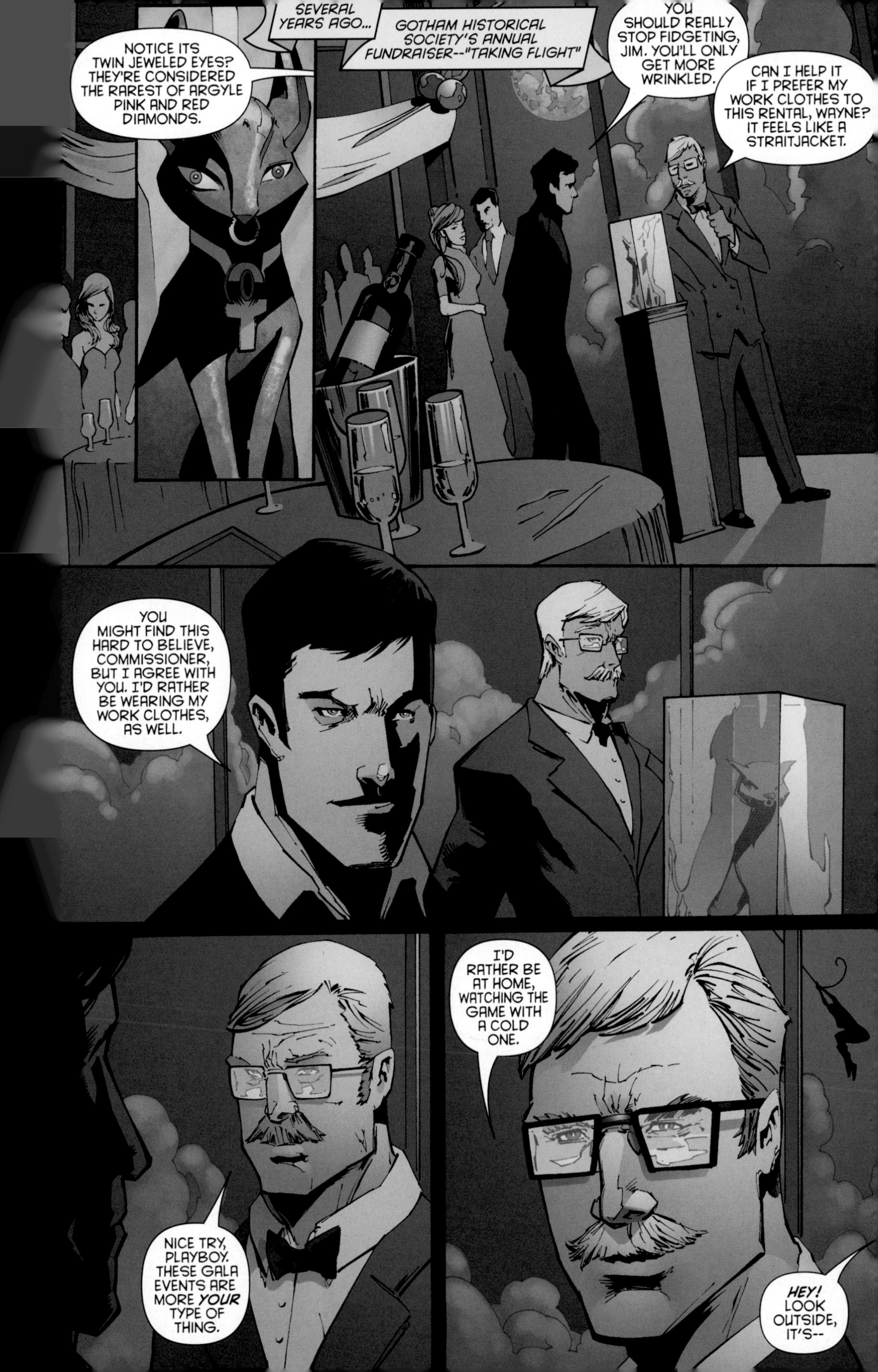
SEVERAL YEARS AGO...
GOTHAM HISTORICAL SOCIETY'S ANNUAL FUNDRAISER--"TAKING FLIGHT"
NOTICE ITS TWIN JEWELED EYES? THEY'RE CONSIDERED THE RAREST OF ARGYLE PINK AND RED DIAMONDS.
YOU SHOULD REALLY STOP FIDGETING, JIM. YOU'LL ONLY GET MORE WRINKLED.
CAN I HELP IT IF I PREFER MY WORK CLOTHES TO THIS RENTAL, WAYNE? IT FEELS LIKE A STRAITJACKET.
YOU MIGHT FIND THIS HARD TO BELIEVE, COMMISSIONER, BUT I AGREE WITH YOU. I'D RATHER BE WEARING MY WORK CLOTHES, AS WELL.
NICE TRY, PLAYBOY. THESE GALA EVENTS ARE MORE *YOUR* TYPE OF THING.
I'D RATHER BE AT HOME, WATCHING THE GAME WITH A COLD ONE.
HEY! LOOK OUTSIDE, IT'S--

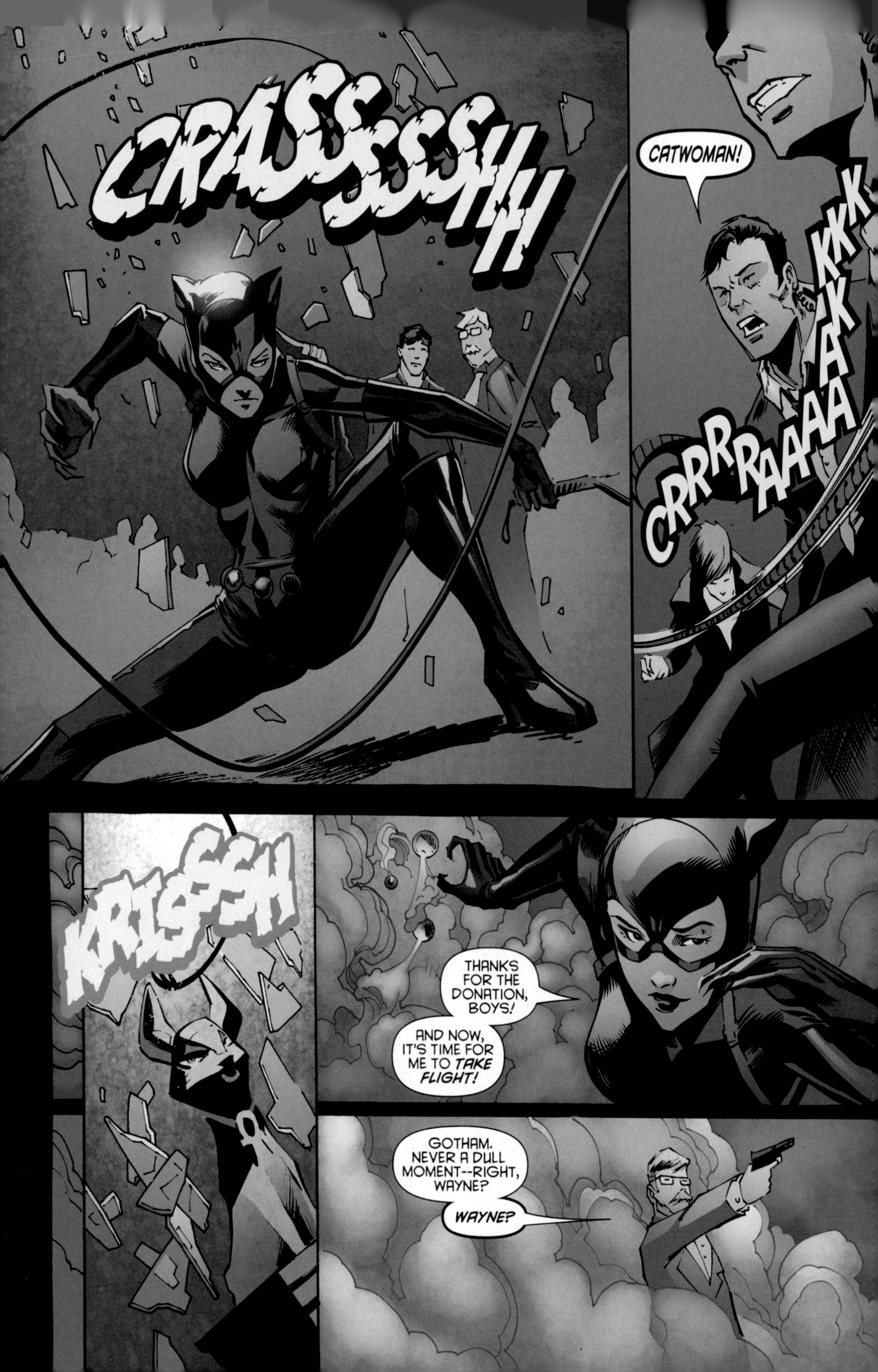
CRASSSSHH
CATWOMAN!
CRRRAAAAAKKK
KRISSCH
THANKS FOR THE DONATION, BOYS!
AND NOW, IT'S TIME FOR ME TO *TAKE FLIGHT!*
GOTHAM. NEVER A DULL MOMENT--RIGHT, WAYNE?
WAYNE?

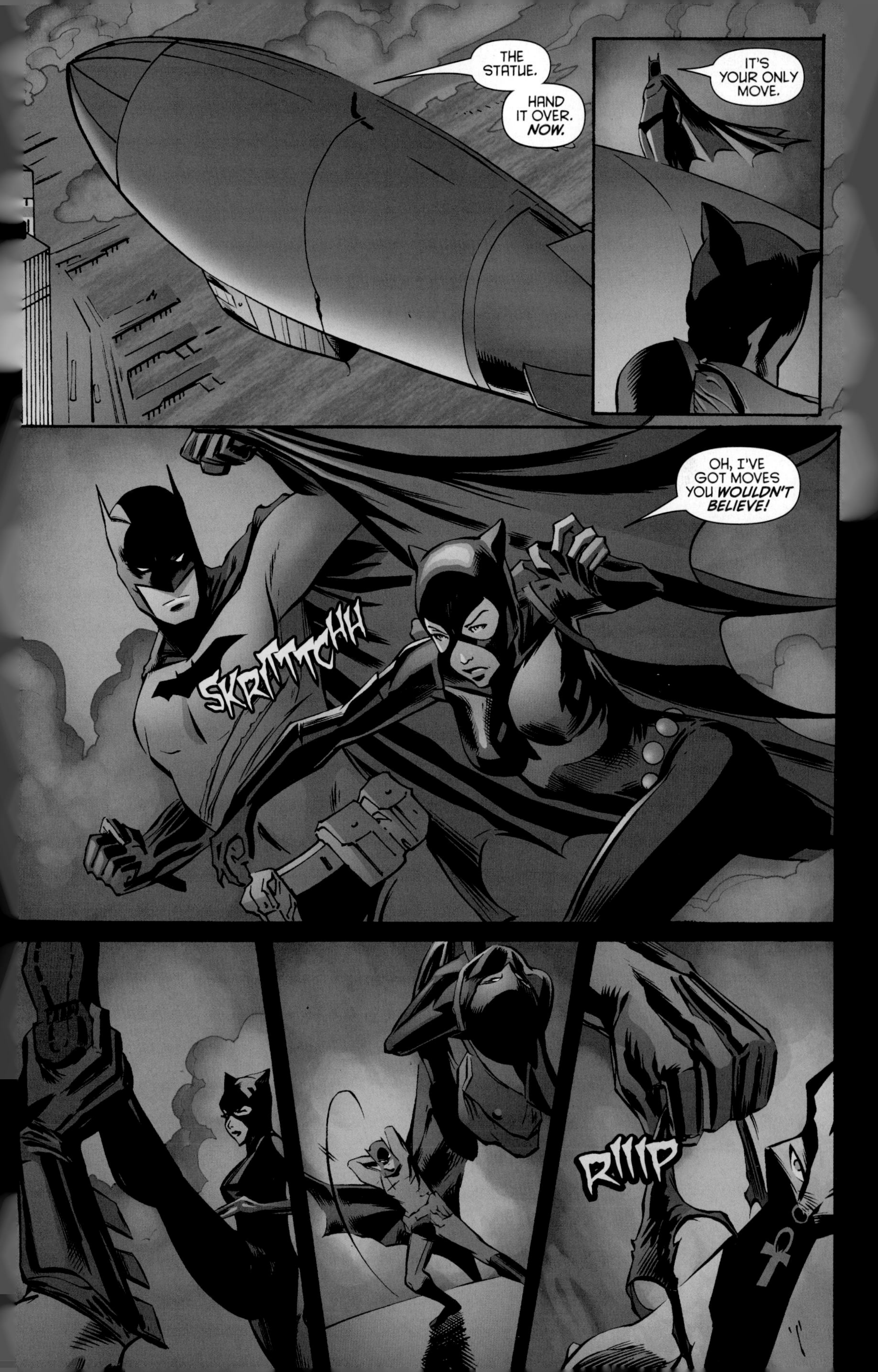
THE STATUE.
HAND IT OVER. *NOW.*
IT'S YOUR ONLY MOVE.
OH, I'VE GOT MOVES YOU *WOULDN'T BELIEVE!*
SKRITTTCHH
RIIIP

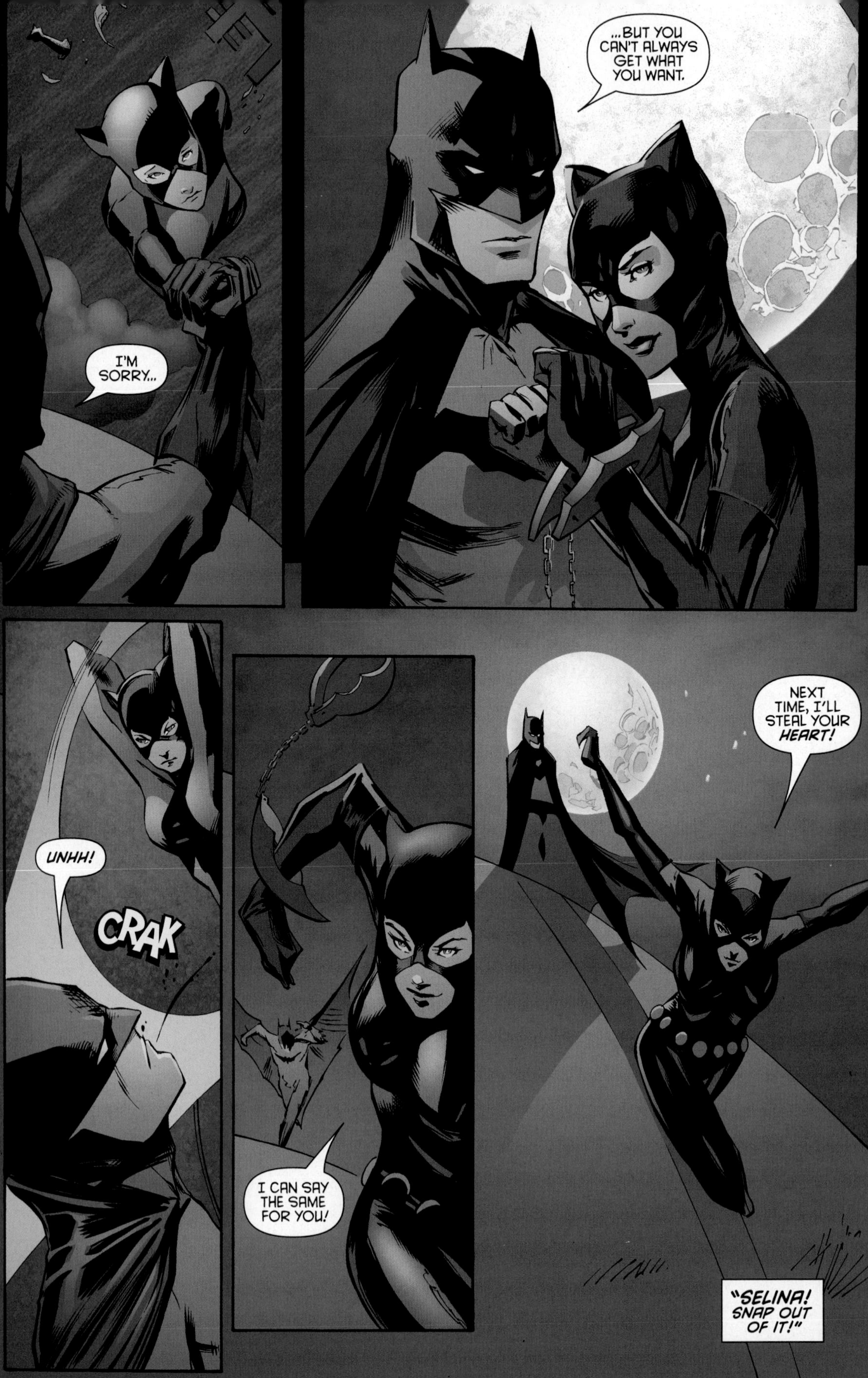
I'M SORRY...
...BUT YOU CAN'T ALWAYS GET WHAT YOU WANT.
UNHH!
CRAK
I CAN SAY THE SAME FOR YOU!
NEXT TIME, I'LL STEAL YOUR HEART!
"SELINA! SNAP OUT OF IT!"

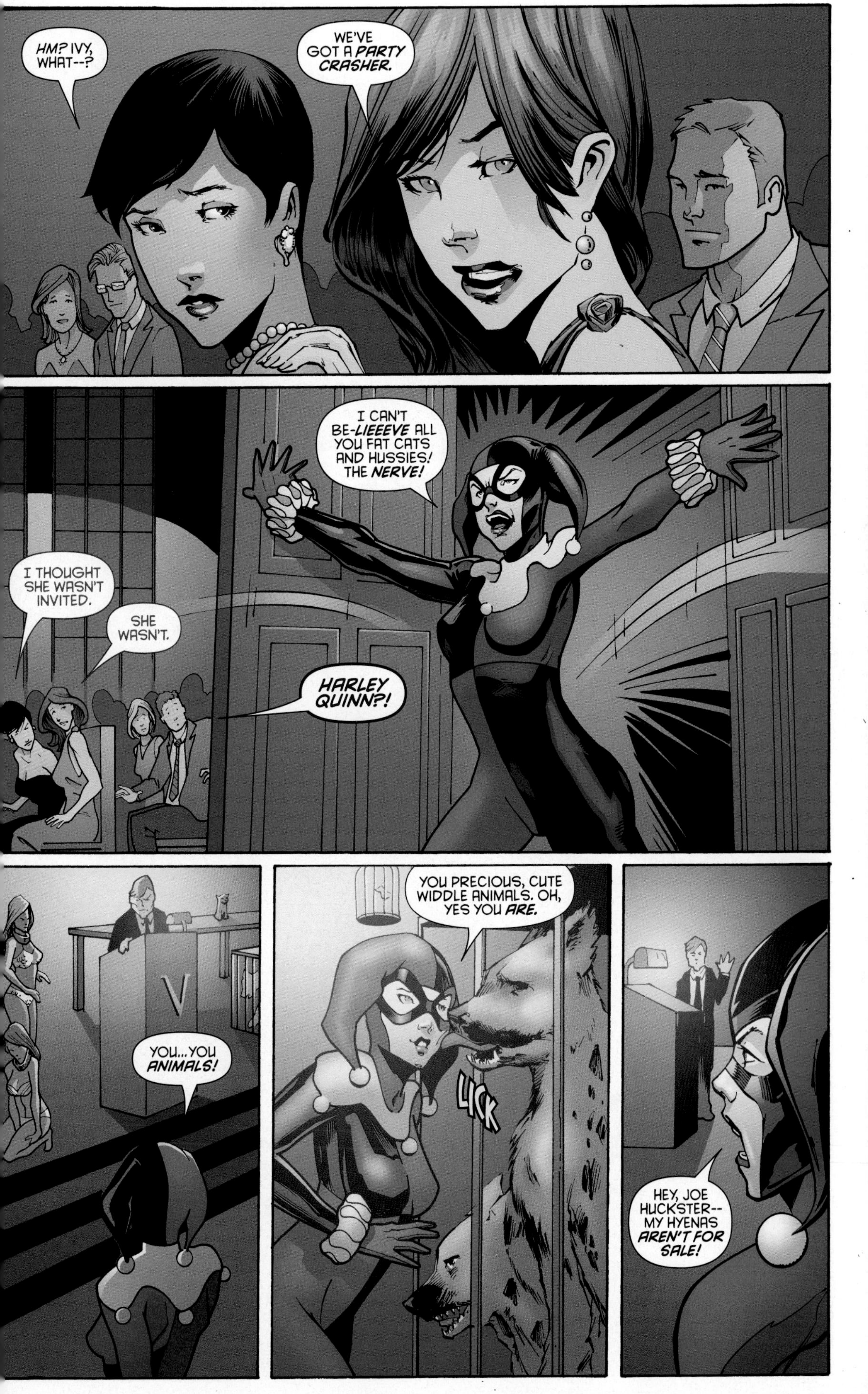
HM? IVY, WHAT--?
WE'VE GOT A PARTY CRASHER.
I CAN'T BE-LIEEEVE ALL YOU FAT CATS AND HUSSIES! THE NERVE!
I THOUGHT SHE WASN'T INVITED.
SHE WASN'T.
HARLEY QUINN?!
YOU...YOU ANIMALS!
YOU PRECIOUS, CUTE WIDDLE ANIMALS. OH, YES YOU ARE.
LICK
HEY, JOE HUCKSTER-- MY HYENAS AREN'T FOR SALE!

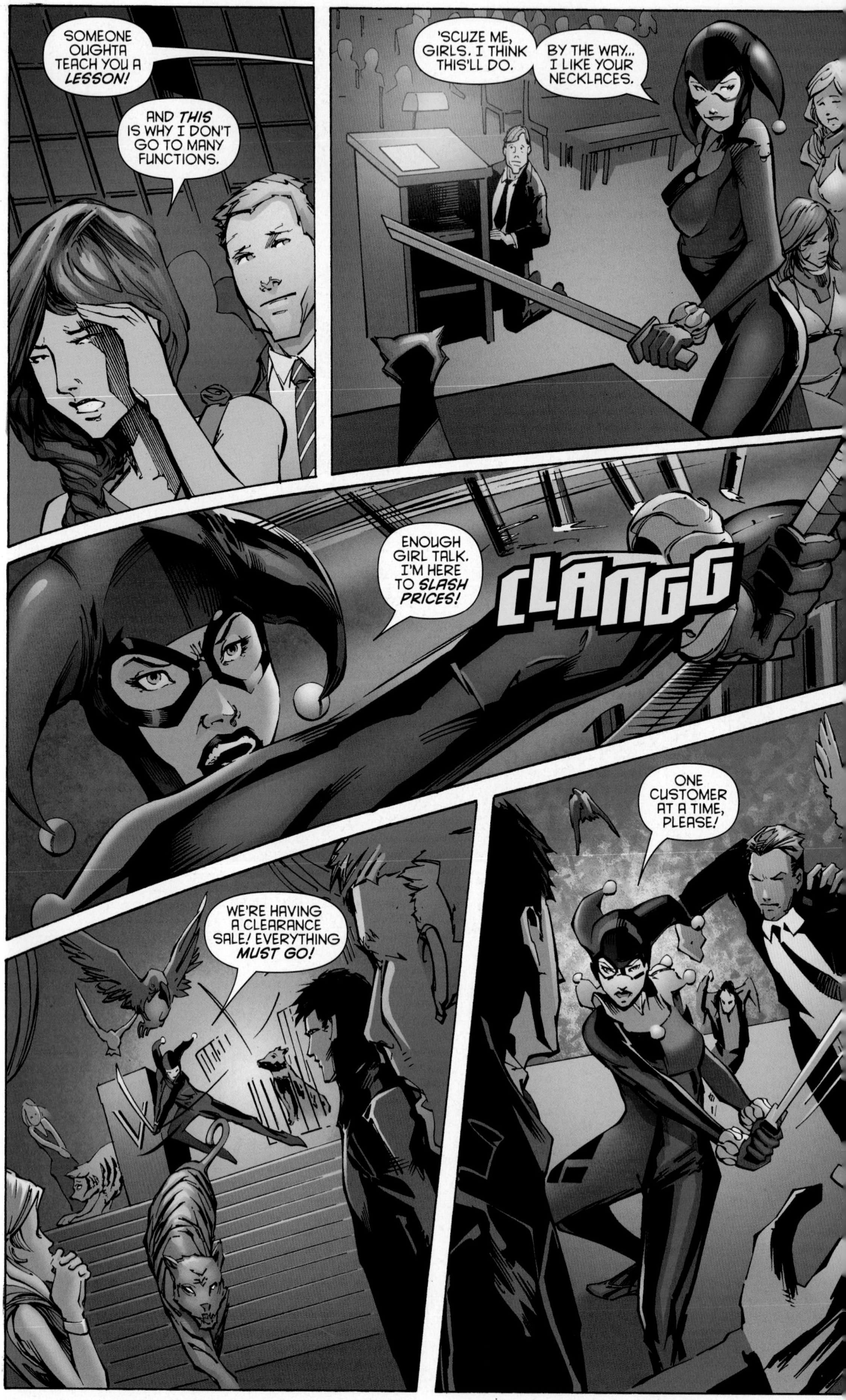
SOMEONE OUGHTA TEACH YOU A LESSON!
AND THIS IS WHY I DON'T GO TO MANY FUNCTIONS.
'SCUZE ME, GIRLS. I THINK THIS'LL DO.
BY THE WAY... I LIKE YOUR NECKLACES.
ENOUGH GIRL TALK. I'M HERE TO SLASH PRICES!
CLANGG
WE'RE HAVING A CLEARANCE SALE! EVERYTHING MUST GO!
ONE CUSTOMER AT A TIME, PLEASE!

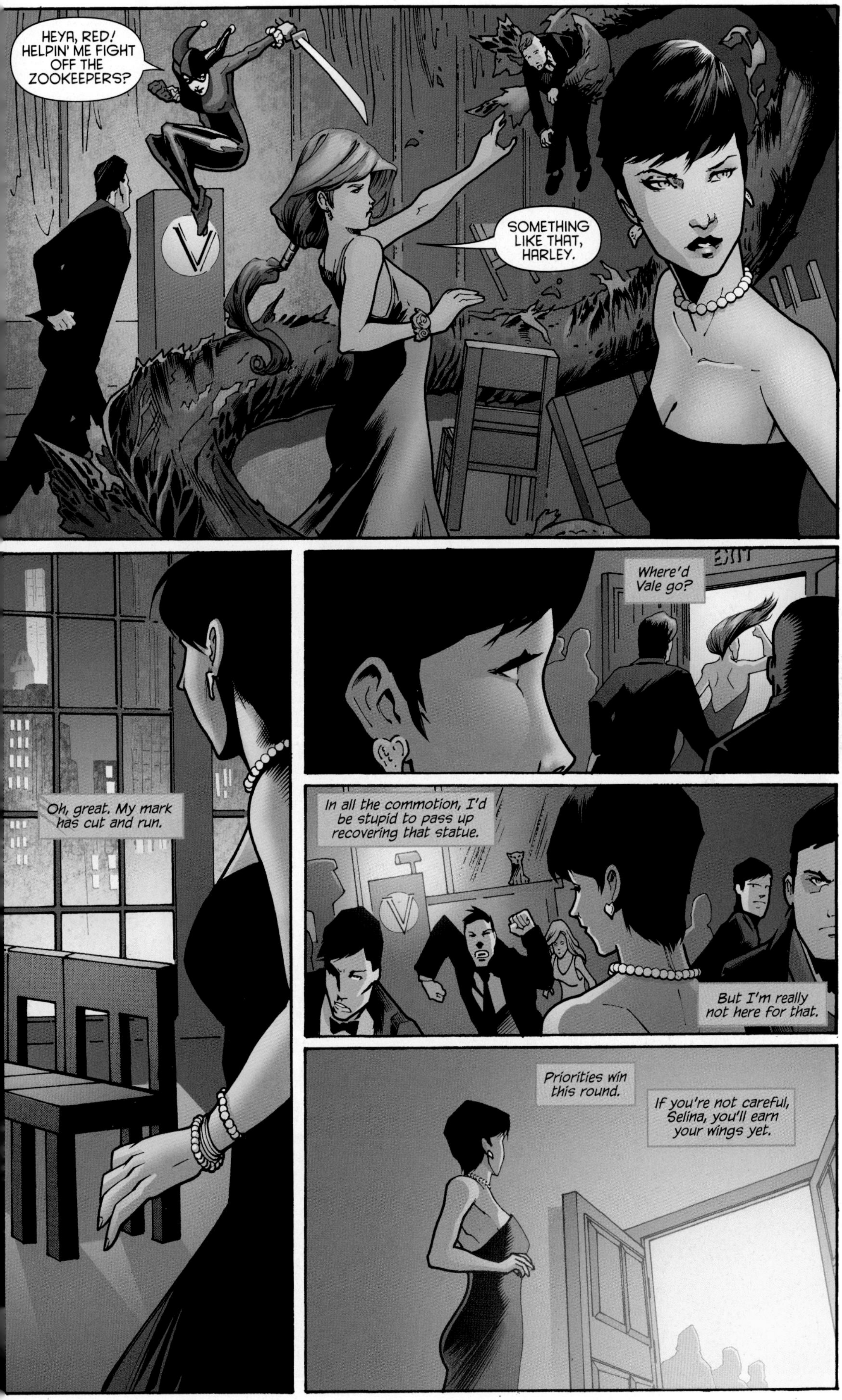
HEYA, RED! HELPIN' ME FIGHT OFF THE ZOOKEEPERS?
SOMETHING LIKE THAT, HARLEY.
Oh, great. My mark has cut and run.
Where'd Vale go?
In all the commotion, I'd be stupid to pass up recovering that statue.
But I'm really not here for that.
Priorities win this round.
If you're not careful, Selina, you'll earn your wings yet.

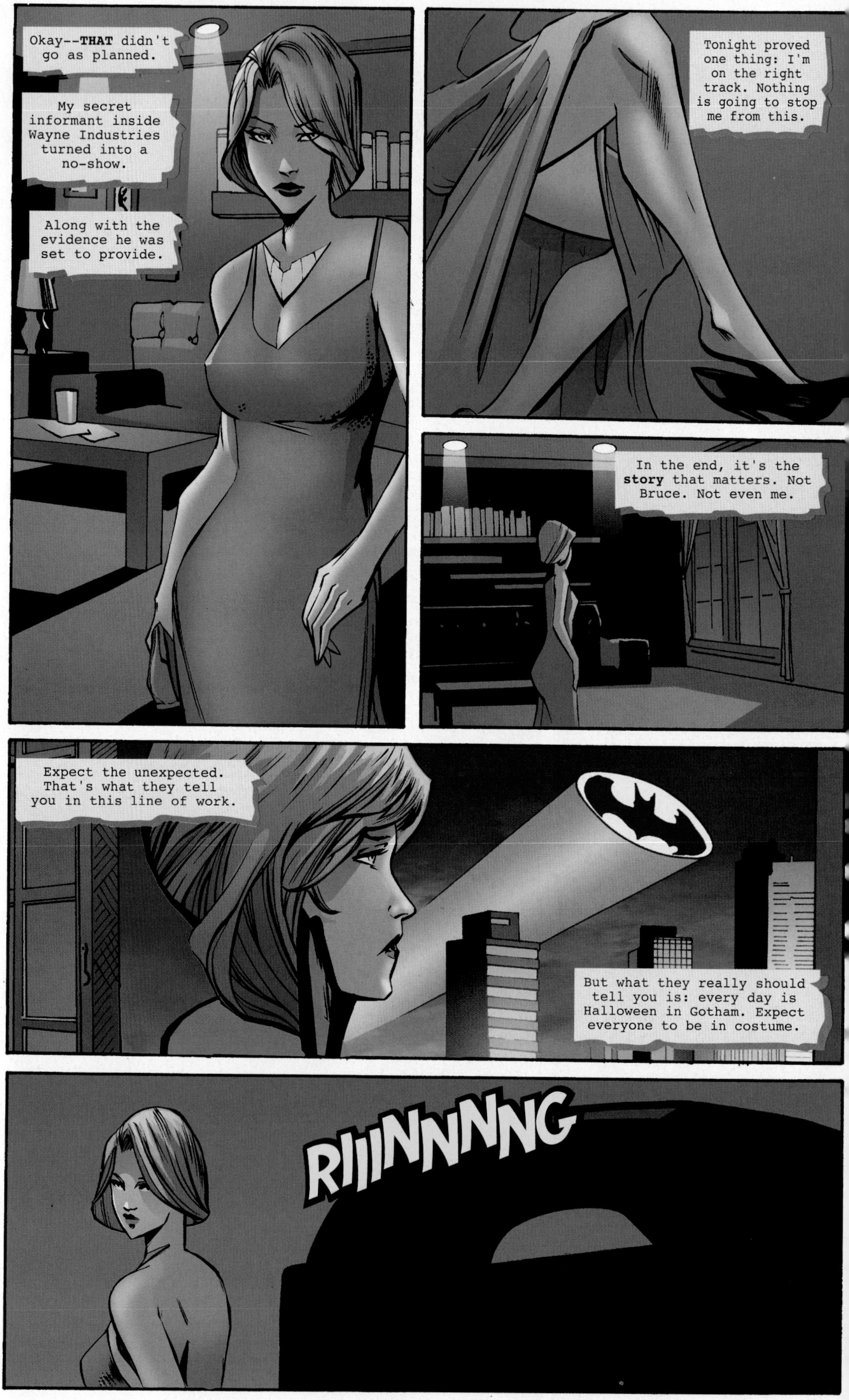

Okay--**THAT** didn't go as planned.
My secret informant inside Wayne Industries turned into a no-show.
Along with the evidence he was set to provide.
Tonight proved one thing: I'm on the right track. Nothing is going to stop me from this.
In the end, it's the **story** that matters. Not Bruce. Not even me.
Expect the unexpected. That's what they tell you in this line of work.
But what they really should tell you is: every day is Halloween in Gotham. Expect everyone to be in costume.
RIIINNNNG

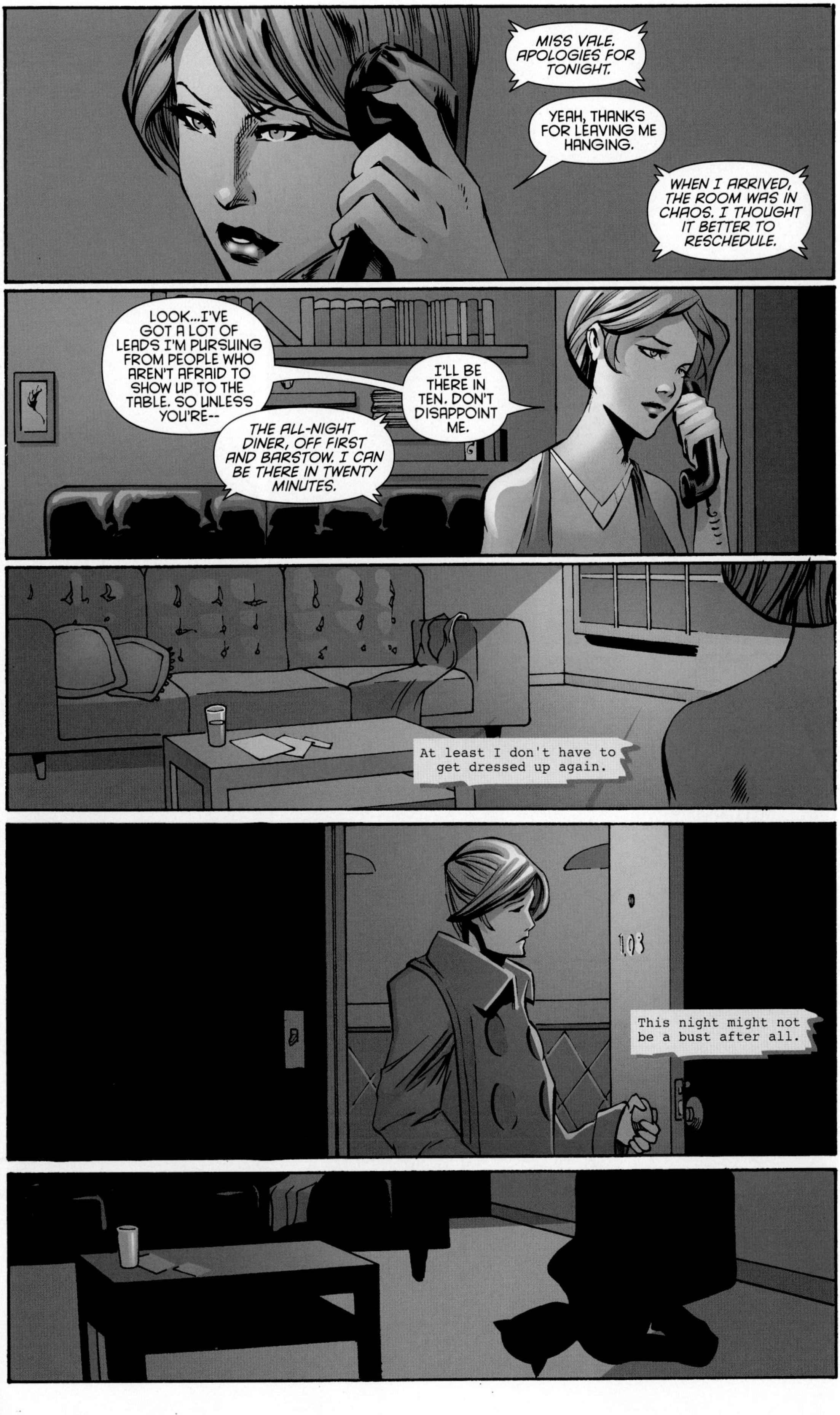
MISS VALE. APOLOGIES FOR TONIGHT.
YEAH, THANKS FOR LEAVING ME HANGING.
WHEN I ARRIVED, THE ROOM WAS IN CHAOS. I THOUGHT IT BETTER TO RESCHEDULE.
LOOK...I'VE GOT A LOT OF LEADS I'M PURSUING FROM PEOPLE WHO AREN'T AFRAID TO SHOW UP TO THE TABLE. SO UNLESS YOU'RE--
THE ALL-NIGHT DINER, OFF FIRST AND BARSTOW. I CAN BE THERE IN TWENTY MINUTES.
I'LL BE THERE IN TEN. DON'T DISAPPOINT ME.
At least I don't have to get dressed up again.
103
This night might not be a bust after all.

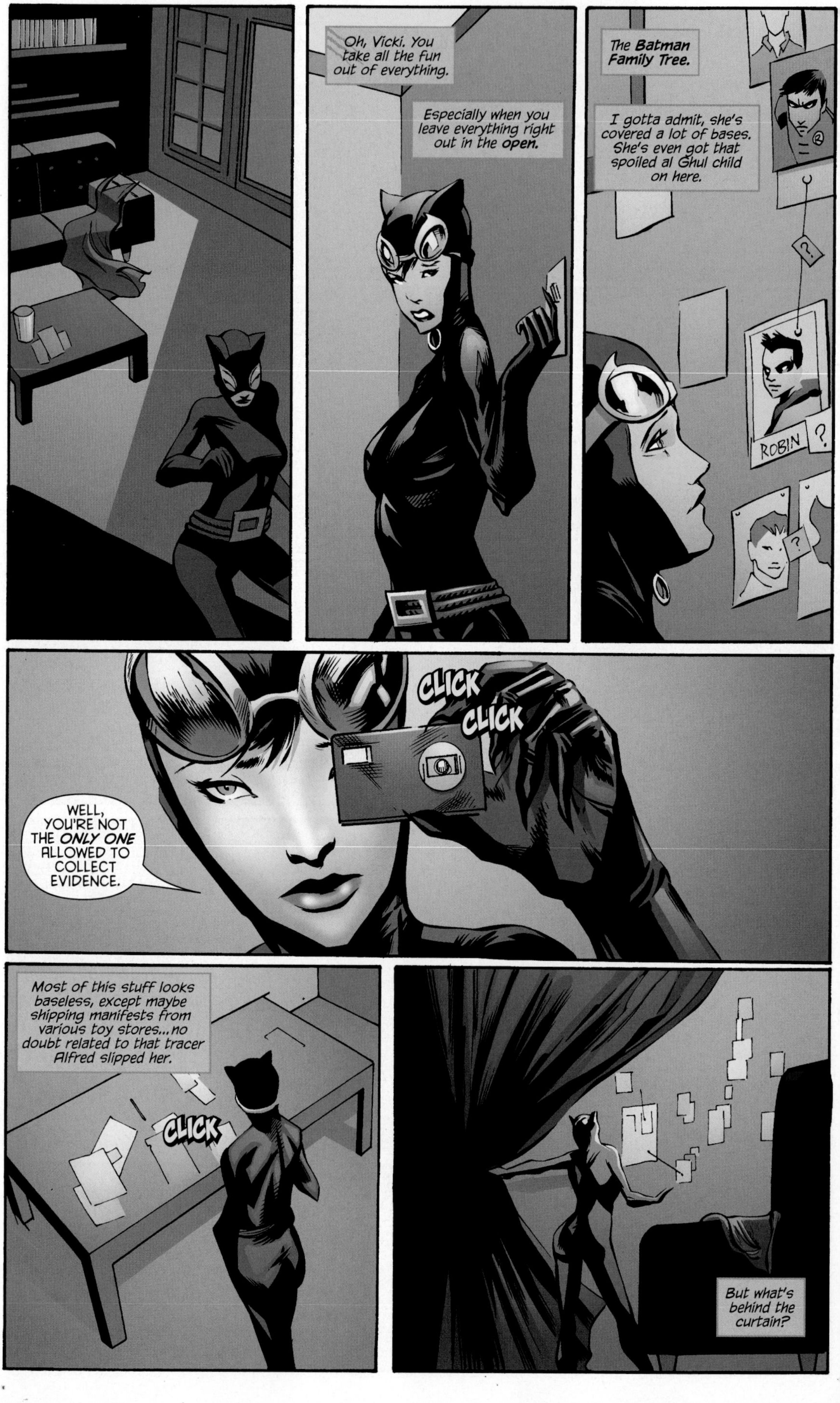

Oh, Vicki. You take all the fun out of everything.
Especially when you leave everything right out in the **open.**
The **Batman Family Tree.**
I gotta admit, she's covered a lot of bases. She's even got that spoiled al Ghul child on here.
ROBIN ?
CLICK
CLICK
WELL, YOU'RE NOT THE ***ONLY ONE*** ALLOWED TO COLLECT EVIDENCE.
Most of this stuff looks baseless, except maybe shipping manifests from various toy stores...no doubt related to that tracer Alfred slipped her.
CLICK
But what's behind the curtain?

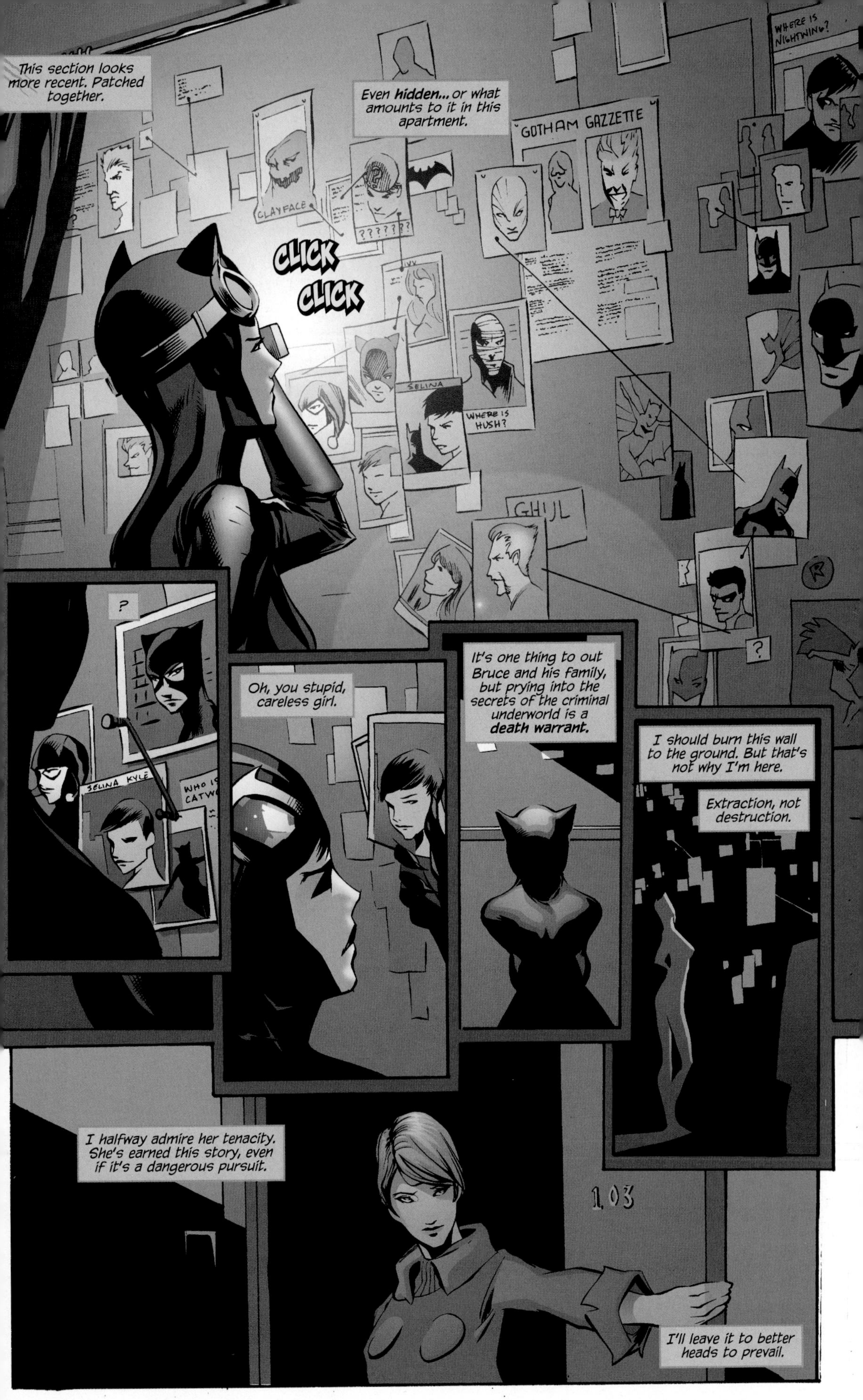

This section looks more recent. Patched together.
Even hidden... or what amounts to it in this apartment.
GOTHAM GAZZETTE
CLAYFACE
??????
CLICK
CLICK
IVY
SELINA
WHERE IS HUSH?
WHERE IS NIGHTWING?
GHUL
?
SELINA KYLE
Oh, you stupid, careless girl.
It's one thing to out Bruce and his family, but prying into the secrets of the criminal underworld is a death warrant.
I should burn this wall to the ground. But that's not why I'm here.
Extraction, not destruction.
I halfway admire her tenacity. She's earned this story, even if it's a dangerous pursuit.
103
I'll leave it to better heads to prevail.

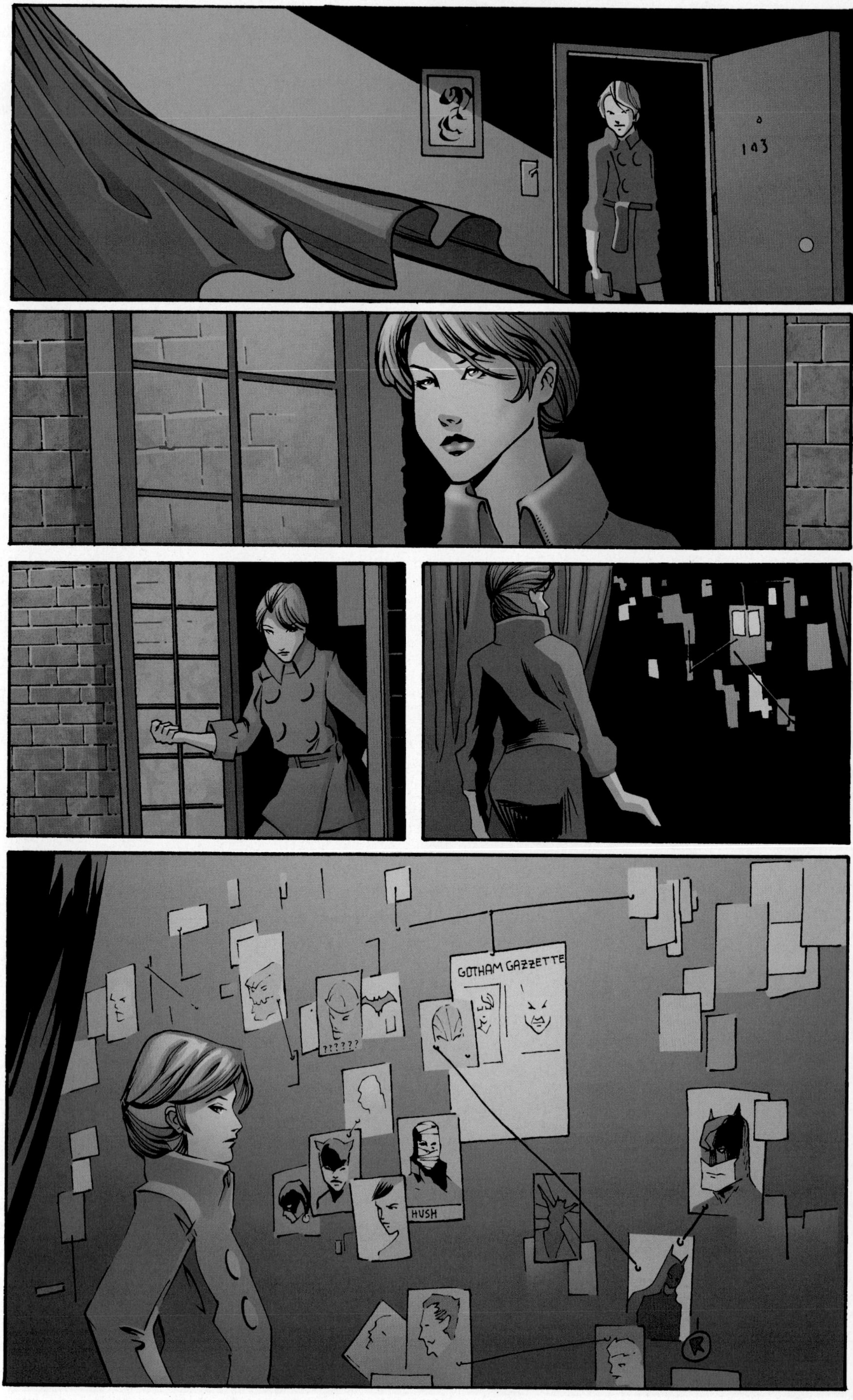

103
GOTHAM GAZZETTE
??????
HUSH

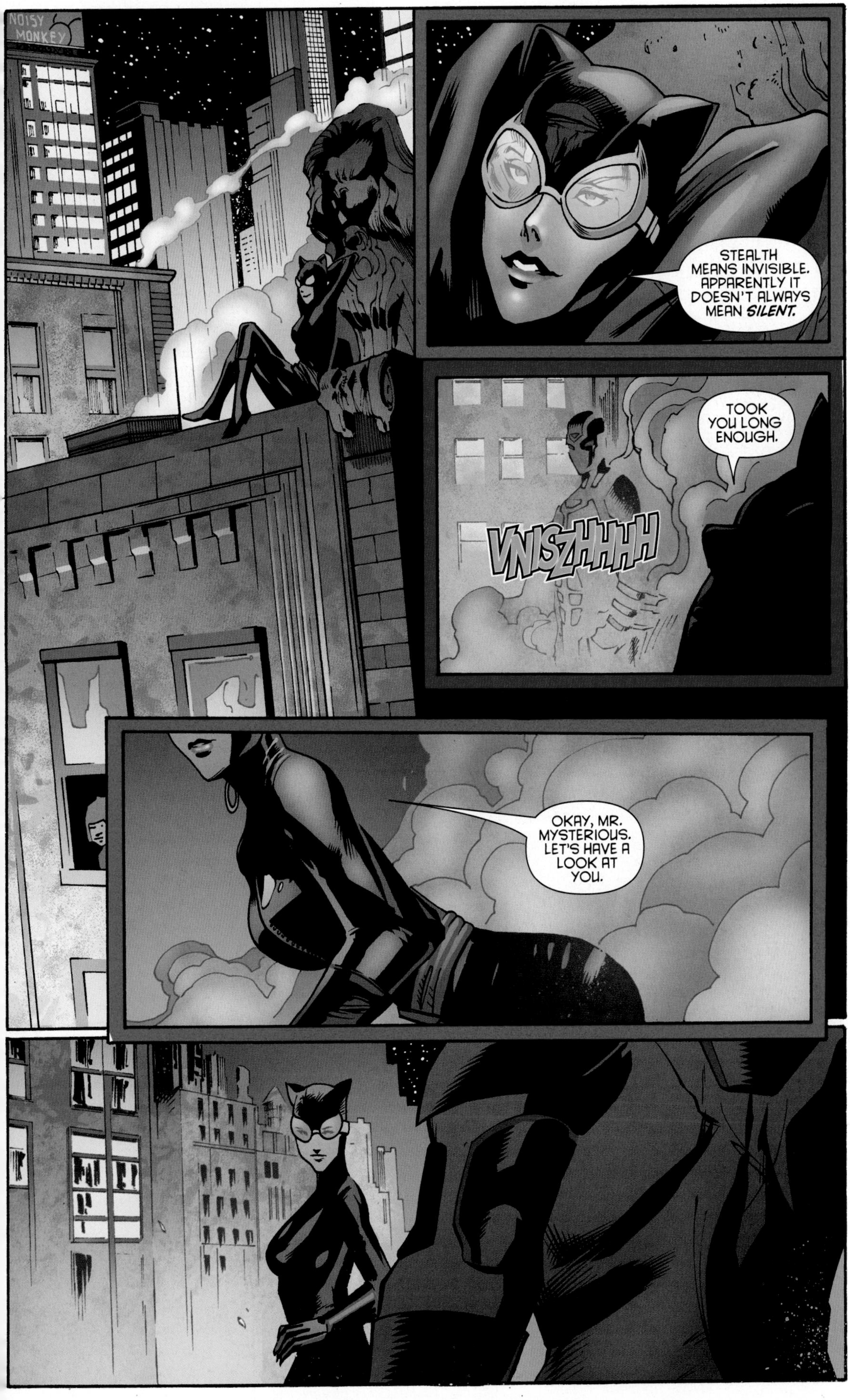
NOISY MONKEY
STEALTH MEANS INVISIBLE. APPARENTLY IT DOESN'T ALWAYS MEAN *SILENT.*
TOOK YOU LONG ENOUGH.
VNISZHHHH
OKAY, MR. MYSTERIOUS. LET'S HAVE A LOOK AT YOU.

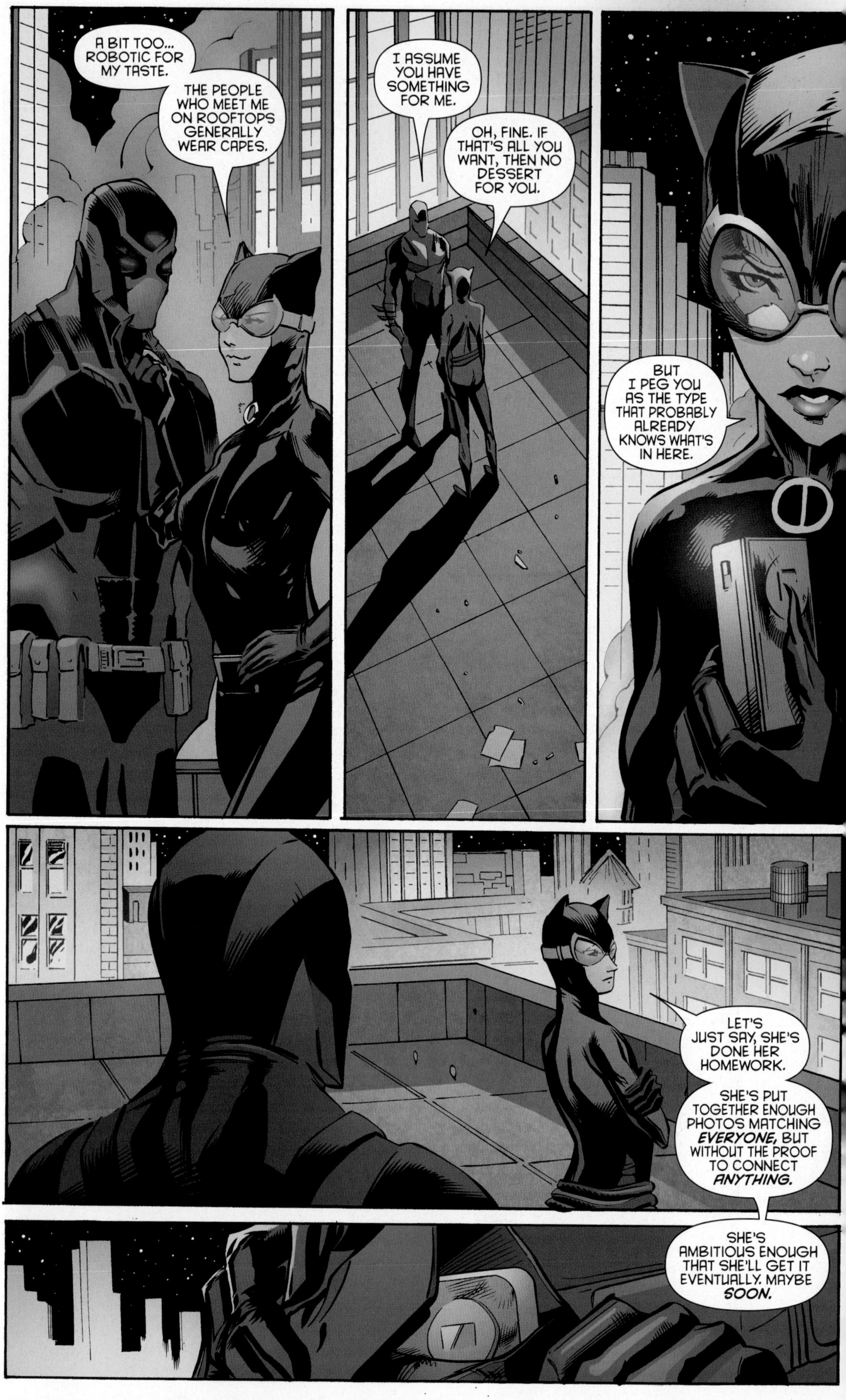
A BIT TOO... ROBOTIC FOR MY TASTE.
THE PEOPLE WHO MEET ME ON ROOFTOPS GENERALLY WEAR CAPES.
I ASSUME YOU HAVE SOMETHING FOR ME.
OH, FINE. IF THAT'S ALL YOU WANT, THEN NO DESSERT FOR YOU.
BUT I PEG YOU AS THE TYPE THAT PROBABLY ALREADY KNOWS WHAT'S IN HERE.
LET'S JUST SAY, SHE'S DONE HER HOMEWORK.
SHE'S PUT TOGETHER ENOUGH PHOTOS MATCHING ***EVERYONE,*** BUT WITHOUT THE PROOF TO CONNECT ***ANYTHING.***
SHE'S AMBITIOUS ENOUGH THAT SHE'LL GET IT EVENTUALLY. MAYBE ***SOON.***

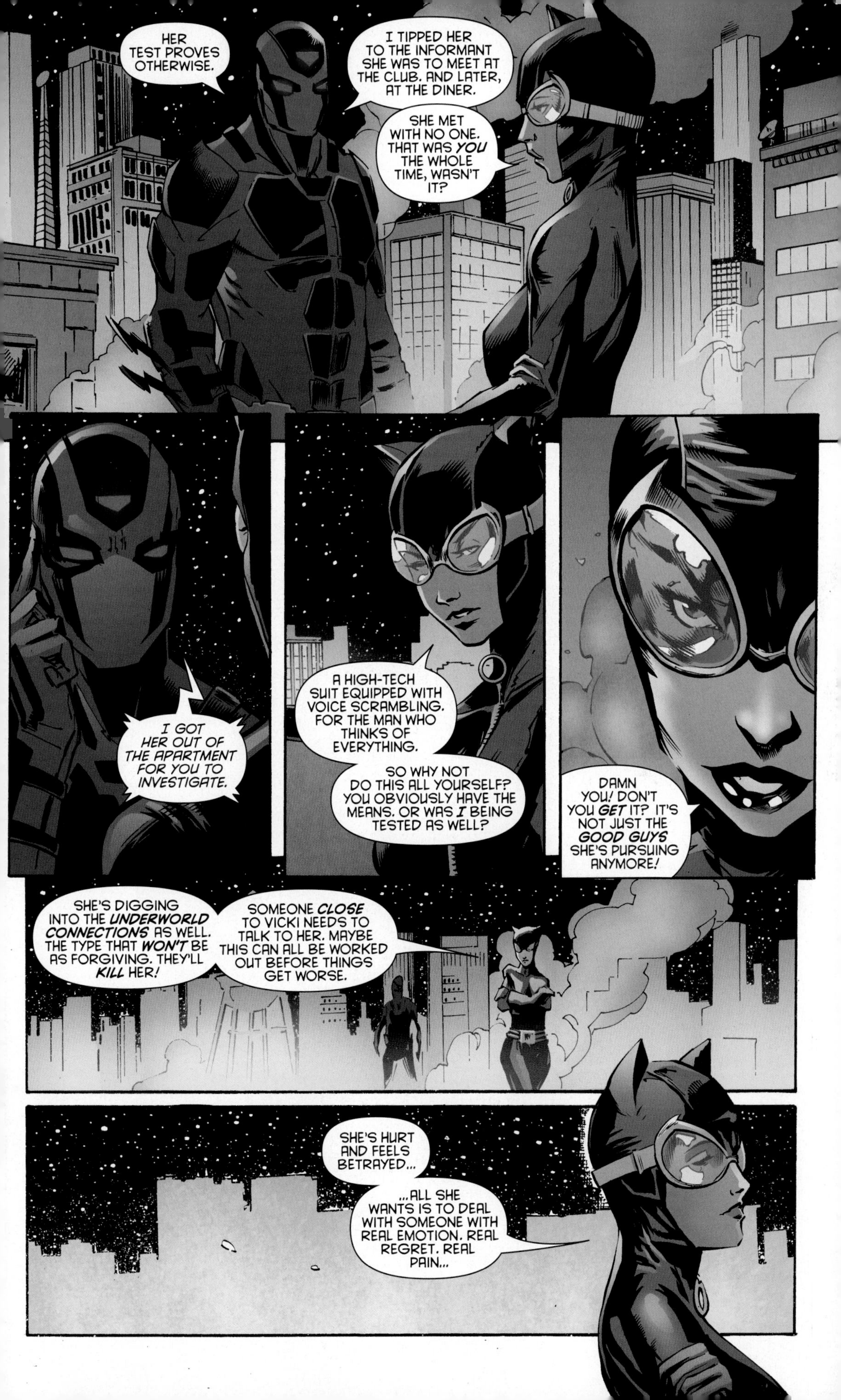
HER TEST PROVES OTHERWISE.
I TIPPED HER TO THE INFORMANT SHE WAS TO MEET AT THE CLUB. AND LATER, AT THE DINER.
SHE MET WITH NO ONE. THAT WAS *YOU* THE WHOLE TIME, WASN'T IT?
I GOT HER OUT OF THE APARTMENT FOR YOU TO INVESTIGATE.
A HIGH-TECH SUIT EQUIPPED WITH VOICE SCRAMBLING. FOR THE MAN WHO THINKS OF EVERYTHING.
SO WHY NOT DO THIS ALL YOURSELF? YOU OBVIOUSLY HAVE THE MEANS. OR WAS *I* BEING TESTED AS WELL?
DAMN YOU! DON'T YOU *GET* IT? IT'S NOT JUST THE ***GOOD GUYS*** SHE'S PURSUING ANYMORE!
SHE'S DIGGING INTO THE ***UNDERWORLD CONNECTIONS*** AS WELL. THE TYPE THAT ***WON'T*** BE AS FORGIVING. THEY'LL ***KILL*** HER!
SOMEONE ***CLOSE*** TO VICKI NEEDS TO TALK TO HER. MAYBE THIS CAN ALL BE WORKED OUT BEFORE THINGS GET WORSE.
SHE'S HURT AND FEELS BETRAYED...
...ALL SHE WANTS IS TO DEAL WITH SOMEONE WITH REAL EMOTION. REAL REGRET. REAL PAIN...

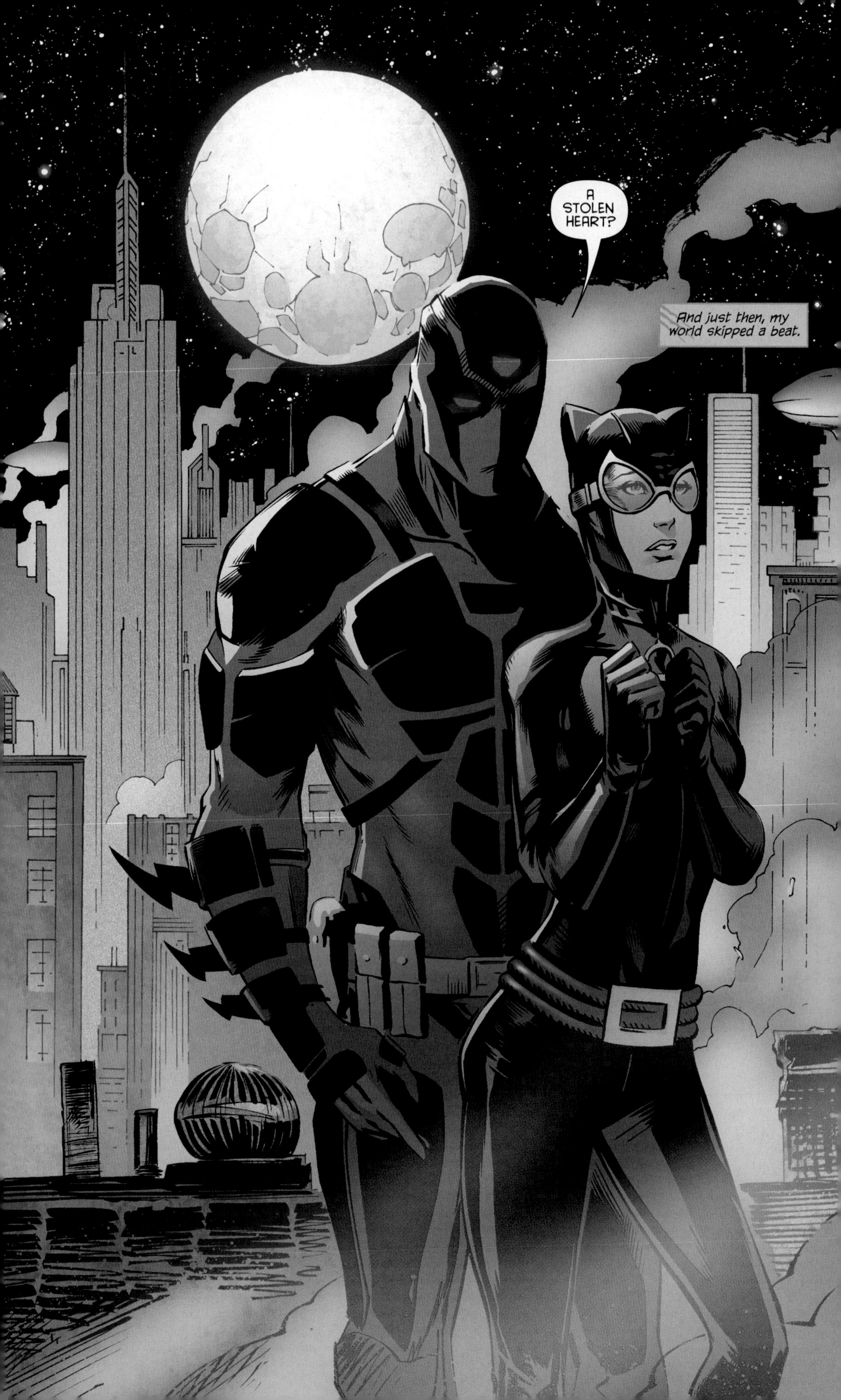

A STOLEN HEART?
And just then, my world skipped a beat.

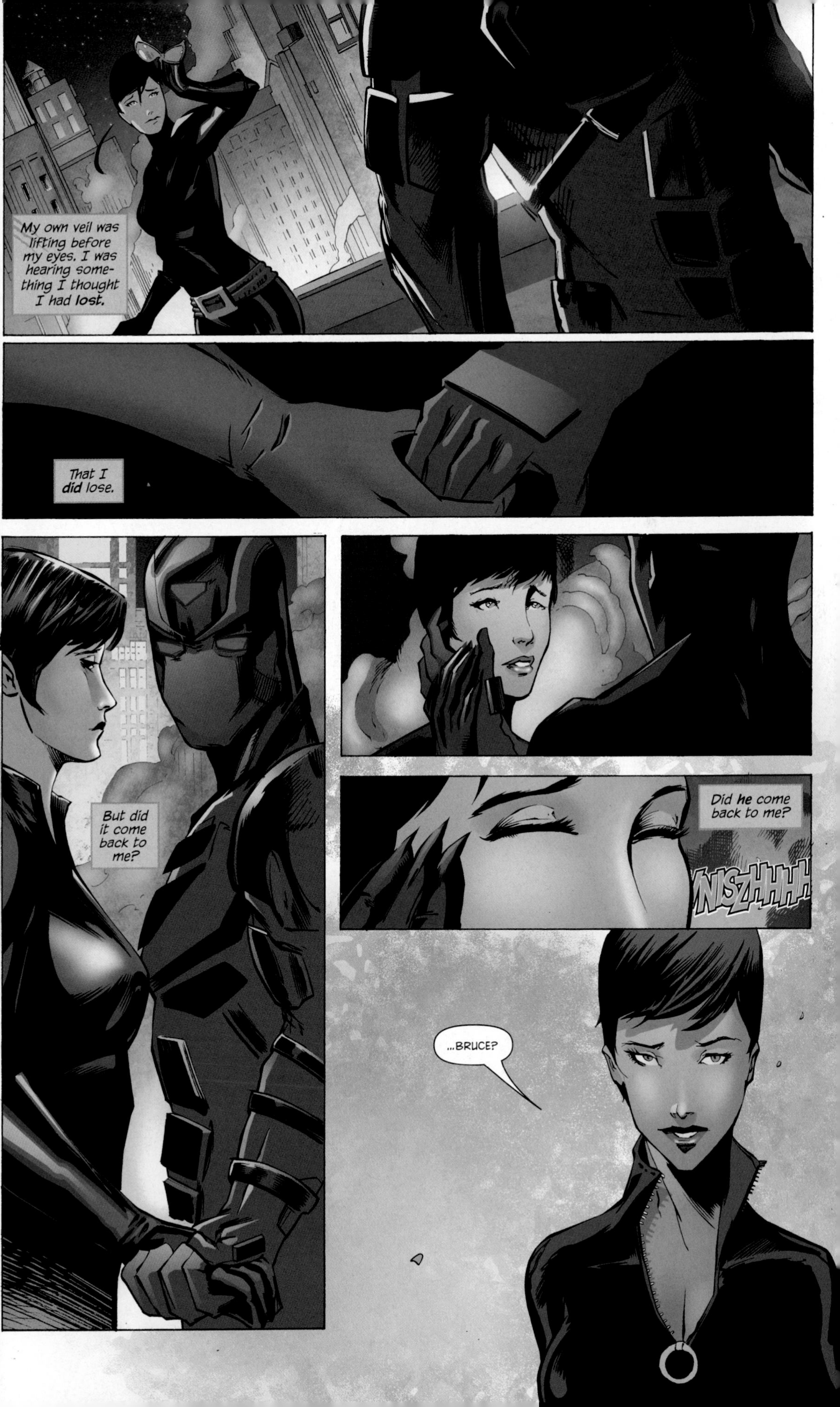

My own veil was lifting before my eyes. I was hearing something I thought I had lost.
That I did lose.
But did it come back to me?
Did he come back to me?
VNISZHHHH
...BRUCE?

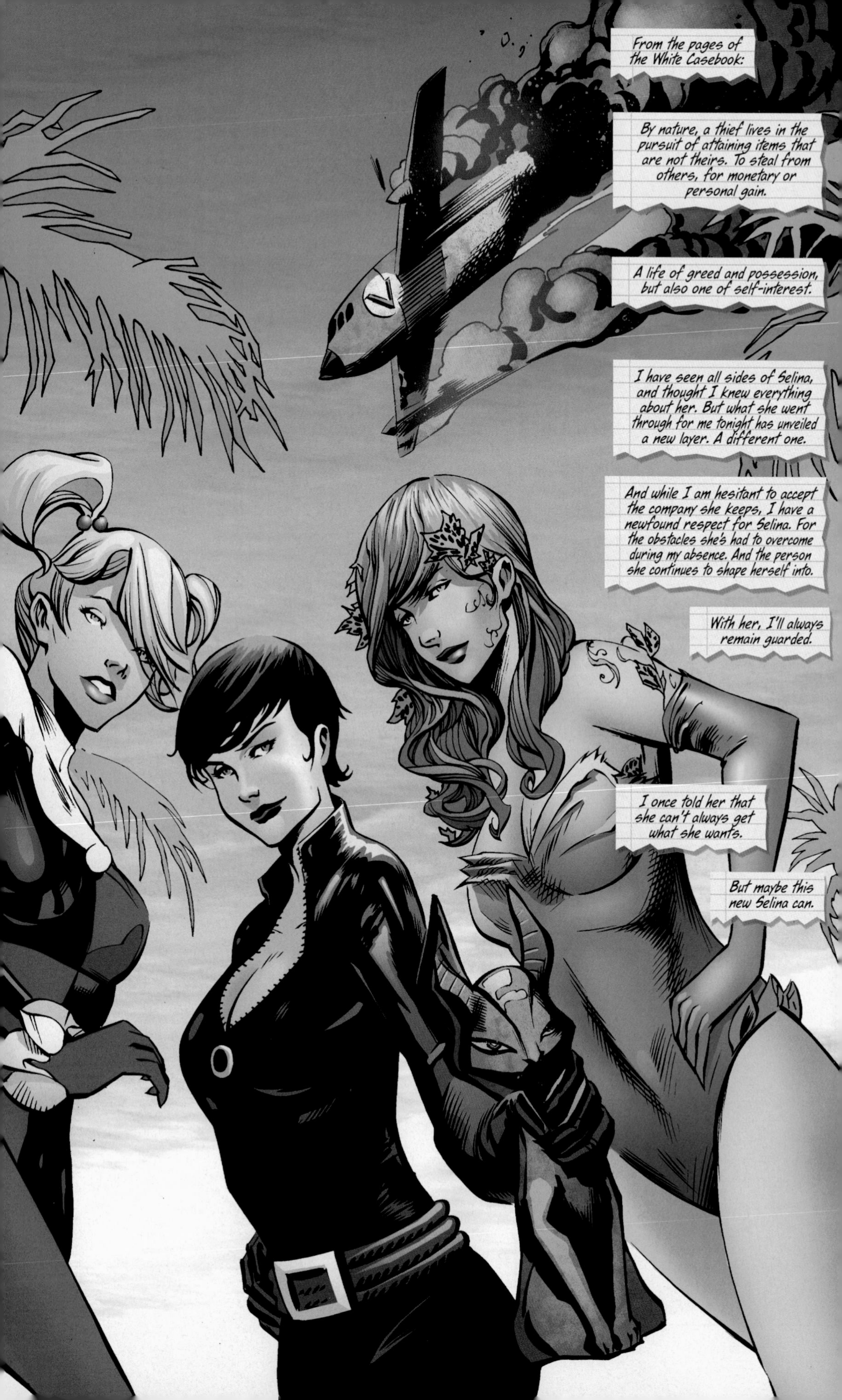
From the pages of the White Casebook:
By nature, a thief lives in the pursuit of attaining items that are not theirs. To steal from others, for monetary or personal gain.
A life of greed and possession, but also one of self-interest.
I have seen all sides of Selina, and thought I knew everything about her. But what she went through for me tonight has unveiled a new layer. A different one.
And while I am hesitant to accept the company she keeps, I have a newfound respect for Selina. For the obstacles she's had to overcome during my absence. And the person she continues to shape herself into.
With her, I'll always remain guarded.
I once told her that she can't always get what she wants.
But maybe this new Selina can.

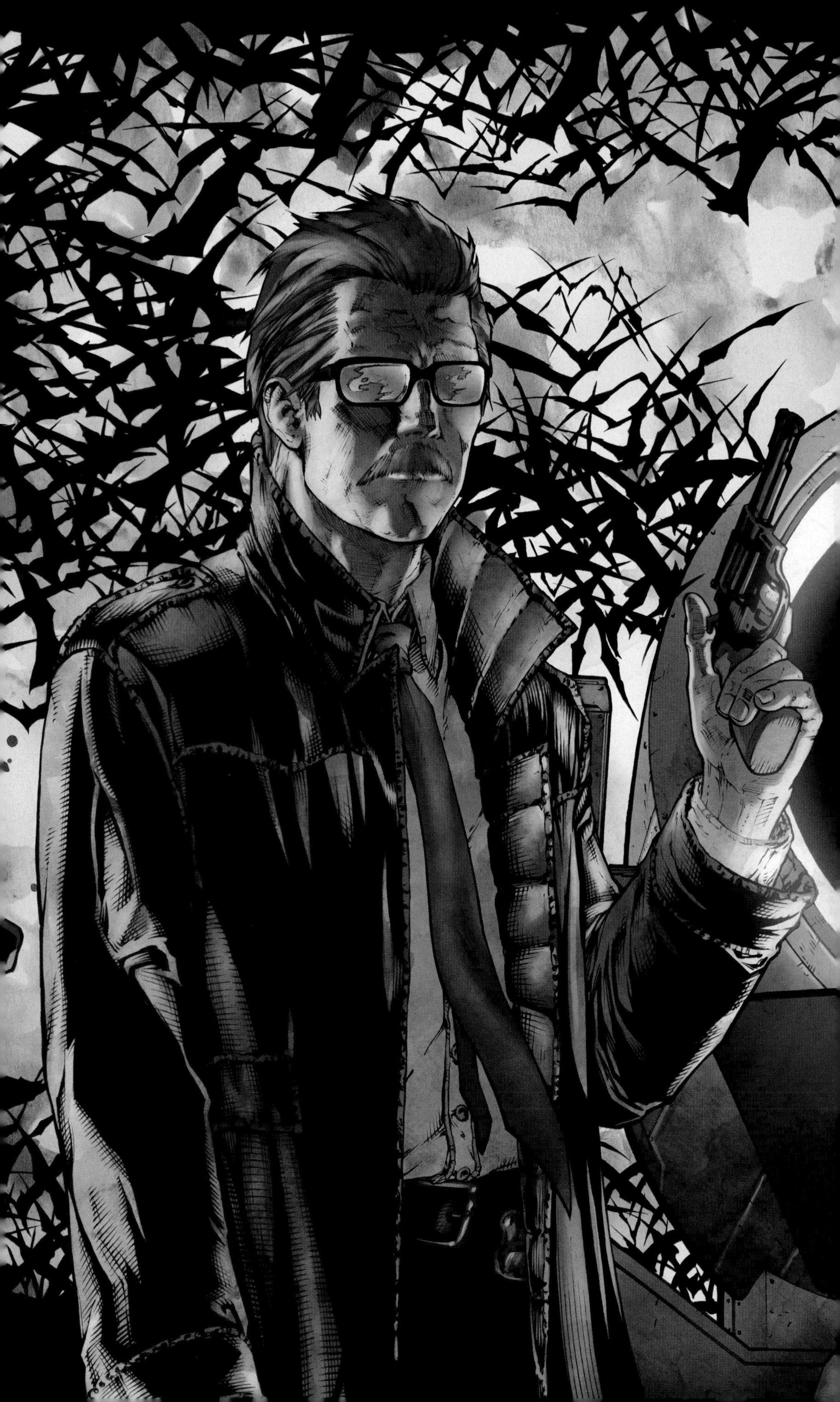

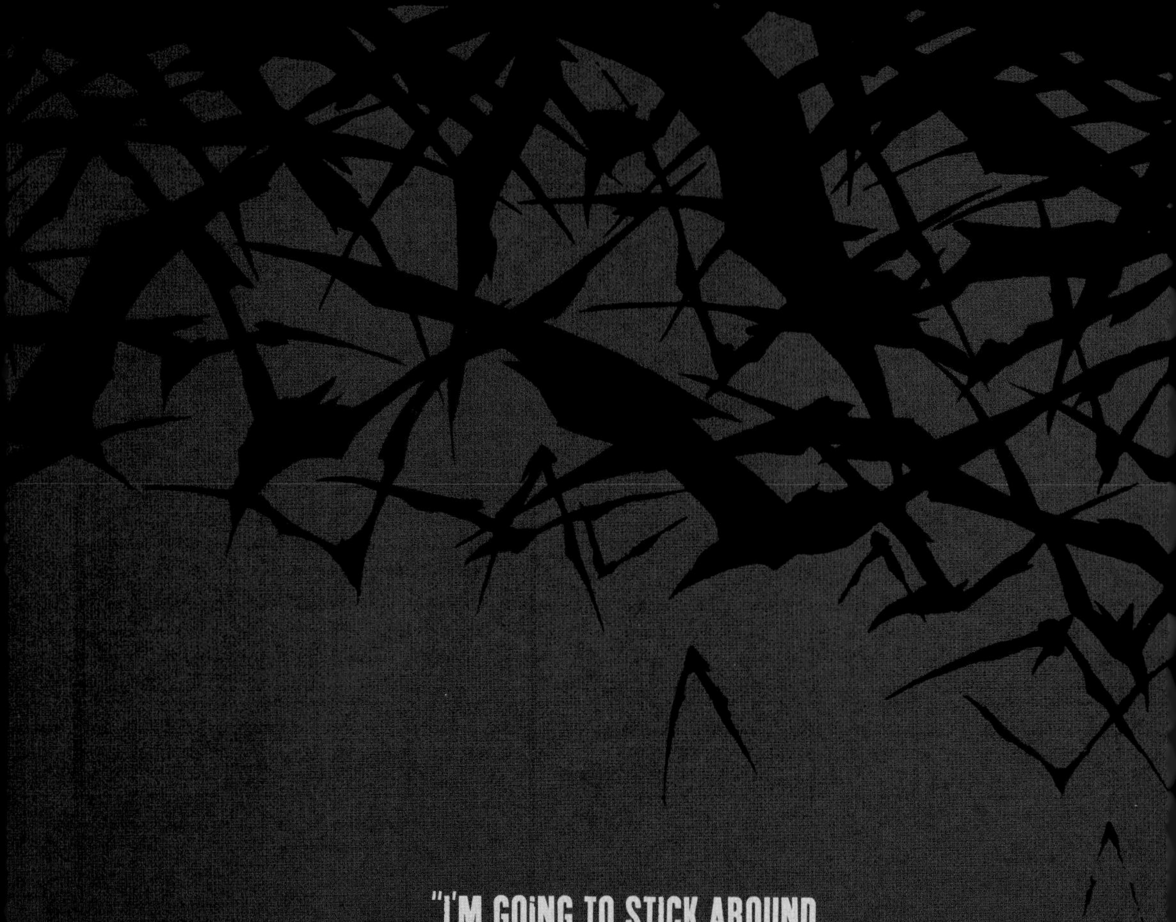

"I'M GOING TO STICK AROUND
AS LONG AS GOTHAM NEEDS ME."

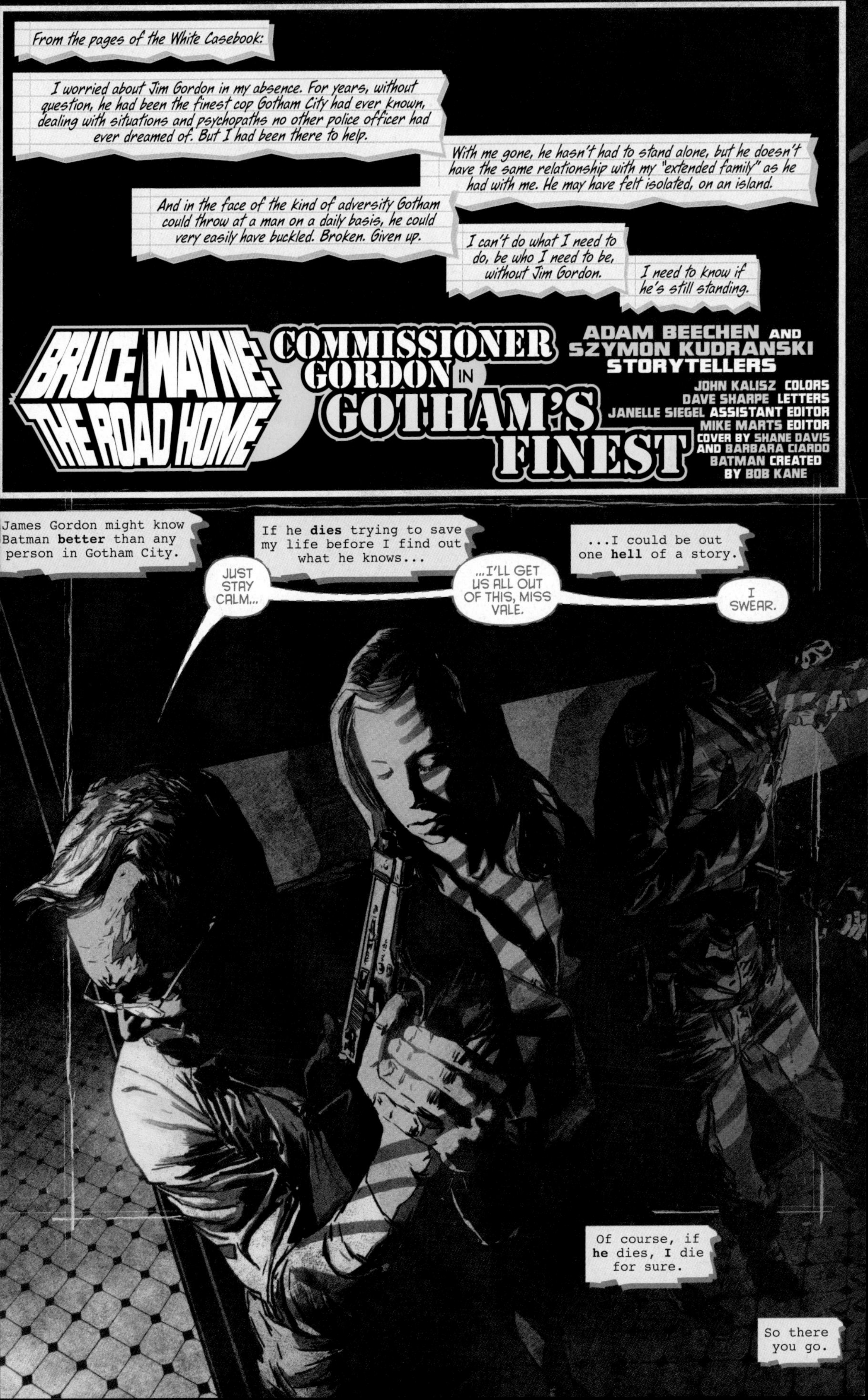
From the pages of the White Casebook:
I worried about Jim Gordon in my absence. For years, without question, he had been the finest cop Gotham City had ever known, dealing with situations and psychopaths no other police officer had ever dreamed of. But I had been there to help.
With me gone, he hasn't had to stand alone, but he doesn't have the same relationship with my "extended family" as he had with me. He may have felt isolated, on an island.
And in the face of the kind of adversity Gotham could throw at a man on a daily basis, he could very easily have buckled. Broken. Given up.
I can't do what I need to do, be who I need to be, without Jim Gordon.
I need to know if he's still standing.
BRUCE WAYNE: THE ROAD HOME
COMMISSIONER GORDON IN GOTHAM'S FINEST
ADAM BEECHEN AND SZYMON KUDRANSKI STORYTELLERS
JOHN KALISZ COLORS
DAVE SHARPE LETTERS
JANELLE SIEGEL ASSISTANT EDITOR
MIKE MARTS EDITOR
COVER BY SHANE DAVIS AND BARBARA CIARDO
BATMAN CREATED BY BOB KANE
James Gordon might know Batman better than any person in Gotham City.
JUST STAY CALM...
If he dies trying to save my life before I find out what he knows...
...I'LL GET US ALL OUT OF THIS, MISS VALE.
...I could be out one hell of a story.
I SWEAR.
Of course, if he dies, I die for sure.
So there you go.

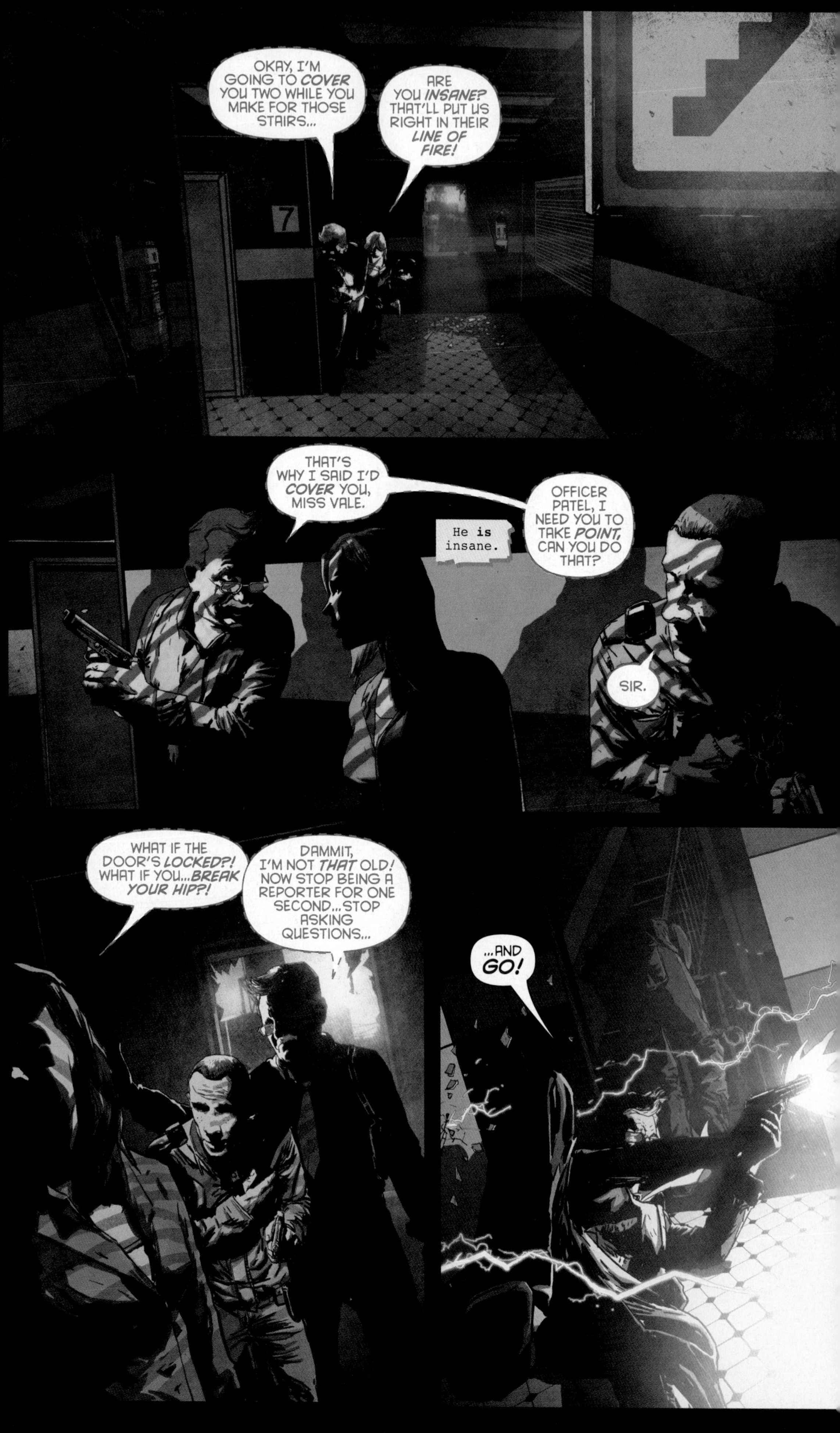
OKAY, I'M GOING TO *COVER* YOU TWO WHILE YOU MAKE FOR THOSE STAIRS...
ARE YOU *INSANE?* THAT'LL PUT US RIGHT IN THEIR *LINE OF FIRE!*
THAT'S WHY I SAID I'D *COVER* YOU, MISS VALE.
He **is** insane.
OFFICER PATEL, I NEED YOU TO TAKE *POINT,* CAN YOU DO THAT?
SIR.
WHAT IF THE DOOR'S *LOCKED?!* WHAT IF YOU...*BREAK YOUR HIP?!*
DAMMIT, I'M NOT *THAT* OLD! NOW STOP BEING A REPORTER FOR ONE SECOND...STOP ASKING QUESTIONS...
...AND *GO!*

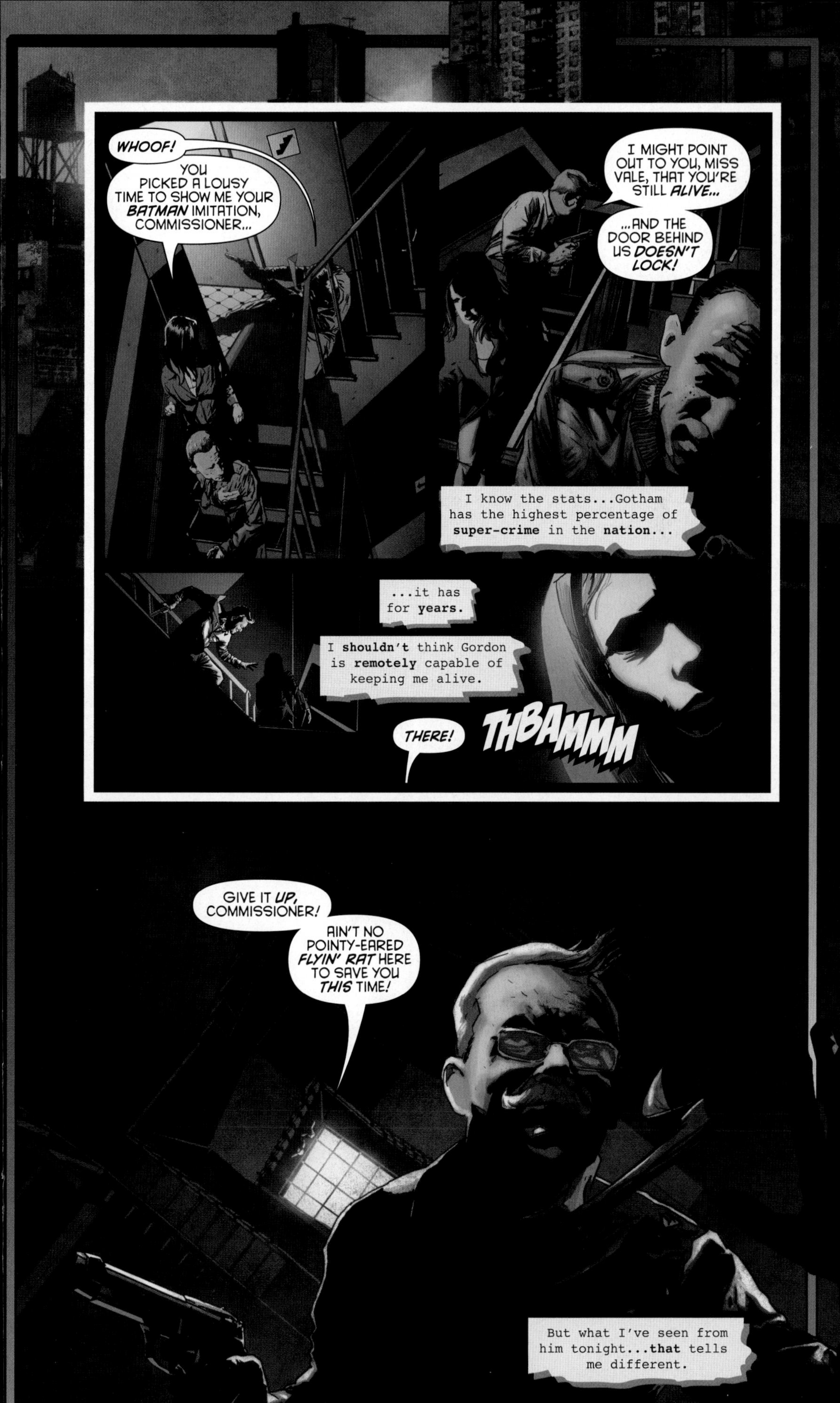
WHOOF!
YOU PICKED A LOUSY TIME TO SHOW ME YOUR BATMAN IMITATION, COMMISSIONER...
I MIGHT POINT OUT TO YOU, MISS VALE, THAT YOU'RE STILL ALIVE...
...AND THE DOOR BEHIND US DOESN'T LOCK!
I know the stats...Gotham has the highest percentage of super-crime in the nation...
...it has for years.
I shouldn't think Gordon is remotely capable of keeping me alive.
THERE!
THBAMMM
GIVE IT UP, COMMISSIONER!
AIN'T NO POINTY-EARED FLYIN' RAT HERE TO SAVE YOU THIS TIME!
But what I've seen from him tonight...that tells me different.

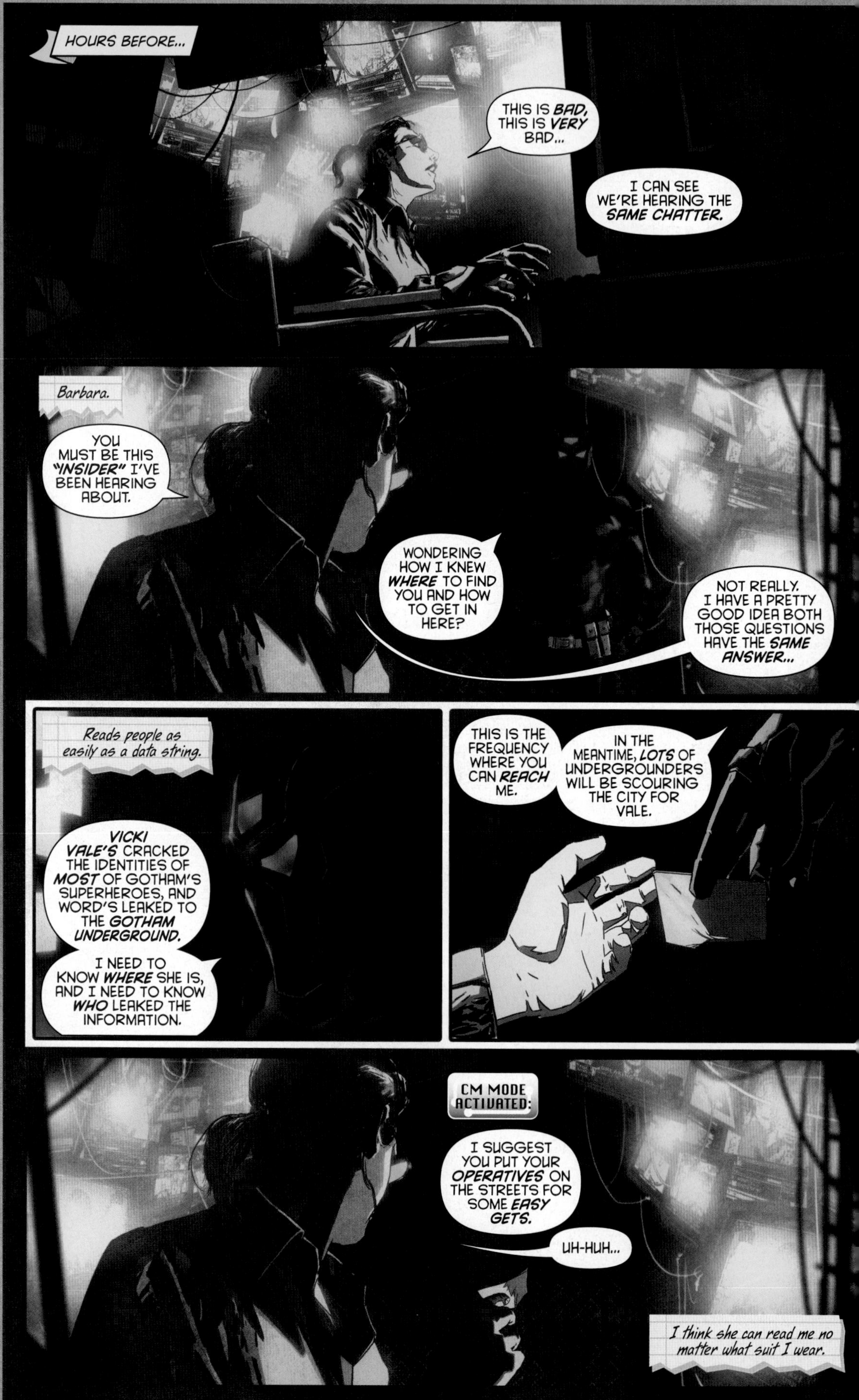
HOURS BEFORE...
THIS IS BAD, THIS IS VERY BAD...
I CAN SEE WE'RE HEARING THE SAME CHATTER.
Barbara.
YOU MUST BE THIS "INSIDER" I'VE BEEN HEARING ABOUT.
WONDERING HOW I KNEW WHERE TO FIND YOU AND HOW TO GET IN HERE?
NOT REALLY. I HAVE A PRETTY GOOD IDEA BOTH THOSE QUESTIONS HAVE THE SAME ANSWER...
Reads people as easily as a data string.
VICKI VALE'S CRACKED THE IDENTITIES OF MOST OF GOTHAM'S SUPERHEROES, AND WORD'S LEAKED TO THE GOTHAM UNDERGROUND.
I NEED TO KNOW WHERE SHE IS, AND I NEED TO KNOW WHO LEAKED THE INFORMATION.
THIS IS THE FREQUENCY WHERE YOU CAN REACH ME.
IN THE MEANTIME, LOTS OF UNDERGROUNDERS WILL BE SCOURING THE CITY FOR VALE.
CM MODE ACTIVATED:
I SUGGEST YOU PUT YOUR OPERATIVES ON THE STREETS FOR SOME EASY GETS.
UH-HUH...
I think she can read me no matter what suit I wear.

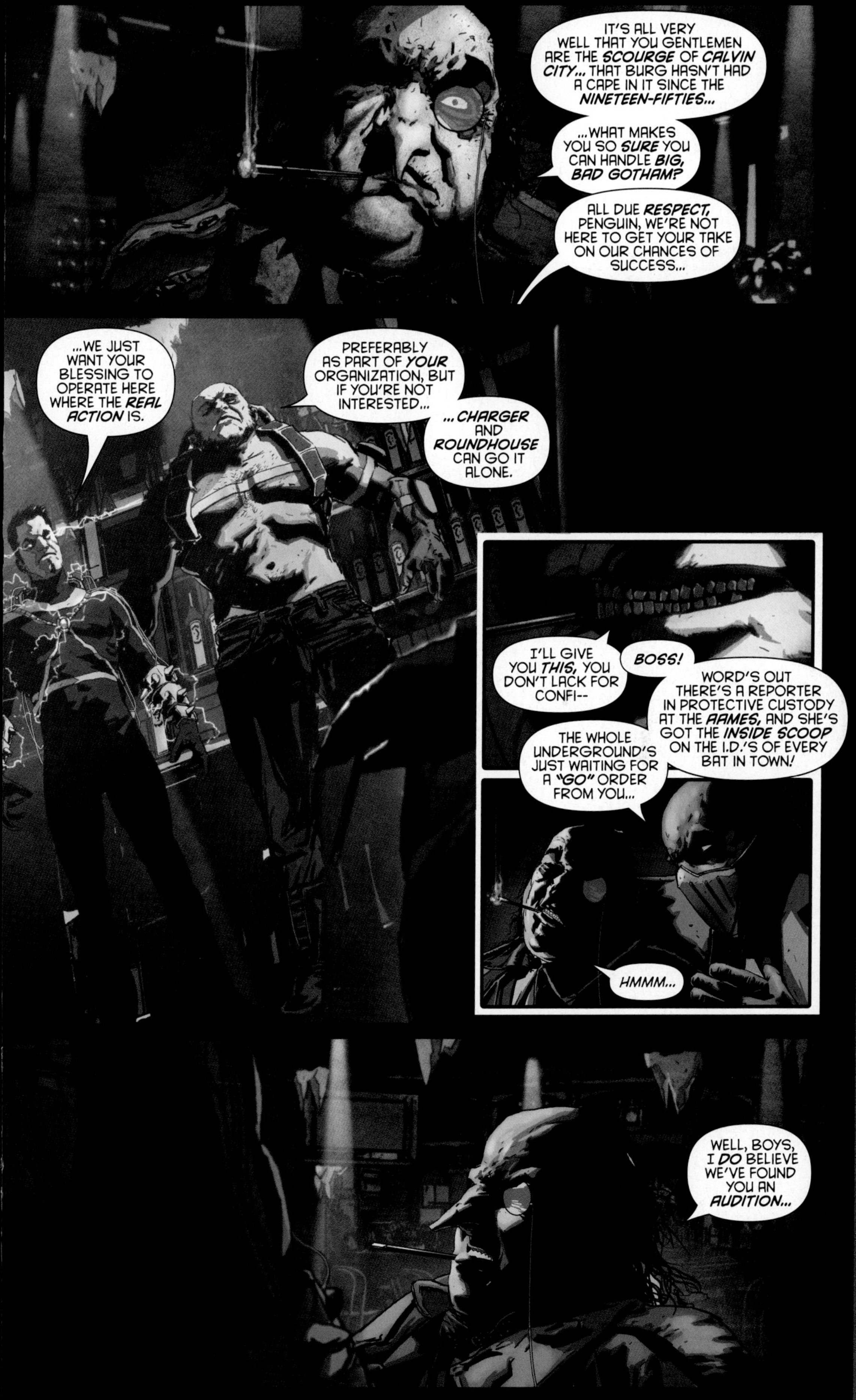
IT'S ALL VERY WELL THAT YOU GENTLEMEN ARE THE SCOURGE OF CALVIN CITY... THAT BURG HASN'T HAD A CAPE IN IT SINCE THE NINETEEN-FIFTIES...
...WHAT MAKES YOU SO SURE YOU CAN HANDLE BIG, BAD GOTHAM?
ALL DUE RESPECT, PENGUIN, WE'RE NOT HERE TO GET YOUR TAKE ON OUR CHANCES OF SUCCESS...
...WE JUST WANT YOUR BLESSING TO OPERATE HERE WHERE THE REAL ACTION IS.
PREFERABLY AS PART OF YOUR ORGANIZATION, BUT IF YOU'RE NOT INTERESTED...
...CHARGER AND ROUNDHOUSE CAN GO IT ALONE.
I'LL GIVE YOU THIS, YOU DON'T LACK FOR CONFI--
BOSS!
WORD'S OUT THERE'S A REPORTER IN PROTECTIVE CUSTODY AT THE AAMES, AND SHE'S GOT THE INSIDE SCOOP ON THE I.D.'S OF EVERY BAT IN TOWN!
THE WHOLE UNDERGROUND'S JUST WAITING FOR A "GO" ORDER FROM YOU...
HMMM...
WELL, BOYS, I DO BELIEVE WE'VE FOUND YOU AN AUDITION...

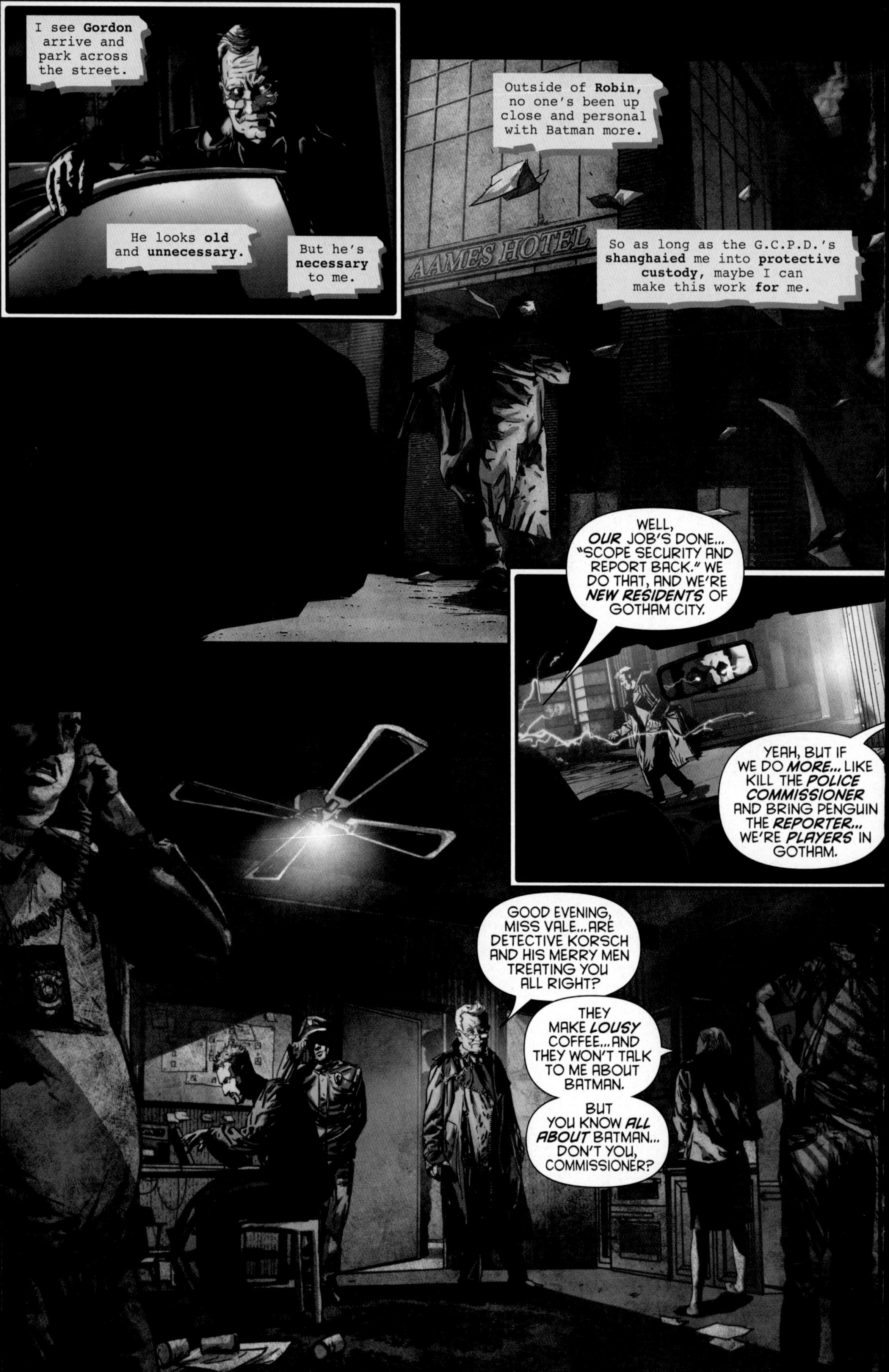

I see Gordon arrive and park across the street.
He looks old and unnecessary.
But he's necessary to me.
Outside of Robin, no one's been up close and personal with Batman more.
AAMES HOTEL
So as long as the G.C.P.D.'s shanghaied me into protective custody, maybe I can make this work for me.
WELL, OUR JOB'S DONE... "SCOPE SECURITY AND REPORT BACK." WE DO THAT, AND WE'RE NEW RESIDENTS OF GOTHAM CITY.
YEAH, BUT IF WE DO MORE... LIKE KILL THE POLICE COMMISSIONER AND BRING PENGUIN THE REPORTER... WE'RE PLAYERS IN GOTHAM.
GOOD EVENING, MISS VALE... ARE DETECTIVE KORSCH AND HIS MERRY MEN TREATING YOU ALL RIGHT?
THEY MAKE LOUSY COFFEE... AND THEY WON'T TALK TO ME ABOUT BATMAN.
BUT YOU KNOW ALL ABOUT BATMAN... DON'T YOU, COMMISSIONER?

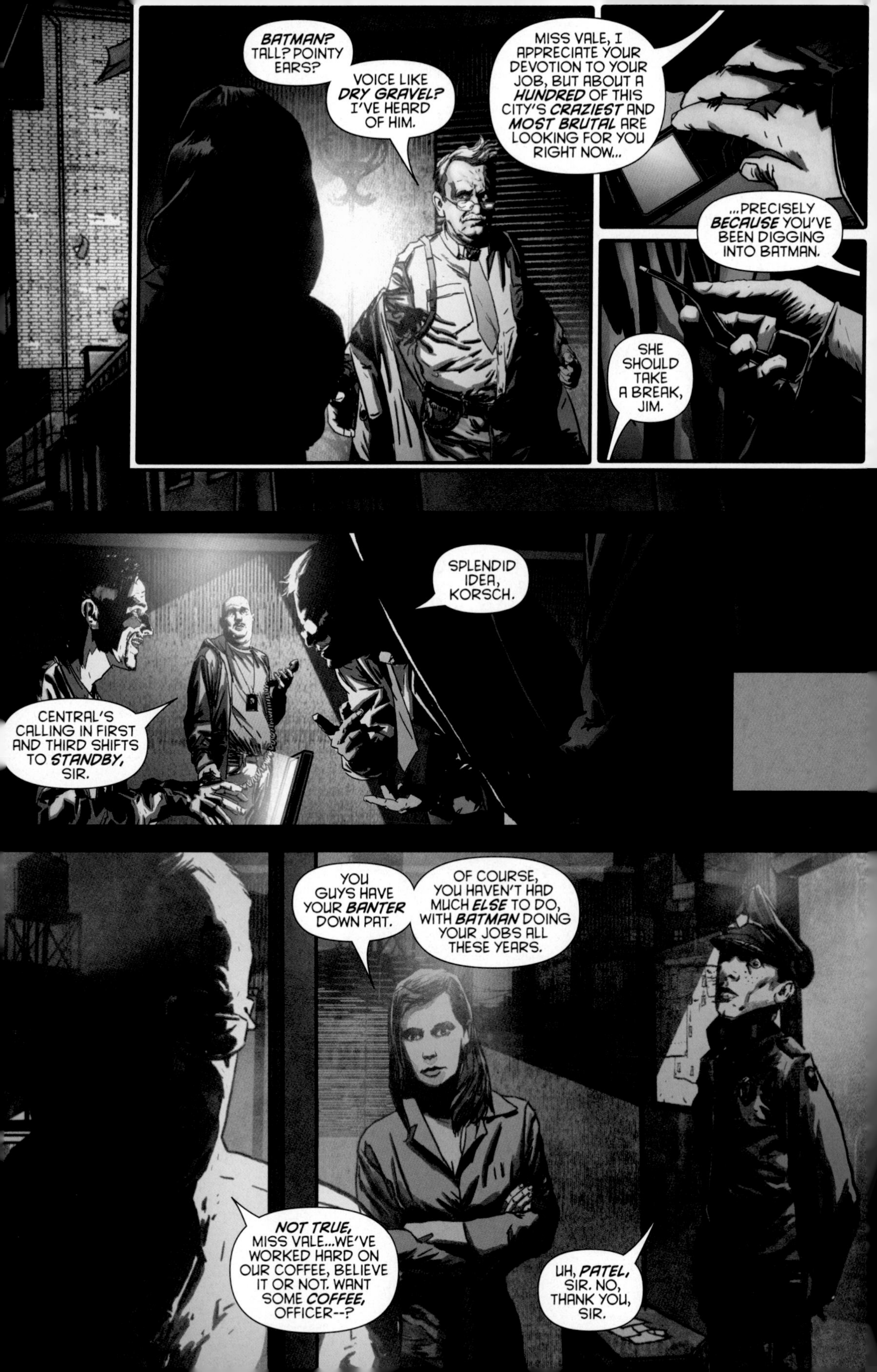
BATMAN? TALL? POINTY EARS?
VOICE LIKE DRY GRAVEL? I'VE HEARD OF HIM.
MISS VALE, I APPRECIATE YOUR DEVOTION TO YOUR JOB, BUT ABOUT A HUNDRED OF THIS CITY'S CRAZIEST AND MOST BRUTAL ARE LOOKING FOR YOU RIGHT NOW...
...PRECISELY BECAUSE YOU'VE BEEN DIGGING INTO BATMAN.
SHE SHOULD TAKE A BREAK, JIM.
SPLENDID IDEA, KORSCH.
CENTRAL'S CALLING IN FIRST AND THIRD SHIFTS TO STANDBY, SIR.
YOU GUYS HAVE YOUR BANTER DOWN PAT.
OF COURSE, YOU HAVEN'T HAD MUCH ELSE TO DO, WITH BATMAN DOING YOUR JOBS ALL THESE YEARS.
NOT TRUE, MISS VALE...WE'VE WORKED HARD ON OUR COFFEE, BELIEVE IT OR NOT. WANT SOME COFFEE, OFFICER--?
UH, PATEL, SIR. NO, THANK YOU, SIR.

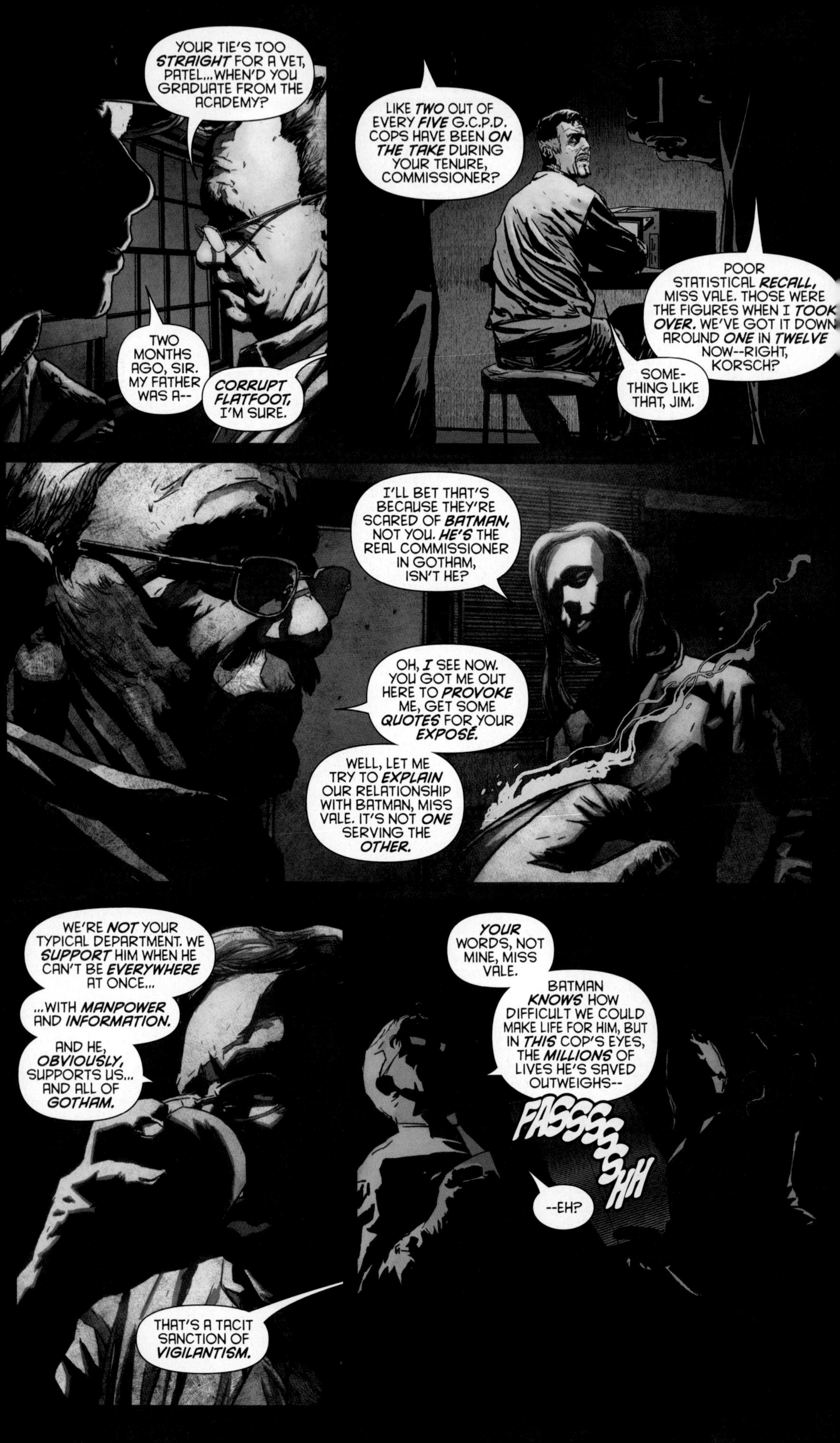

YOUR TIE'S TOO STRAIGHT FOR A VET, PATEL...WHEN'D YOU GRADUATE FROM THE ACADEMY?
TWO MONTHS AGO, SIR. MY FATHER WAS A--
CORRUPT FLATFOOT, I'M SURE.
LIKE TWO OUT OF EVERY FIVE G.C.P.D. COPS HAVE BEEN ON THE TAKE DURING YOUR TENURE, COMMISSIONER?
POOR STATISTICAL RECALL, MISS VALE. THOSE WERE THE FIGURES WHEN I TOOK OVER. WE'VE GOT IT DOWN AROUND ONE IN TWELVE NOW--RIGHT, KORSCH?
SOME-THING LIKE THAT, JIM.
I'LL BET THAT'S BECAUSE THEY'RE SCARED OF BATMAN, NOT YOU. HE'S THE REAL COMMISSIONER IN GOTHAM, ISN'T HE?
OH, I SEE NOW. YOU GOT ME OUT HERE TO PROVOKE ME, GET SOME QUOTES FOR YOUR EXPOSÉ.
WELL, LET ME TRY TO EXPLAIN OUR RELATIONSHIP WITH BATMAN, MISS VALE. IT'S NOT ONE SERVING THE OTHER.
WE'RE NOT YOUR TYPICAL DEPARTMENT. WE SUPPORT HIM WHEN HE CAN'T BE EVERYWHERE AT ONCE...
...WITH MANPOWER AND INFORMATION.
AND HE, OBVIOUSLY, SUPPORTS US... AND ALL OF GOTHAM.
THAT'S A TACIT SANCTION OF VIGILANTISM.
YOUR WORDS, NOT MINE, MISS VALE.
BATMAN KNOWS HOW DIFFICULT WE COULD MAKE LIFE FOR HIM, BUT IN THIS COP'S EYES, THE MILLIONS OF LIVES HE'S SAVED OUTWEIGHS--
FASSSSSHH
--EH?

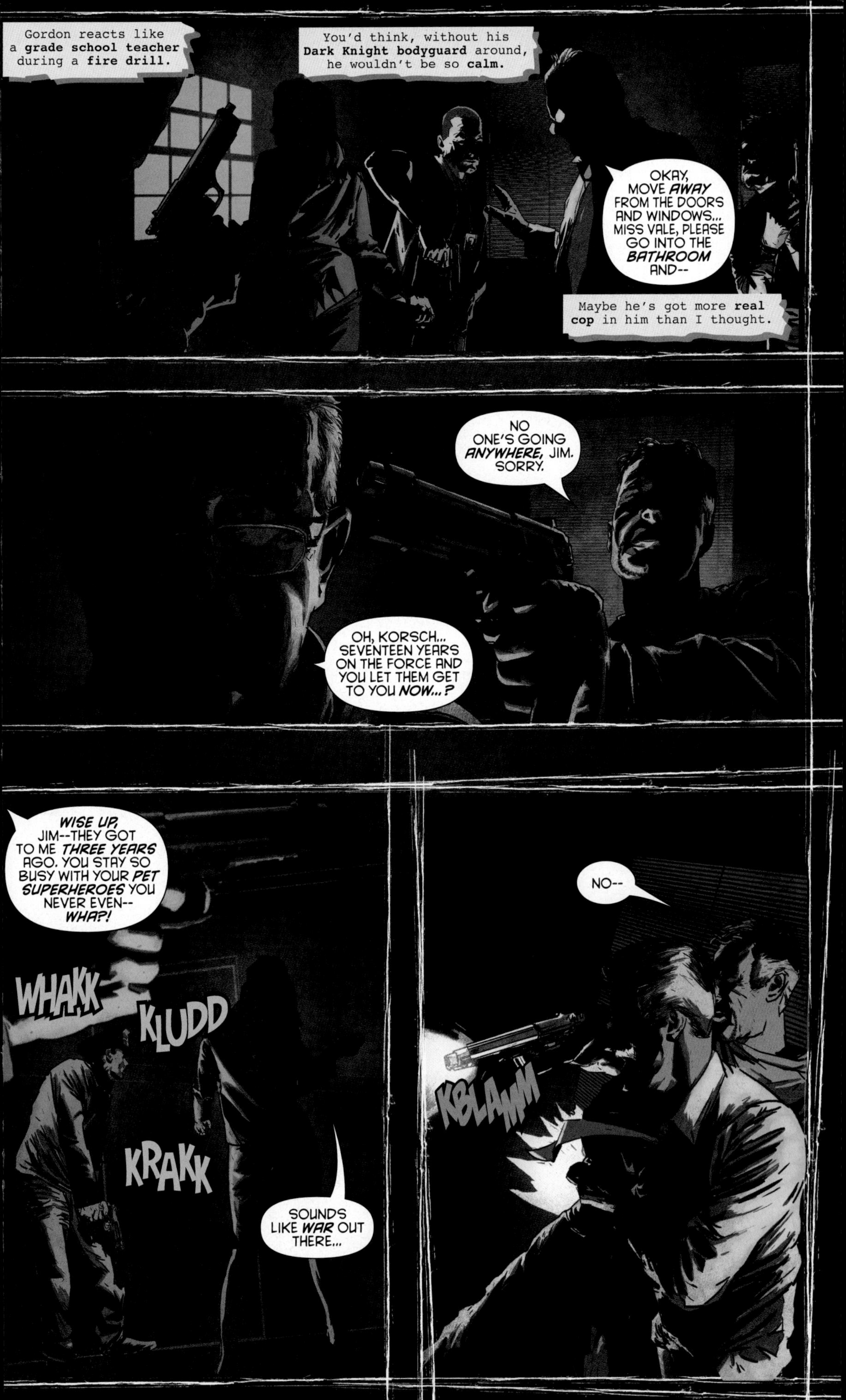
Gordon reacts like a grade school teacher during a fire drill.
You'd think, without his Dark Knight bodyguard around, he wouldn't be so calm.
OKAY, MOVE AWAY FROM THE DOORS AND WINDOWS... MISS VALE, PLEASE GO INTO THE BATHROOM AND--
Maybe he's got more real cop in him than I thought.
NO ONE'S GOING ANYWHERE, JIM. SORRY.
OH, KORSCH... SEVENTEEN YEARS ON THE FORCE AND YOU LET THEM GET TO YOU NOW...?
WISE UP, JIM--THEY GOT TO ME THREE YEARS AGO. YOU STAY SO BUSY WITH YOUR PET SUPERHEROES YOU NEVER EVEN-- WHA?!
WHAKK
KLUDD
KRAKK
SOUNDS LIKE WAR OUT THERE...
NO--
KBLAMM

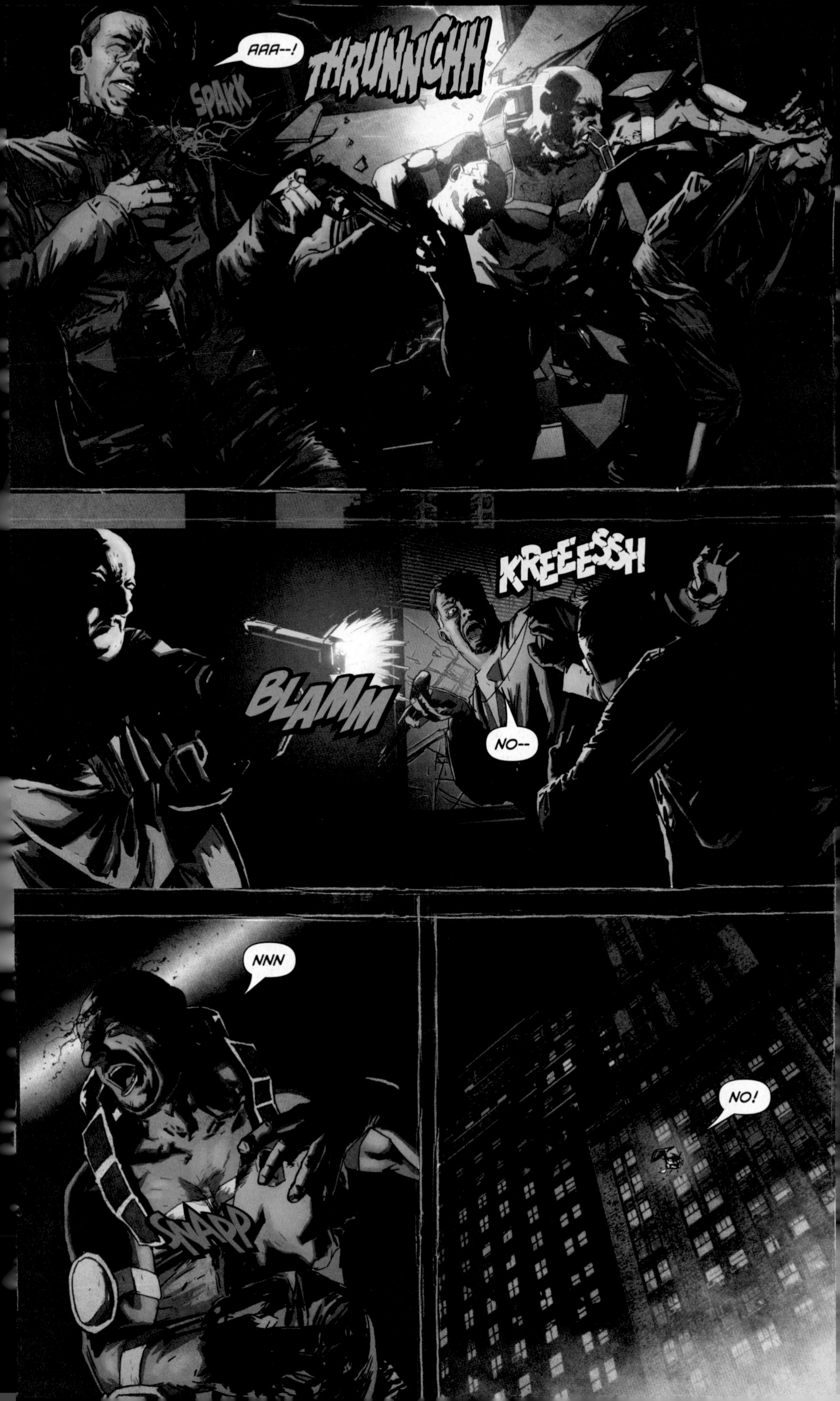
AAA--!
SPAKK
THRUNNCHH
KREEESSH
BLAMM
NO--
NNN
SNAPP
NO!

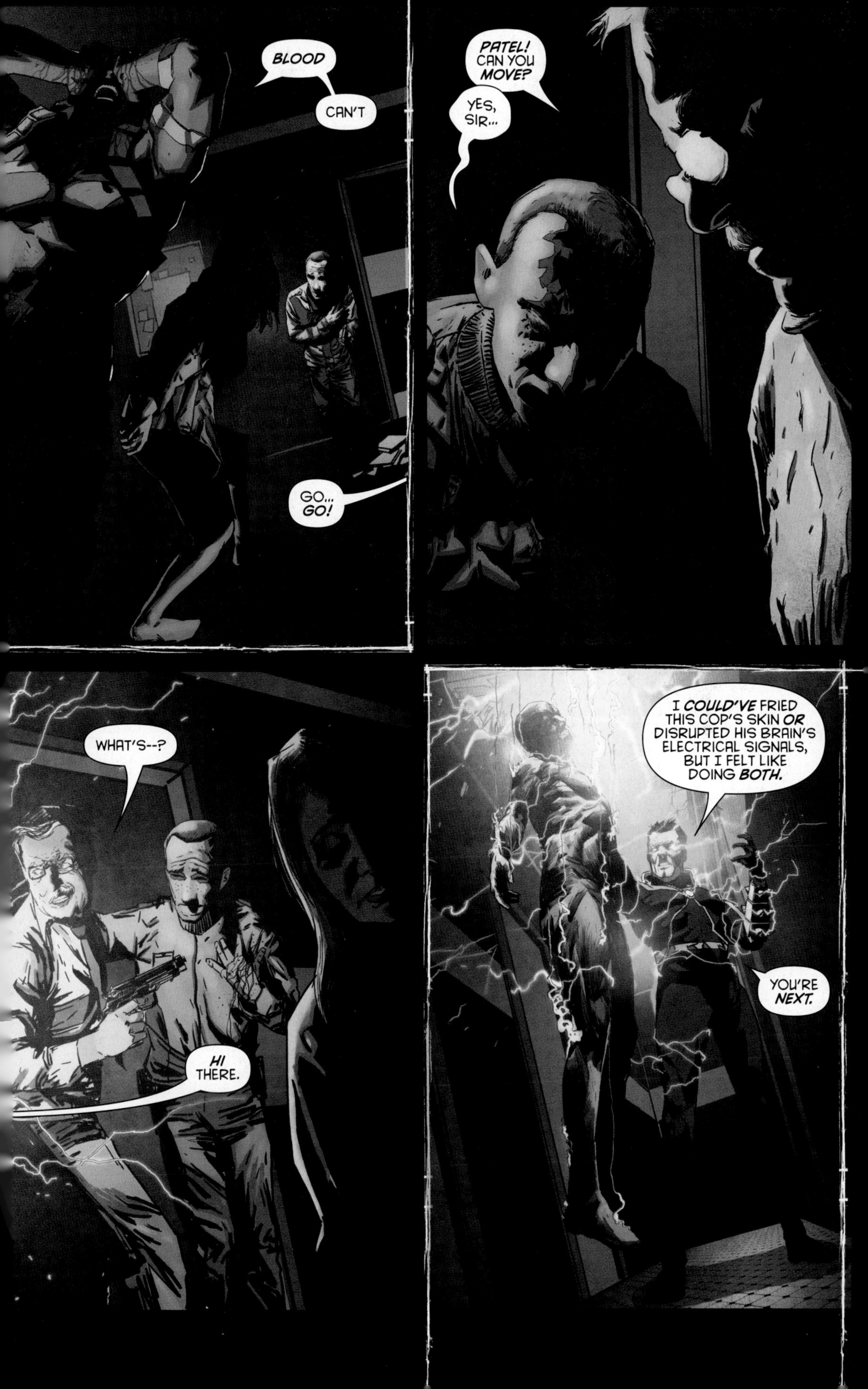
BLOOD
CAN'T
GO... GO!
PATEL! CAN YOU MOVE?
YES, SIR...
WHAT'S--?
HI THERE.
I COULD'VE FRIED THIS COP'S SKIN OR DISRUPTED HIS BRAIN'S ELECTRICAL SIGNALS, BUT I FELT LIKE DOING BOTH.
YOU'RE NEXT.

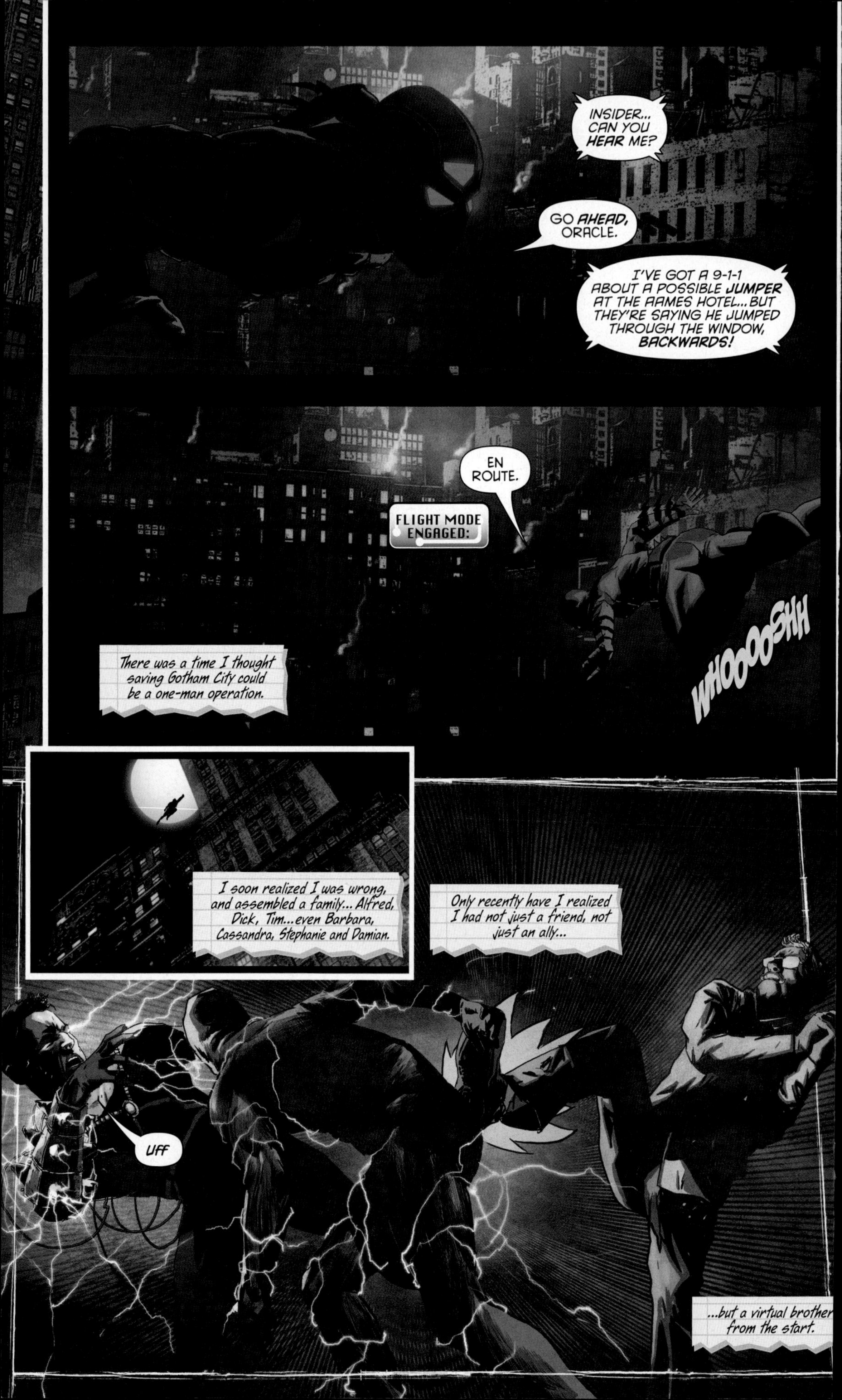
INSIDER... CAN YOU HEAR ME?
GO AHEAD, ORACLE.
I'VE GOT A 9-1-1 ABOUT A POSSIBLE JUMPER AT THE AAMES HOTEL... BUT THEY'RE SAYING HE JUMPED THROUGH THE WINDOW, BACKWARDS!
EN ROUTE.
FLIGHT MODE ENGAGED:
There was a time I thought saving Gotham City could be a one-man operation.
WHOOOOOSHH
I soon realized I was wrong, and assembled a family... Alfred, Dick, Tim...even Barbara, Cassandra, Stephanie and Damian.
Only recently have I realized I had not just a friend, not just an ally...
UFF
...but a virtual brother from the start.

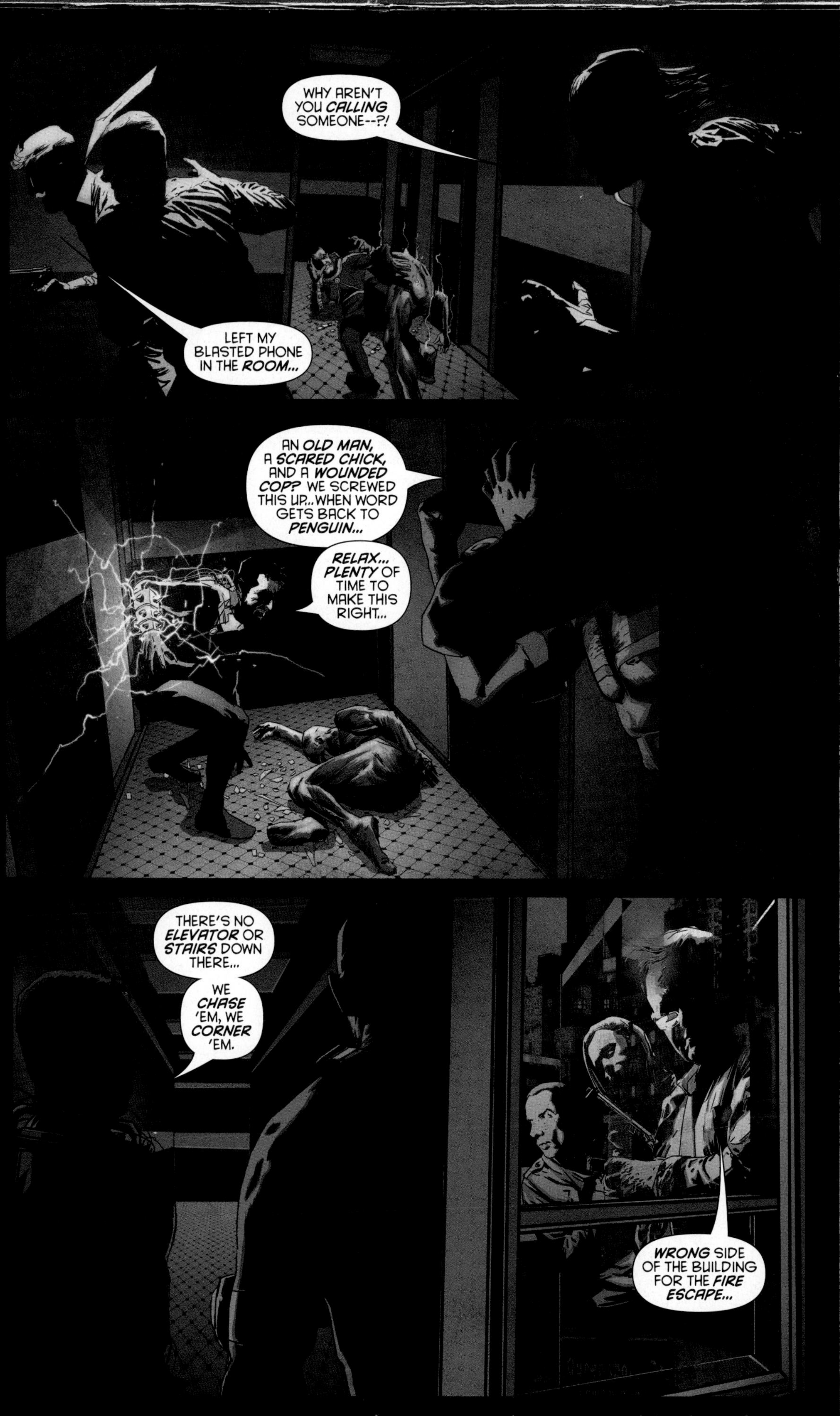

WHY AREN'T YOU *CALLING* SOMEONE--?!
LEFT MY BLASTED PHONE IN THE *ROOM...*
AN *OLD MAN,* A *SCARED CHICK,* AND A *WOUNDED COP?* WE SCREWED THIS UP...WHEN WORD GETS BACK TO *PENGUIN...*
RELAX... PLENTY OF TIME TO MAKE THIS RIGHT...
THERE'S NO *ELEVATOR* OR *STAIRS* DOWN THERE...
WE *CHASE* 'EM, WE *CORNER* 'EM.
WRONG SIDE OF THE BUILDING FOR THE *FIRE ESCAPE...*

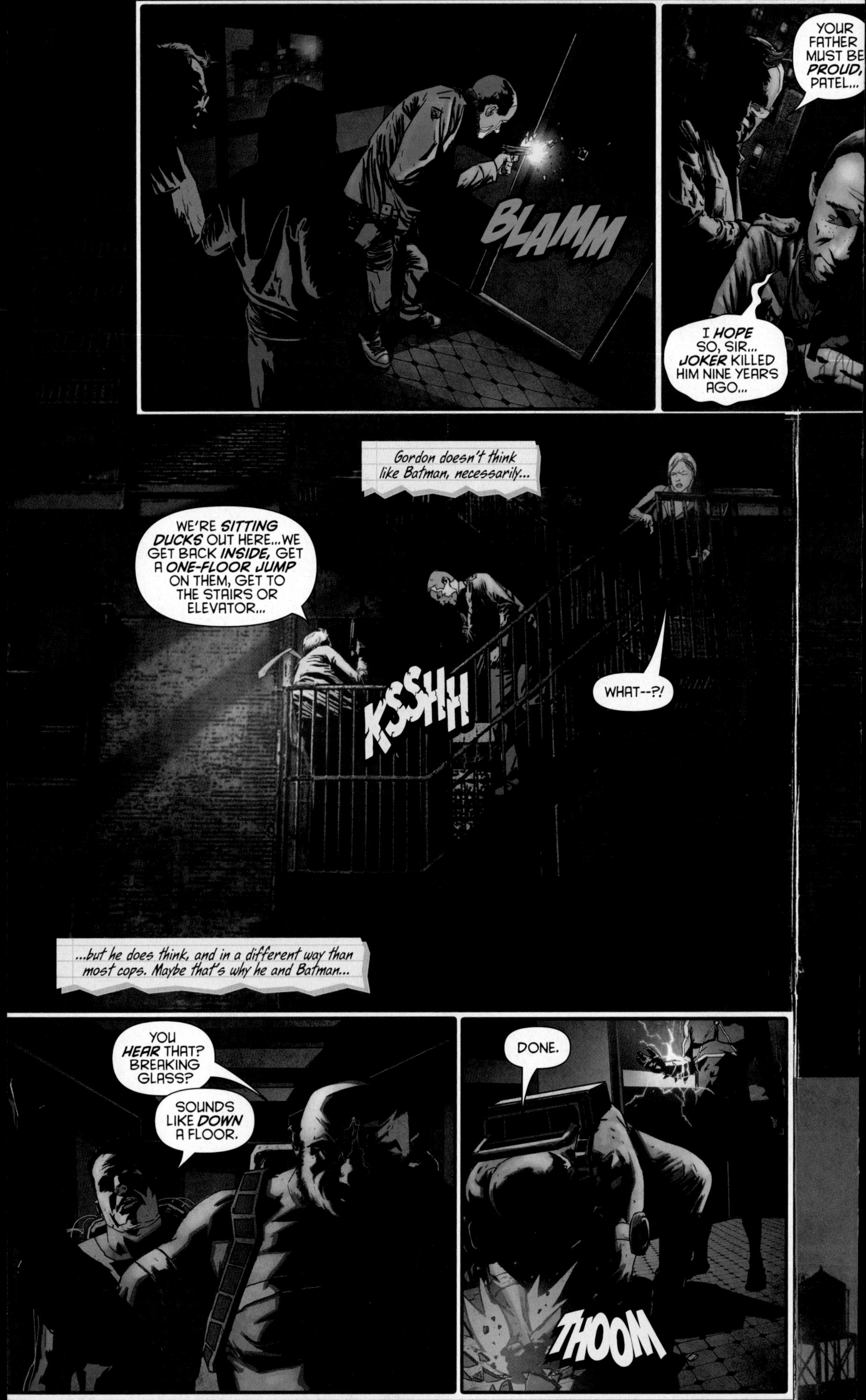
BLAMM
YOUR FATHER MUST BE PROUD, PATEL...
I HOPE SO, SIR... JOKER KILLED HIM NINE YEARS AGO...
Gordon doesn't think like Batman, necessarily...
WE'RE SITTING DUCKS OUT HERE...WE GET BACK INSIDE, GET A ONE-FLOOR JUMP ON THEM, GET TO THE STAIRS OR ELEVATOR...
KSSHH
WHAT--?!
...but he does think, and in a different way than most cops. Maybe that's why he and Batman...
YOU HEAR THAT? BREAKING GLASS?
SOUNDS LIKE DOWN A FLOOR.
DONE.
THOOM

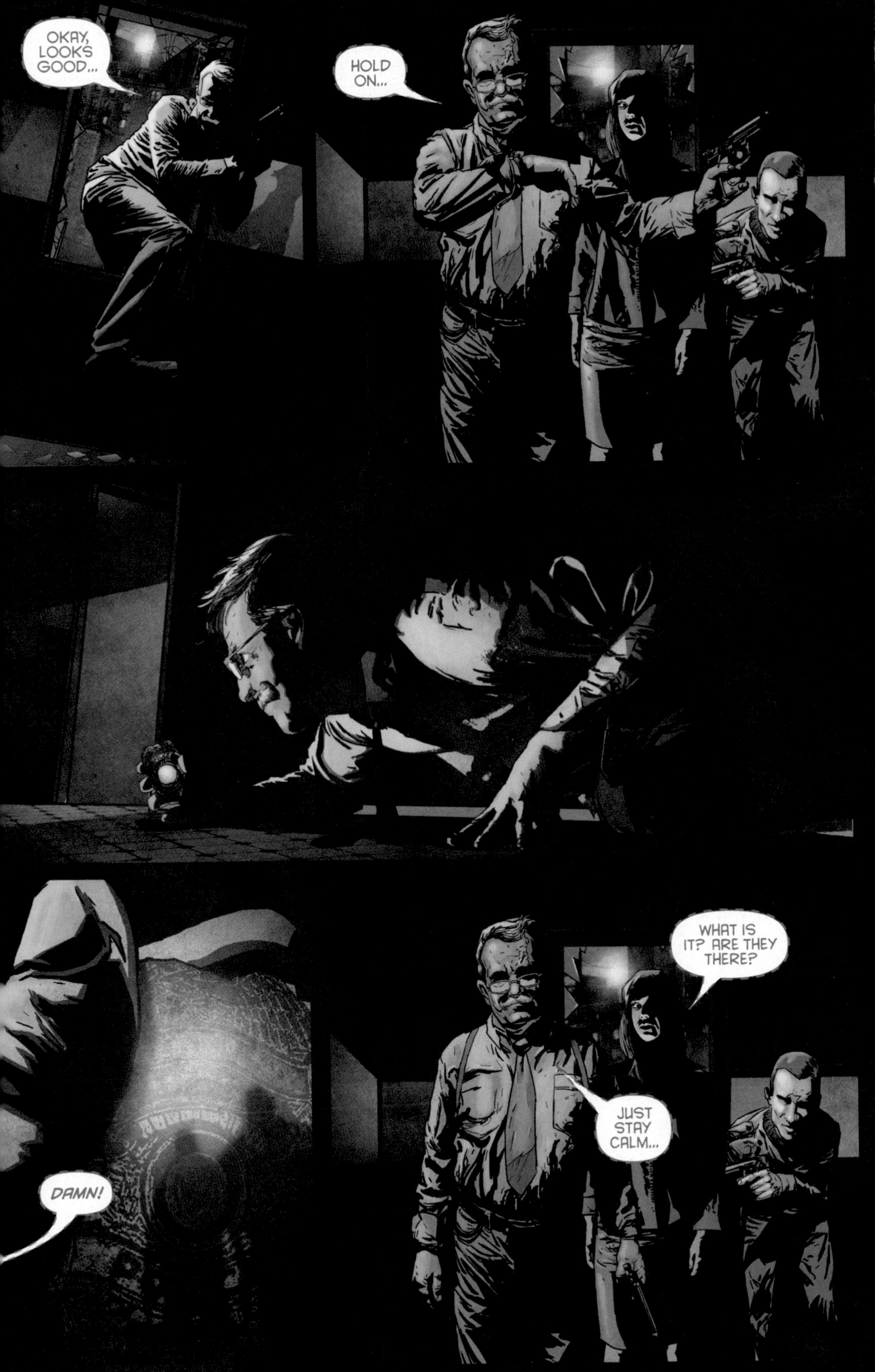
OKAY, LOOKS GOOD...
HOLD ON...
DAMN!
WHAT IS IT? ARE THEY THERE?
JUST STAY CALM...

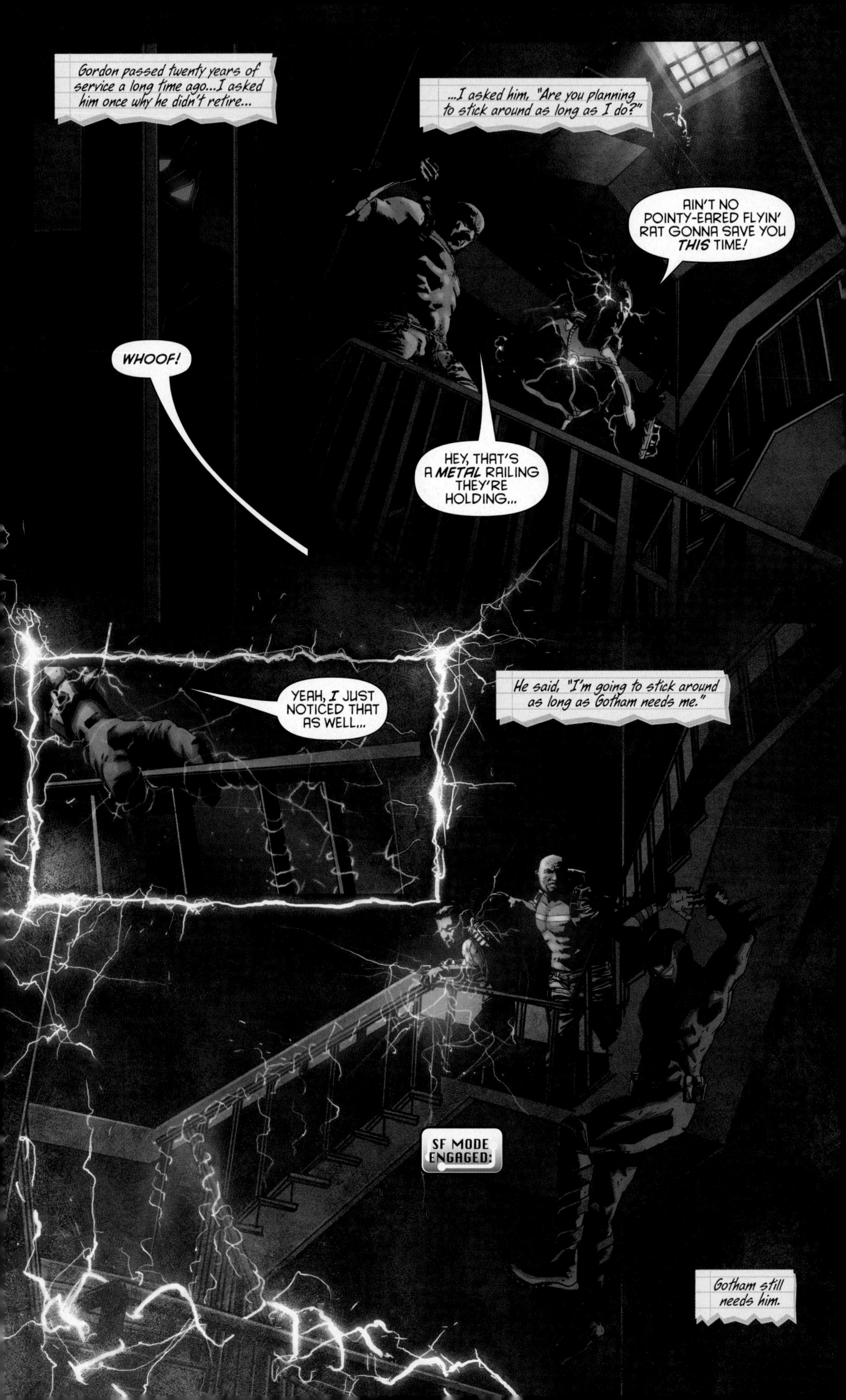
Gordon passed twenty years of service a long time ago...I asked him once why he didn't retire...
...I asked him, "Are you planning to stick around as long as I do?"
AIN'T NO POINTY-EARED FLYIN' RAT GONNA SAVE YOU THIS TIME!
WHOOF!
HEY, THAT'S A METAL RAILING THEY'RE HOLDING...
YEAH, I JUST NOTICED THAT AS WELL...
He said, "I'm going to stick around as long as Gotham needs me."
SF MODE ENGAGED:
Gotham still needs him.

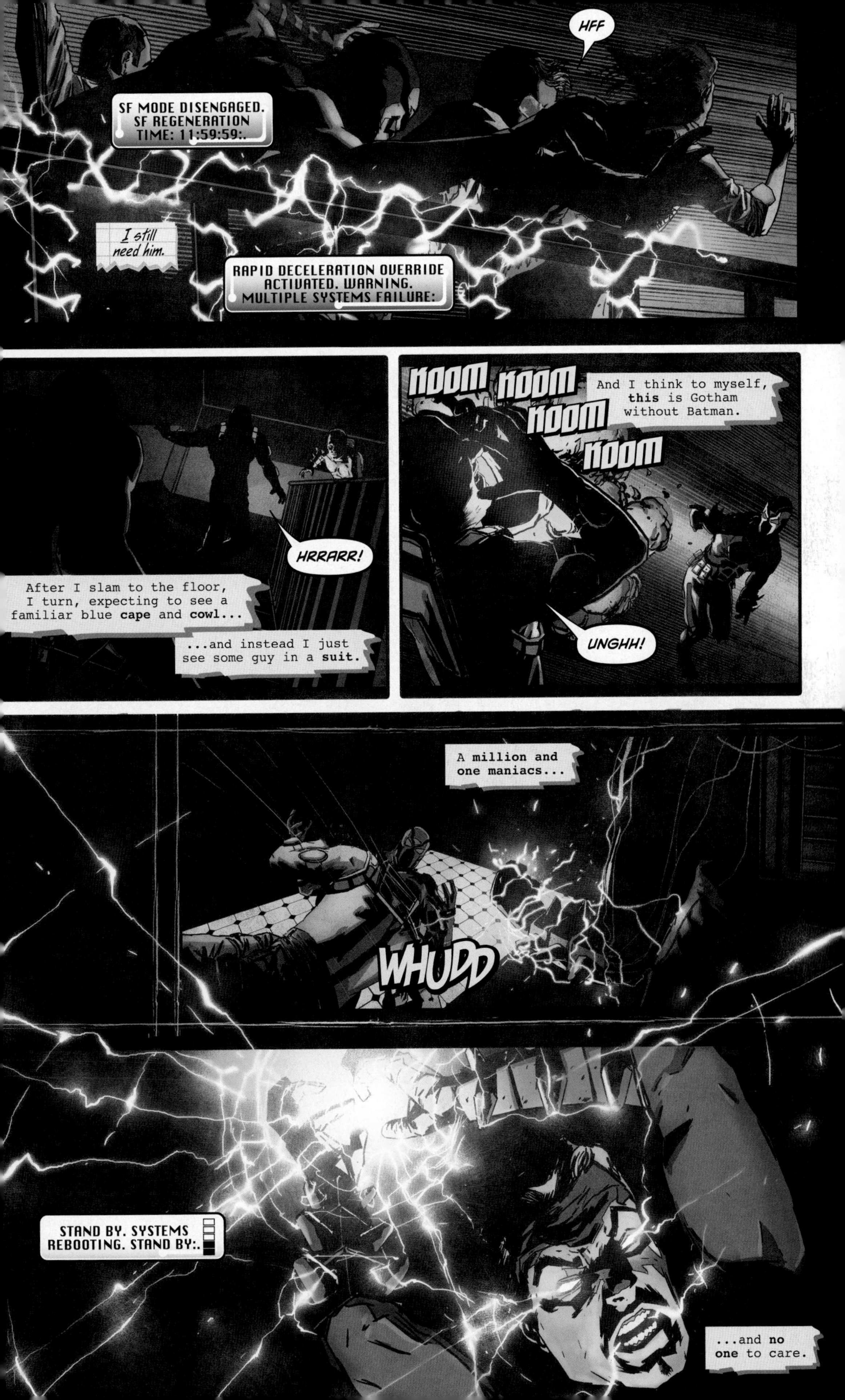

HFF
SF MODE DISENGAGED. SF REGENERATION TIME: 11:59:59:.
I still need him.
RAPID DECELERATION OVERRIDE ACTIVATED. WARNING. MULTIPLE SYSTEMS FAILURE:
HRRARR!
After I slam to the floor, I turn, expecting to see a familiar blue cape and cowl...
...and instead I just see some guy in a suit.
KOOM KOOM KOOM KOOM
And I think to myself, this is Gotham without Batman.
UNGHH!
A million and one maniacs...
WHUDD
STAND BY. SYSTEMS REBOOTING. STAND BY:.
...and no one to care.

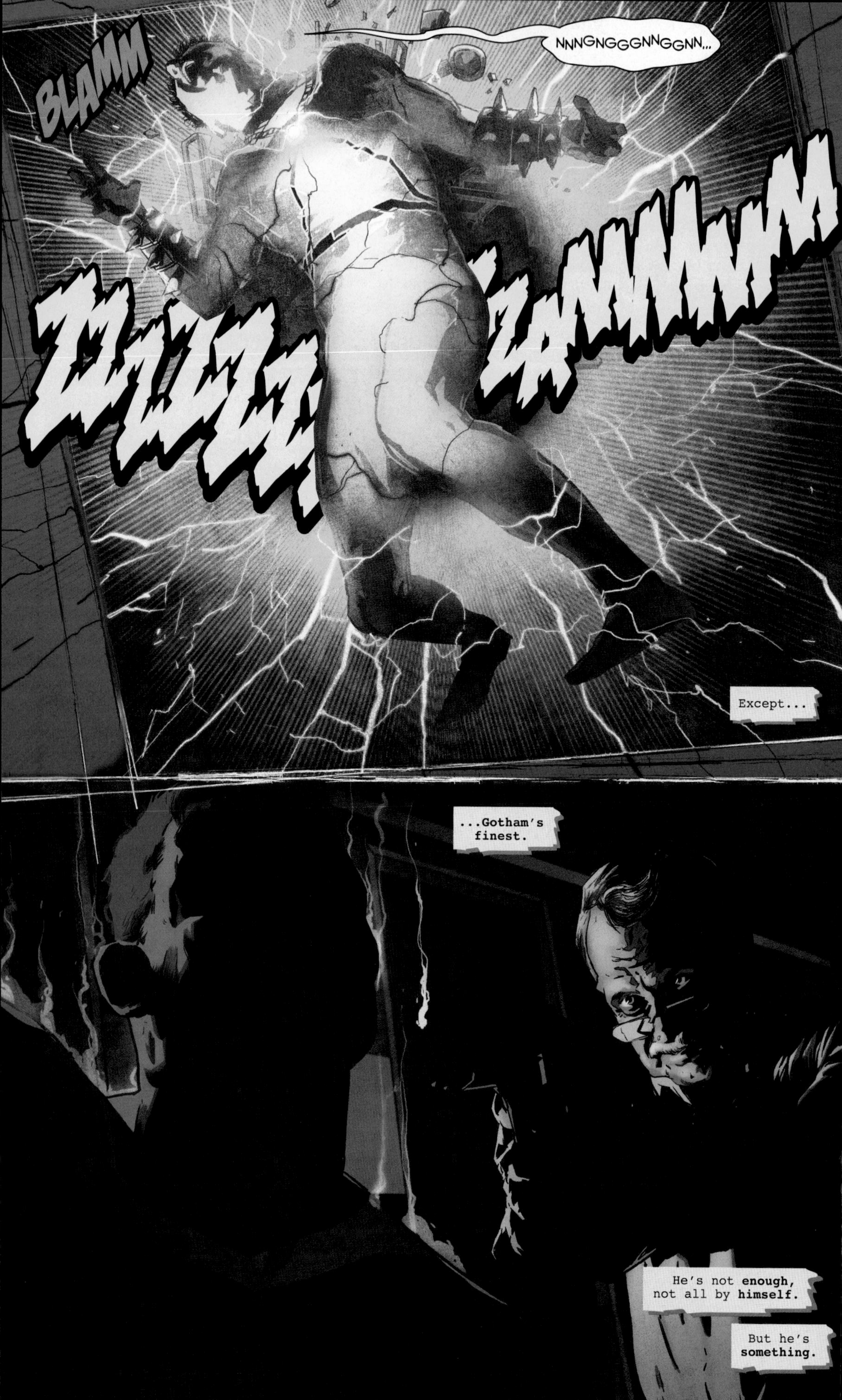
BLAMM
NNNGNGGGNNGGNN...
ZZZZZZMMMMM
Except...
...Gotham's finest.
He's not **enough**, not all by **himself**.
But he's **something**.

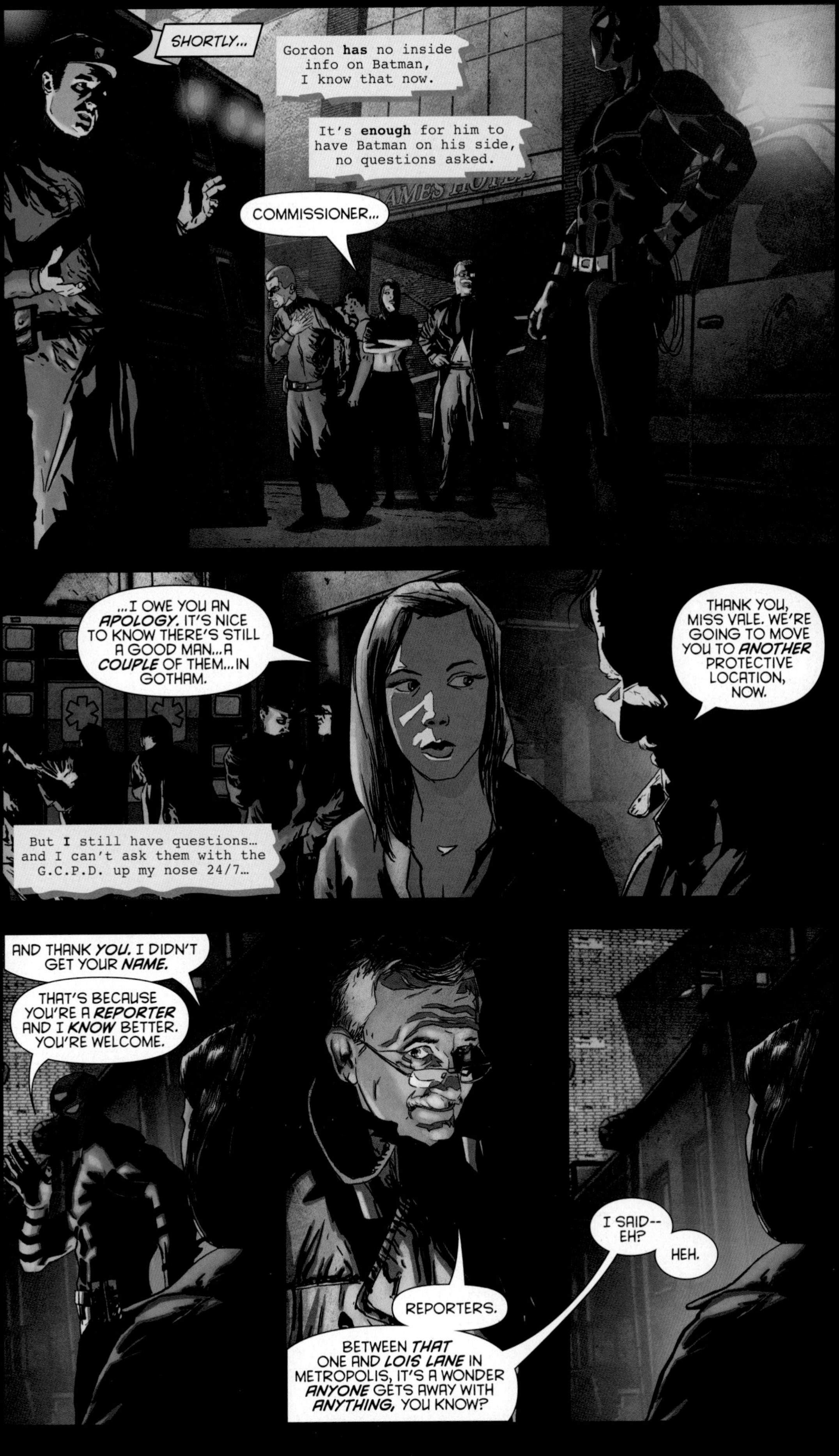
SHORTLY...
Gordon has no inside info on Batman, I know that now.
It's enough for him to have Batman on his side, no questions asked.
AMES HOTEL
COMMISSIONER...
...I OWE YOU AN APOLOGY. IT'S NICE TO KNOW THERE'S STILL A GOOD MAN...A COUPLE OF THEM...IN GOTHAM.
THANK YOU, MISS VALE. WE'RE GOING TO MOVE YOU TO ANOTHER PROTECTIVE LOCATION, NOW.
But I still have questions... and I can't ask them with the G.C.P.D. up my nose 24/7...
AND THANK YOU. I DIDN'T GET YOUR NAME.
THAT'S BECAUSE YOU'RE A REPORTER AND I KNOW BETTER. YOU'RE WELCOME.
REPORTERS.
BETWEEN THAT ONE AND LOIS LANE IN METROPOLIS, IT'S A WONDER ANYONE GETS AWAY WITH ANYTHING, YOU KNOW?
I SAID-- EH?
HEH.

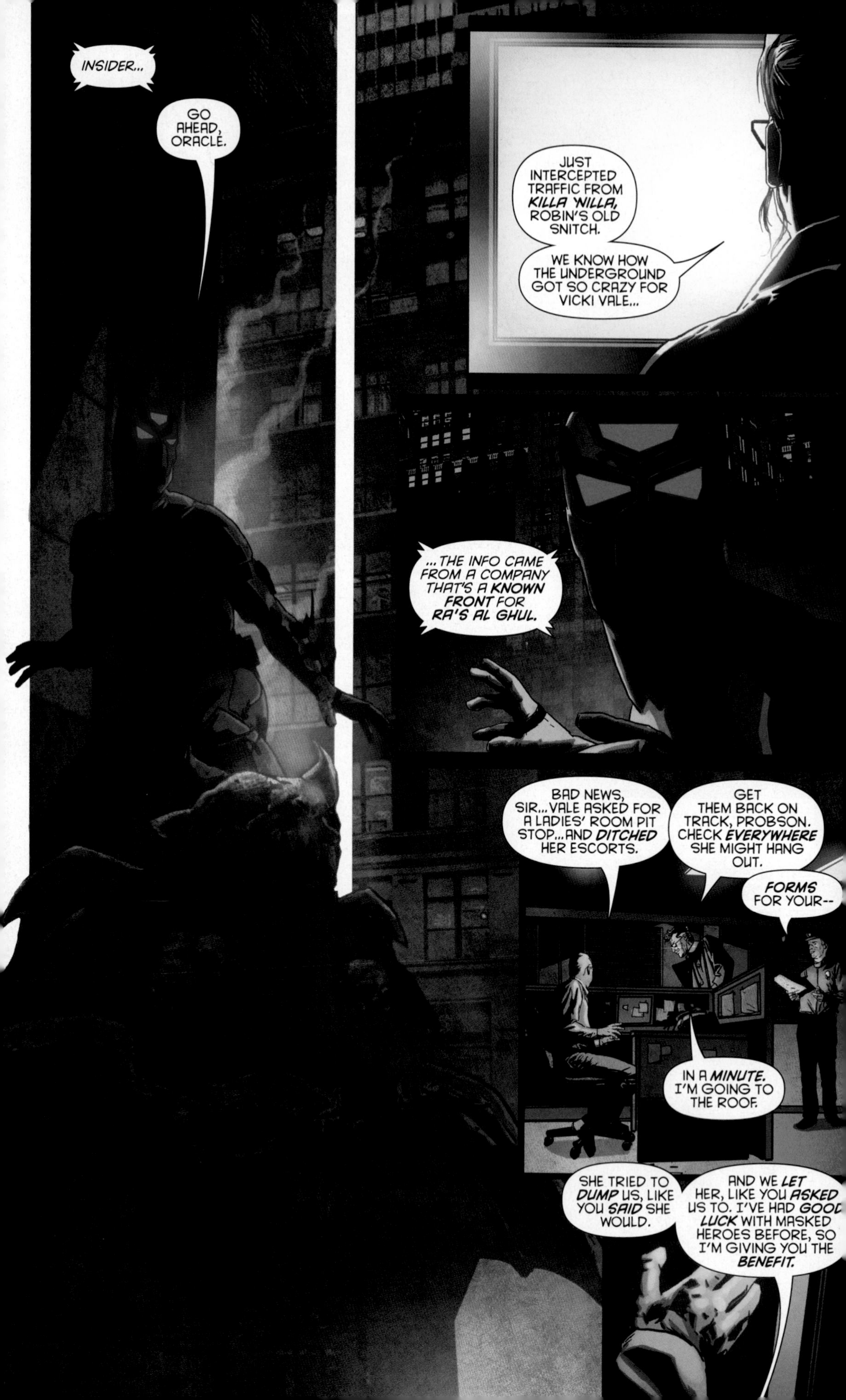
INSIDER...
GO AHEAD, ORACLE.
JUST INTERCEPTED TRAFFIC FROM KILLA 'NILLA, ROBIN'S OLD SNITCH.
WE KNOW HOW THE UNDERGROUND GOT SO CRAZY FOR VICKI VALE...
...THE INFO CAME FROM A COMPANY THAT'S A KNOWN FRONT FOR RA'S AL GHUL.
BAD NEWS, SIR...VALE ASKED FOR A LADIES' ROOM PIT STOP...AND DITCHED HER ESCORTS.
GET THEM BACK ON TRACK, PROBSON. CHECK EVERYWHERE SHE MIGHT HANG OUT.
FORMS FOR YOUR--
IN A MINUTE. I'M GOING TO THE ROOF.
SHE TRIED TO DUMP US, LIKE YOU SAID SHE WOULD.
AND WE LET HER, LIKE YOU ASKED US TO. I'VE HAD GOOD LUCK WITH MASKED HEROES BEFORE, SO I'M GIVING YOU THE BENEFIT.

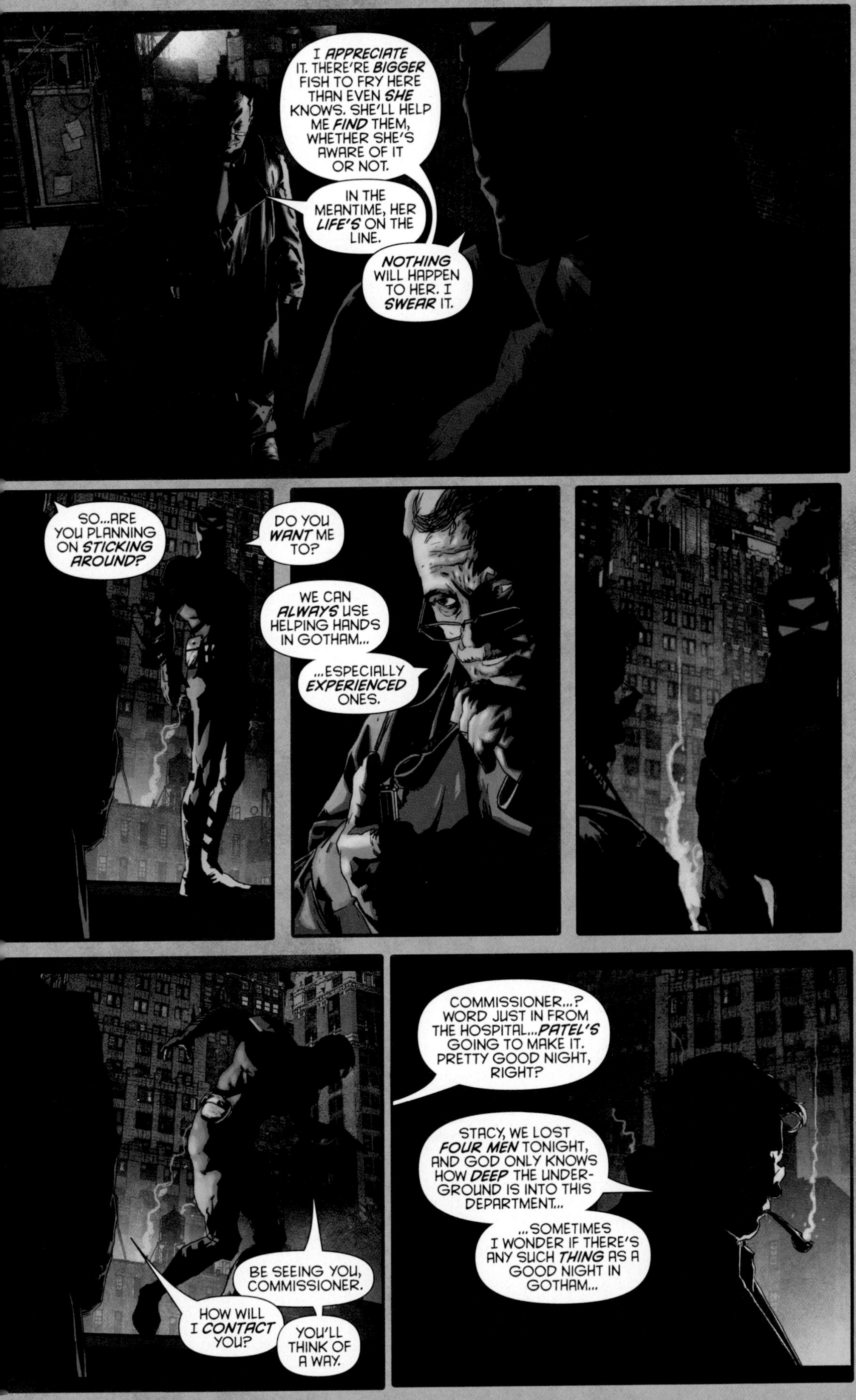

I APPRECIATE IT. THERE'RE BIGGER FISH TO FRY HERE THAN EVEN SHE KNOWS. SHE'LL HELP ME FIND THEM, WHETHER SHE'S AWARE OF IT OR NOT.
IN THE MEANTIME, HER LIFE'S ON THE LINE.
NOTHING WILL HAPPEN TO HER. I SWEAR IT.
SO...ARE YOU PLANNING ON STICKING AROUND?
DO YOU WANT ME TO?
WE CAN ALWAYS USE HELPING HANDS IN GOTHAM...
...ESPECIALLY EXPERIENCED ONES.
BE SEEING YOU, COMMISSIONER.
HOW WILL I CONTACT YOU?
YOU'LL THINK OF A WAY.
COMMISSIONER...? WORD JUST IN FROM THE HOSPITAL...PATEL'S GOING TO MAKE IT. PRETTY GOOD NIGHT, RIGHT?
STACY, WE LOST FOUR MEN TONIGHT, AND GOD ONLY KNOWS HOW DEEP THE UNDER-GROUND IS INTO THIS DEPARTMENT...
...SOMETIMES I WONDER IF THERE'S ANY SUCH THING AS A GOOD NIGHT IN GOTHAM...

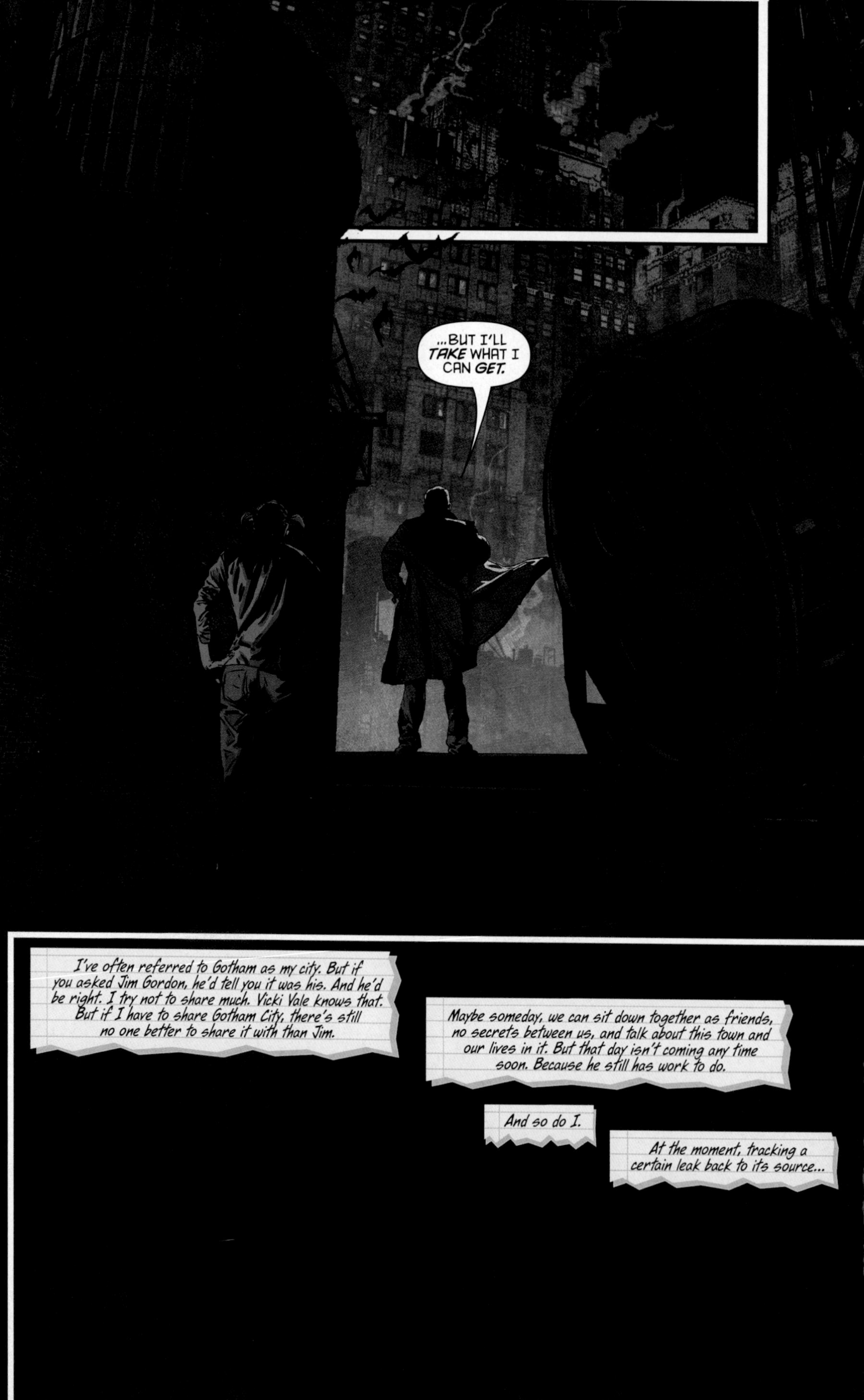
...BUT I'LL TAKE WHAT I CAN GET.
I've often referred to Gotham as my city. But if you asked Jim Gordon, he'd tell you it was his. And he'd be right. I try not to share much. Vicki Vale knows that. But if I have to share Gotham City, there's still no one better to share it with than Jim.
Maybe someday, we can sit down together as friends, no secrets between us, and talk about this town and our lives in it. But that day isn't coming any time soon. Because he still has work to do.
And so do I.
At the moment, tracking a certain leak back to its source...

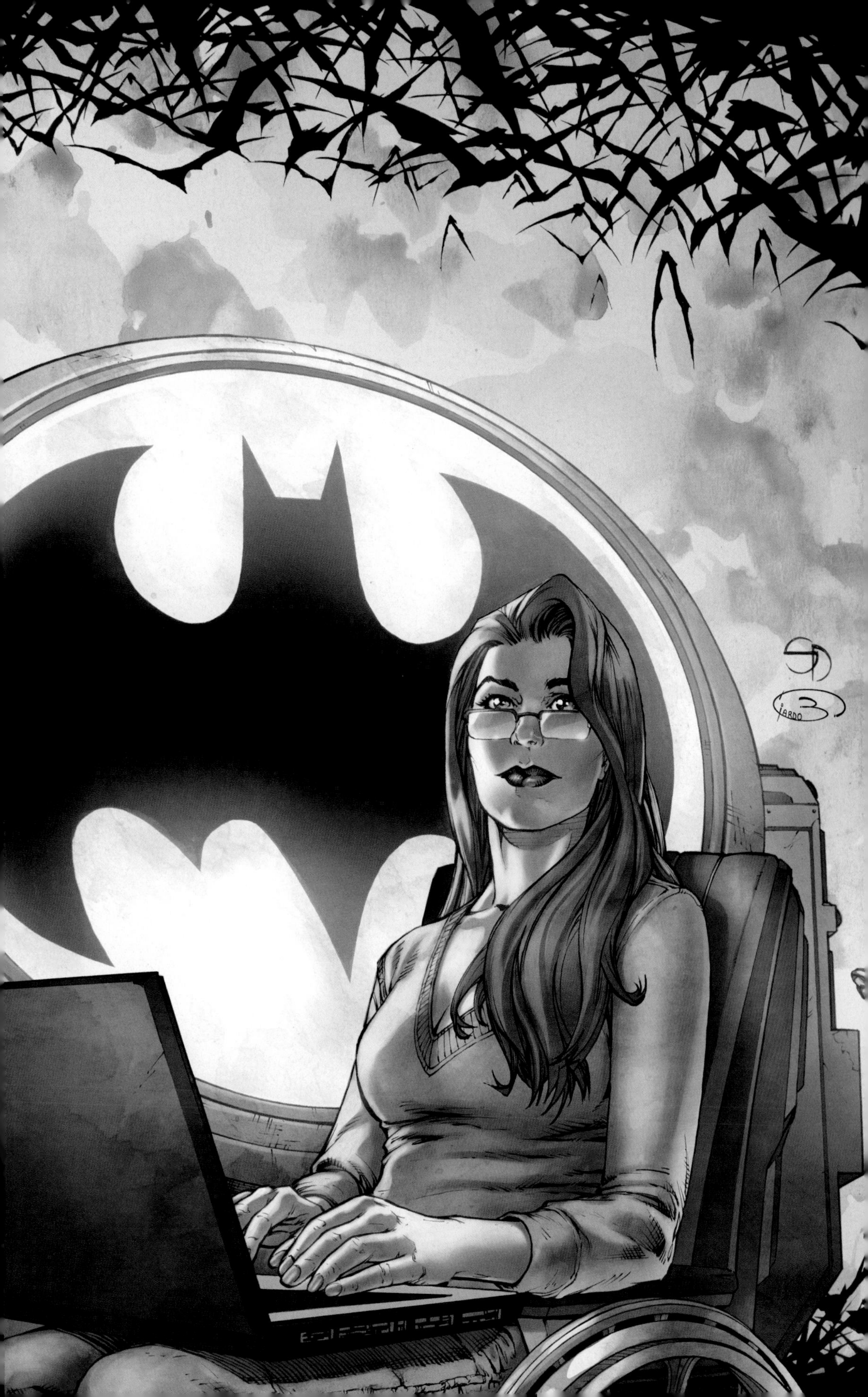

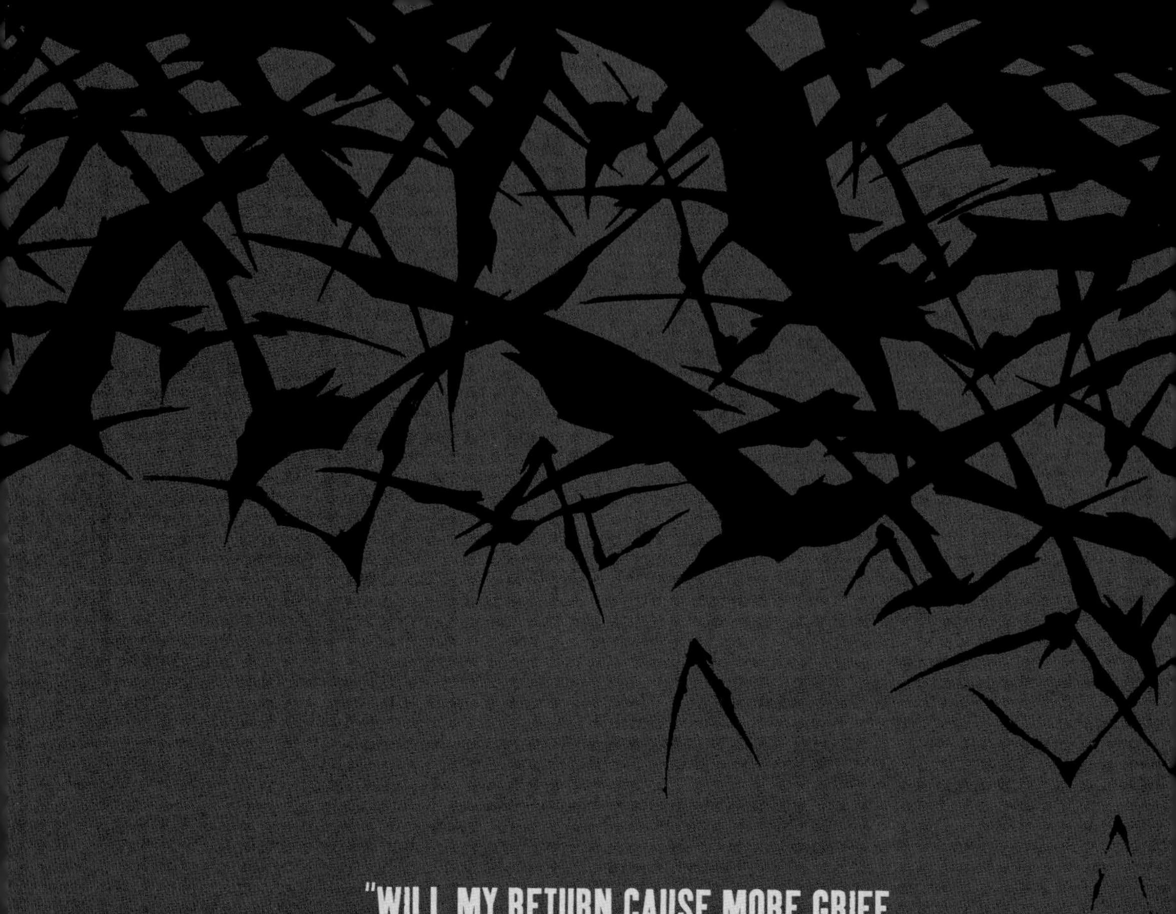

"WILL MY RETURN CAUSE MORE GRIEF
THAN WHEN I WAS GONE?"

OH, CRAP.

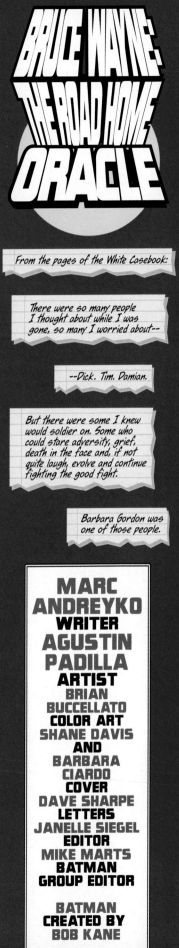

BRUCE WAYNE: THE ROAD HOME ORACLE

From the pages of the White Casebook:

There were so many people I thought about while I was gone, so many I worried about--

--Dick. Tim. Damian.

But there were some I knew would soldier on. Some who could stare adversity, grief, death in the face and, if not quite laugh, evolve and continue fighting the good fight.

Barbara Gordon was one of those people.

MARC ANDREYKO WRITER
AGUSTIN PADILLA ARTIST
BRIAN BUCCELLATO COLOR ART
SHANE DAVIS AND **BARBARA CIARDO** COVER
DAVE SHARPE LETTERS
JANELLE SIEGEL EDITOR
MIKE MARTS BATMAN GROUP EDITOR

BATMAN CREATED BY BOB KANE

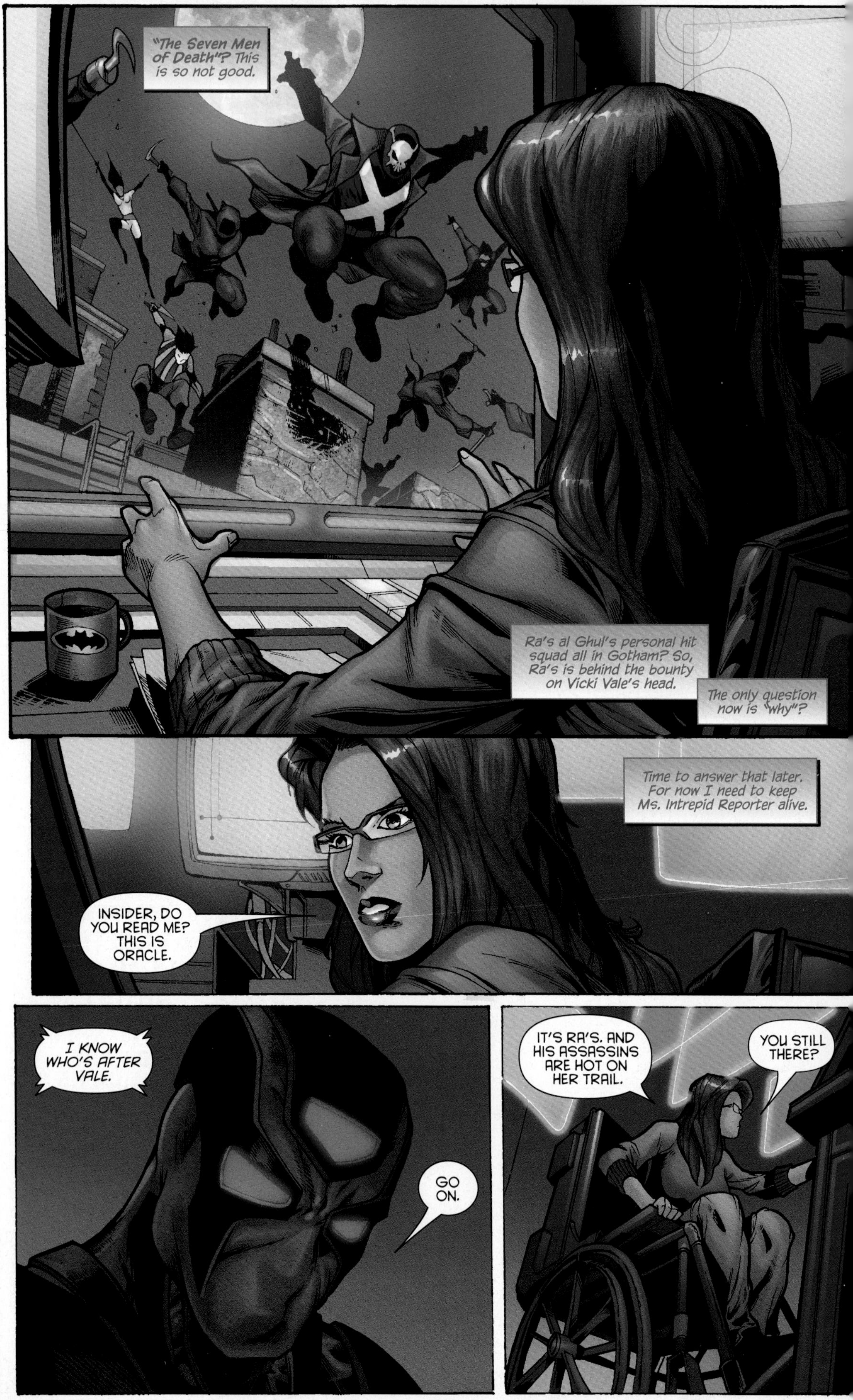
"The Seven Men of Death"? This is so not good.
Ra's al Ghul's personal hit squad all in Gotham? So, Ra's is behind the bounty on Vicki Vale's head.
The only question now is "why"?
Time to answer that later. For now I need to keep Ms. Intrepid Reporter alive.
INSIDER, DO YOU READ ME? THIS IS ORACLE.
I KNOW WHO'S AFTER VALE.
GO ON.
IT'S RA'S. AND HIS ASSASSINS ARE HOT ON HER TRAIL.
YOU STILL THERE?

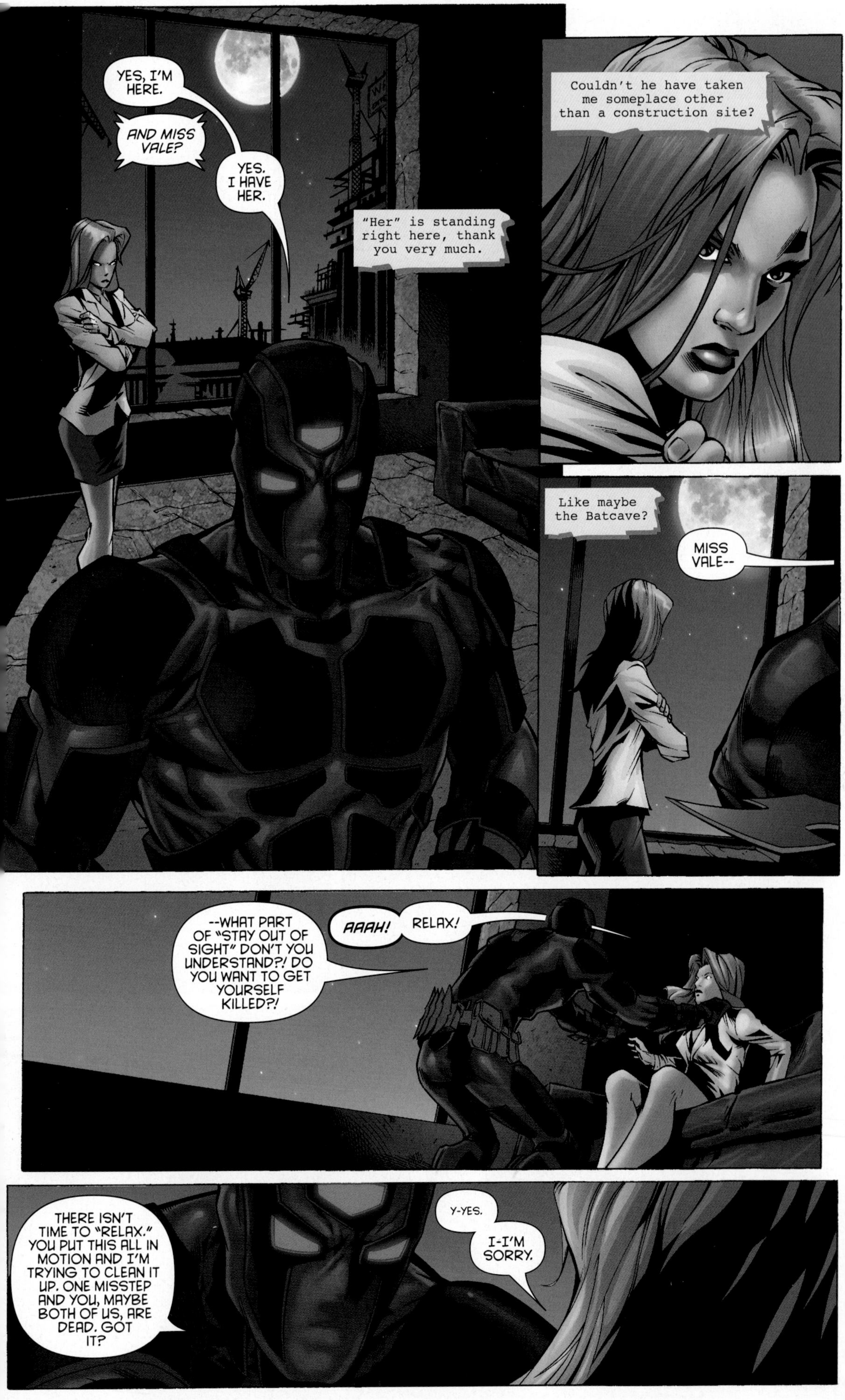
YES, I'M HERE.
AND MISS VALE?
YES. I HAVE HER.
"Her" is standing right here, thank you very much.
Couldn't he have taken me someplace other than a construction site?
Like maybe the Batcave?
MISS VALE--
--WHAT PART OF "STAY OUT OF SIGHT" DON'T YOU UNDERSTAND?! DO YOU WANT TO GET YOURSELF KILLED?!
AAAH!
RELAX!
THERE ISN'T TIME TO "RELAX." YOU PUT THIS ALL IN MOTION AND I'M TRYING TO CLEAN IT UP. ONE MISSTEP AND YOU, MAYBE BOTH OF US, ARE DEAD. GOT IT?
Y-YES.
I-I'M SORRY.

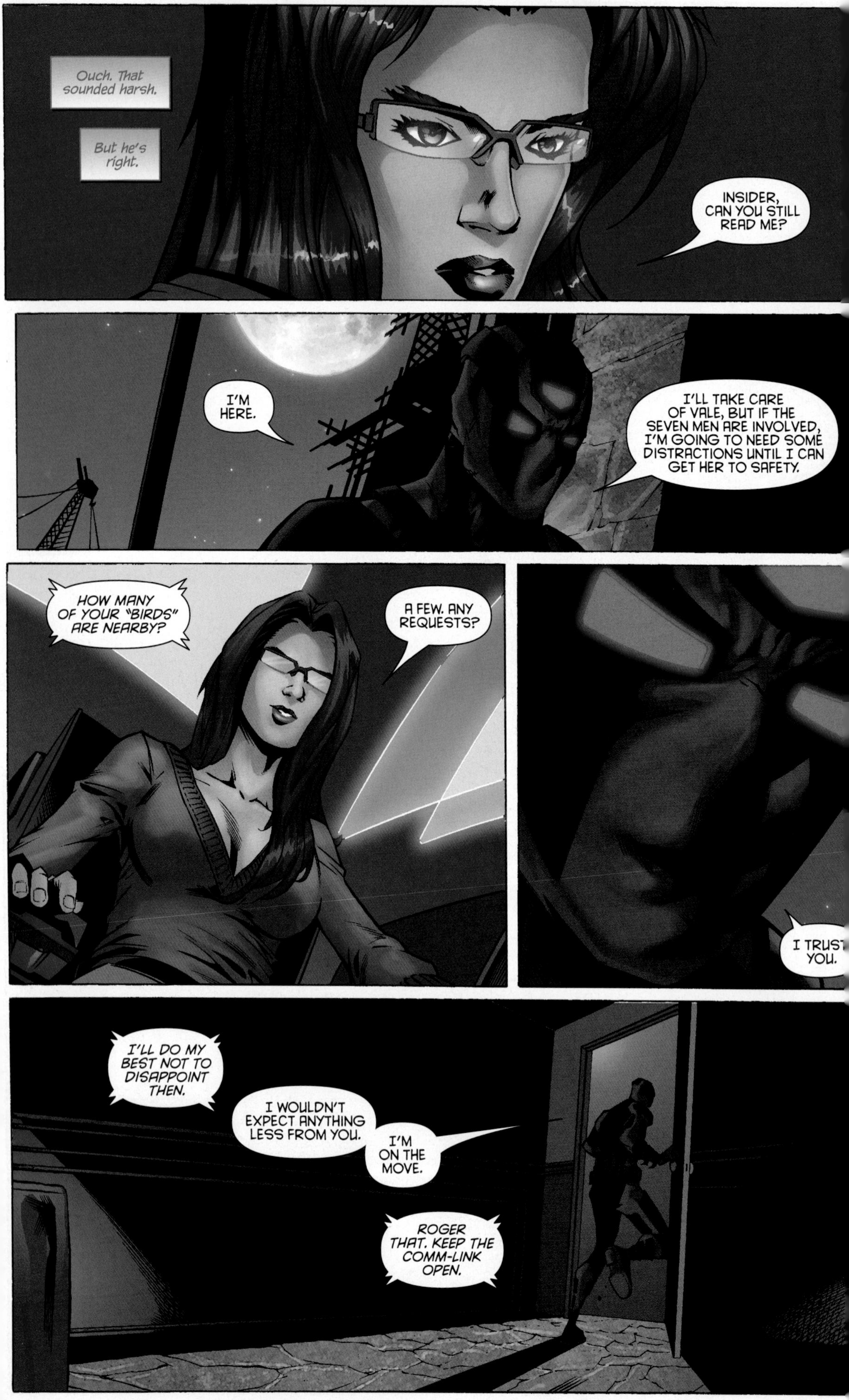
Ouch. That sounded harsh.
But he's right.
INSIDER, CAN YOU STILL READ ME?
I'M HERE.
I'LL TAKE CARE OF VALE, BUT IF THE SEVEN MEN ARE INVOLVED, I'M GOING TO NEED SOME DISTRACTIONS UNTIL I CAN GET HER TO SAFETY.
HOW MANY OF YOUR "BIRDS" ARE NEARBY?
A FEW. ANY REQUESTS?
I TRUST YOU.
I'LL DO MY BEST NOT TO DISAPPOINT THEN.
I WOULDN'T EXPECT ANYTHING LESS FROM YOU.
I'M ON THE MOVE.
ROGER THAT. KEEP THE COMM-LINK OPEN.

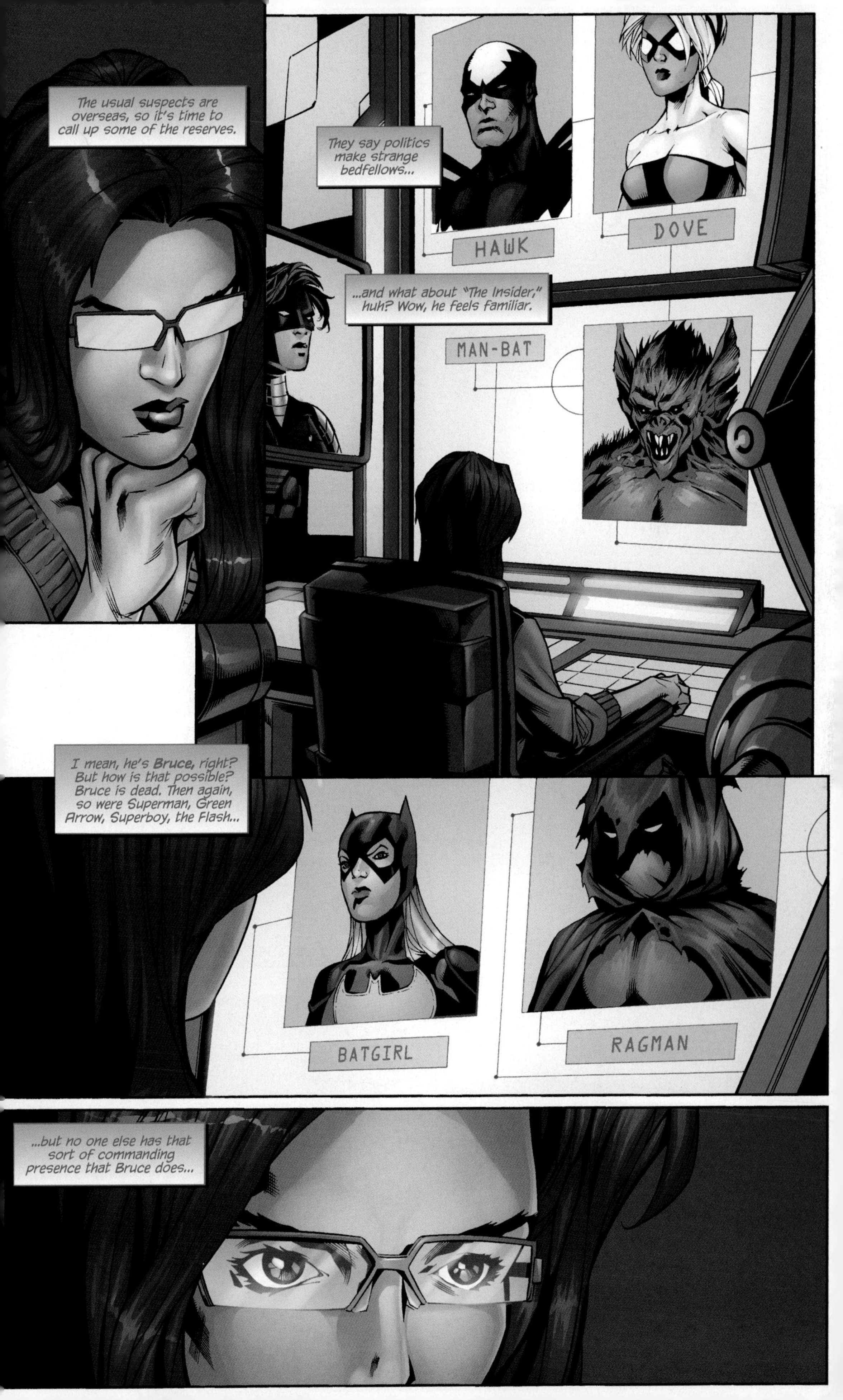
The usual suspects are overseas, so it's time to call up some of the reserves.
They say politics make strange bedfellows...
HAWK
DOVE
...and what about "The Insider," huh? Wow, he feels familiar.
MAN-BAT
I mean, he's **Bruce**, right? But how is that possible? Bruce is dead. Then again, so were Superman, Green Arrow, Superboy, the Flash...
BATGIRL
RAGMAN
...but no one else has that sort of commanding presence that Bruce does...

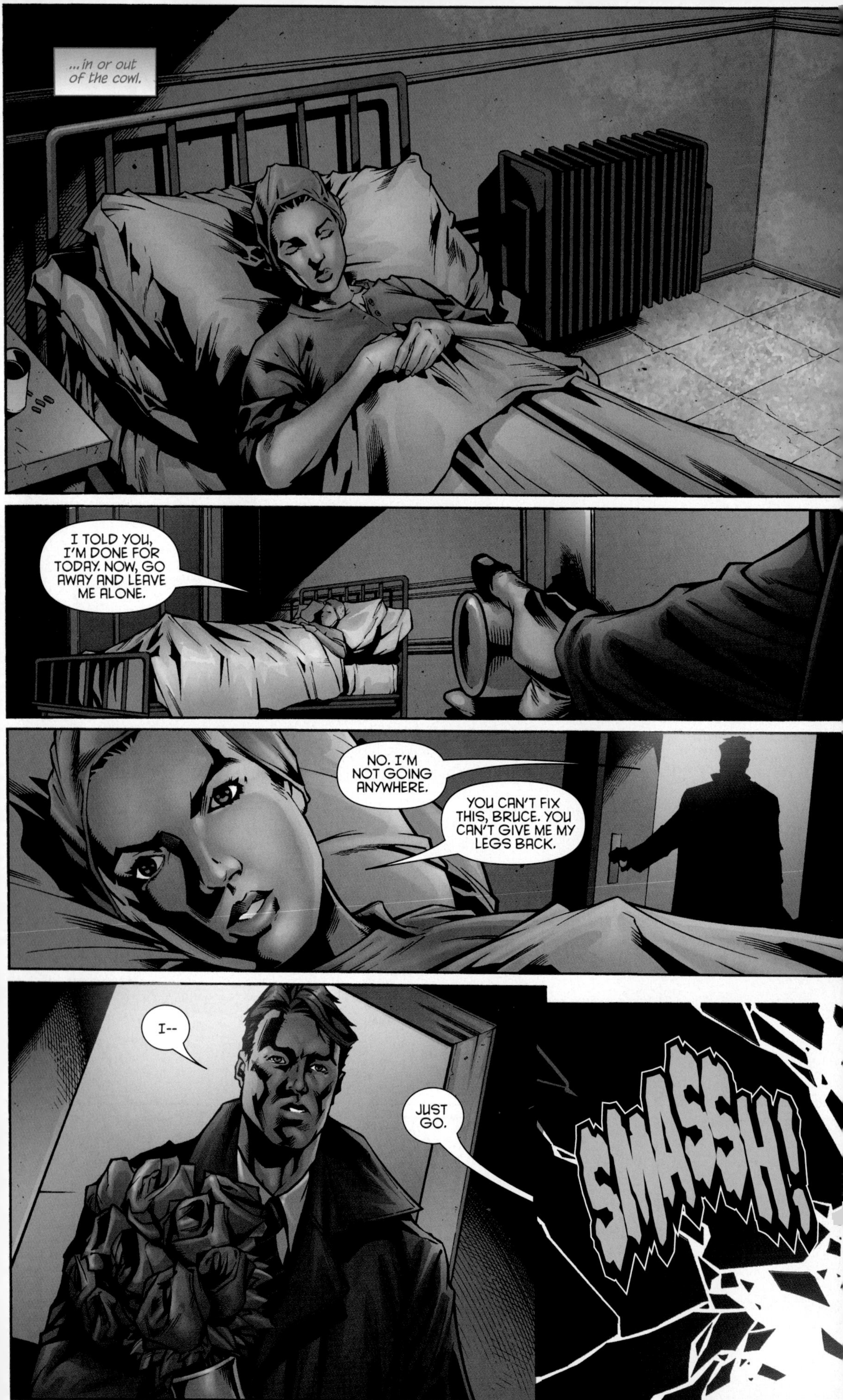

...in or out of the cowl.
I TOLD YOU, I'M DONE FOR TODAY. NOW, GO AWAY AND LEAVE ME ALONE.
NO. I'M NOT GOING ANYWHERE.
YOU CAN'T FIX THIS, BRUCE. YOU CAN'T GIVE ME MY LEGS BACK.
I--
JUST GO.
SMASSH!

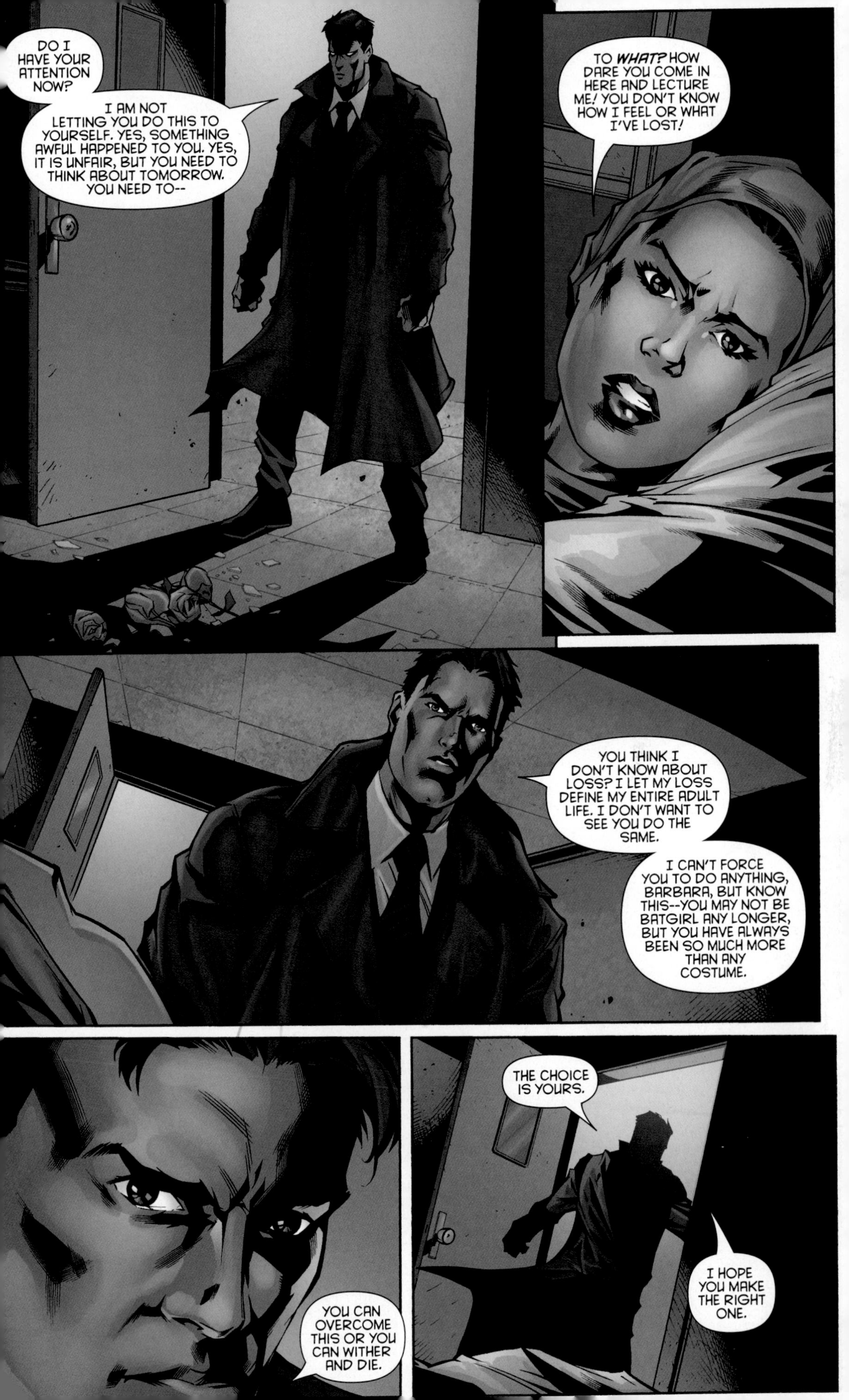
DO I HAVE YOUR ATTENTION NOW?
I AM NOT LETTING YOU DO THIS TO YOURSELF. YES, SOMETHING AWFUL HAPPENED TO YOU. YES, IT IS UNFAIR, BUT YOU NEED TO THINK ABOUT TOMORROW. YOU NEED TO--
TO *WHAT?* HOW DARE YOU COME IN HERE AND LECTURE ME! YOU DON'T KNOW HOW I FEEL OR WHAT I'VE LOST!
YOU THINK I DON'T KNOW ABOUT LOSS? I LET MY LOSS DEFINE MY ENTIRE ADULT LIFE. I DON'T WANT TO SEE YOU DO THE SAME.
I CAN'T FORCE YOU TO DO ANYTHING, BARBARA, BUT KNOW THIS--YOU MAY NOT BE BATGIRL ANY LONGER, BUT YOU HAVE ALWAYS BEEN SO MUCH MORE THAN ANY COSTUME.
YOU CAN OVERCOME THIS OR YOU CAN WITHER AND DIE.
THE CHOICE IS YOURS.
I HOPE YOU MAKE THE RIGHT ONE.

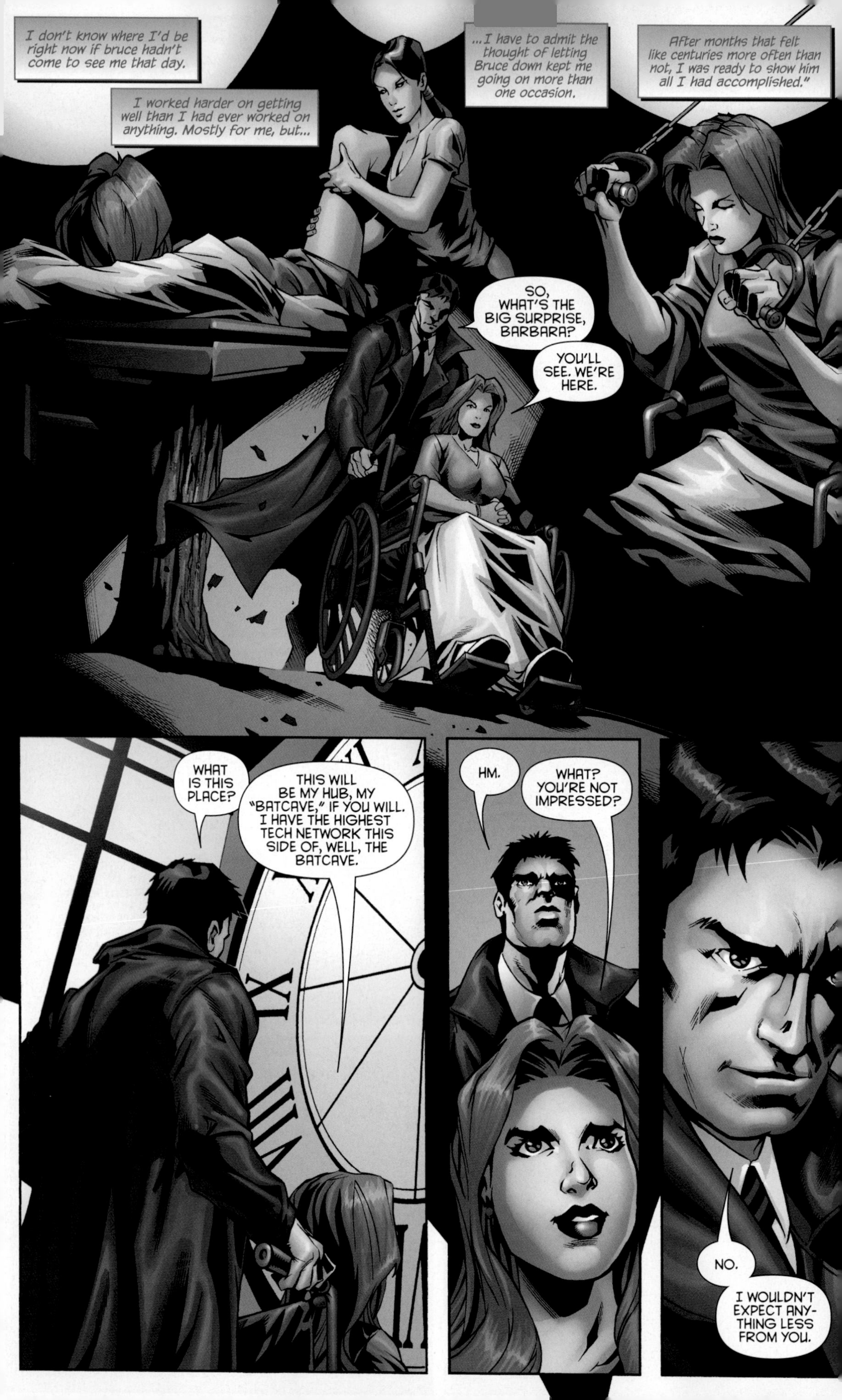

I don't know where I'd be right now if Bruce hadn't come to see me that day.
I worked harder on getting well than I had ever worked on anything. Mostly for me, but...
...I have to admit the thought of letting Bruce down kept me going on more than one occasion.
After months that felt like centuries more often than not, I was ready to show him all I had accomplished."
SO, WHAT'S THE BIG SURPRISE, BARBARA?
YOU'LL SEE. WE'RE HERE.
WHAT IS THIS PLACE?
THIS WILL BE MY HUB, MY "BATCAVE," IF YOU WILL. I HAVE THE HIGHEST TECH NETWORK THIS SIDE OF, WELL, THE BATCAVE.
HM.
WHAT? YOU'RE NOT IMPRESSED?
NO.
I WOULDN'T EXPECT ANYTHING LESS FROM YOU.

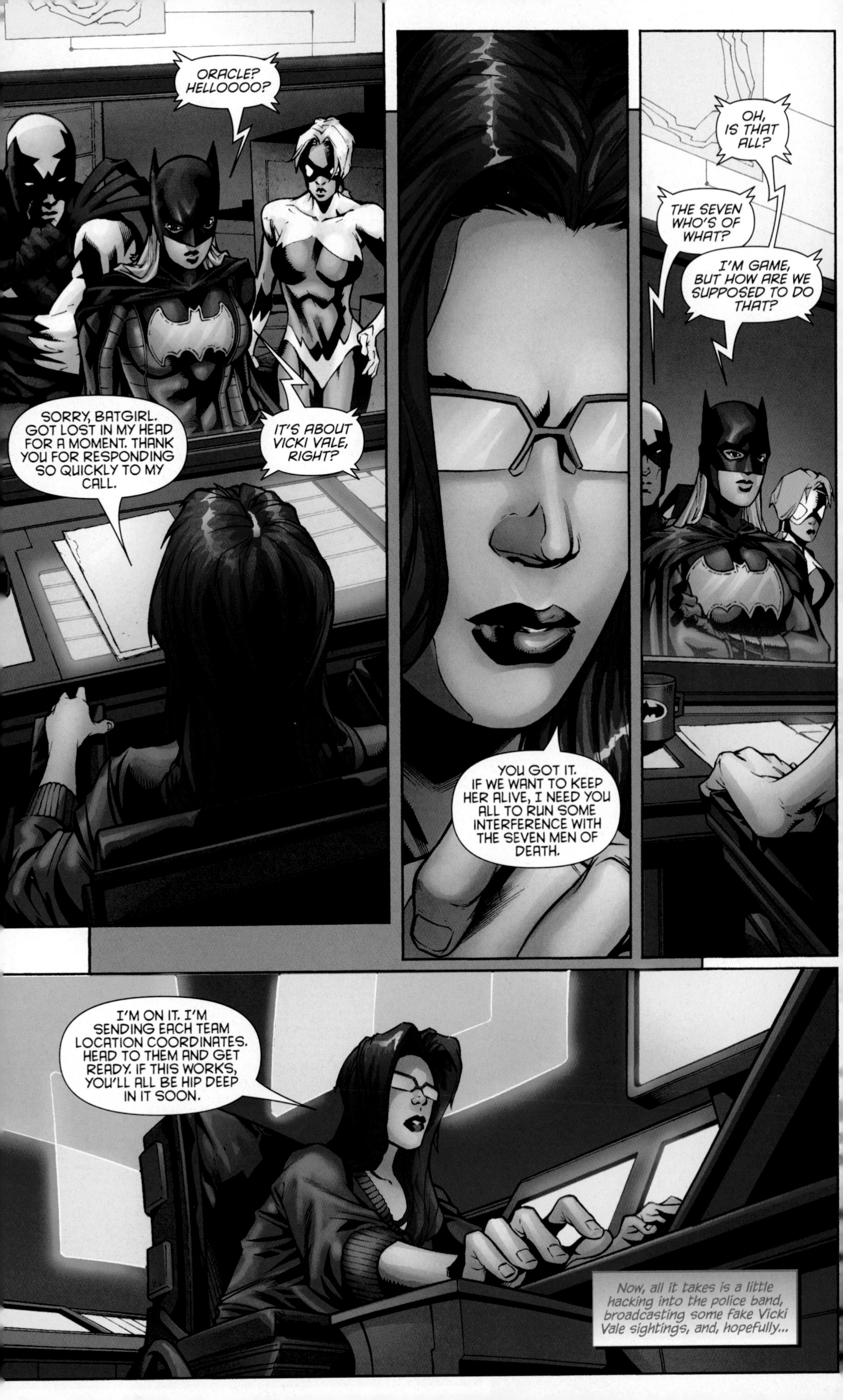
ORACLE? HELLOOOO?
SORRY, BATGIRL. GOT LOST IN MY HEAD FOR A MOMENT. THANK YOU FOR RESPONDING SO QUICKLY TO MY CALL.
IT'S ABOUT VICKI VALE, RIGHT?
YOU GOT IT. IF WE WANT TO KEEP HER ALIVE, I NEED YOU ALL TO RUN SOME INTERFERENCE WITH THE SEVEN MEN OF DEATH.
OH, IS THAT ALL?
THE SEVEN WHO'S OF WHAT?
I'M GAME, BUT HOW ARE WE SUPPOSED TO DO THAT?
I'M ON IT. I'M SENDING EACH TEAM LOCATION COORDINATES. HEAD TO THEM AND GET READY. IF THIS WORKS, YOU'LL ALL BE HIP DEEP IN IT SOON.
Now, all it takes is a little hacking into the police band, broadcasting some fake Vicki Vale sightings, and, hopefully...

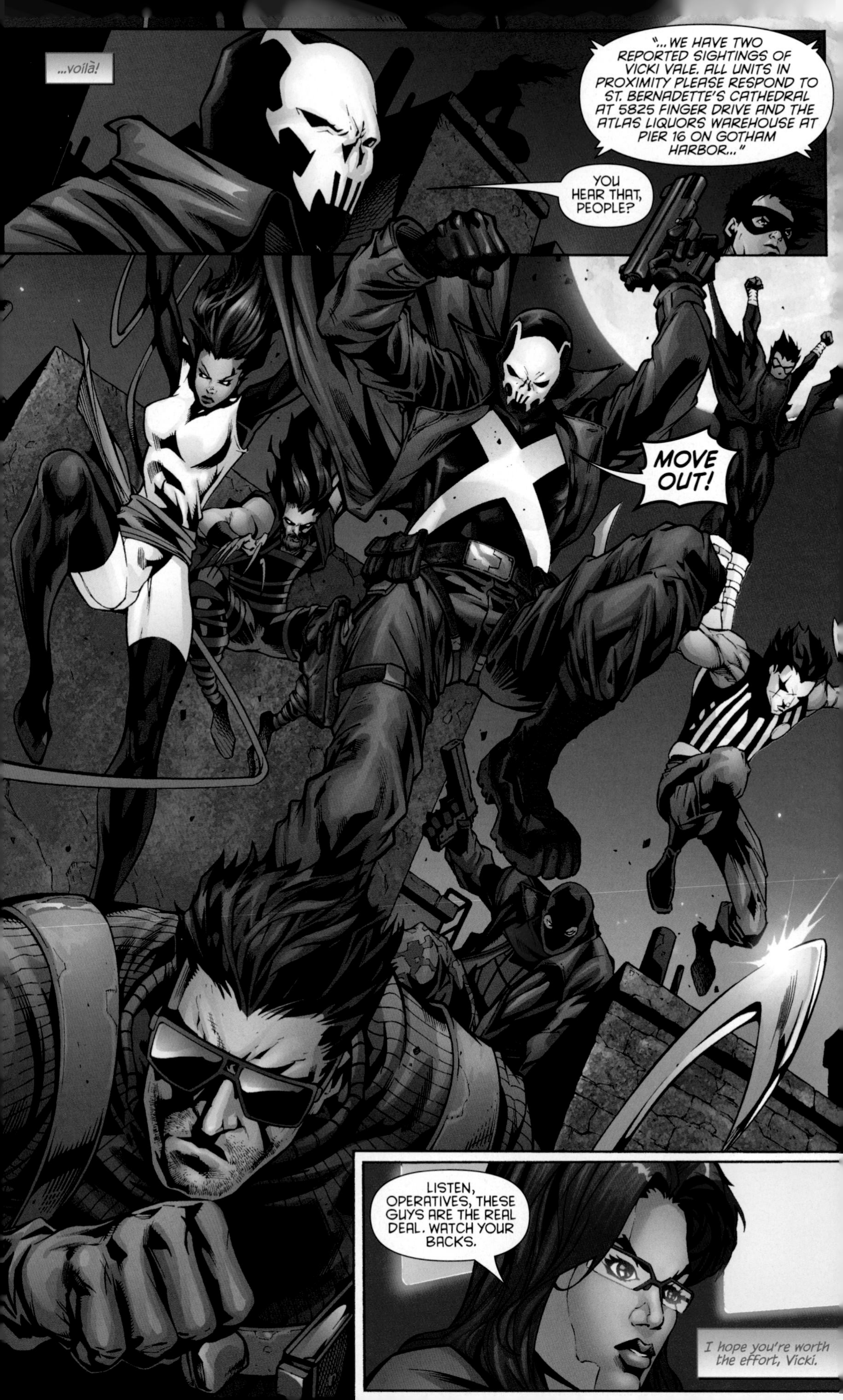

...voilà!
"...WE HAVE TWO REPORTED SIGHTINGS OF VICKI VALE. ALL UNITS IN PROXIMITY PLEASE RESPOND TO ST. BERNADETTE'S CATHEDRAL AT 5825 FINGER DRIVE AND THE ATLAS LIQUORS WAREHOUSE AT PIER 16 ON GOTHAM HARBOR..."
YOU HEAR THAT, PEOPLE?
MOVE OUT!
LISTEN, OPERATIVES, THESE GUYS ARE THE REAL DEAL. WATCH YOUR BACKS.
I hope you're worth the effort, Vicki.

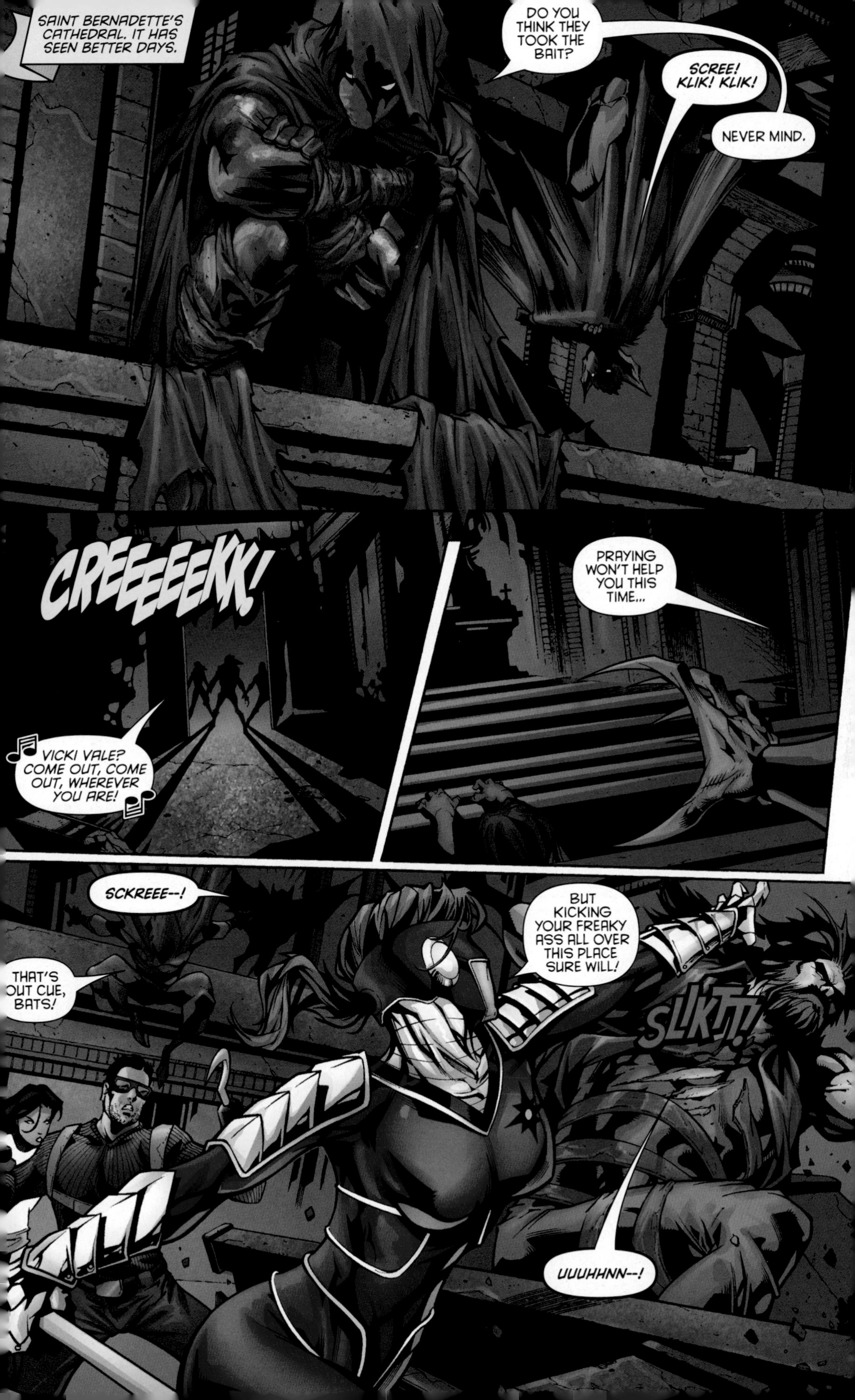
SAINT BERNADETTE'S CATHEDRAL. IT HAS SEEN BETTER DAYS.
DO YOU THINK THEY TOOK THE BAIT?
SCREE! KLIK! KLIK!
NEVER MIND.
CREEEEEEKK!
VICKI VALE? COME OUT, COME OUT, WHEREVER YOU ARE!
PRAYING WON'T HELP YOU THIS TIME...
SCKREEE--!
THAT'S OUT CUE, BATS!
BUT KICKING YOUR FREAKY ASS ALL OVER THIS PLACE SURE WILL!
SLIKTT!
UUUHHNN--!

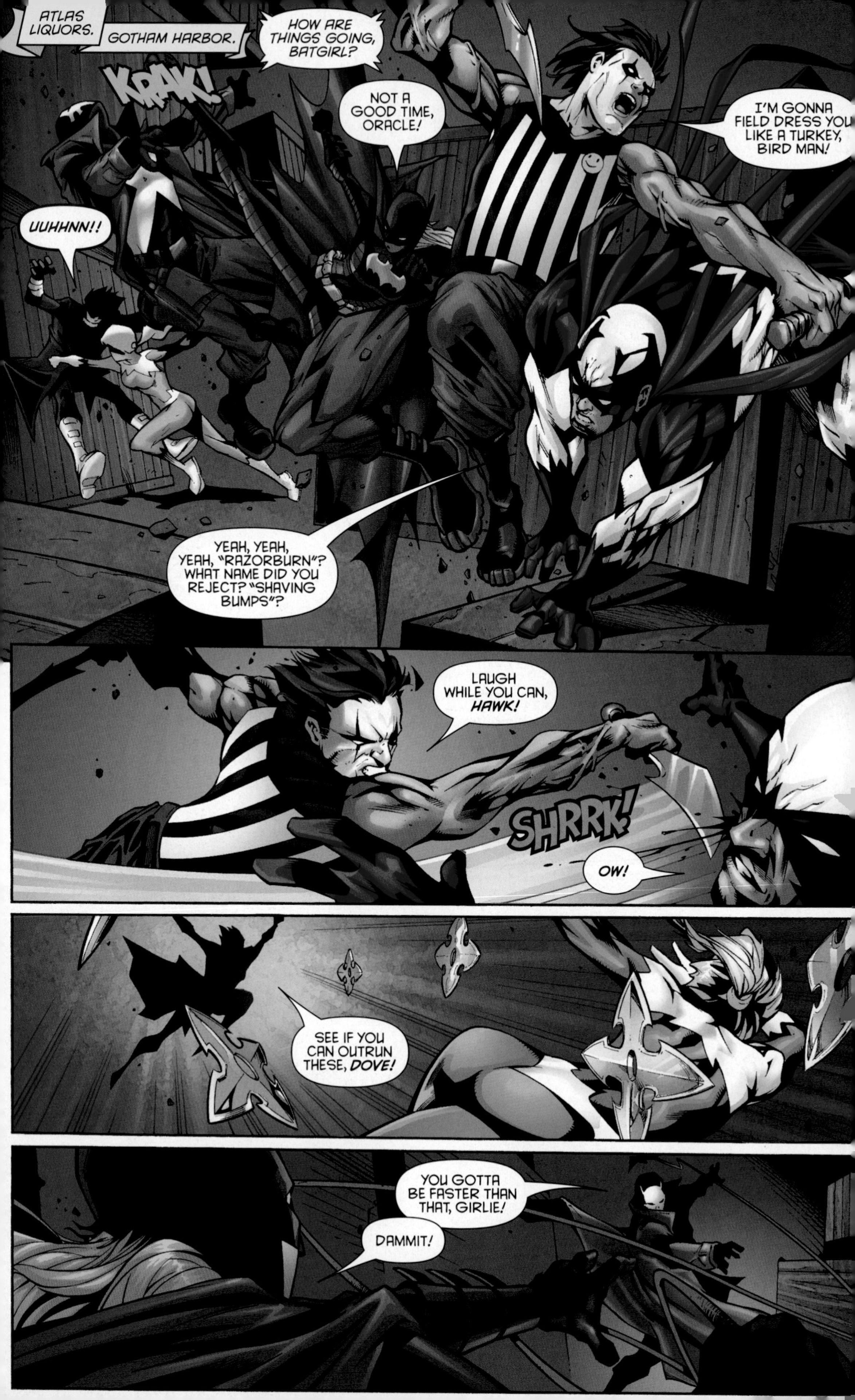
ATLAS LIQUORS.
GOTHAM HARBOR.
HOW ARE THINGS GOING, BATGIRL?
KRAK!
NOT A GOOD TIME, ORACLE!
I'M GONNA FIELD DRESS YOU LIKE A TURKEY, BIRD MAN!
UUHHNN!!
YEAH, YEAH, YEAH, "RAZORBURN"? WHAT NAME DID YOU REJECT? "SHAVING BUMPS"?
LAUGH WHILE YOU CAN, HAWK!
SHRRK!
OW!
SEE IF YOU CAN OUTRUN THESE, DOVE!
YOU GOTTA BE FASTER THAN THAT, GIRLIE!
DAMMIT!

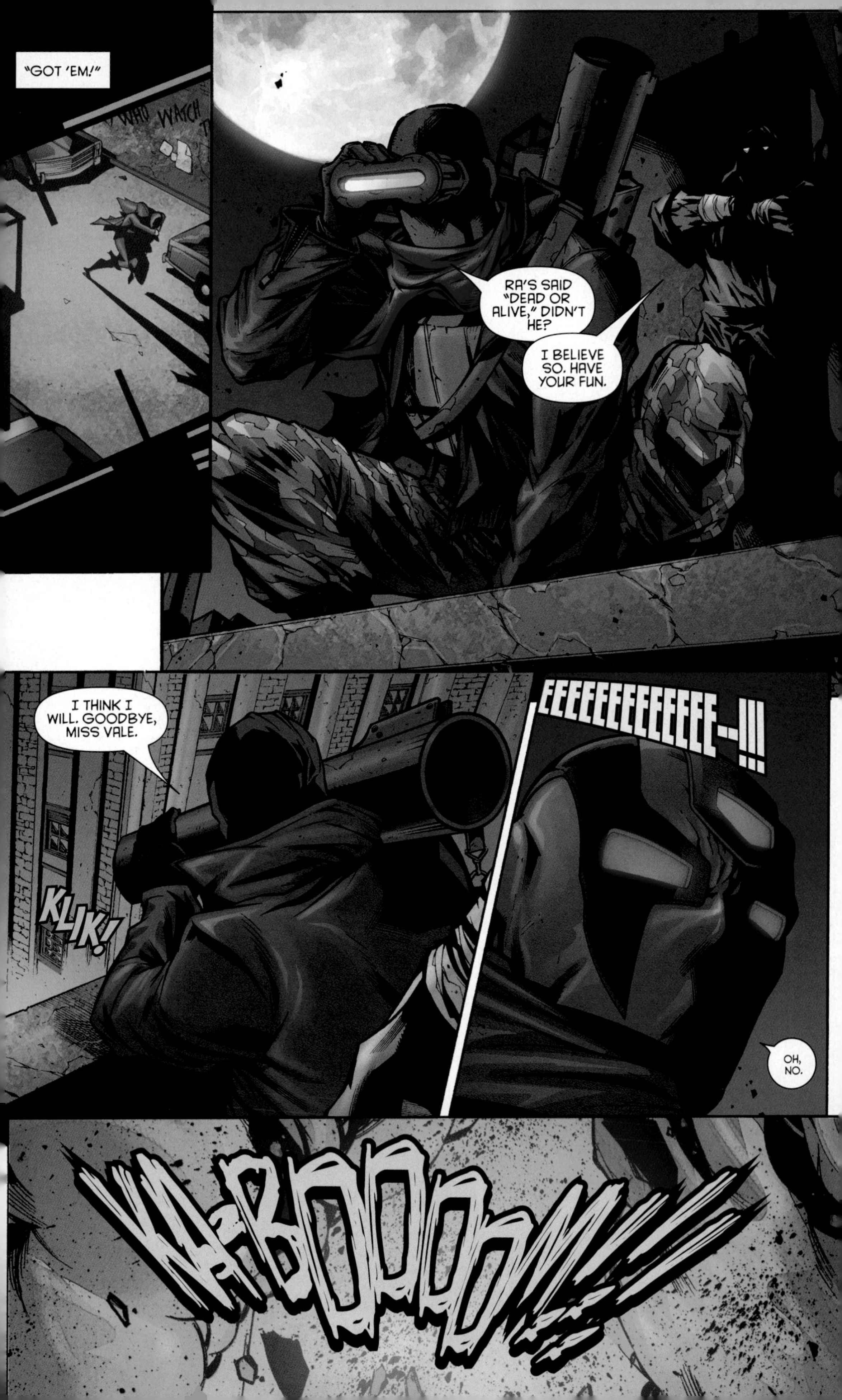
"GOT 'EM!"
RA'S SAID "DEAD OR ALIVE," DIDN'T HE?
I BELIEVE SO. HAVE YOUR FUN.
I THINK I WILL. GOODBYE, MISS VALE.
KLIK!
EEEEEEEEEEEEE--!!!
OH, NO.

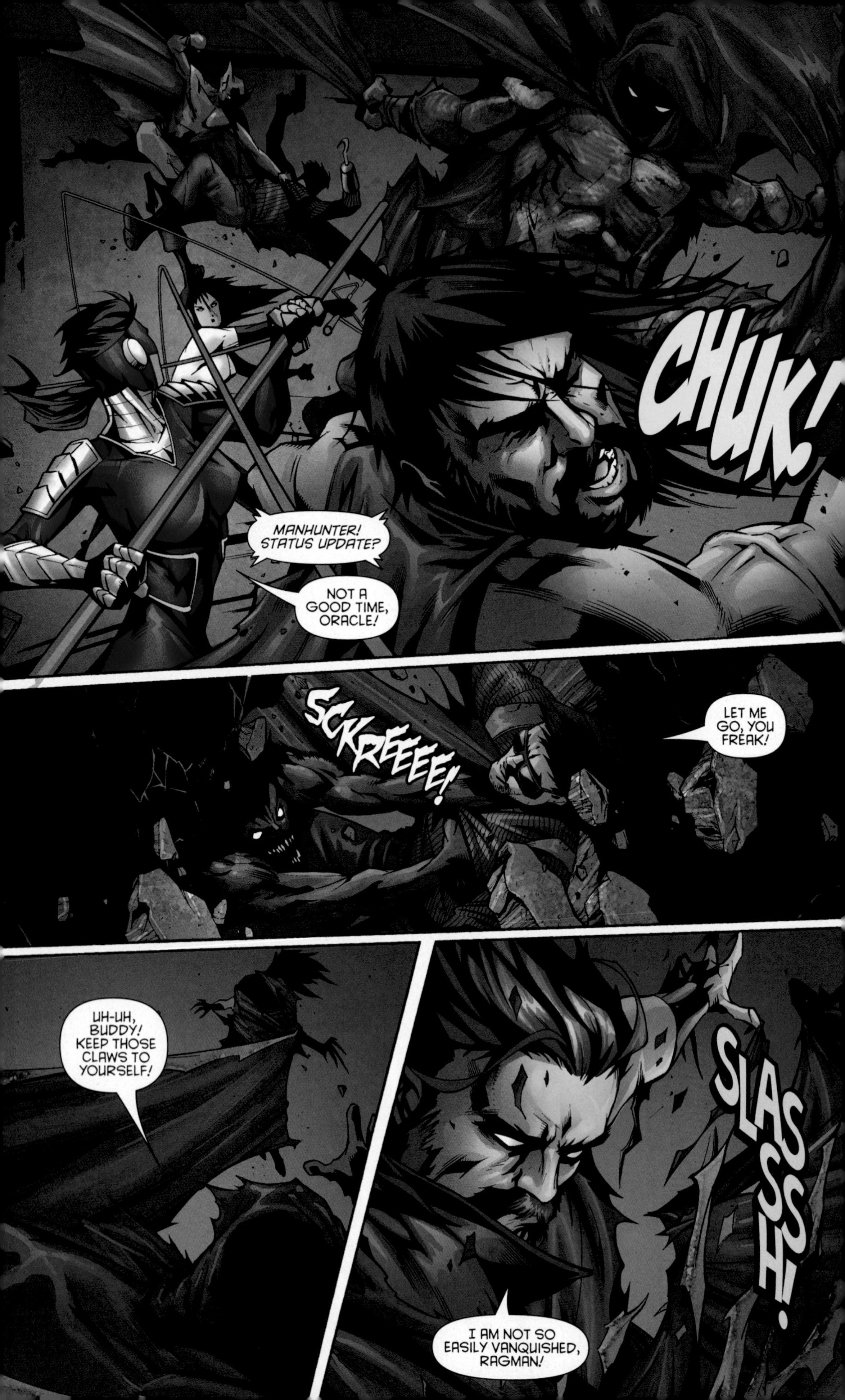
CHUK!
MANHUNTER! STATUS UPDATE?
NOT A GOOD TIME, ORACLE!
SCKREEEEE!
LET ME GO, YOU FREAK!
UH-UH, BUDDY! KEEP THOSE CLAWS TO YOURSELF!
SLASSSH!
I AM NOT SO EASILY VANQUISHED, RAGMAN!

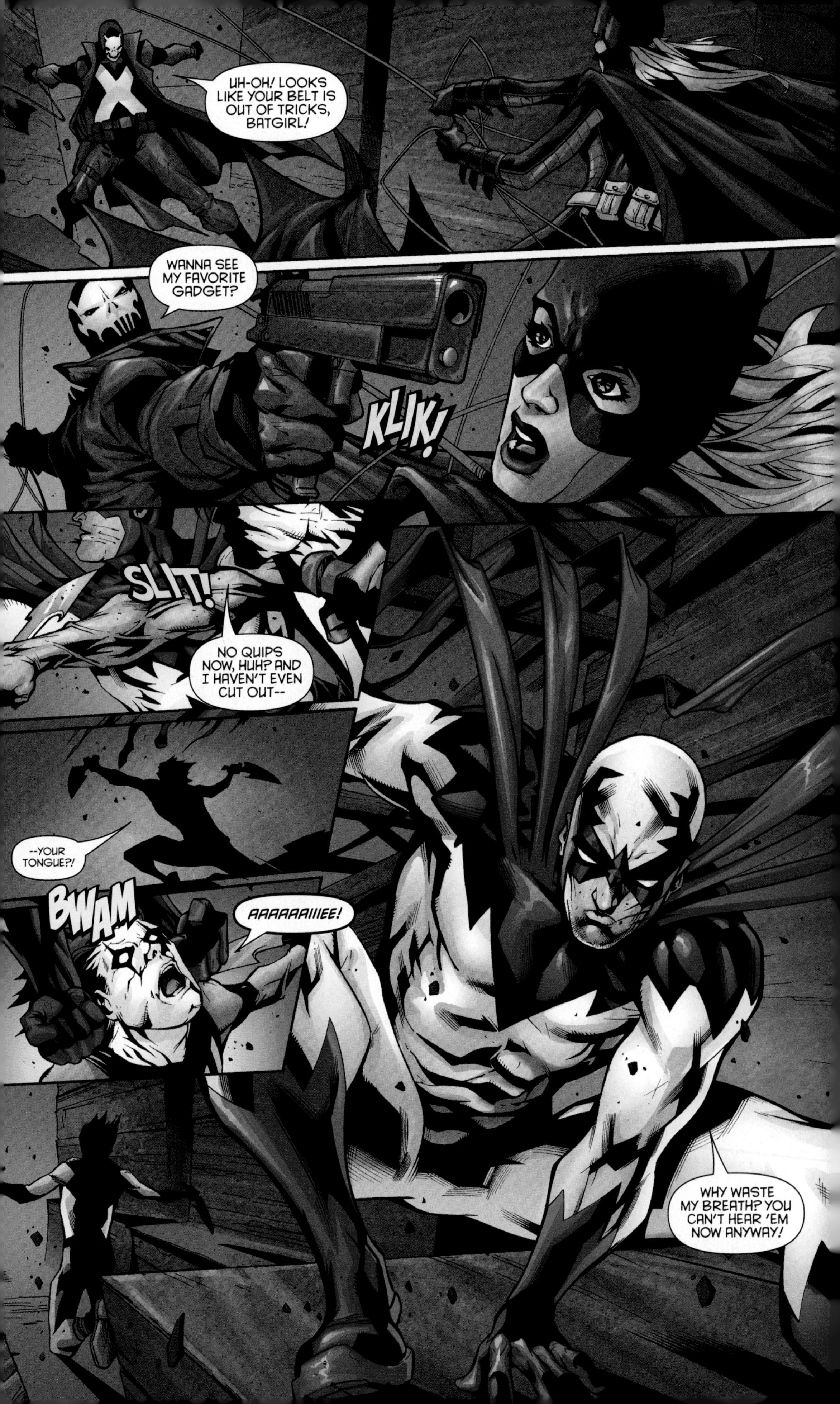
UH-OH! LOOKS LIKE YOUR BELT IS OUT OF TRICKS, BATGIRL!
WANNA SEE MY FAVORITE GADGET?
KLIK!
SLIT!
NO QUIPS NOW, HUH? AND I HAVEN'T EVEN CUT OUT--
--YOUR TONGUE?!
BWAM
AAAAAAIIIEE!
WHY WASTE MY BREATH? YOU CAN'T HEAR 'EM NOW ANYWAY!

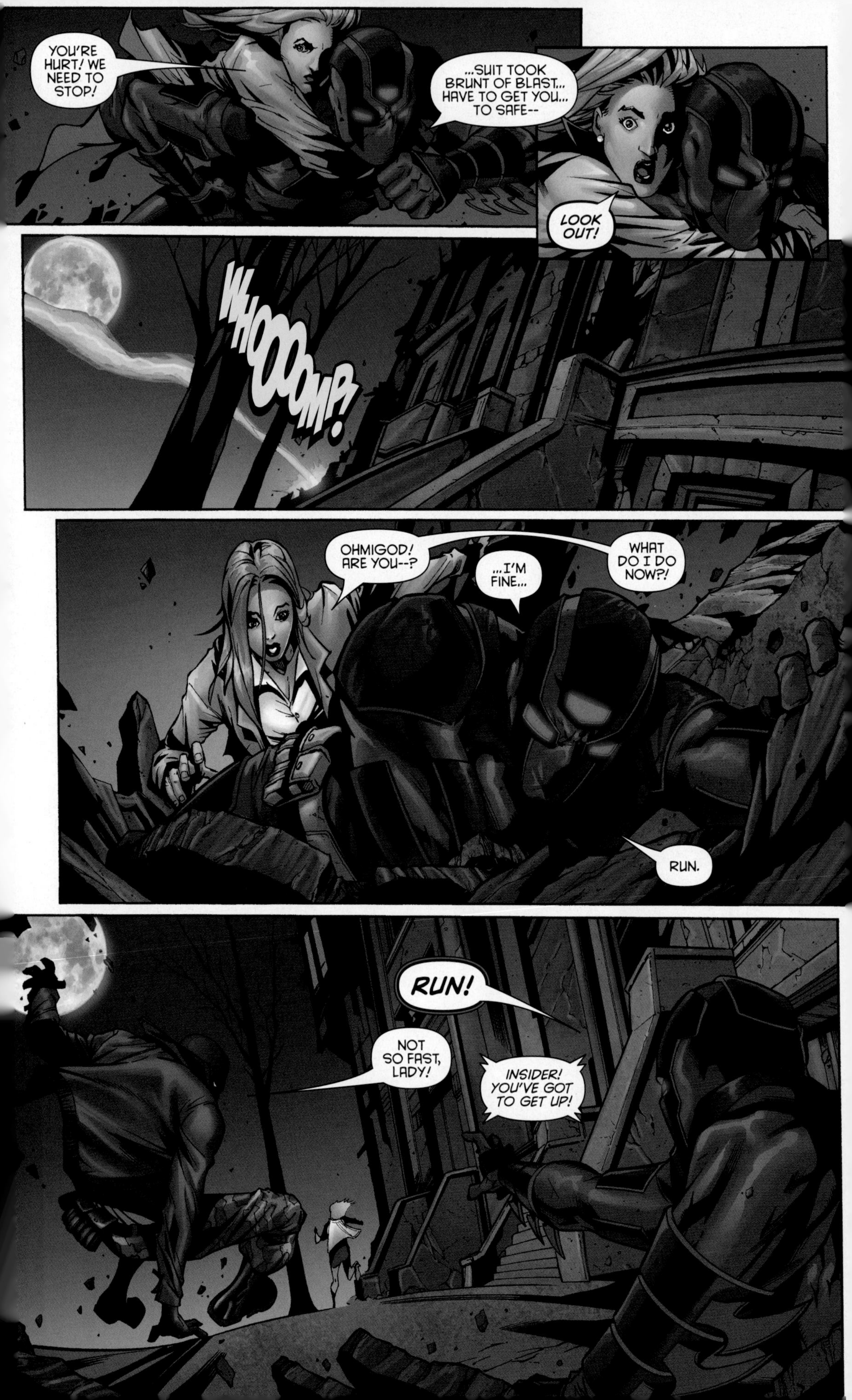
YOU'RE HURT! WE NEED TO STOP!
...SUIT TOOK BRUNT OF BLAST... HAVE TO GET YOU... TO SAFE--
LOOK OUT!
WHOOOOOM!?!
OHMIGOD! ARE YOU--?
...I'M FINE...
WHAT DO I DO NOW?!
RUN.
RUN!
NOT SO FAST, LADY!
INSIDER! YOU'VE GOT TO GET UP!

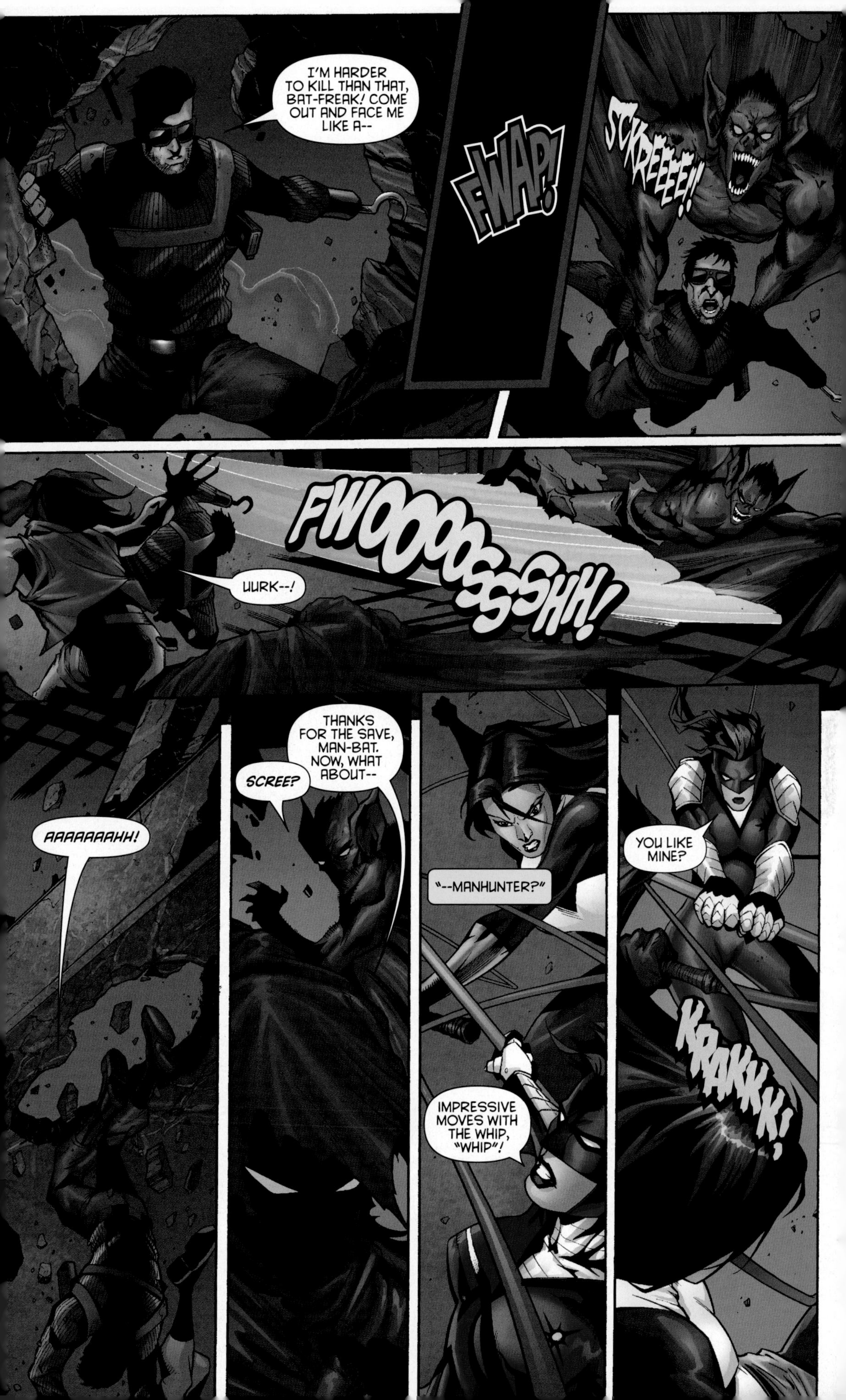
I'M HARDER TO KILL THAN THAT, BAT-FREAK! COME OUT AND FACE ME LIKE A--
FWAP!
SCKREEEEE!!
FWOOOOSSSHH!
UURK--!
AAAAAAAHH!
SCREE?
THANKS FOR THE SAVE, MAN-BAT. NOW, WHAT ABOUT--
"--MANHUNTER?"
IMPRESSIVE MOVES WITH THE WHIP, "WHIP"!
YOU LIKE MINE?
KRAKKK!

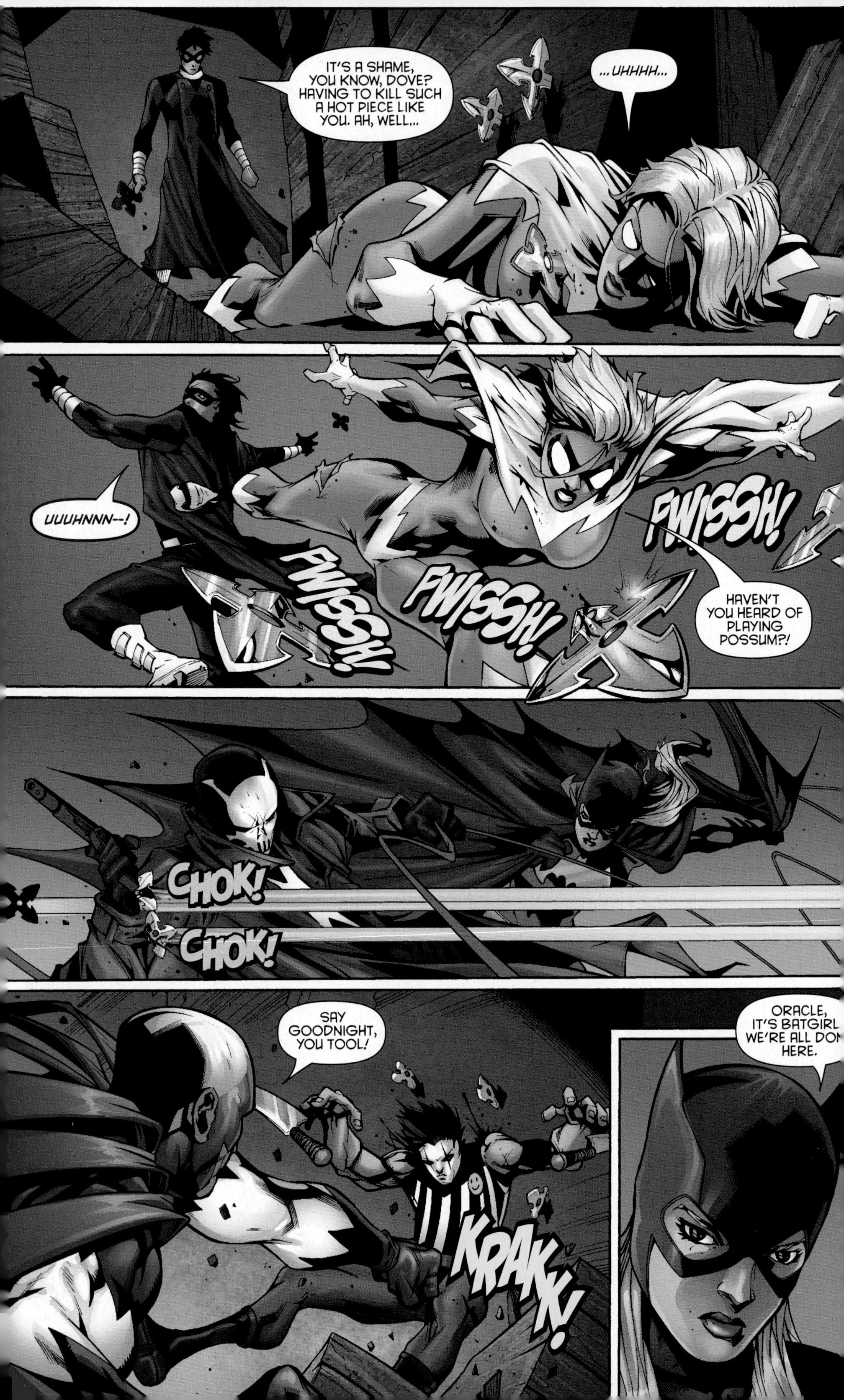

IT'S A SHAME, YOU KNOW, DOVE? HAVING TO KILL SUCH A HOT PIECE LIKE YOU. AH, WELL...
...UHHHH...
UUUHNNN--!
FWISSH!
FWISSH!
FWISSH!
HAVEN'T YOU HEARD OF PLAYING POSSUM?!
CHOK!
CHOK!
SAY GOODNIGHT, YOU TOOL!
KRAKK!
ORACLE, IT'S BATGIRL WE'RE ALL DON HERE.

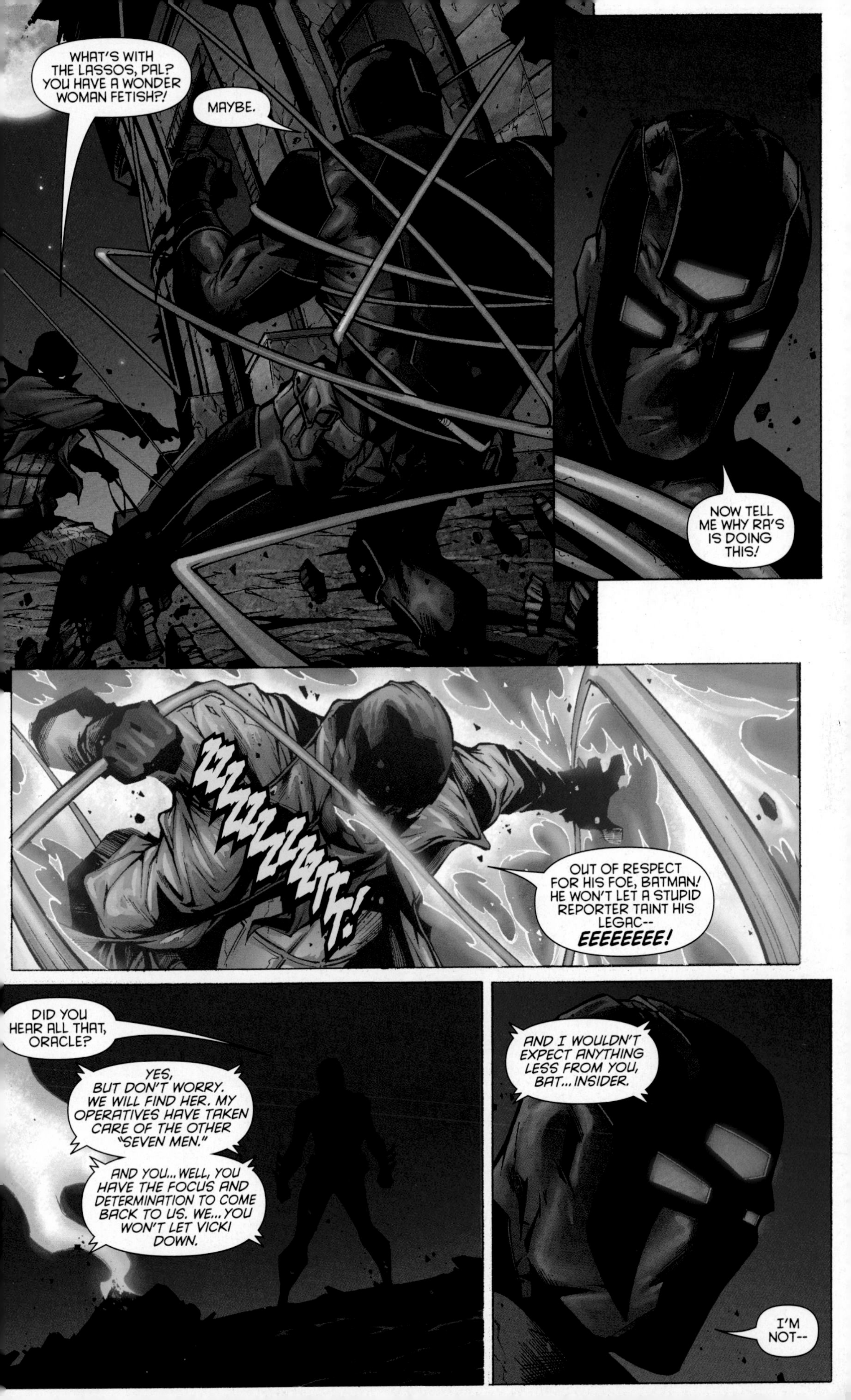
WHAT'S WITH THE LASSOS, PAL? YOU HAVE A WONDER WOMAN FETISH?!
MAYBE.
NOW TELL ME WHY RA'S IS DOING THIS!
ZZZZZZZZZZZTTT!
OUT OF RESPECT FOR HIS FOE, BATMAN! HE WON'T LET A STUPID REPORTER TAINT HIS LEGAC-- EEEEEEEE!
DID YOU HEAR ALL THAT, ORACLE?
YES, BUT DON'T WORRY. WE WILL FIND HER. MY OPERATIVES HAVE TAKEN CARE OF THE OTHER "SEVEN MEN."
AND YOU... WELL, YOU HAVE THE FOCUS AND DETERMINATION TO COME BACK TO US. WE... YOU WON'T LET VICKI DOWN.
AND I WOULDN'T EXPECT ANYTHING LESS FROM YOU, BAT... INSIDER.
I'M NOT--

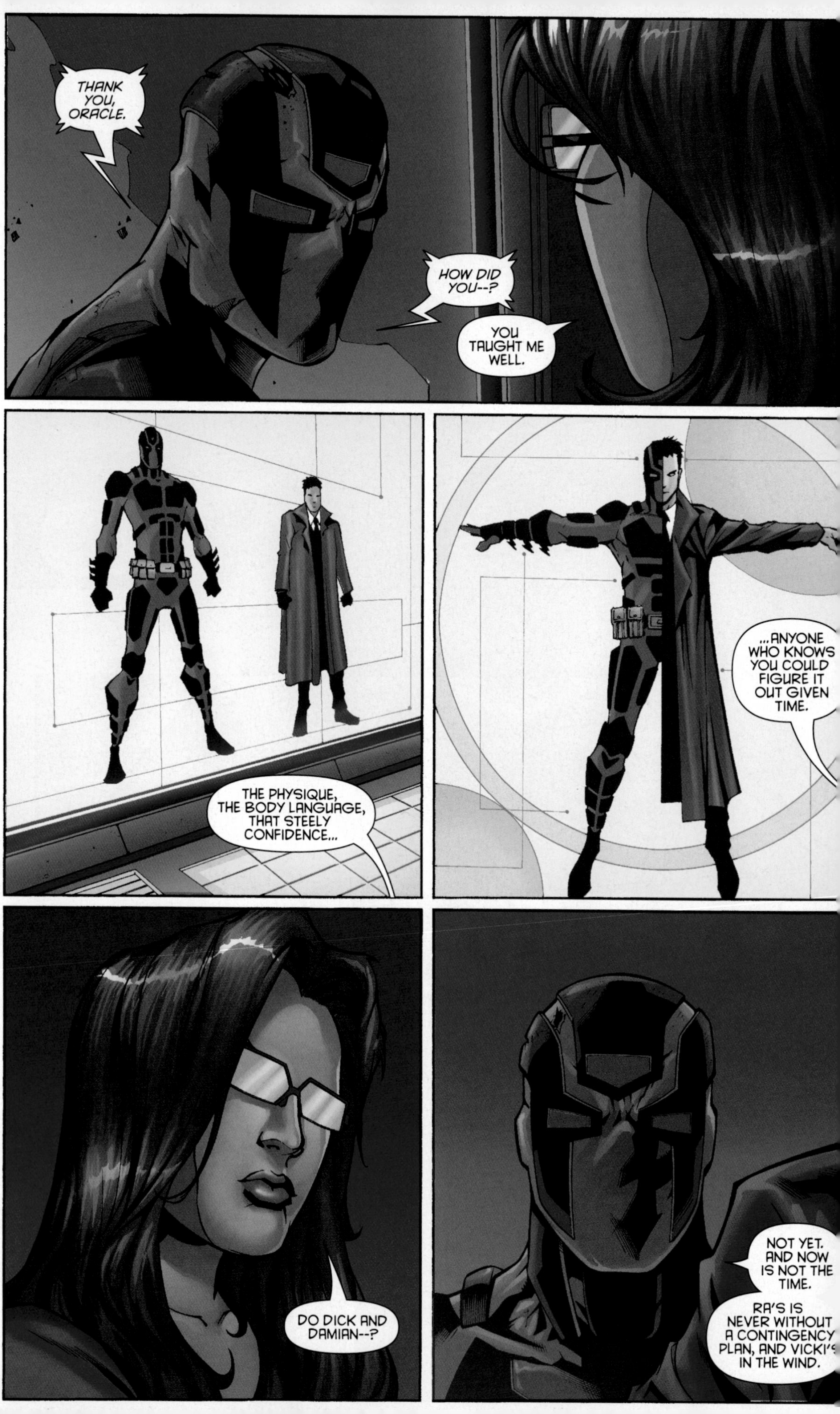
THANK YOU, ORACLE.
HOW DID YOU--?
YOU TAUGHT ME WELL.
THE PHYSIQUE, THE BODY LANGUAGE, THAT STEELY CONFIDENCE...
...ANYONE WHO KNOWS YOU COULD FIGURE IT OUT GIVEN TIME.
DO DICK AND DAMIAN--?
NOT YET. AND NOW IS NOT THE TIME.
RA'S IS NEVER WITHOUT A CONTINGENCY PLAN, AND VICKI'S IN THE WIND.

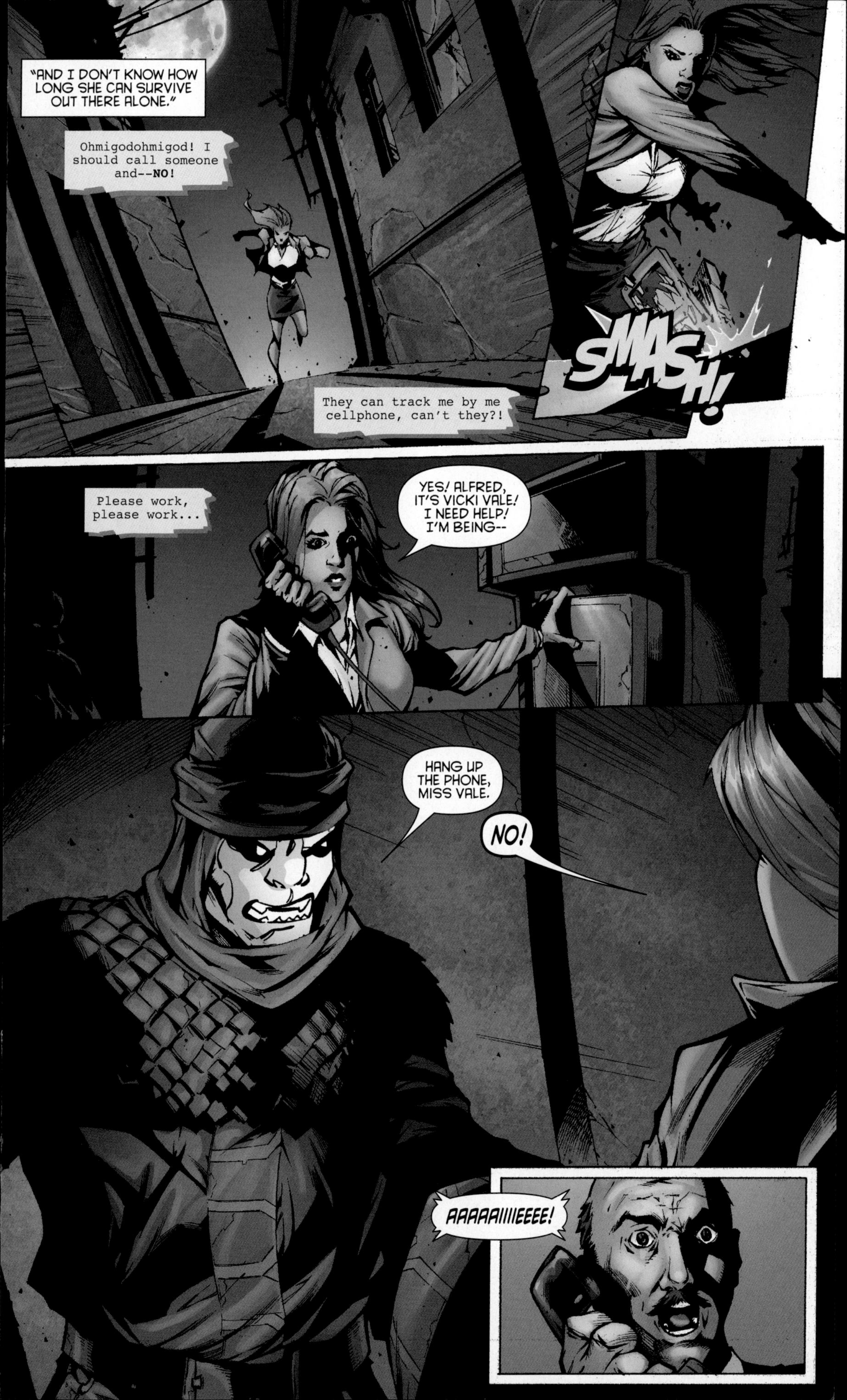
"AND I DON'T KNOW HOW LONG SHE CAN SURVIVE OUT THERE ALONE."
Ohmigodohmigod! I should call someone and--NO!
They can track me by me cellphone, can't they?!
SMASH!
Please work, please work...
YES! ALFRED, IT'S VICKI VALE! I NEED HELP! I'M BEING--
HANG UP THE PHONE, MISS VALE.
NO!
AAAAAIIIIEEEE!

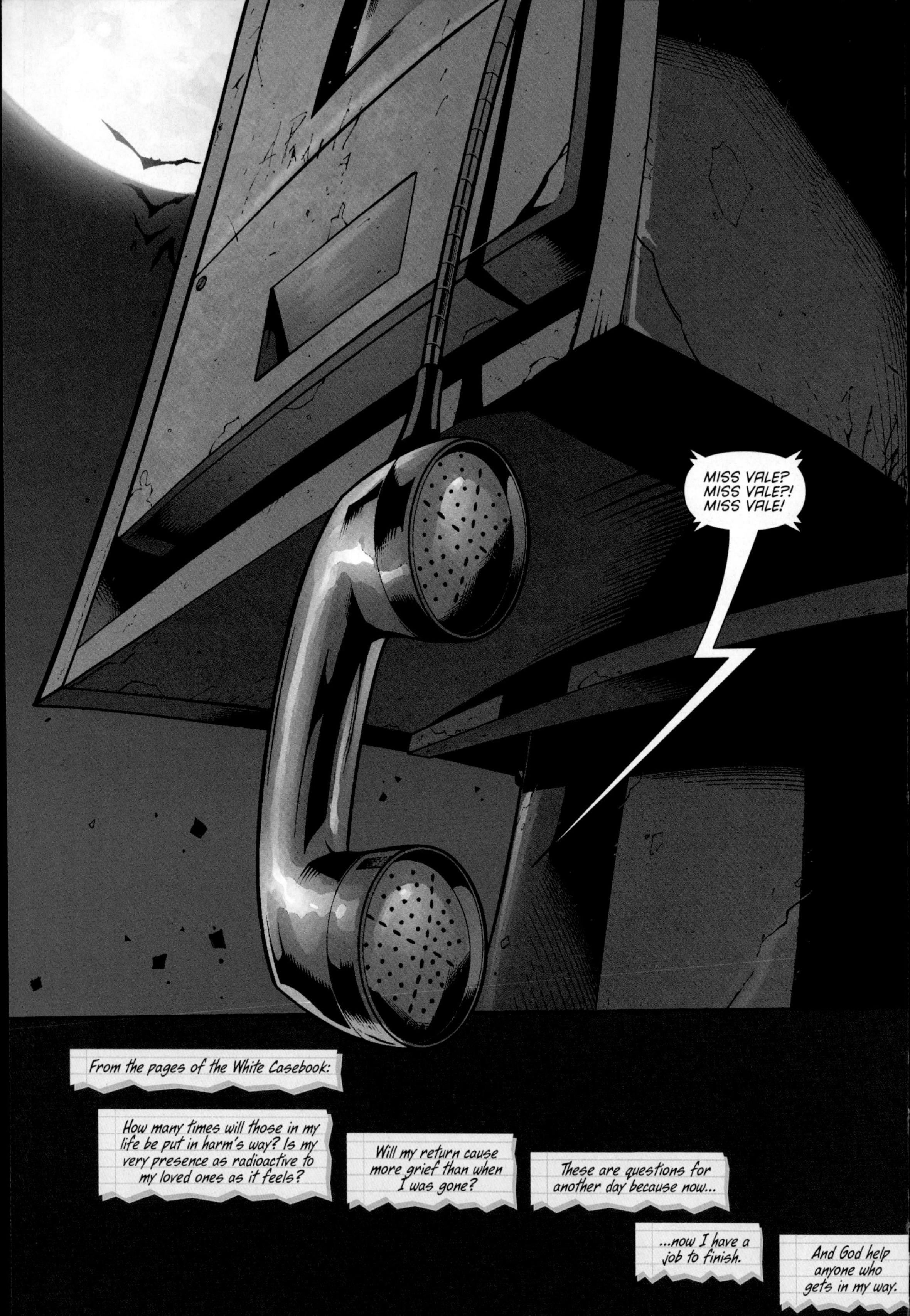
MISS VALE? MISS VALE?! MISS VALE!
From the pages of the White Casebook:
How many times will those in my life be put in harm's way? Is my very presence as radioactive to my loved ones as it feels?
Will my return cause more grief than when I was gone?
These are questions for another day because now...
...now I have a job to finish.
And God help anyone who gets in my way.

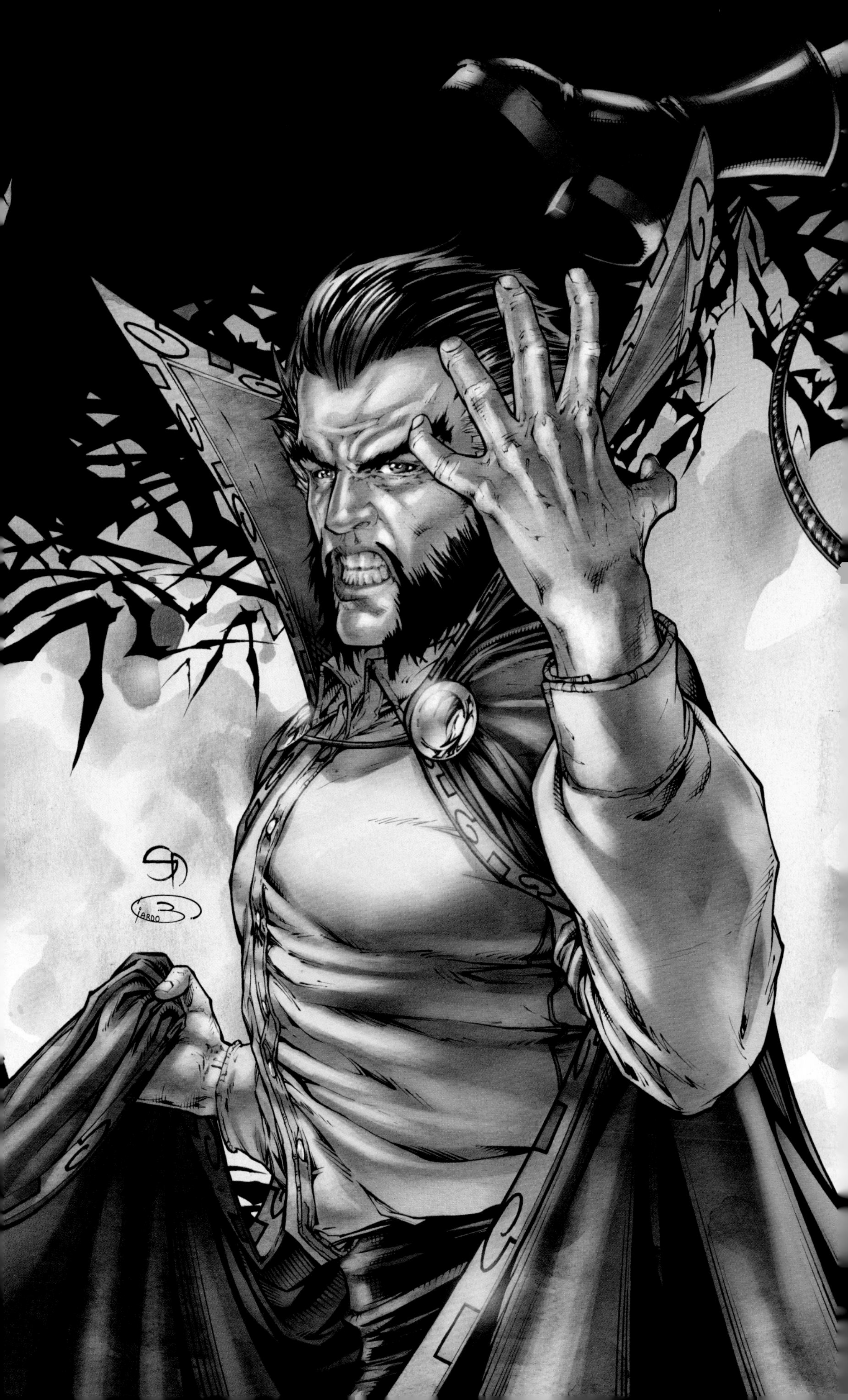

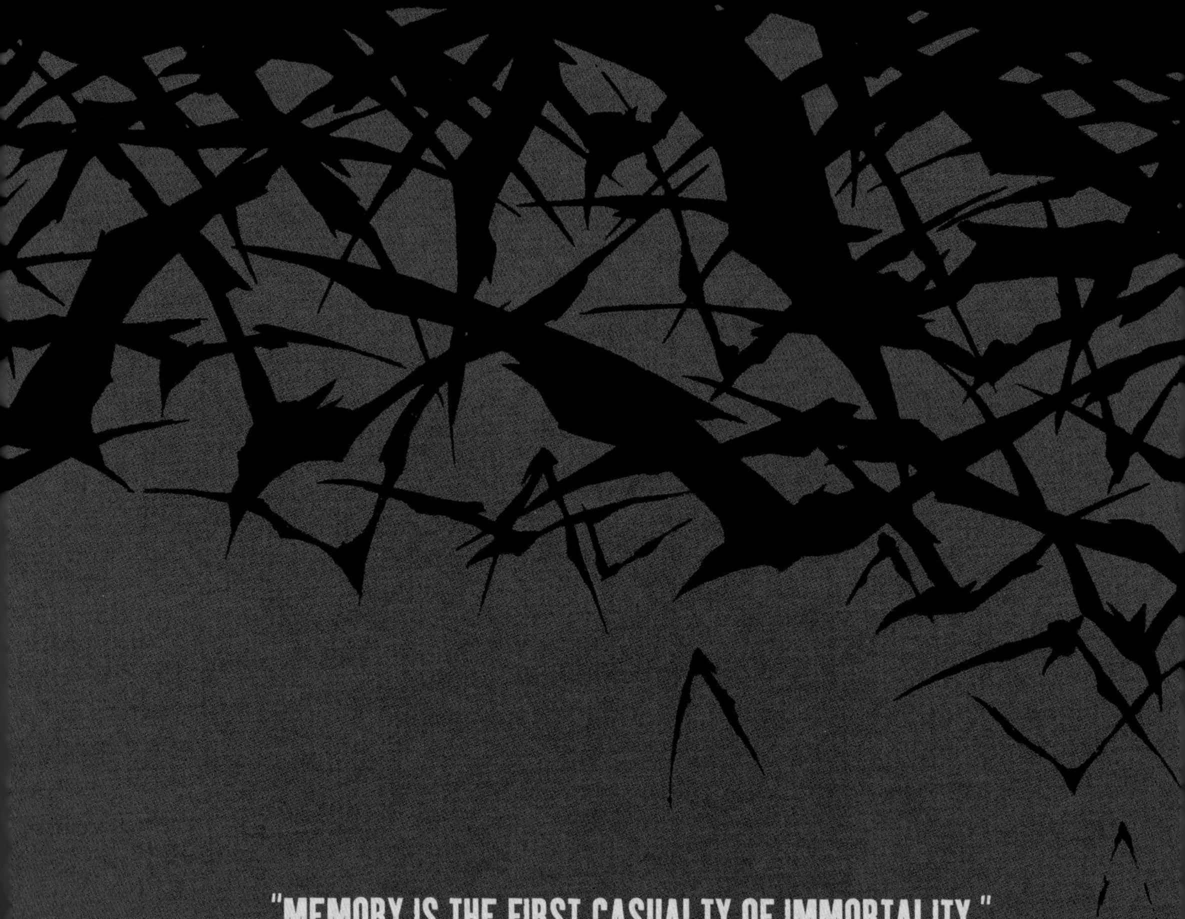

"MEMORY IS THE FIRST CASUALTY OF IMMORTALITY."

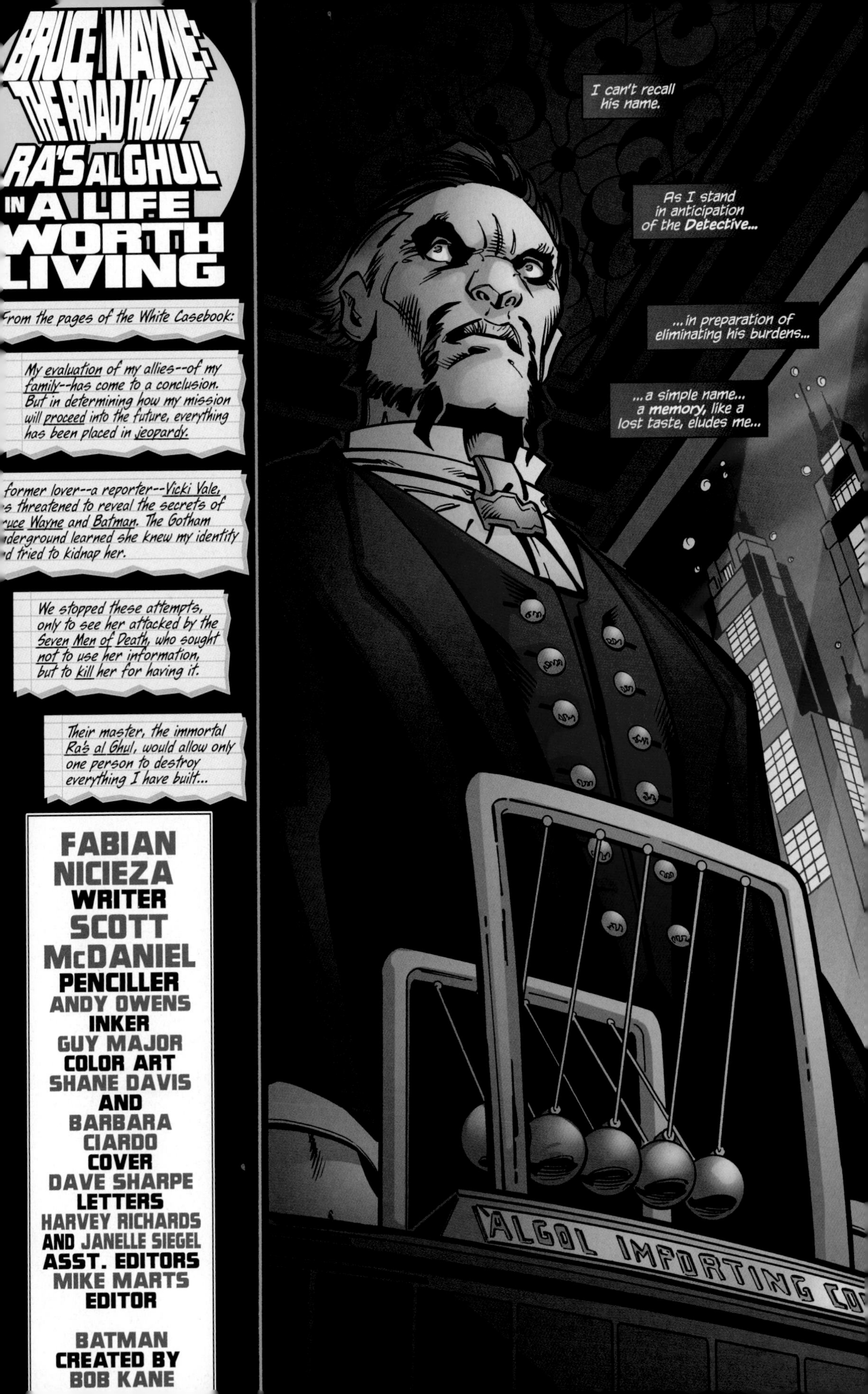

BRUCE WAYNE: THE ROAD HOME
RA'S AL GHUL IN A LIFE WORTH LIVING
From the pages of the White Casebook:
My evaluation of my allies--of my family--has come to a conclusion. But in determining how my mission will proceed into the future, everything has been placed in jeopardy.
former lover--a reporter--Vicki Vale, s threatened to reveal the secrets of ruce Wayne and Batman. The Gotham derground learned she knew my identity d tried to kidnap her.
We stopped these attempts, only to see her attacked by the Seven Men of Death, who sought not to use her information, but to kill her for having it.
Their master, the immortal Ra's al Ghul, would allow only one person to destroy everything I have built...
FABIAN NICIEZA WRITER SCOTT McDANIEL PENCILLER ANDY OWENS INKER GUY MAJOR COLOR ART SHANE DAVIS AND BARBARA CIARDO COVER DAVE SHARPE LETTERS HARVEY RICHARDS AND JANELLE SIEGEL ASST. EDITORS MIKE MARTS EDITOR
BATMAN CREATED BY BOB KANE
I can't recall his name.
As I stand in anticipation of the Detective...
...in preparation of eliminating his burdens...
...a simple name... a memory, like a lost taste, eludes me...
ALGOL IMPORTING CO

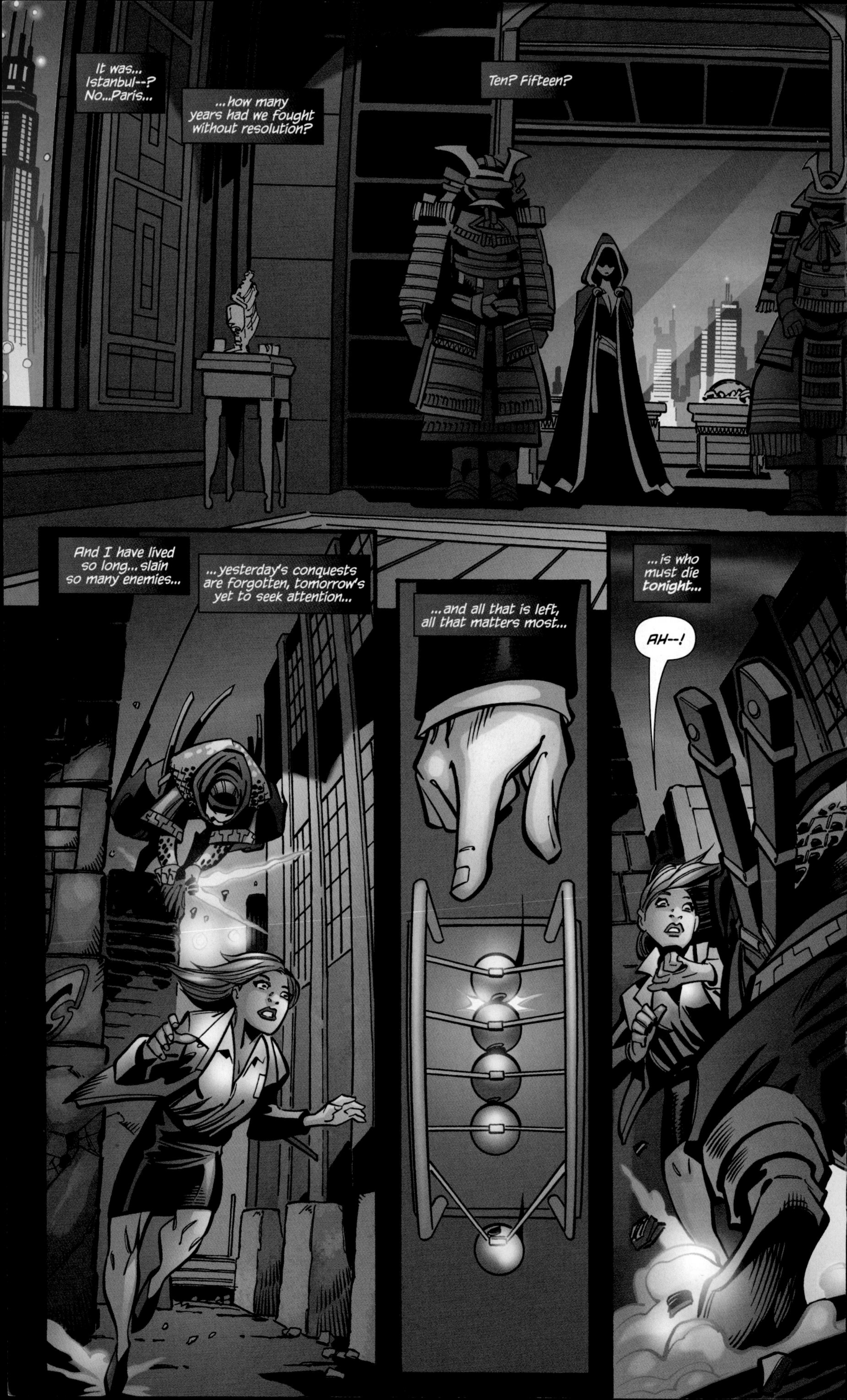
It was... Istanbul--? No...Paris...
...how many years had we fought without resolution?
Ten? Fifteen?
And I have lived so long... slain so many enemies...
...yesterday's conquests are forgotten, tomorrow's yet to seek attention...
...and all that is left, all that matters most...
...is who must die tonight...
AH--!

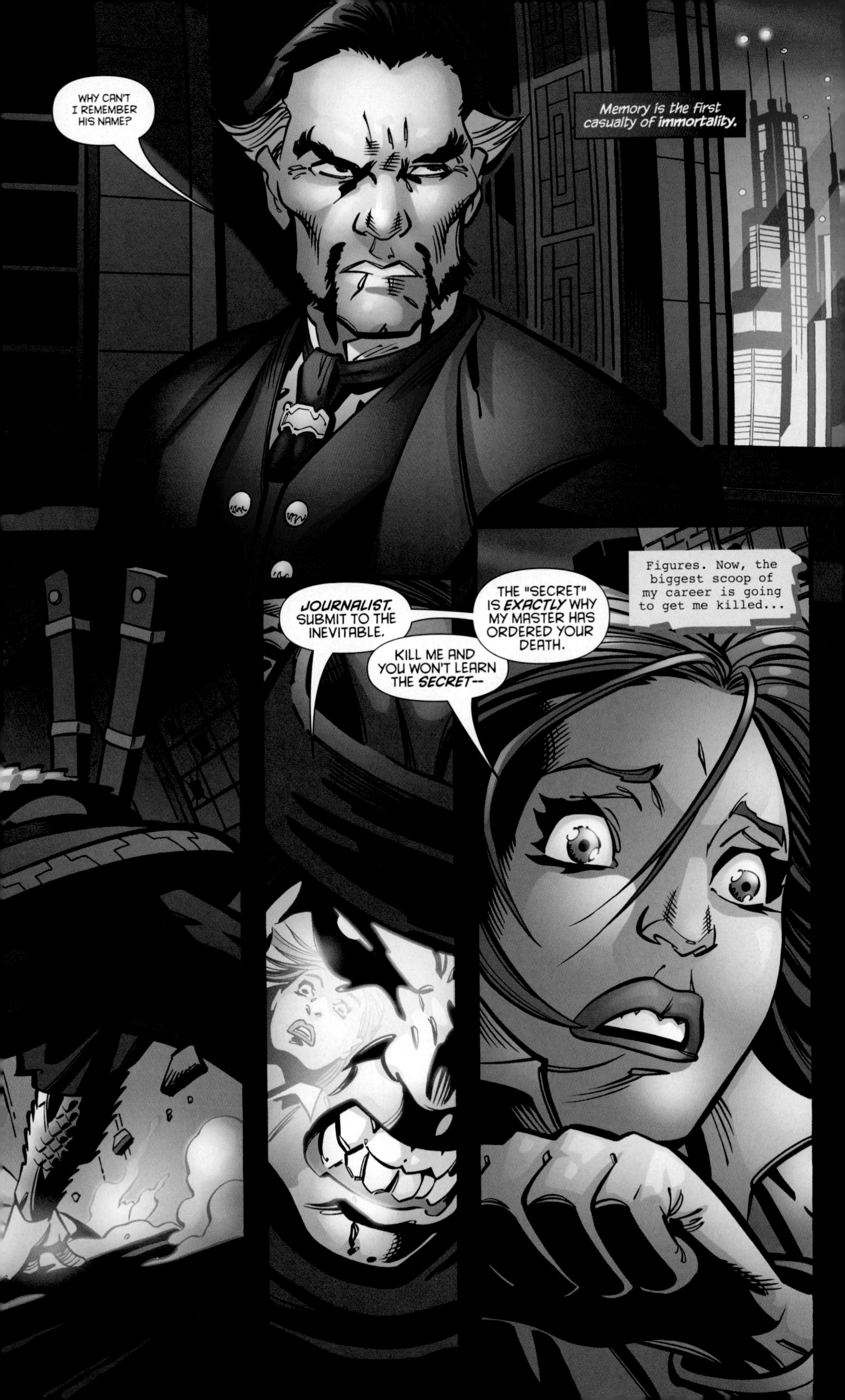
WHY CAN'T I REMEMBER HIS NAME?
Memory is the first casualty of immortality.
Figures. Now, the biggest scoop of my career is going to get me killed...
JOURNALIST. SUBMIT TO THE INEVITABLE.
KILL ME AND YOU WON'T LEARN THE SECRET--
THE "SECRET" IS EXACTLY WHY MY MASTER HAS ORDERED YOUR DEATH.

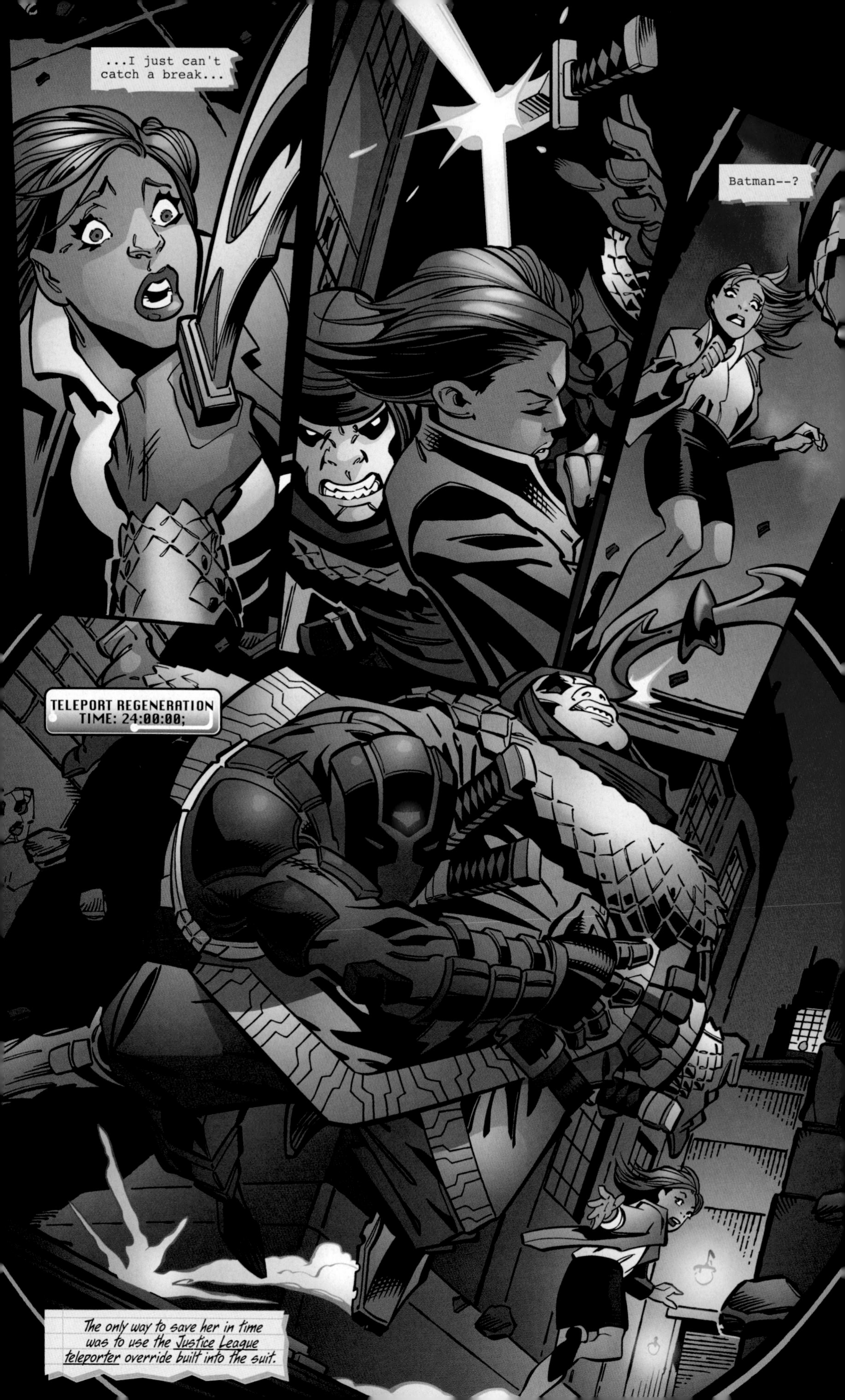
...I just can't catch a break...
Batman--?
TELEPORT REGENERATION TIME: 24:00:00;
The only way to save her in time was to use the Justice League teleporter override built into the suit.

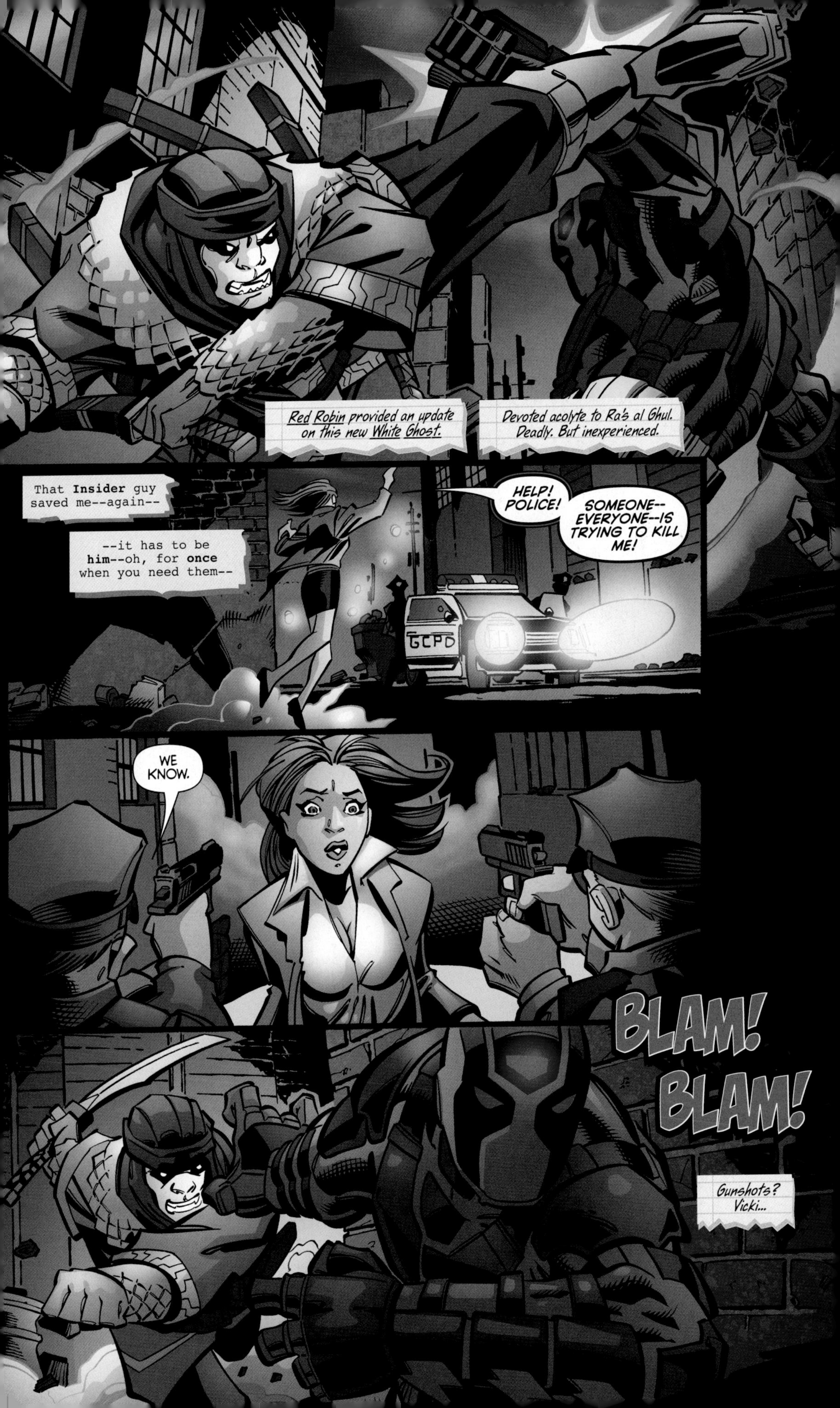
Red Robin provided an update on this new White Ghost.
Devoted acolyte to Ra's al Ghul. Deadly. But inexperienced.
That Insider guy saved me--again--
--it has to be him--oh, for once when you need them--
HELP! POLICE!
SOMEONE--EVERYONE--IS TRYING TO KILL ME!
GCPD
WE KNOW.
BLAM!
BLAM!
Gunshots? Vicki...

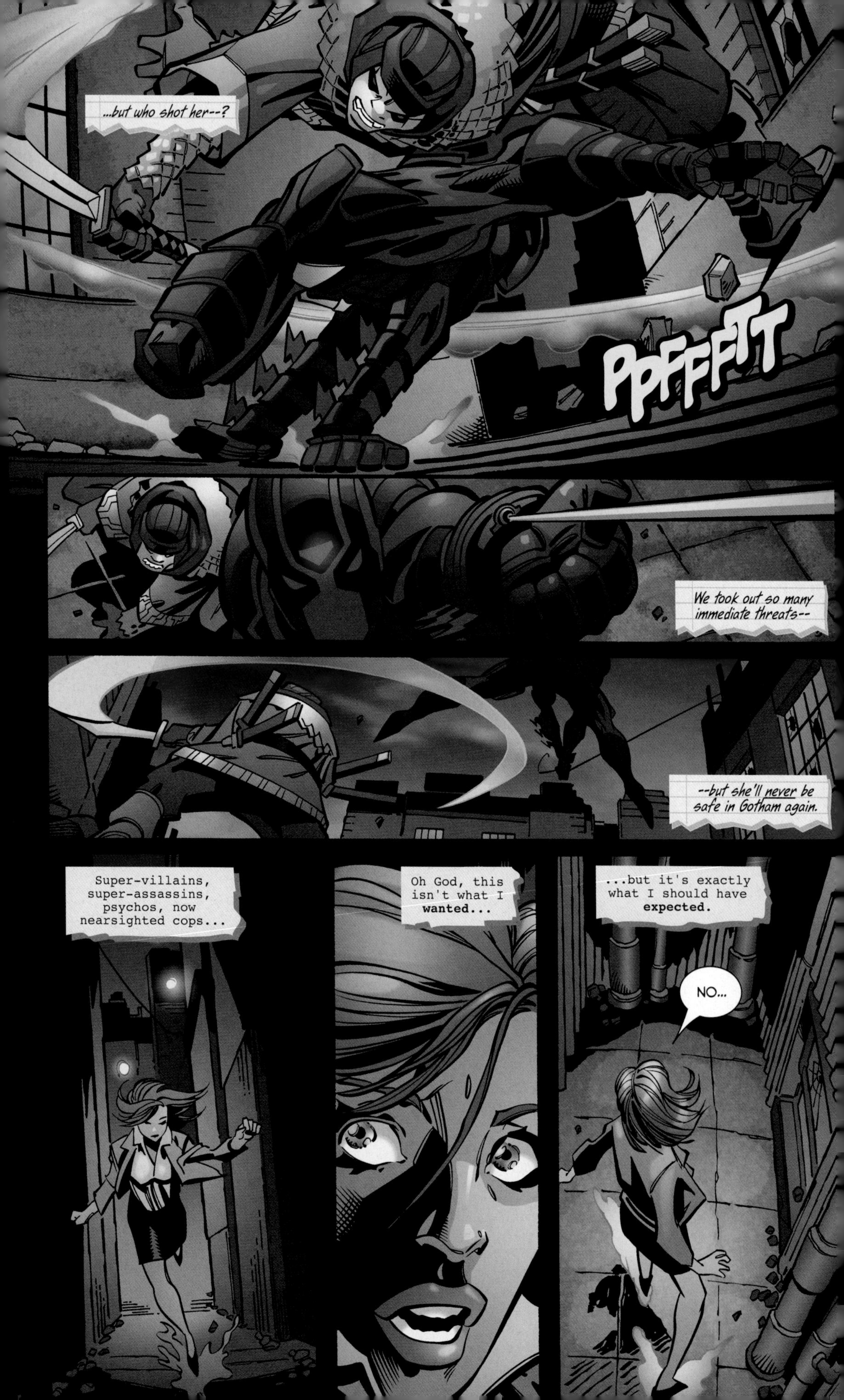
...but who shot her--?
PPFFFTT
We took out so many immediate threats--
--but she'll never be safe in Gotham again.
Super-villains, super-assassins, psychos, now nearsighted cops...
Oh God, this isn't what I wanted...
...but it's exactly what I should have expected.
NO...

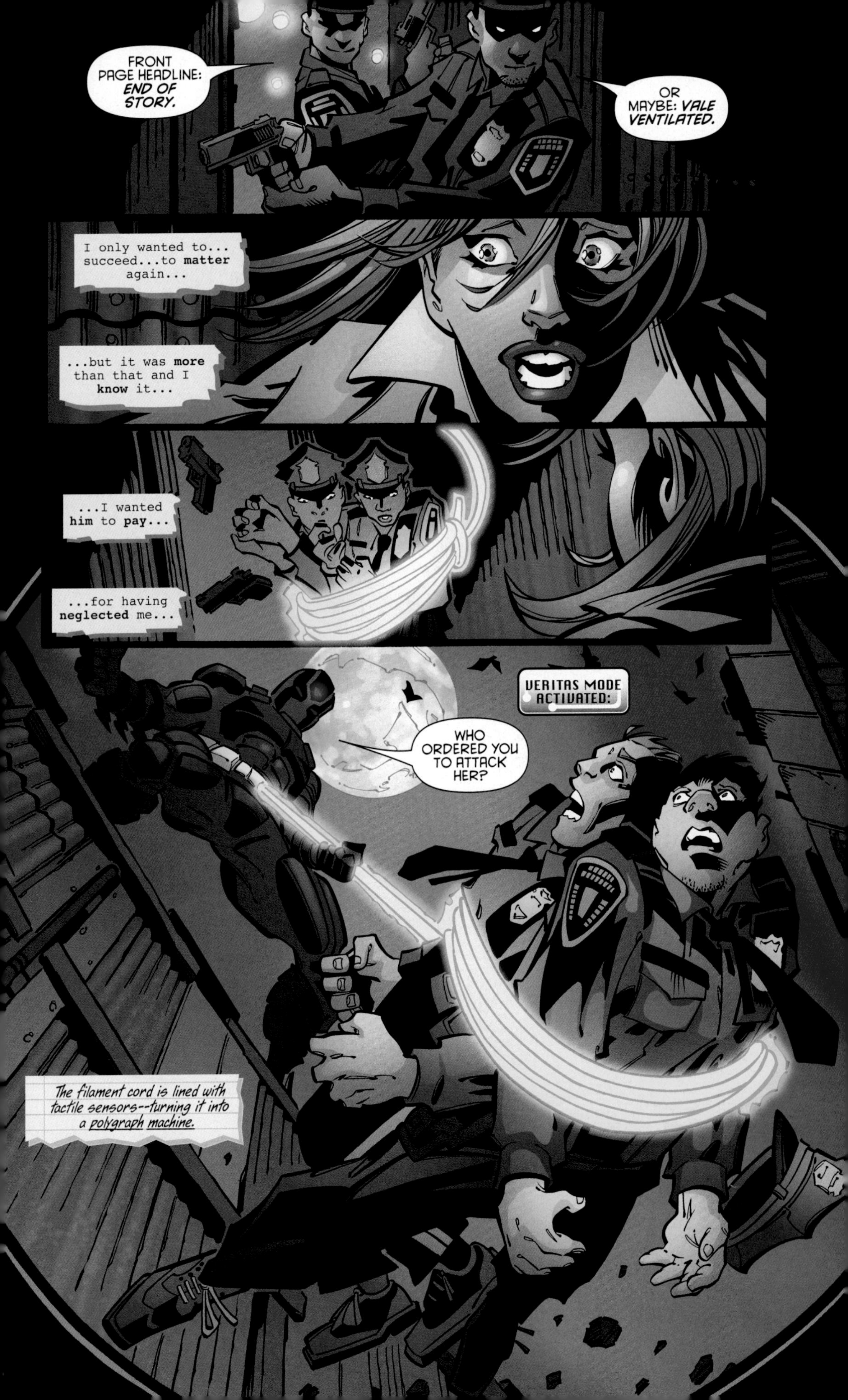
FRONT PAGE HEADLINE: END OF STORY.
OR MAYBE: VALE VENTILATED.
I only wanted to... succeed...to matter again...
...but it was more than that and I know it...
...I wanted him to pay...
...for having neglected me...
VERITAS MODE ACTIVATED:
WHO ORDERED YOU TO ATTACK HER?
The filament cord is lined with tactile sensors--turning it into a polygraph machine.

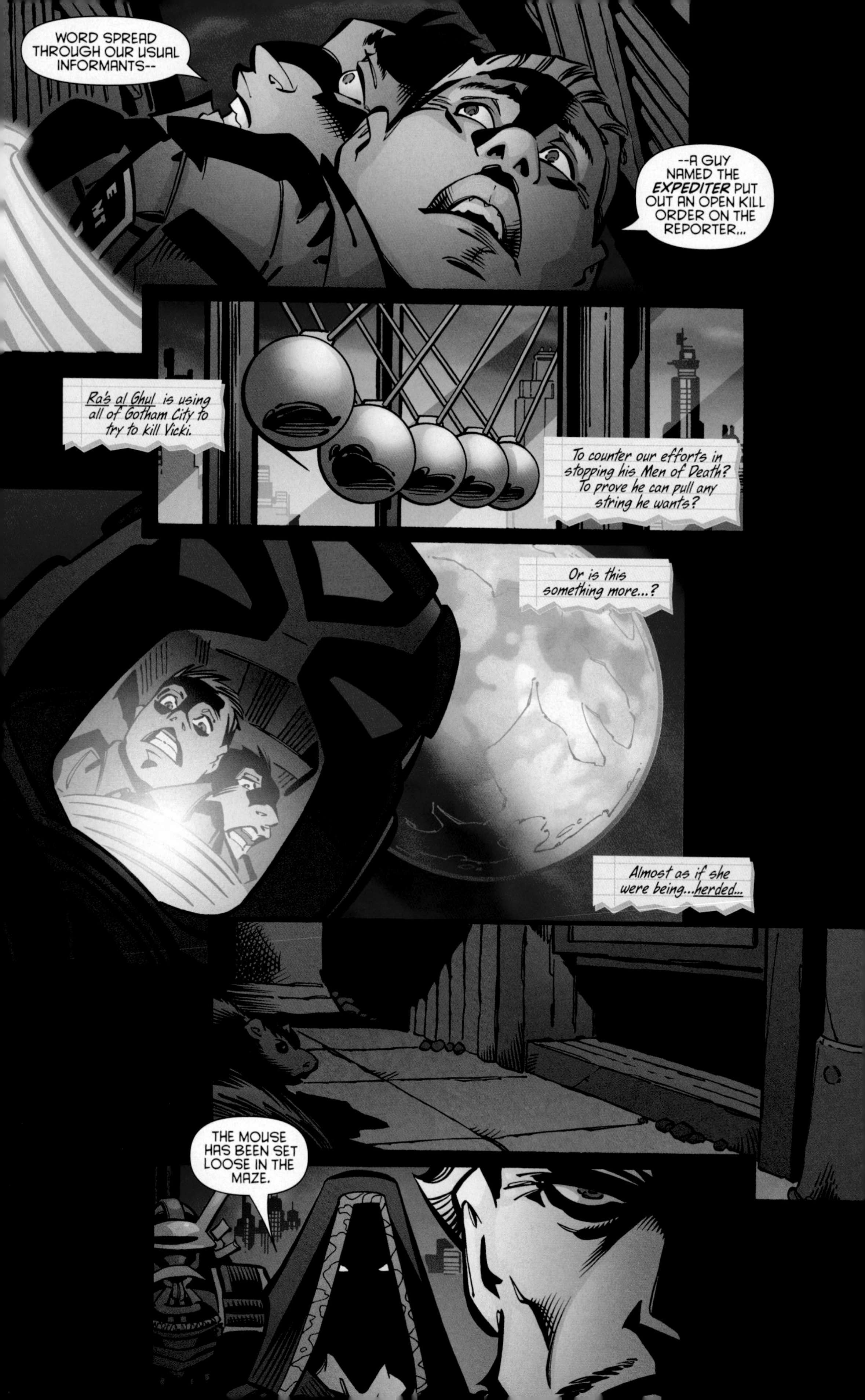
WORD SPREAD THROUGH OUR USUAL INFORMANTS--
--A GUY NAMED THE EXPEDITER PUT OUT AN OPEN KILL ORDER ON THE REPORTER...
Ra's al Ghul is using all of Gotham City to try to kill Vicki.
To counter our efforts in stopping his Men of Death? To prove he can pull any string he wants?
Or is this something more...?
Almost as if she were being...herded...
THE MOUSE HAS BEEN SET LOOSE IN THE MAZE.

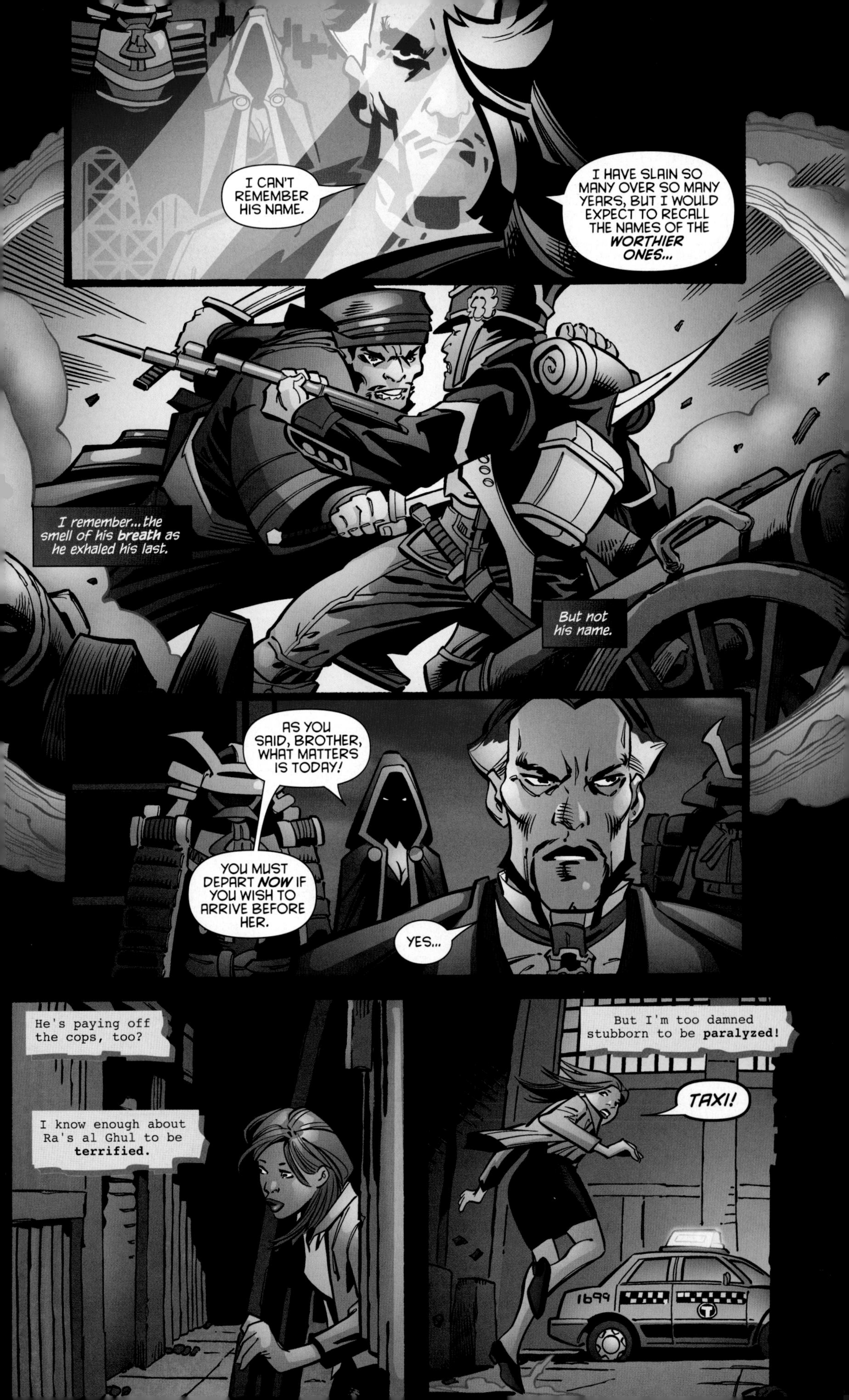
I CAN'T REMEMBER HIS NAME.
I HAVE SLAIN SO MANY OVER SO MANY YEARS, BUT I WOULD EXPECT TO RECALL THE NAMES OF THE WORTHIER ONES...
I remember... the smell of his breath as he exhaled his last.
But not his name.
AS YOU SAID, BROTHER, WHAT MATTERS IS TODAY!
YOU MUST DEPART NOW IF YOU WISH TO ARRIVE BEFORE HER.
YES...
He's paying off the cops, too?
I know enough about Ra's al Ghul to be terrified.
But I'm too damned stubborn to be paralyzed!
TAXI!
1699

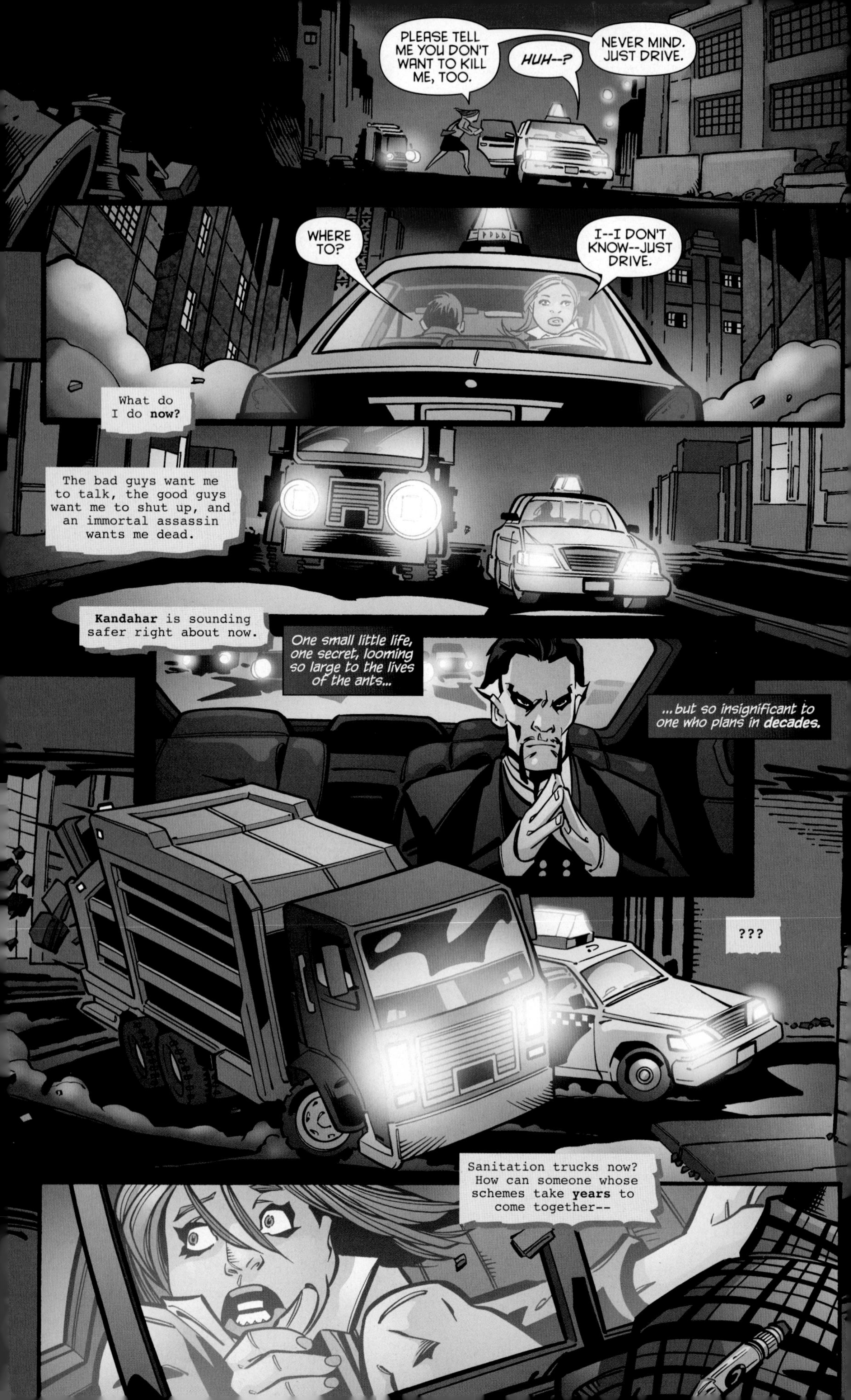

PLEASE TELL ME YOU DON'T WANT TO KILL ME, TOO.
HUH--?
NEVER MIND. JUST DRIVE.
WHERE TO?
I--I DON'T KNOW--JUST DRIVE.
What do I do now?
The bad guys want me to talk, the good guys want me to shut up, and an immortal assassin wants me dead.
Kandahar is sounding safer right about now.
One small little life, one secret, looming so large to the lives of the ants...
...but so insignificant to one who plans in decades.
???
Sanitation trucks now? How can someone whose schemes take years to come together--

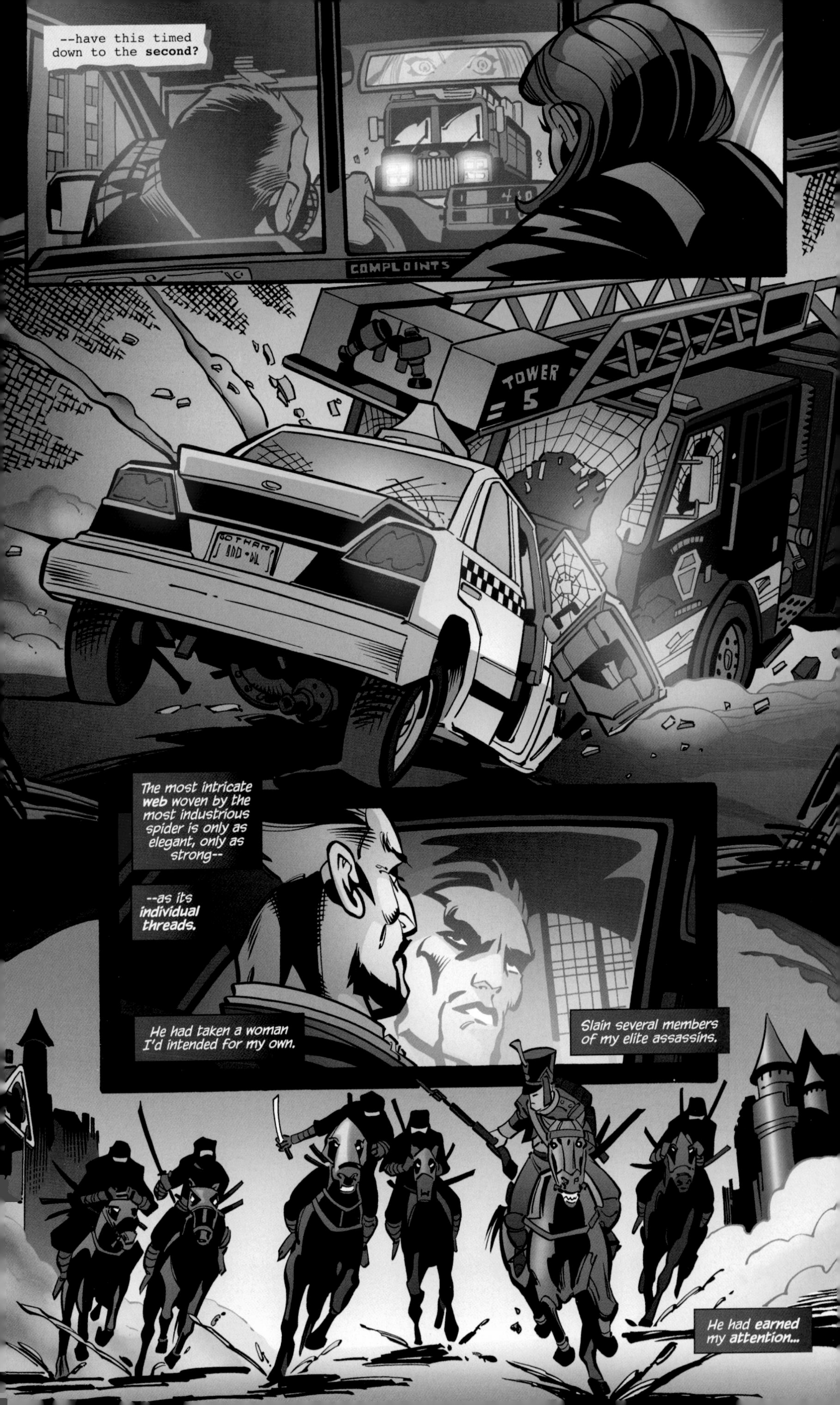
--have this timed down to the **second?**
COMPLOINTS
TOWER 5
GOTHAM
The most intricate **web** woven by the most industrious spider is only as elegant, only as strong--
--as its **individual threads.**
He had taken a woman I'd intended for my own.
Slain several members of my elite assassins.
He had earned my **attention...**

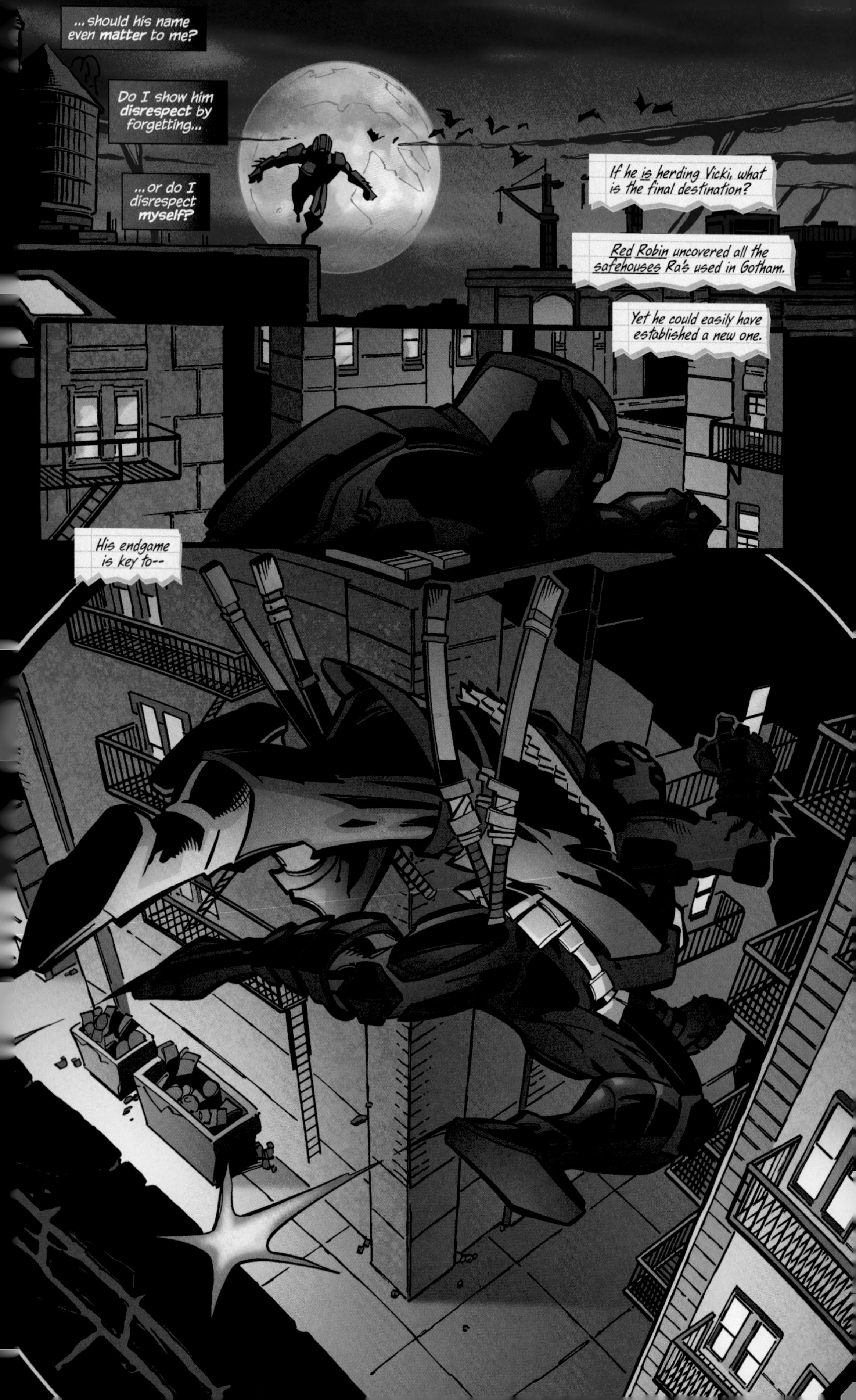
...should his name even matter to me?
Do I show him disrespect by forgetting...
...or do I disrespect myself?
If he is herding Vicki, what is the final destination?
Red Robin uncovered all the safehouses Ra's used in Gotham.
Yet he could easily have established a new one.
His endgame is key to--

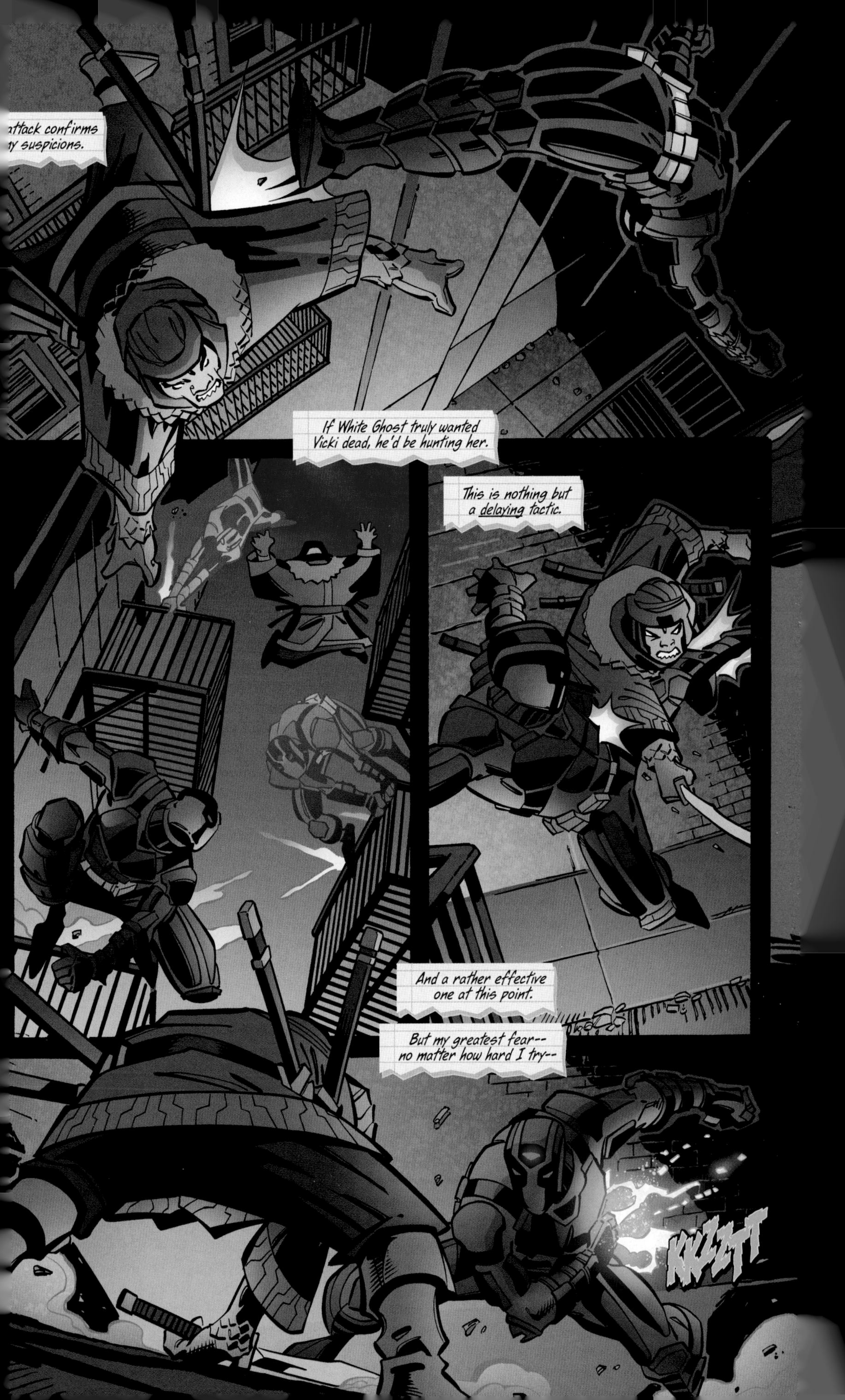
attack confirms
my suspicions.
If White Ghost truly wanted Vicki dead, he'd be hunting her.
This is nothing but a delaying tactic.
And a rather effective one at this point.
But my greatest fear-- no matter how hard I try--
KKZZTT

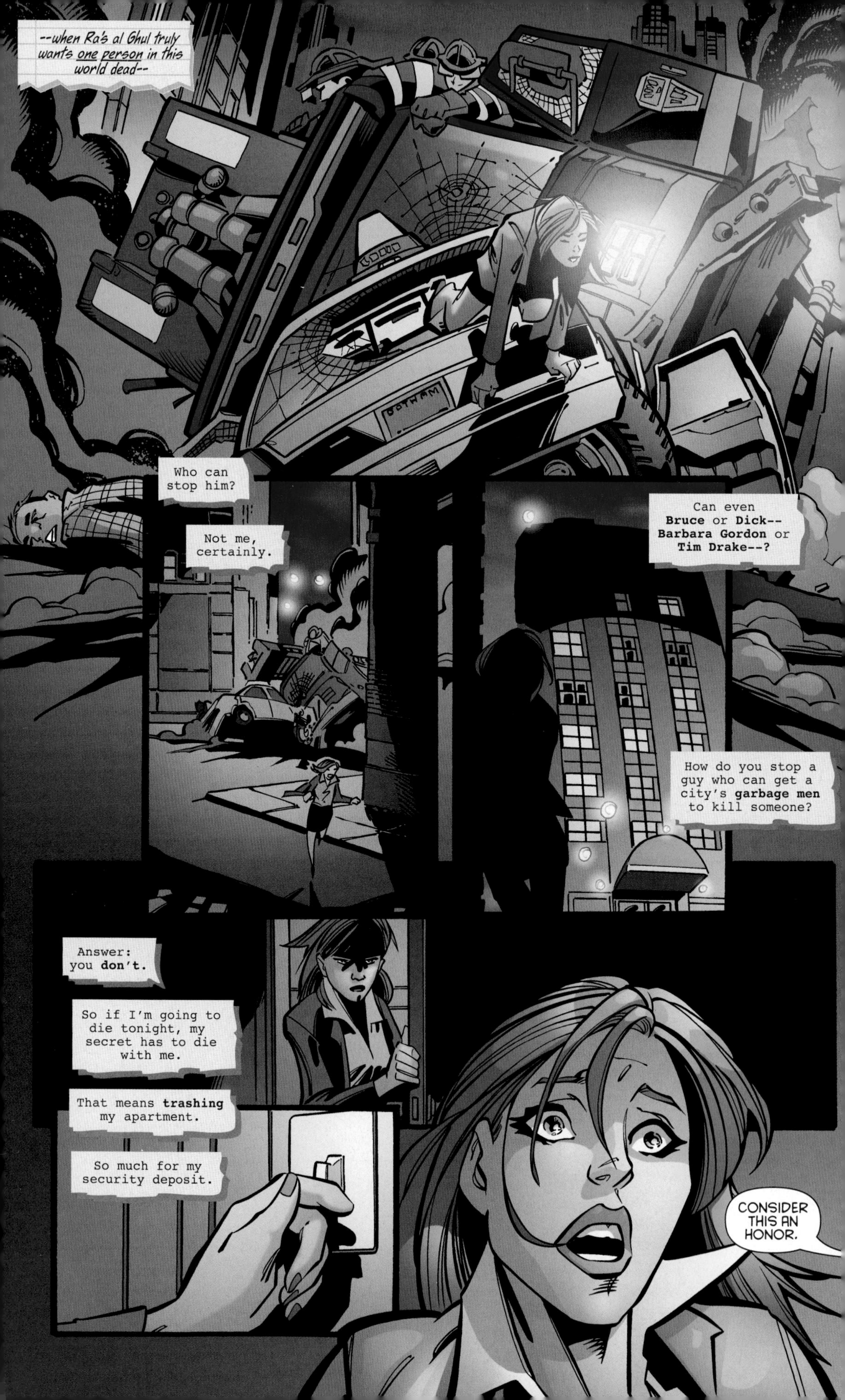
--when Ra's al Ghul truly wants one person in this world dead--
Who can stop him?
Not me, certainly.
Can even Bruce or Dick-- Barbara Gordon or Tim Drake--?
How do you stop a guy who can get a city's garbage men to kill someone?
Answer: you don't.
So if I'm going to die tonight, my secret has to die with me.
That means trashing my apartment.
So much for my security deposit.
CONSIDER THIS AN HONOR.

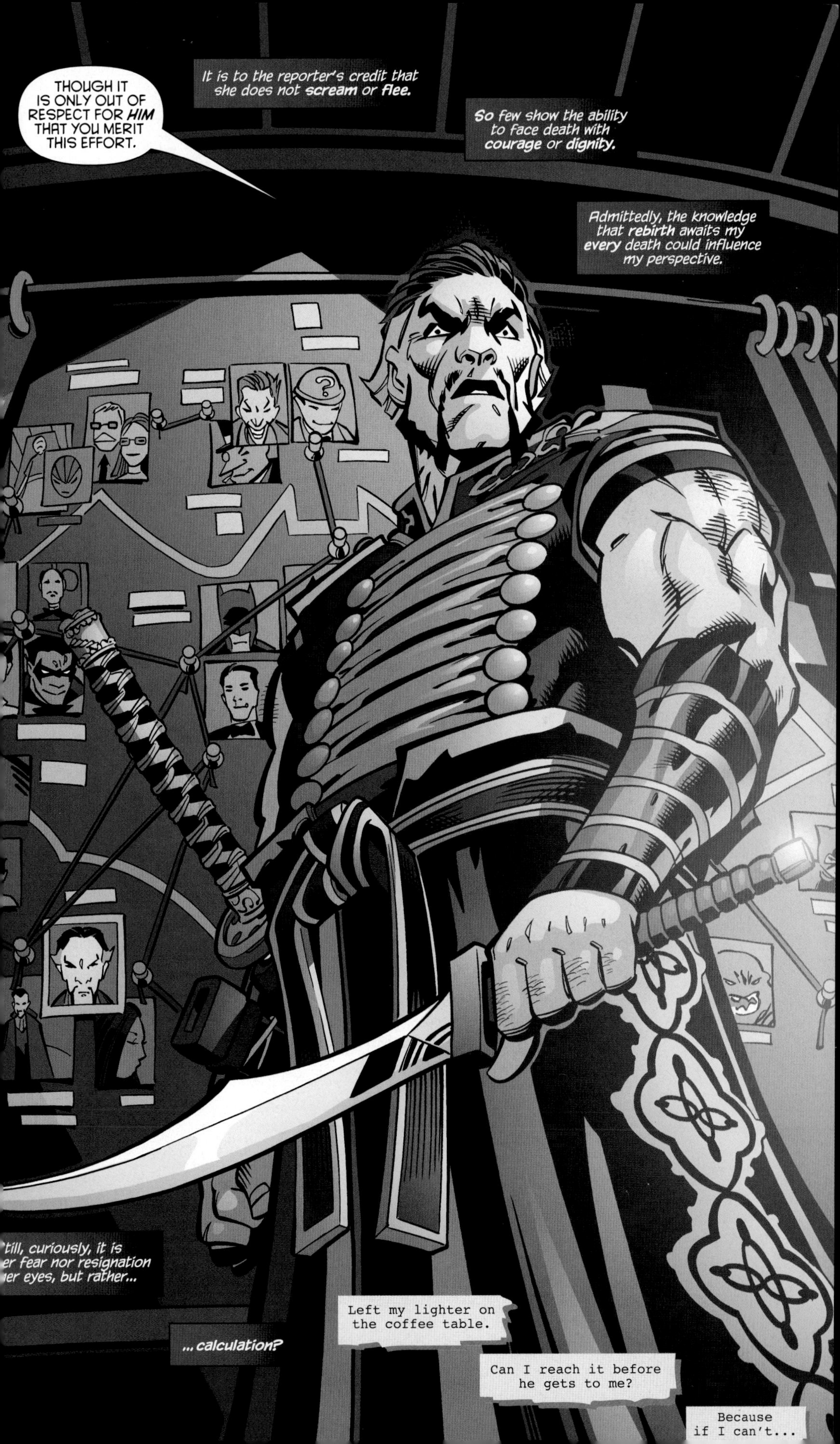
THOUGH IT IS ONLY OUT OF RESPECT FOR HIM THAT YOU MERIT THIS EFFORT.
It is to the reporter's credit that she does not scream or flee.
So few show the ability to face death with courage or dignity.
Admittedly, the knowledge that rebirth awaits my every death could influence my perspective.
till, curiously, it is
er fear nor resignation
er eyes, but rather...
...calculation?
Left my lighter on the coffee table.
Can I reach it before he gets to me?
Because if I can't...

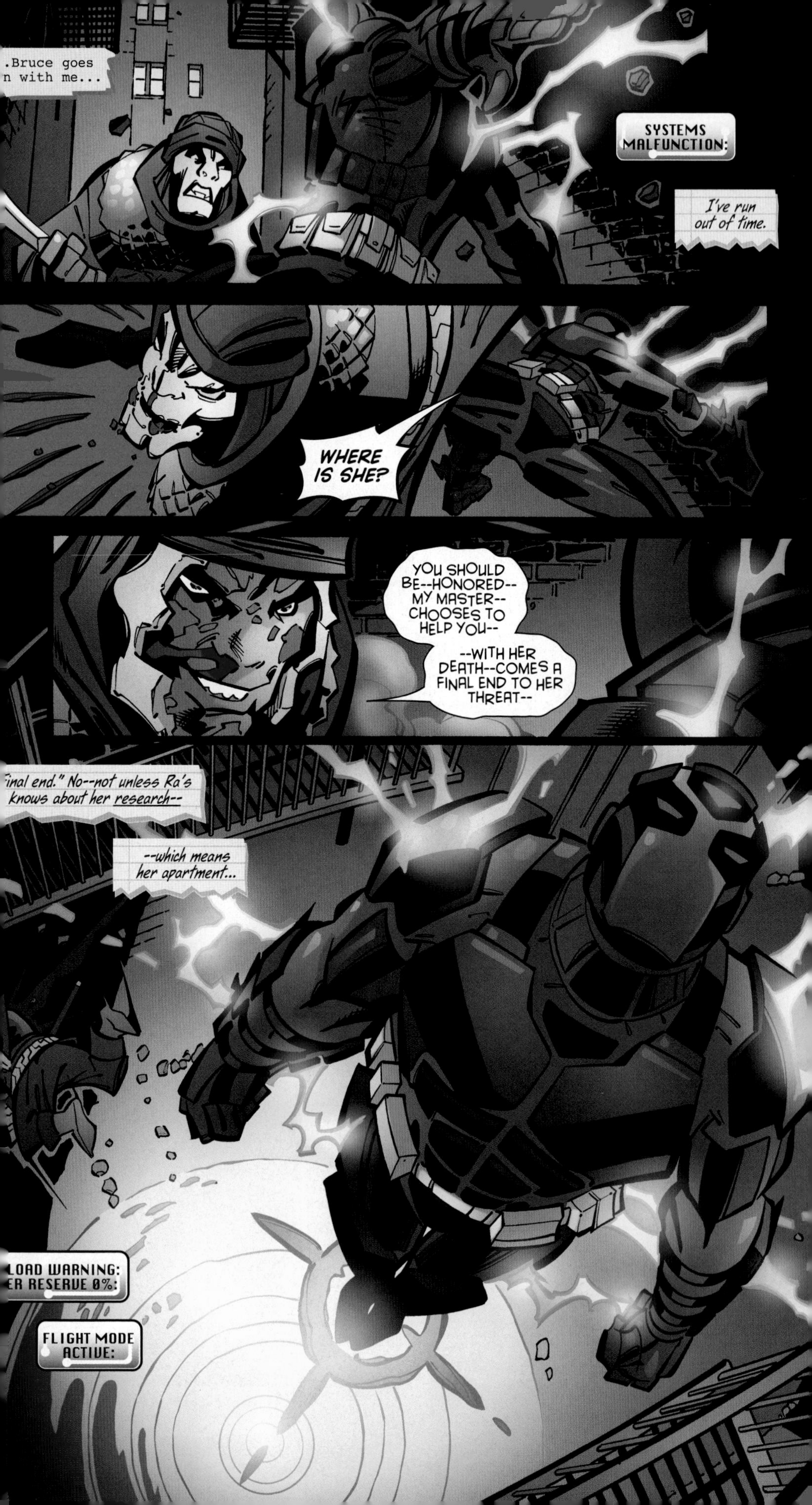
.Bruce goes
n with me...
SYSTEMS MALFUNCTION:
I've run out of time.
WHERE IS SHE?
YOU SHOULD BE--HONORED--MY MASTER--CHOOSES TO HELP YOU--
--WITH HER DEATH--COMES A FINAL END TO HER THREAT--
Final end." No--not unless Ra's knows about her research--
--which means her apartment...
LOAD WARNING:
ER RESERVE 0%:
FLIGHT MODE ACTIVE:

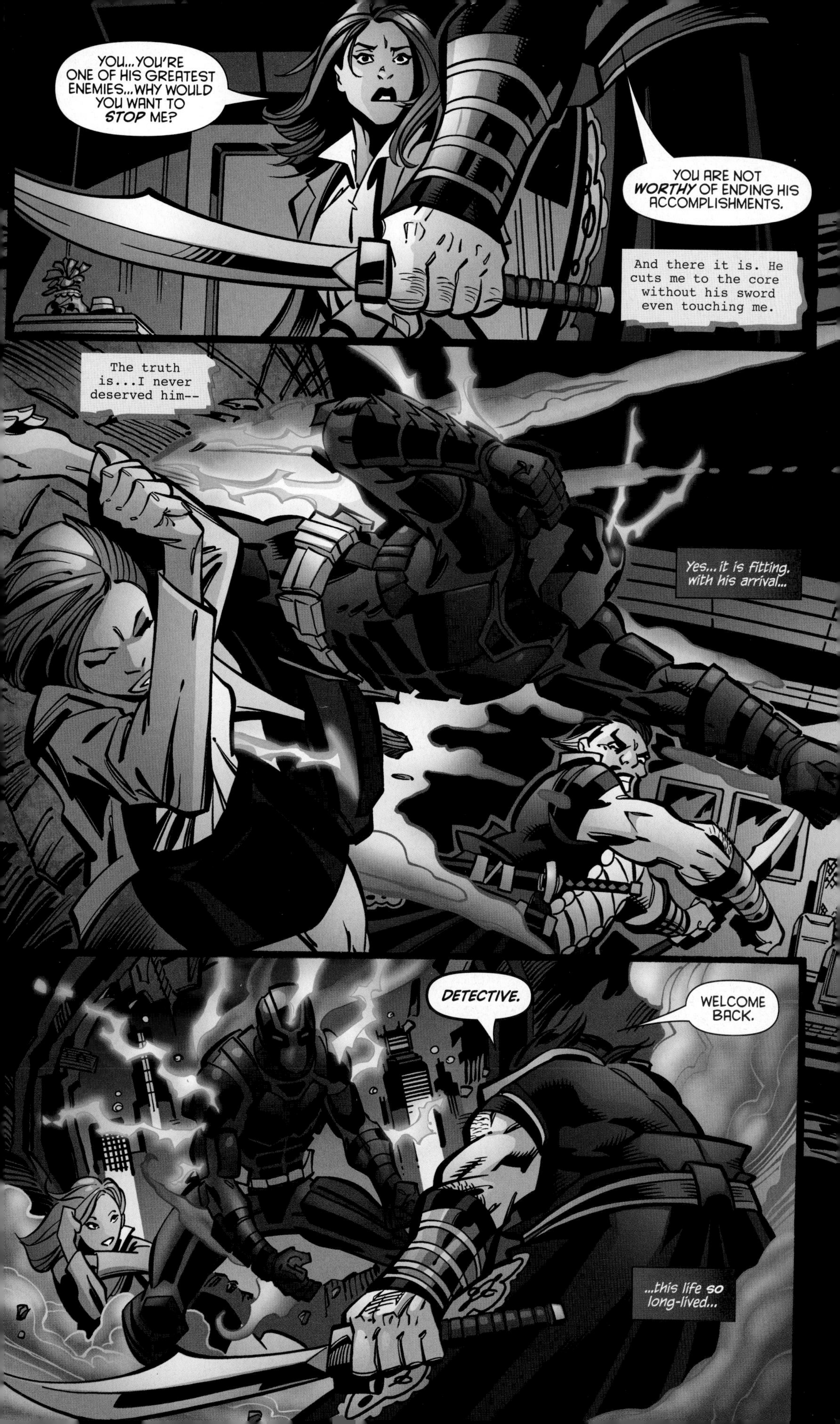
YOU...YOU'RE ONE OF HIS GREATEST ENEMIES...WHY WOULD YOU WANT TO *STOP* ME?
YOU ARE NOT *WORTHY* OF ENDING HIS ACCOMPLISHMENTS.
And there it is. He cuts me to the core without his sword even touching me.
The truth is...I never deserved him--
Yes...it is fitting, with his arrival...
DETECTIVE.
WELCOME BACK.
*...this life **so** long-lived...*

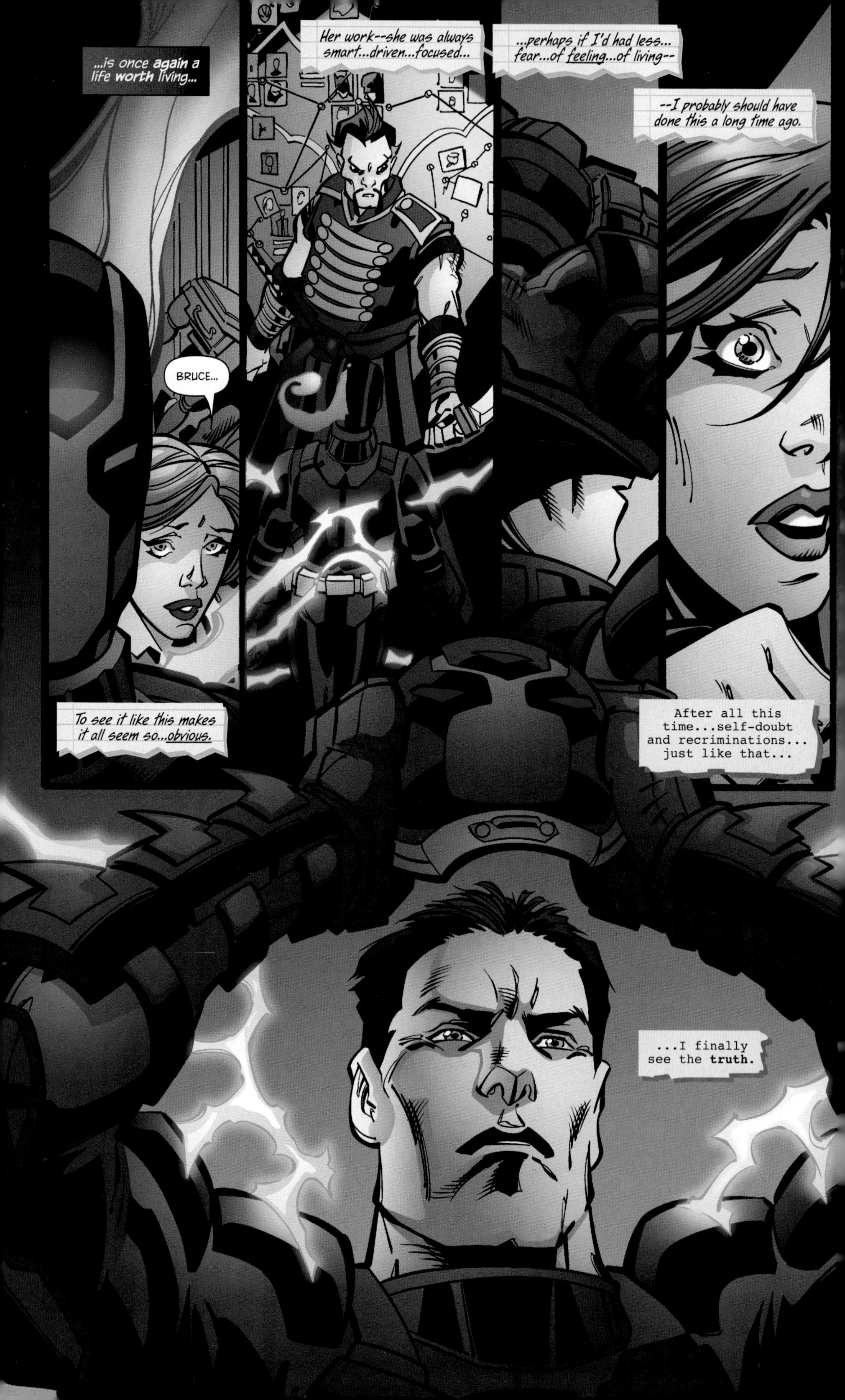
...is once again a life worth living...
Her work--she was always smart...driven...focused...
...perhaps if I'd had less... fear...of feeling...of living--
--I probably should have done this a long time ago.
BRUCE...
To see it like this makes it all seem so...obvious.
After all this time...self-doubt and recriminations... just like that...
...I finally see the truth.

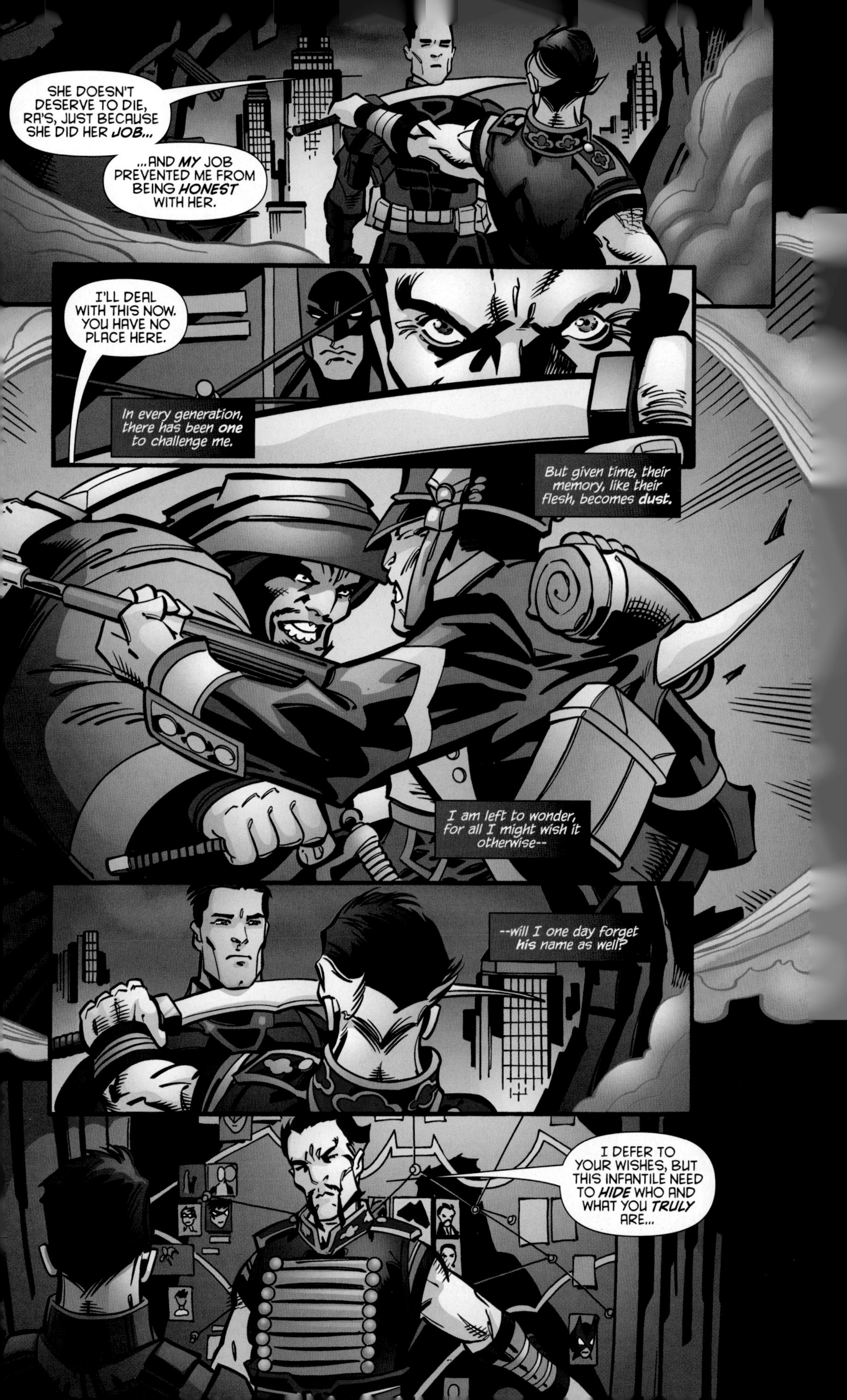
SHE DOESN'T DESERVE TO DIE, RA'S, JUST BECAUSE SHE DID HER JOB...
...AND MY JOB PREVENTED ME FROM BEING HONEST WITH HER.
I'LL DEAL WITH THIS NOW. YOU HAVE NO PLACE HERE.
In every generation, there has been one to challenge me.
But given time, their memory, like their flesh, becomes dust.
I am left to wonder, for all I might wish it otherwise--
--will I one day forget his name as well?
I DEFER TO YOUR WISHES, BUT THIS INFANTILE NEED TO HIDE WHO AND WHAT YOU TRULY ARE...

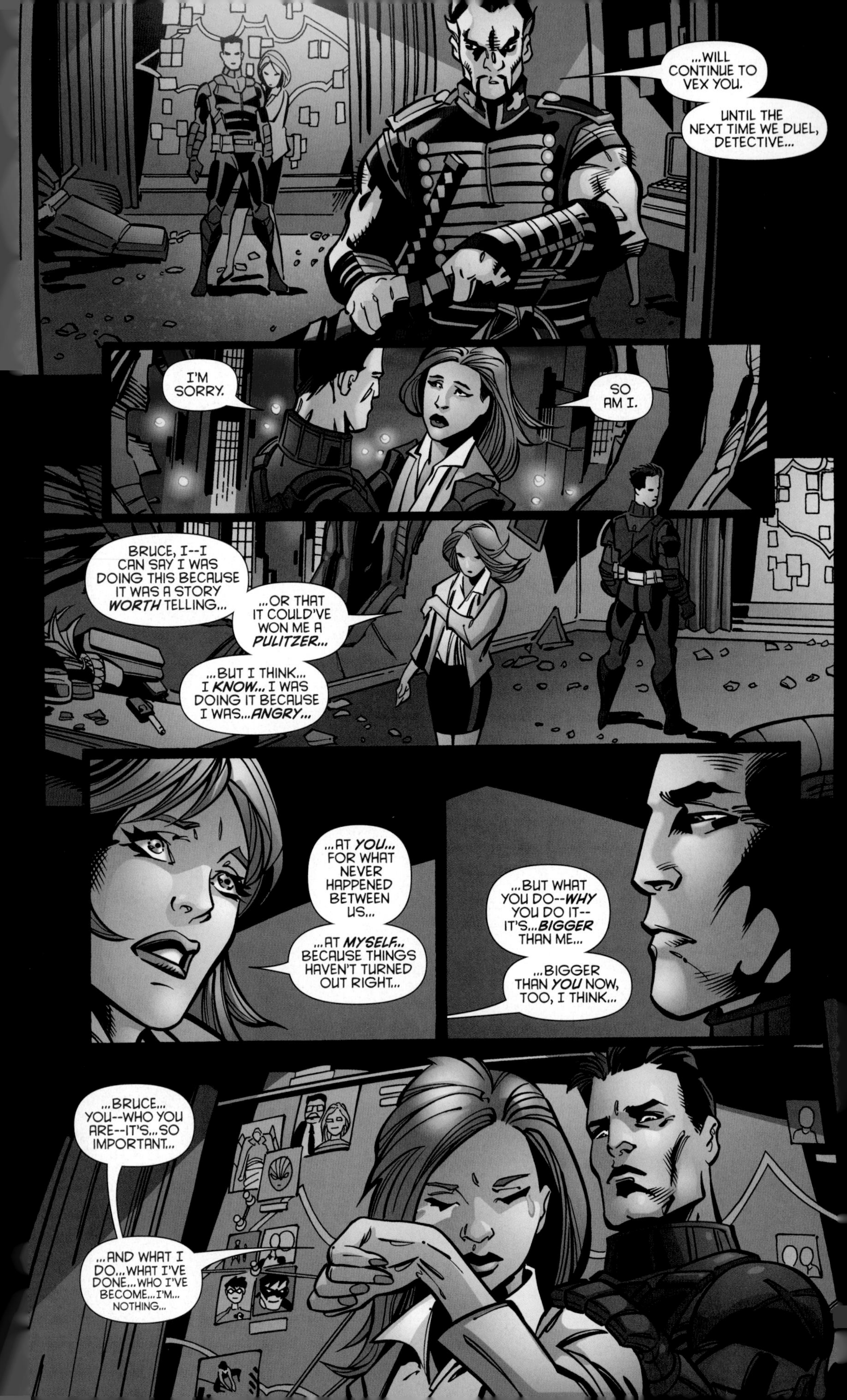
...WILL CONTINUE TO VEX YOU.
UNTIL THE NEXT TIME WE DUEL, DETECTIVE...
I'M SORRY.
SO AM I.
BRUCE, I--I CAN SAY I WAS DOING THIS BECAUSE IT WAS A STORY WORTH TELLING...
...OR THAT IT COULD'VE WON ME A PULITZER...
...BUT I THINK... I KNOW... I WAS DOING IT BECAUSE I WAS...ANGRY...
...AT YOU... FOR WHAT NEVER HAPPENED BETWEEN US...
...AT MYSELF... BECAUSE THINGS HAVEN'T TURNED OUT RIGHT...
...BUT WHAT YOU DO--WHY YOU DO IT--IT'S...BIGGER THAN ME...
...BIGGER THAN YOU NOW, TOO, I THINK...
...BRUCE... YOU--WHO YOU ARE--IT'S...SO IMPORTANT...
...AND WHAT I DO...WHAT I'VE DONE...WHO I'VE BECOME...I'M... NOTHING...

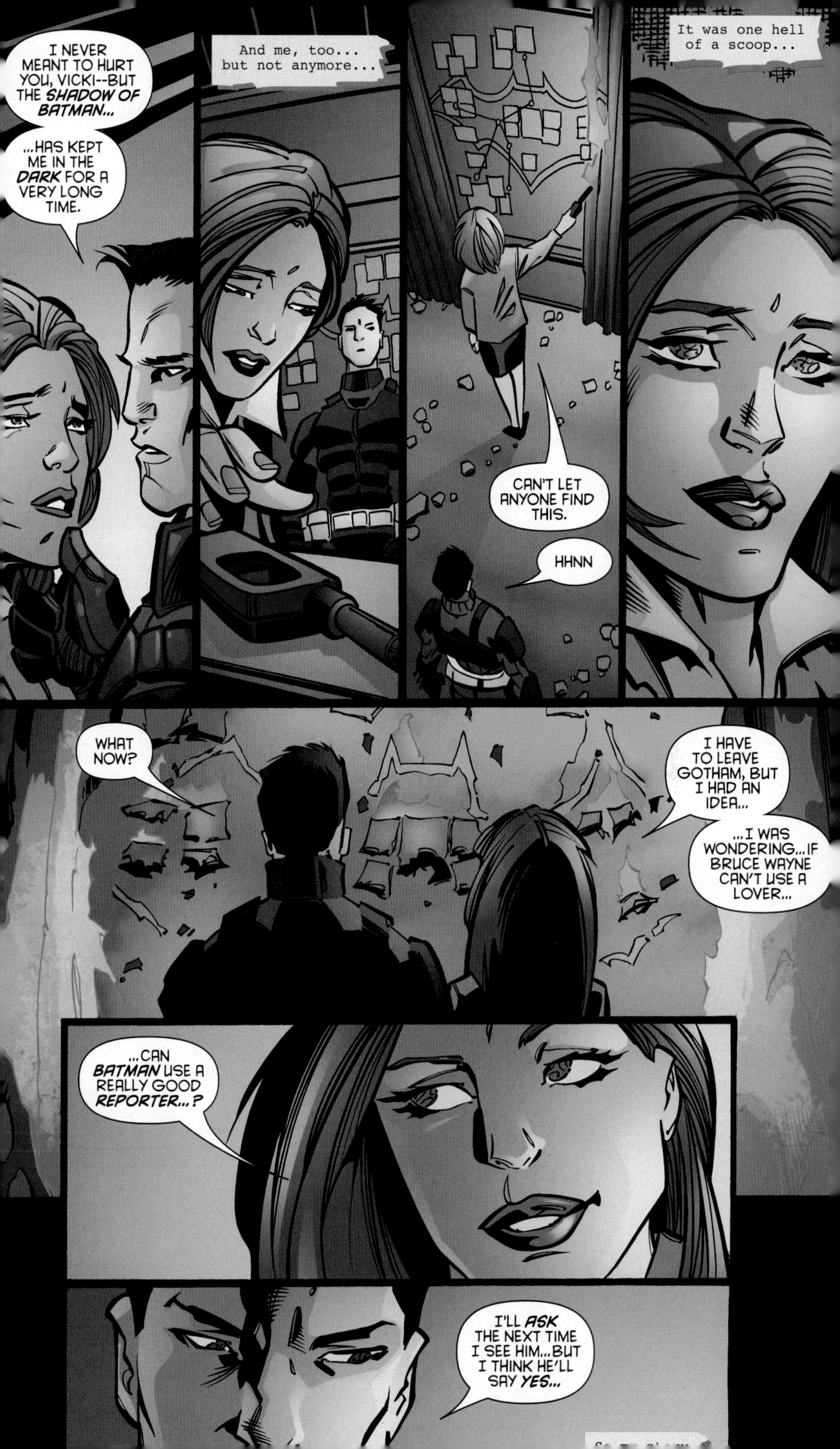
I NEVER MEANT TO HURT YOU, VICKI--BUT THE SHADOW OF BATMAN...
...HAS KEPT ME IN THE DARK FOR A VERY LONG TIME.
And me, too... but not anymore...
CAN'T LET ANYONE FIND THIS.
HHNN
It was one hell of a scoop...
WHAT NOW?
I HAVE TO LEAVE GOTHAM, BUT I HAD AN IDEA...
...I WAS WONDERING...IF BRUCE WAYNE CAN'T USE A LOVER...
...CAN BATMAN USE A REALLY GOOD REPORTER...?
I'LL ASK THE NEXT TIME I SEE HIM...BUT I THINK HE'LL SAY YES...

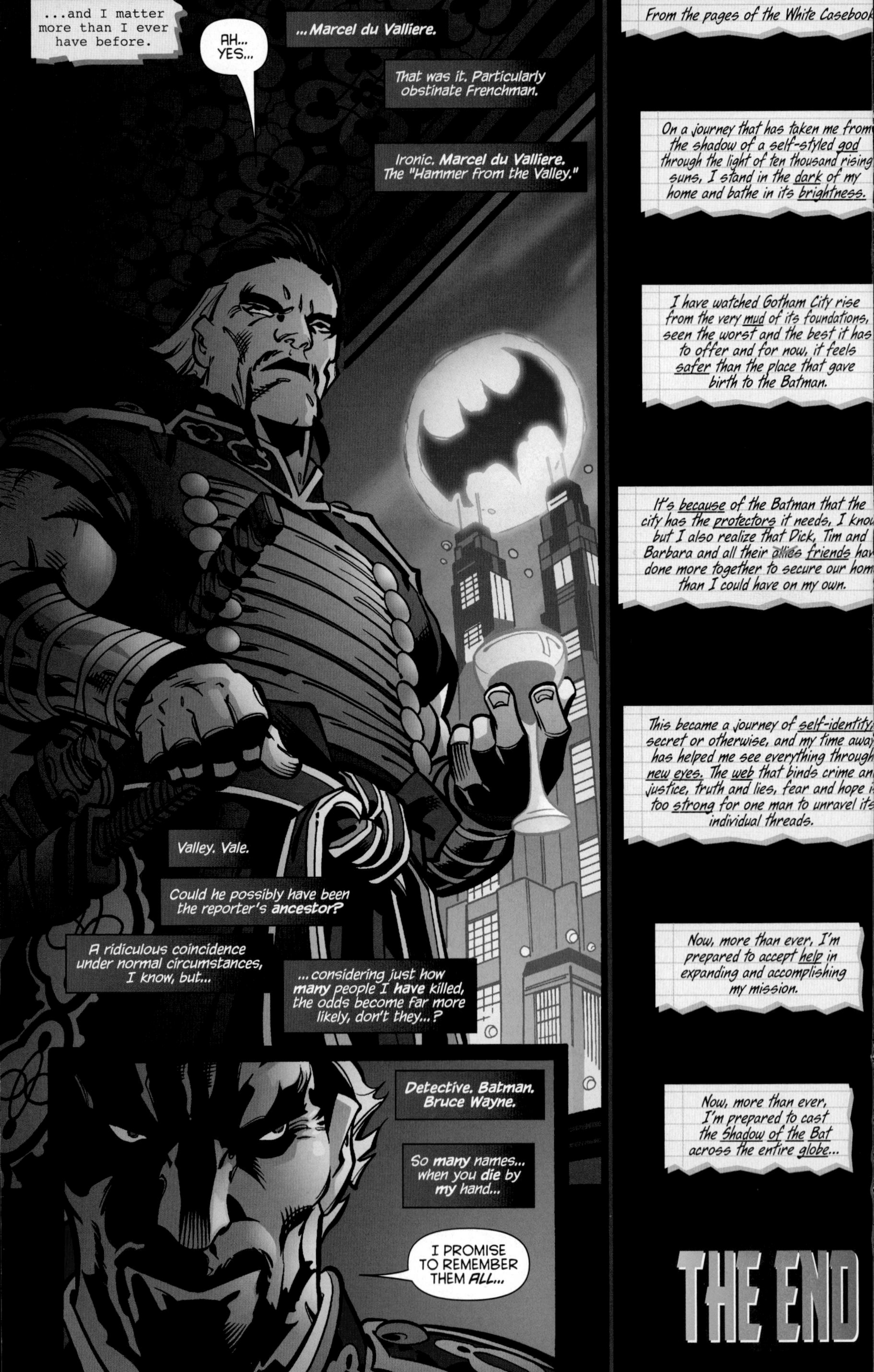

...and I matter more than I ever have before.

AH... YES...

...Marcel du Valliere.

That was it. Particularly obstinate Frenchman.

Ironic. **Marcel du Valliere.** The "Hammer from the Valley."

Valley. Vale.

Could he possibly have been the reporter's **ancestor?**

A ridiculous coincidence under normal circumstances, I know, but...

...considering just how **many** people I **have** killed, the odds become far more likely, don't they...?

Detective. Batman. Bruce Wayne.

So **many** names... when you **die** by **my** hand...

I PROMISE TO REMEMBER THEM **ALL**...

From the pages of the White Casebook

On a journey that has taken me from the shadow of a self-styled god through the light of ten thousand rising suns, I stand in the dark of my home and bathe in its brightness.

I have watched Gotham City rise from the very mud of its foundations, seen the worst and the best it has to offer and for now, it feels safer than the place that gave birth to the Batman.

It's because of the Batman that the city has the protectors it needs, I know, but I also realize that Dick, Tim and Barbara and all their allies friends have done more together to secure our home than I could have on my own.

This became a journey of self-identity, secret or otherwise, and my time away has helped me see everything through new eyes. The web that binds crime and justice, truth and lies, fear and hope is too strong for one man to unravel its individual threads.

Now, more than ever, I'm prepared to accept help in expanding and accomplishing my mission.

Now, more than ever, I'm prepared to cast the Shadow of the Bat across the entire globe...

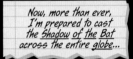

THE END

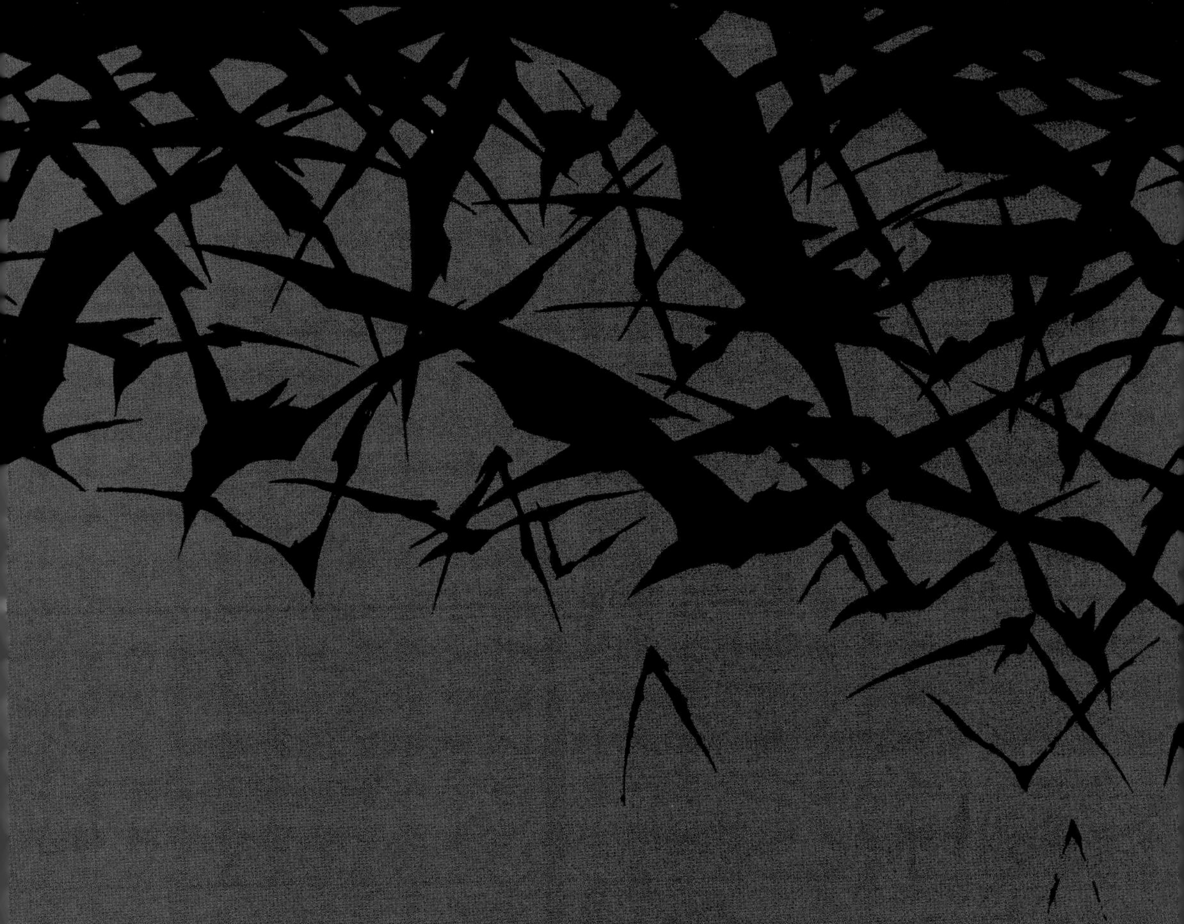

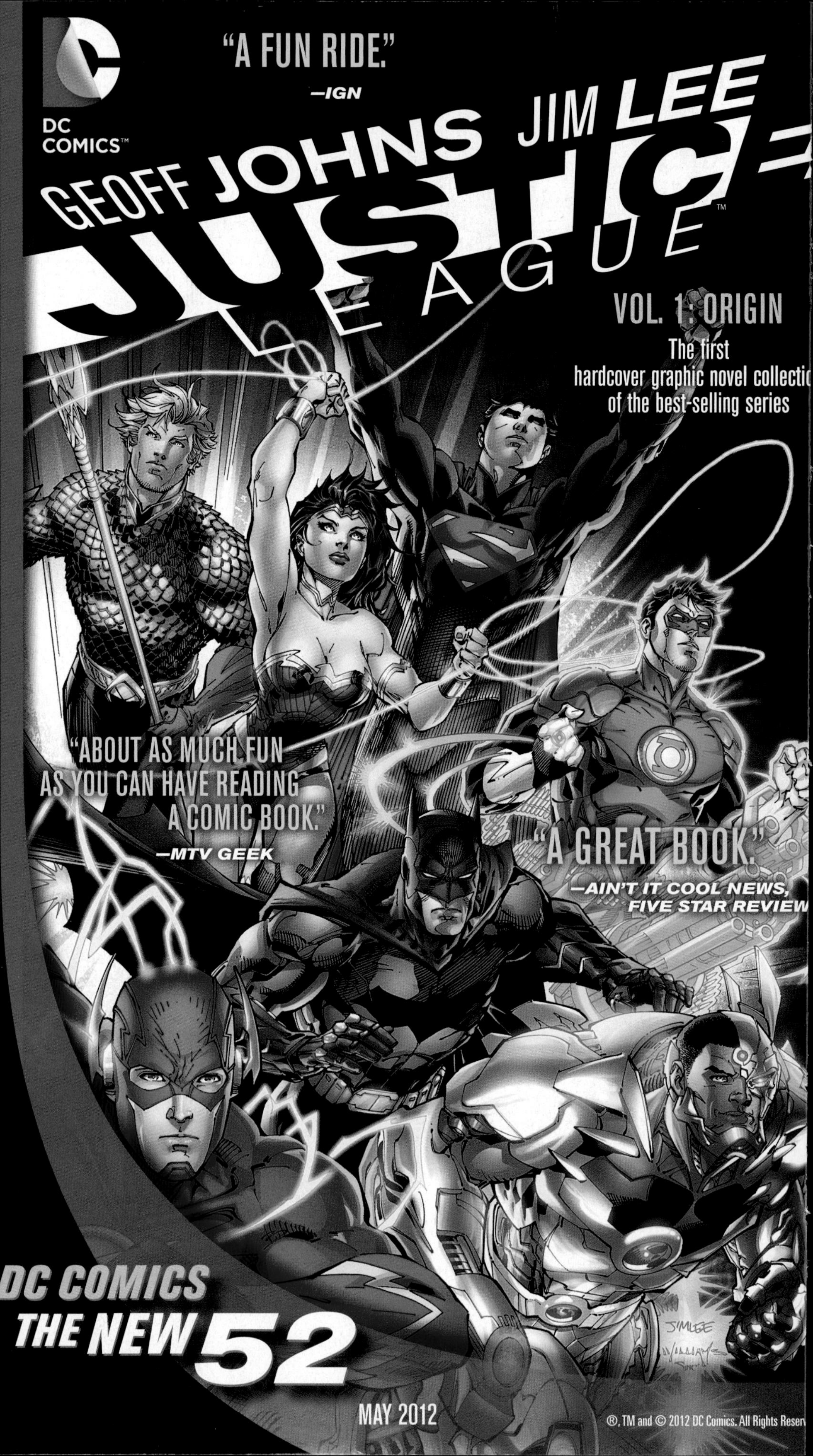
DC COMICS™
"A FUN RIDE."
—IGN
GEOFF JOHNS JIM LEE
JUSTICE LEAGUE™
VOL. 1: ORIGIN
The first
hardcover graphic novel collecti
of the best-selling series
"ABOUT AS MUCH FUN
AS YOU CAN HAVE READING
A COMIC BOOK."
—MTV GEEK
"A GREAT BOOK."
—AIN'T IT COOL NEWS,
FIVE STAR REVIEW
DC COMICS
THE NEW 52
MAY 2012
®, TM and © 2012 DC Comics. All Rights Reserv

DC COMICS-THE NEW 52!
GRAPHIC NOVELS RELEASE SCHEDULE

MAY
- ☐ Animal Man Vol 1: The Hunt
- ☐ Batman Vol 1: The Court of Owls
- ☐ Catwoman Vol 1: The Game
- ☐ Green Arrow Vol 1: The Midas Touch
- ☐ Green Lantern Vol 1: Sinestro
- ☐ Justice League International Vol 1: The Signal Masters
- ☐ Justice League Vol 1: Origin
- ☐ Stormwatch Vol 1: The Dark Side
- ☐ Wonder Woman Vol 1: Blood

JUNE
- ☐ Batman: Detective Comics Vol 1: Faces of Death
- ☐ Batwoman Vol 1: Hydrology
- ☐ Frankenstein Agent of S.H.A.D.E. Vol 1: War of The Monsters
- ☐ Legion of Super-Heroes Vol 1: Hostile World
- ☐ Mister Terrific Vol 1: Mind Games
- ☐ Red Lanterns Vol 1: Blood and Rage
- ☐ Static Shock Vol 1: Supercharged

JULY
- ☐ Batgirl Vol 1: The Darkest Reflection
- ☐ Batwing Vol 1: The Lost Kingdom
- ☐ Batman and Robin Vol 1: Born to Kill
- ☐ Demon Knights Vol 1: Seven Against the Dark
- ☐ Grifter Vol 1: Most Wanted
- ☐ Men of War Vol 1: Uneasy Company
- ☐ Suicide Squad Vol 1: Kicked in the Teeth

AUGUST
- ☐ Deathstroke Vol 1: Legacy
- ☐ Hawk and Dove Vol 1: First Strikes
- ☐ O.M.A.C. Vol 1: Omactivate!
- ☐ Resurrection Man Vol 1: Dead Again
- ☐ Superman: Action Comics Vol 1: Superman and The Men of Steel
- ☐ Superboy Vol 1: Incubation
- ☐ Swamp Thing Vol 1: Raise Them Bones

SEPTEMBER
- ☐ Aquaman Vol 1: The Trench
- ☐ Birds of Prey Vol 1: Trouble in Mind
- ☐ The Fury of Firestorm: The Nuclear Men Vol 1: God Particle
- ☐ Green Lantern Corps Vol 1: Fearsome
- ☐ Legion Lost Vol 1: Run from Tomorrow
- ☐ Teen Titans Vol 1: It's Our Right to Fight
- ☐ Voodoo Vol 1: What Lies Beneath

OCTOBER
- ☐ All-Star Western Vol 1: Guns and Gotham
- ☐ Batman: The Dark Knight Vol 1: Knight Terrors
- ☐ Green Lantern: New Guardians Vol 1: The Ring Bearer
- ☐ I, Vampire Vol 1: Tainted Love
- ☐ Justice League Dark Vol 1: In the Dark
- ☐ Nightwing Vol 1: Traps and Trapezes
- ☐ The Savage Hawkman Vol 1: Darkness Rising
- ☐ Supergirl Vol 1: The Last Daughter of Krypton

NOVEMBER
- ☐ Blackhawks Vol 1: The Great Leap Forward
- ☐ Blue Beetle Vol 1: Metamorphosis
- ☐ Captain Atom Vol 1: Evolution
- ☐ DC Universe Presents Vol 1 Featuring Deadman & Challengers of the Unknown
- ☐ The Flash Vol 1: Move Forward
- ☐ Red Hood and The Outlaws Vol 1: Redemption
- ☐ Superman Vol 1: What Price Tomorrow?

The First Volumes of the Decade's Biggest Comics Event

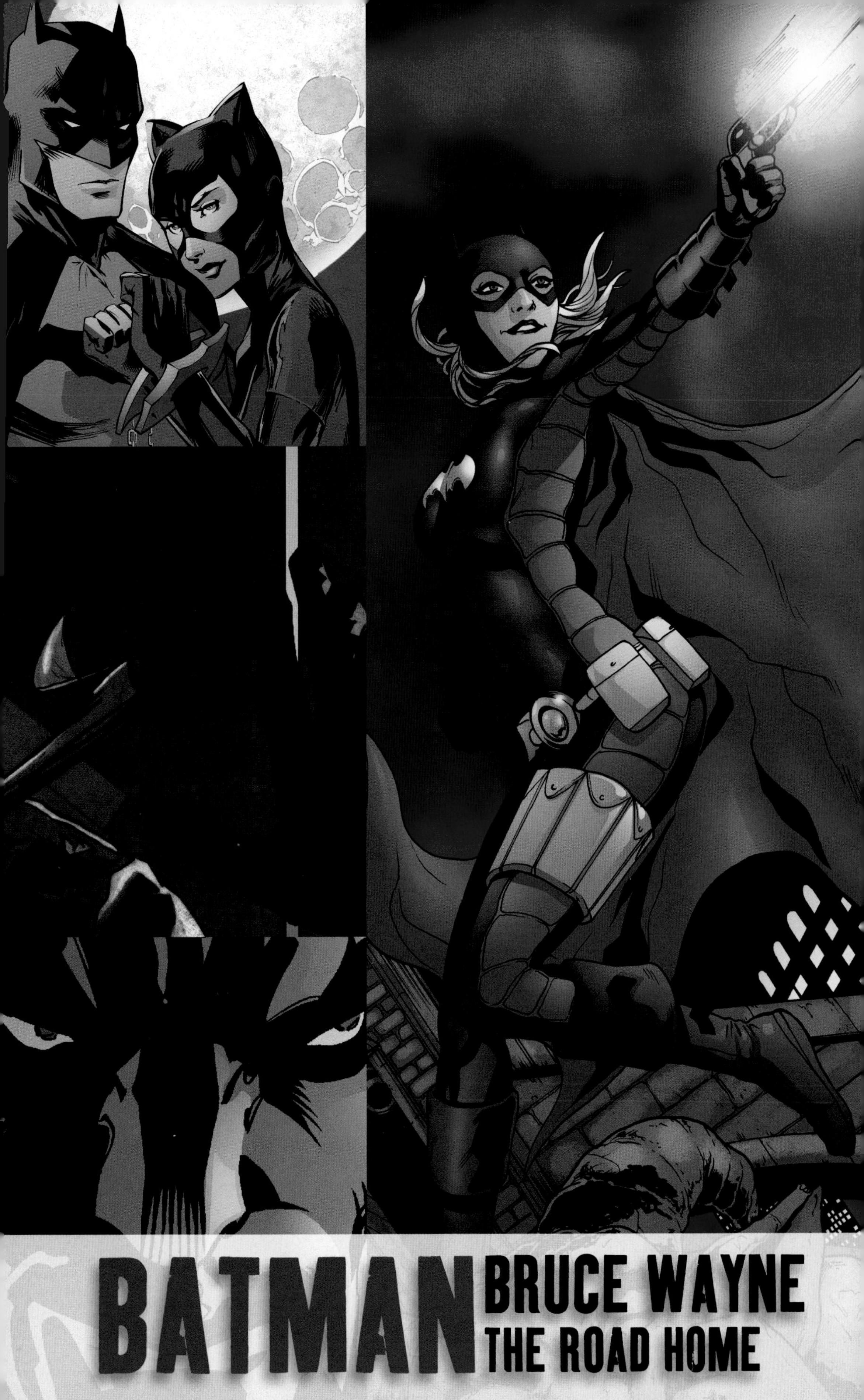

BATMAN BRUCE WAYNE THE ROAD HOME

Aike Marts Sean Ryan Harvey Richards Janelle Siegel Editors – Original Series
Scott Nybakken Editor
Robbin Brosterman Design Director – Books

Eddie Berganza Executive Editor
Bob Harras VP – Editor-in-Chief

Diane Nelson President
Dan DiDio and Jim Lee Co-Publishers
Geoff Johns Chief Creative Officer
ohn Rood Executive VP – Sales, Marketing and Business Development
my Genkins Senior VP – Business and Legal Affairs
Nairi Gardiner Senior VP – Finance
eff Boison VP – Publishing Operations
Mark Chiarello VP – Art Direction and Design
ohn Cunningham VP – Marketing
erri Cunningham VP – Talent Relations and Services
Alison Gill Senior VP – Manufacturing and Operations
David Hyde VP – Publicity
Hank Kanalz Senior VP – Digital
ay Kogan VP – Business and Legal Affairs, Publishing
ack Mahan VP – Business Affairs, Talent
Nick Napolitano VP – Manufacturing Administration
ue Pohja VP – Book Sales
Courtney Simmons Senior VP – Publicity
Bob Wayne Senior VP – Sales

BATMAN: BRUCE WAYNE — THE ROAD HOME

DC Comics, 1700 Broadway, New York, NY 10019
A Warner Bros. Entertainment Company
Printed by RR Donnelley, Salem, VA, USA. 4/13/12. First Printing.
ISBN: 978-1-4012-3347-1

SUSTAINABLE FORESTRY INITIATIVE
Certified Chain of Custody
At Least 25% Certified Forest Content
www.sfiprogram.org
SFI-01042
APPLIES TO TEXT STOCK ONLY

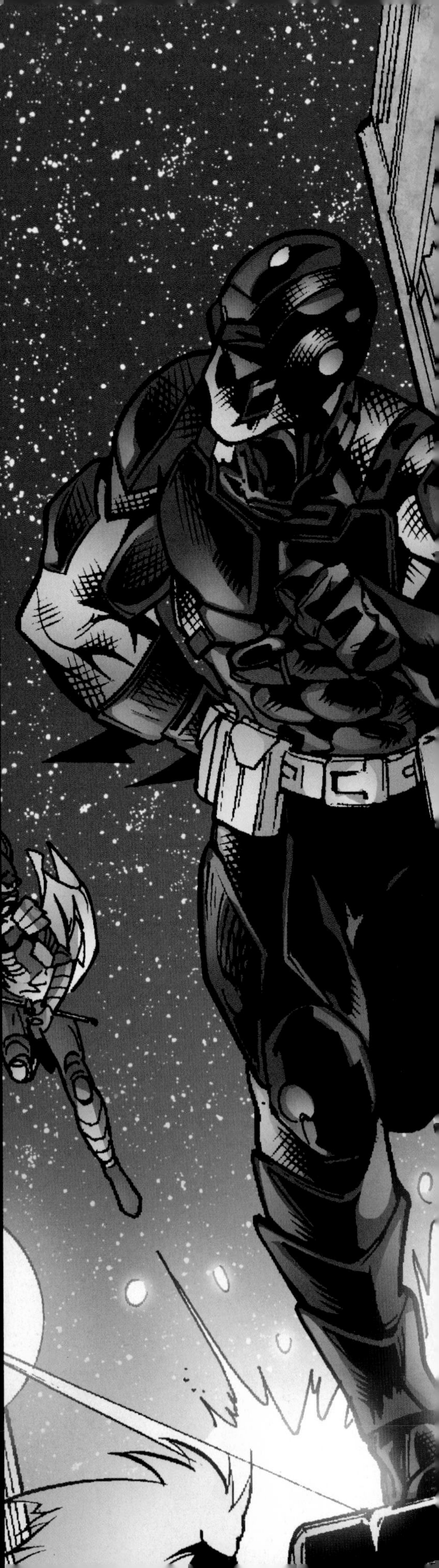

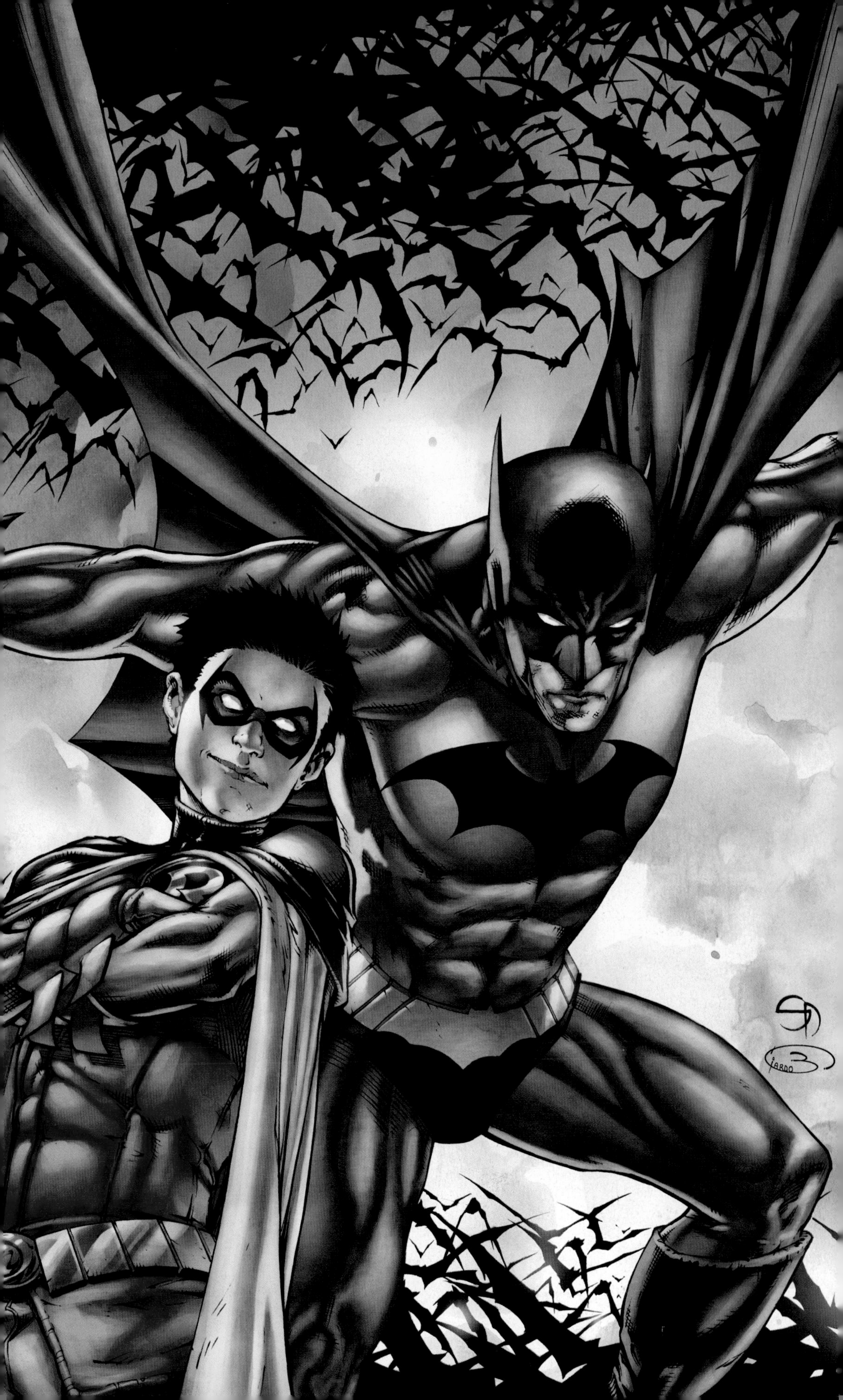

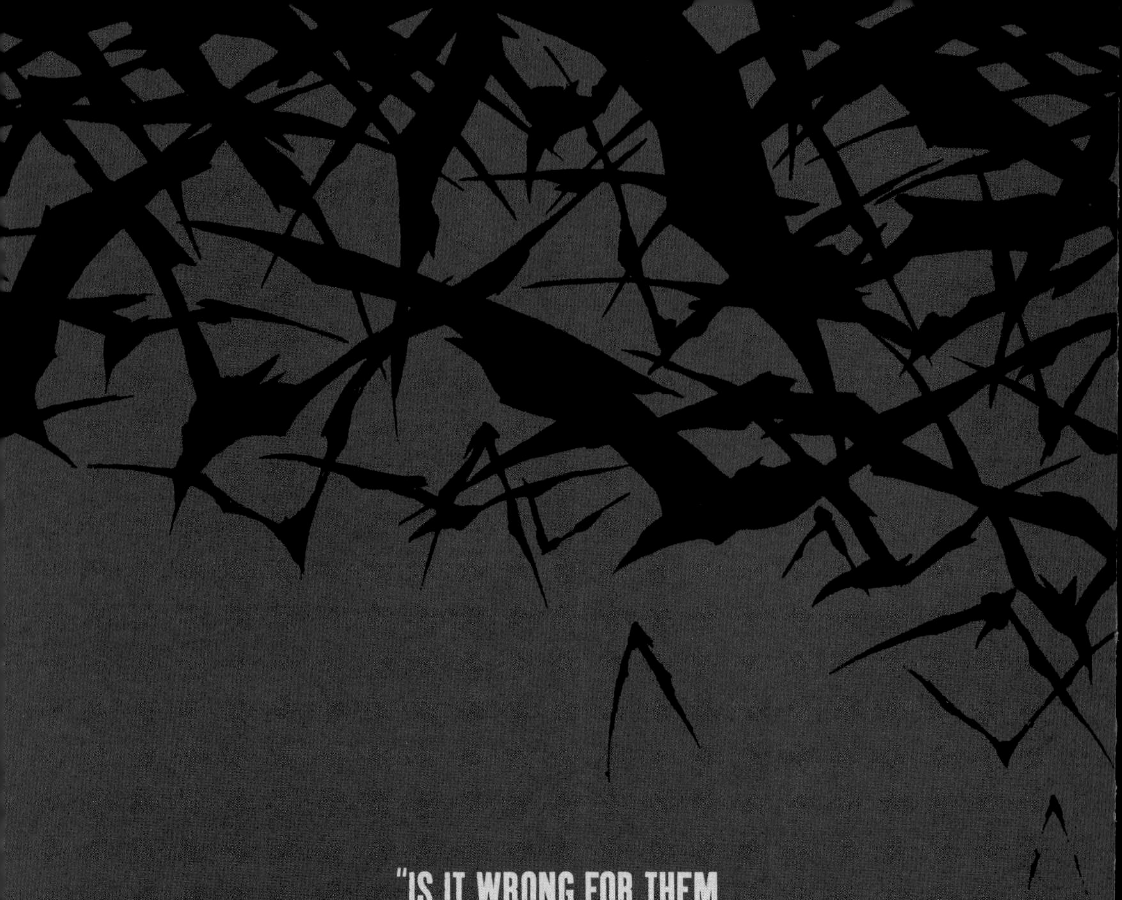

"IS IT WRONG FOR THEM
TO MAKE THIS AN ADVENTURE
RATHER THAN AN OBSESSION?"

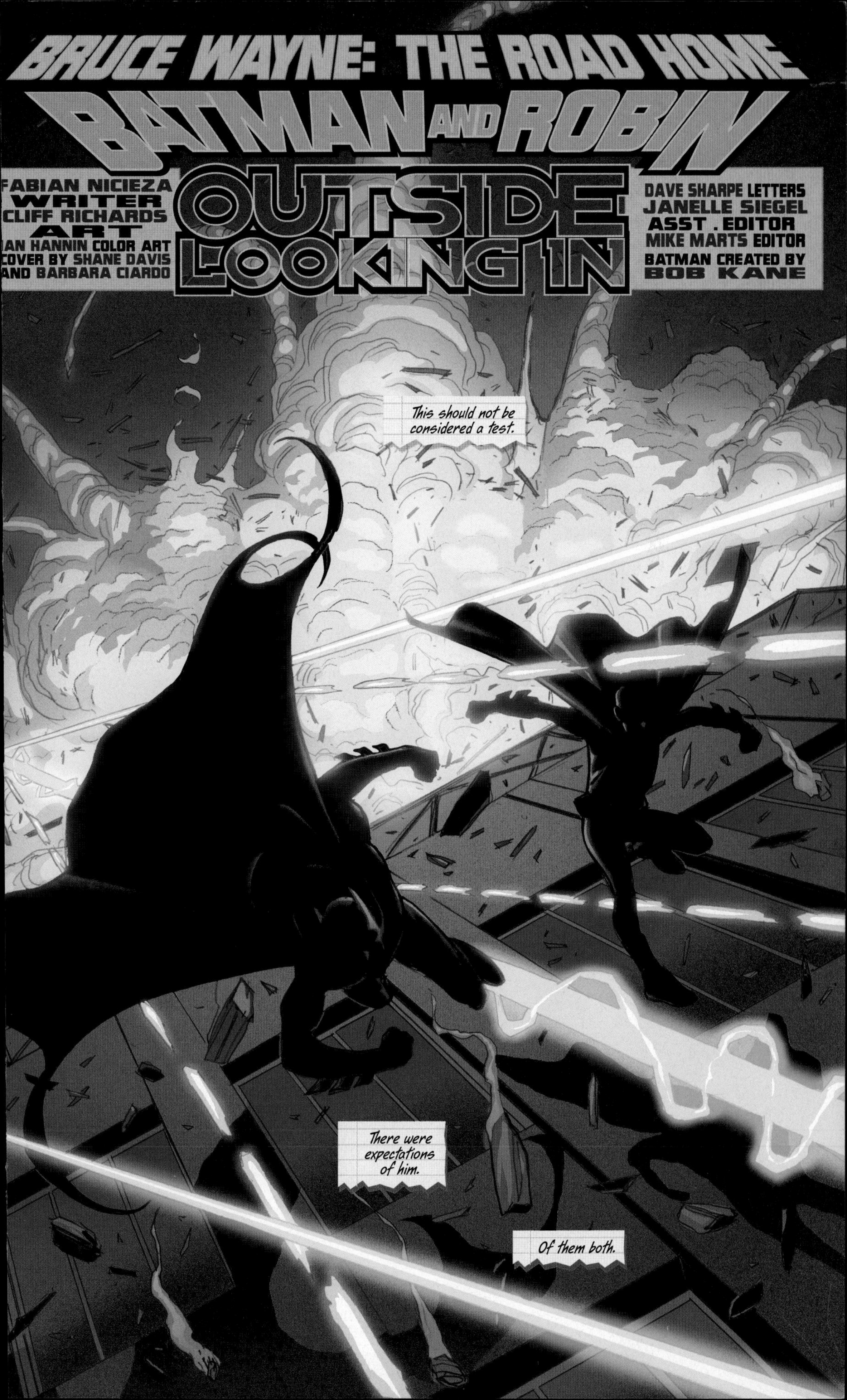

BRUCE WAYNE: THE ROAD HOME
BATMAN AND ROBIN
FABIAN NICIEZA WRITER
CLIFF RICHARDS ART
AN HANNIN COLOR ART
COVER BY SHANE DAVIS AND BARBARA CIARDO
OUTSIDE LOOKING IN
DAVE SHARPE LETTERS
JANELLE SIEGEL ASST. EDITOR
MIKE MARTS EDITOR
BATMAN CREATED BY BOB KANE
This should not be considered a test.
There were expectations of him.
Of them both.

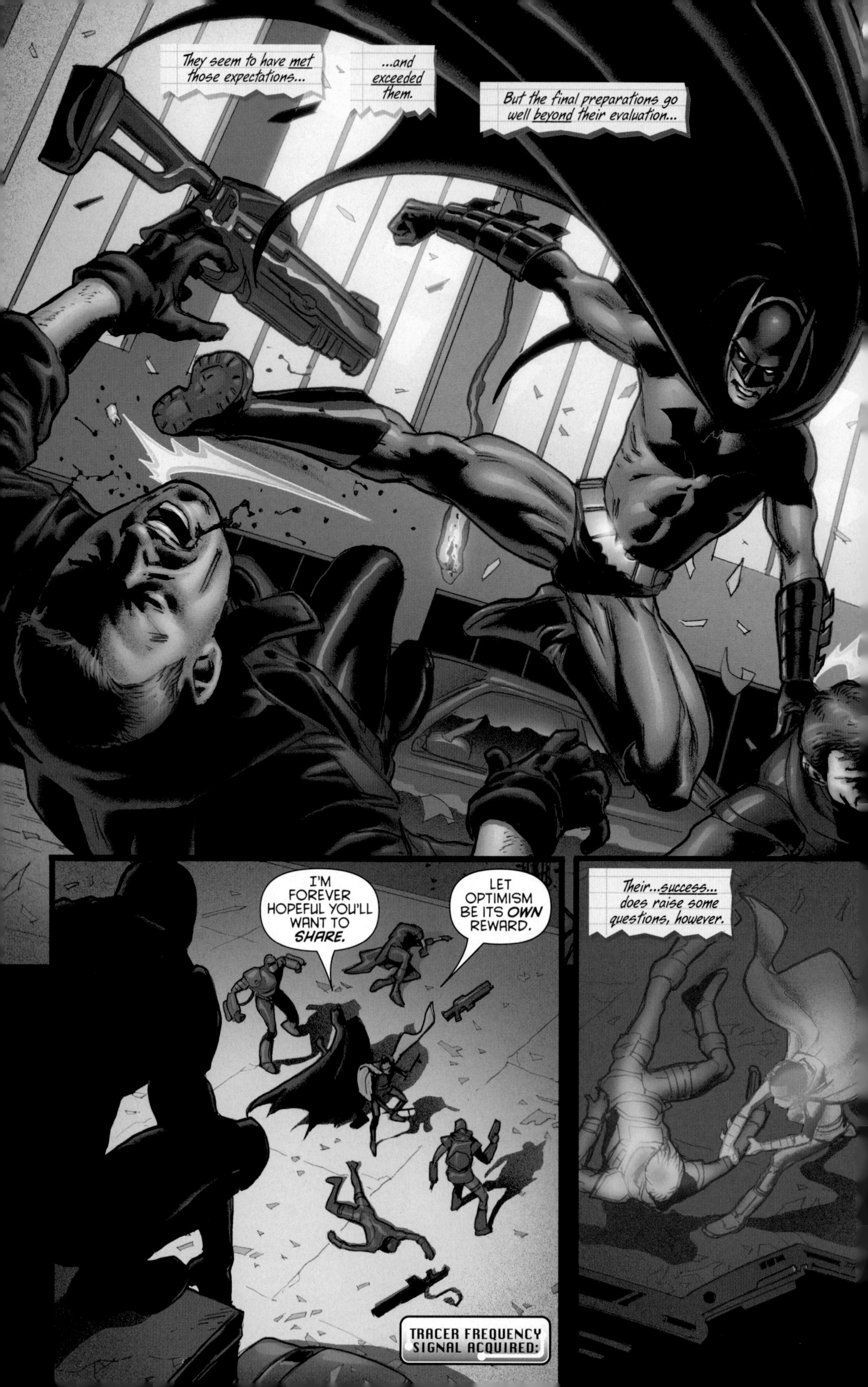
They seem to have met those expectations...
...and exceeded them.
But the final preparations go well beyond their evaluation...
I'M FOREVER HOPEFUL YOU'LL WANT TO SHARE.
LET OPTIMISM BE ITS OWN REWARD.
TRACER FREQUENCY SIGNAL ACQUIRED:
Their...success... does raise some questions, however.

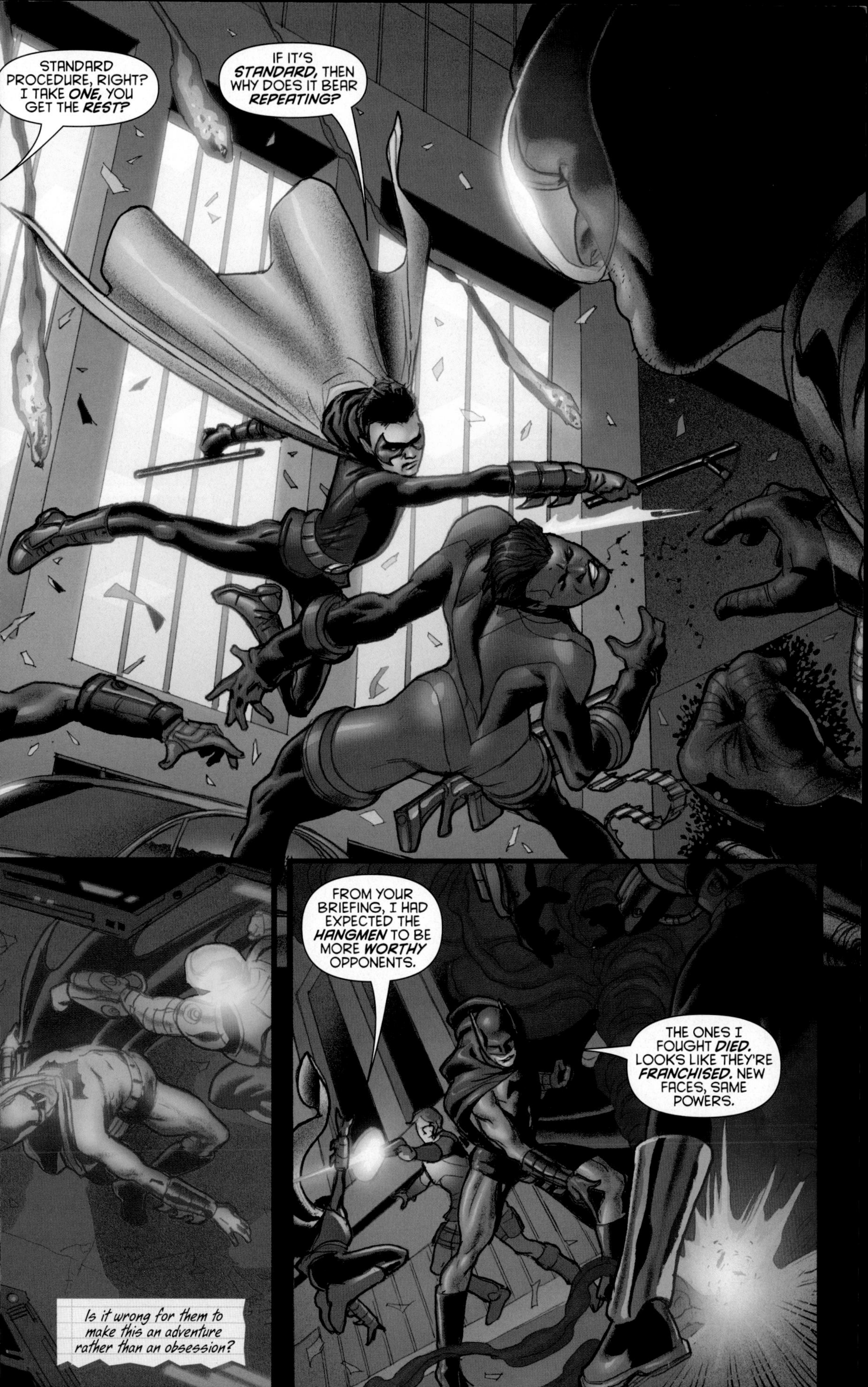
STANDARD PROCEDURE, RIGHT? I TAKE ONE, YOU GET THE REST?
IF IT'S STANDARD, THEN WHY DOES IT BEAR REPEATING?
Is it wrong for them to make this an adventure rather than an obsession?
FROM YOUR BRIEFING, I HAD EXPECTED THE HANGMEN TO BE MORE WORTHY OPPONENTS.
THE ONES I FOUGHT DIED. LOOKS LIKE THEY'RE FRANCHISED. NEW FACES, SAME POWERS.

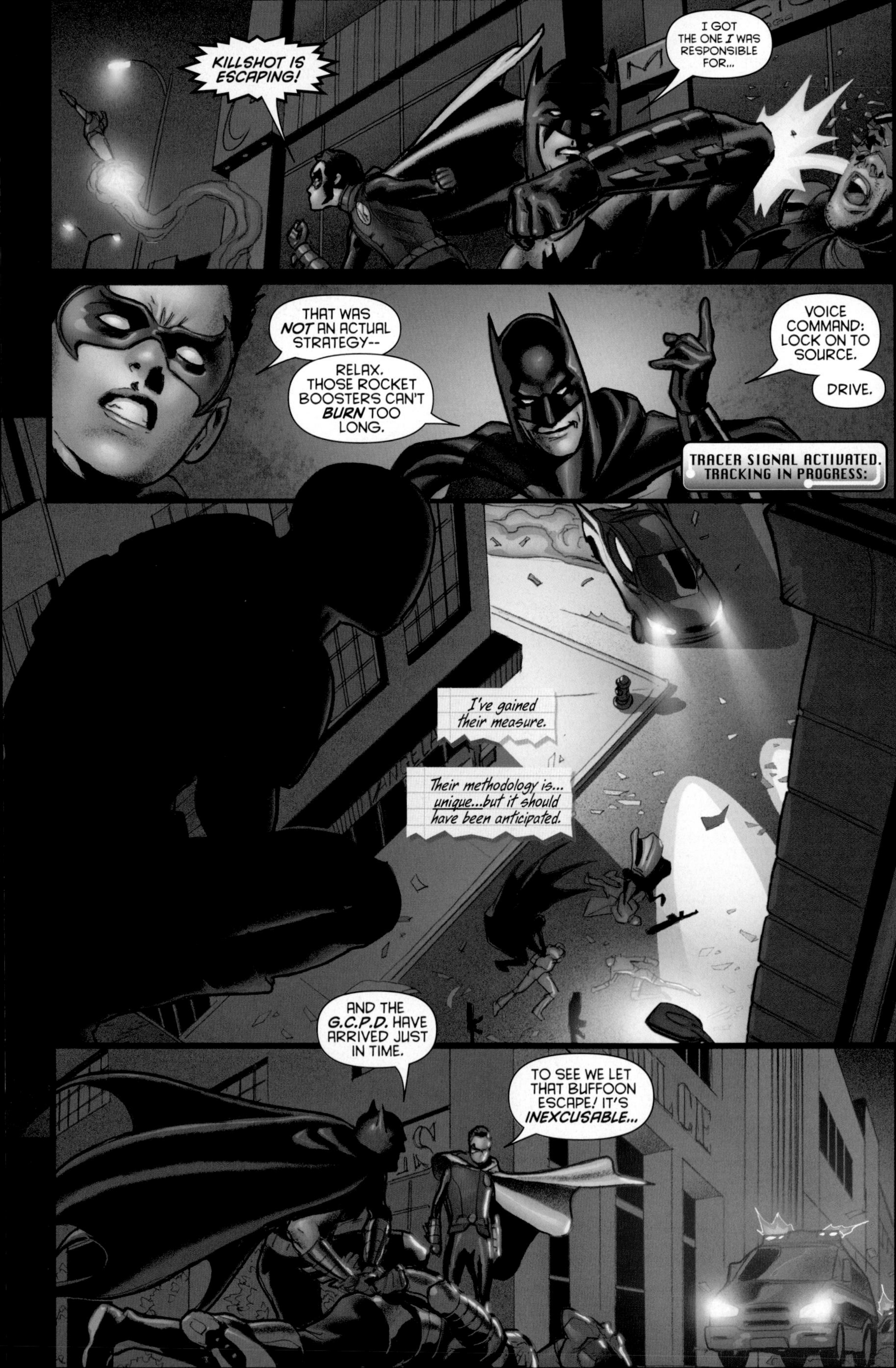
KILLSHOT IS ESCAPING!
I GOT THE ONE I WAS RESPONSIBLE FOR...
THAT WAS NOT AN ACTUAL STRATEGY--
RELAX. THOSE ROCKET BOOSTERS CAN'T BURN TOO LONG.
VOICE COMMAND: LOCK ON TO SOURCE.
DRIVE.
TRACER SIGNAL ACTIVATED. TRACKING IN PROGRESS:
I've gained their measure.
Their methodology is... unique...but it should have been anticipated.
AND THE G.C.P.D. HAVE ARRIVED JUST IN TIME.
TO SEE WE LET THAT BUFFOON ESCAPE! IT'S INEXCUSABLE...

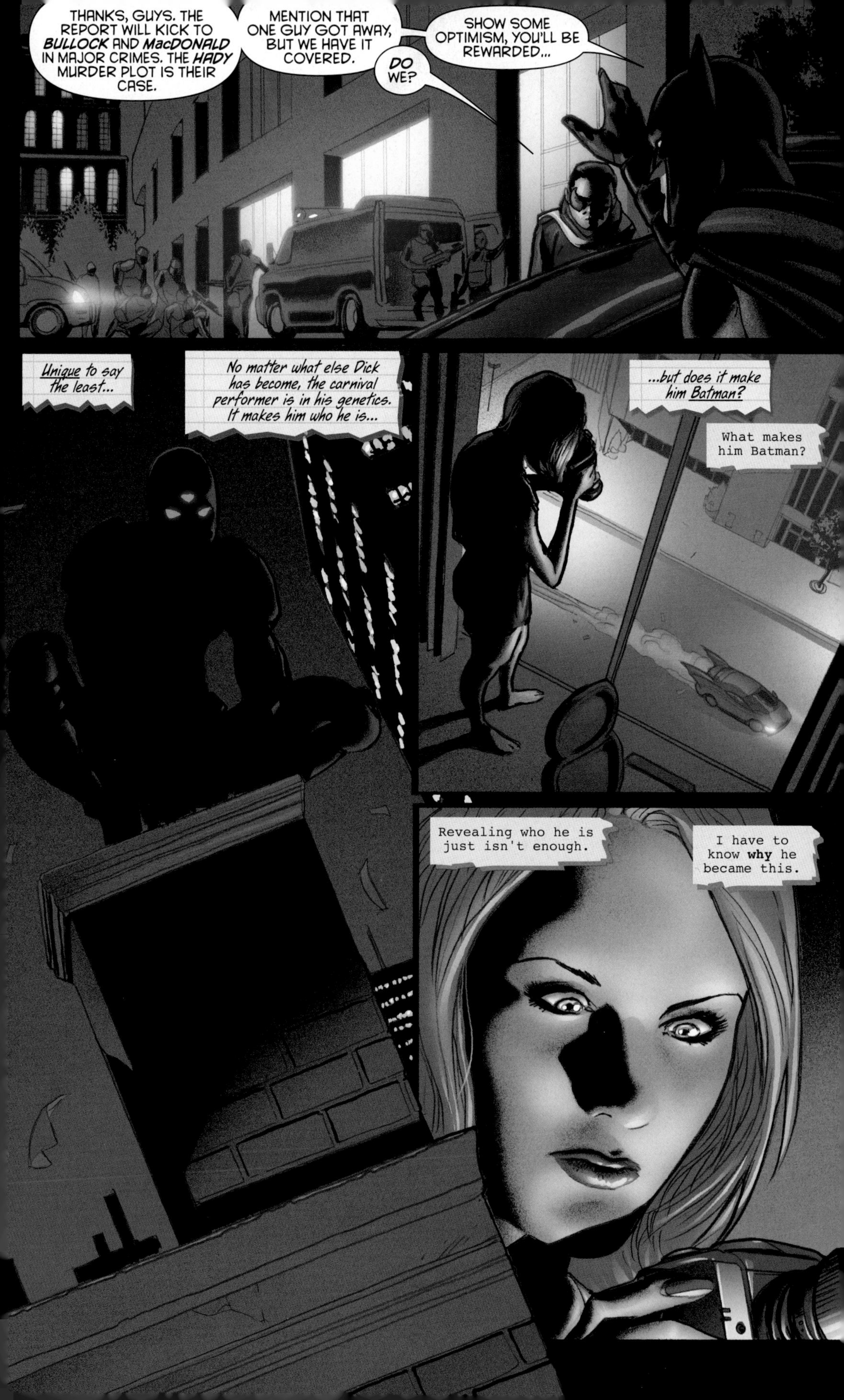
THANKS, GUYS. THE REPORT WILL KICK TO BULLOCK AND MacDONALD IN MAJOR CRIMES. THE HADY MURDER PLOT IS THEIR CASE.
MENTION THAT ONE GUY GOT AWAY, BUT WE HAVE IT COVERED.
DO WE?
SHOW SOME OPTIMISM, YOU'LL BE REWARDED...
Unique to say the least...
No matter what else Dick has become, the carnival performer is in his genetics. It makes him who he is...
...but does it make him Batman?
What makes him Batman?
Revealing who he is just isn't enough.
I have to know why he became this.

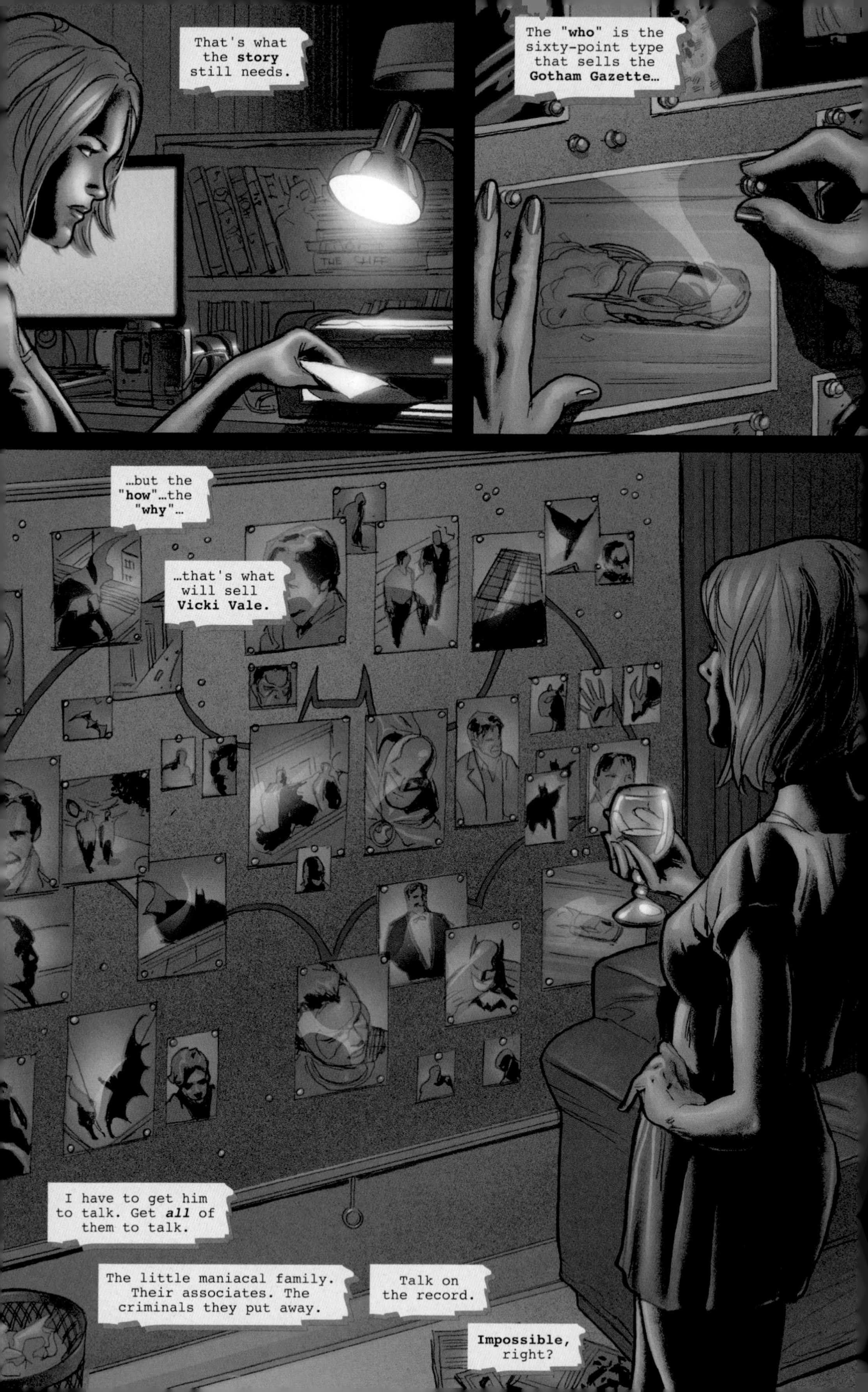
That's what the **story** still needs.
The "**who**" is the sixty-point type that sells the **Gotham Gazette**...
...but the "**how**"...the "**why**"...
...that's what will sell **Vicki Vale.**
I have to get him to talk. Get ***all*** of them to talk.
The little maniacal family. Their associates. The criminals they put away.
Talk on the record.
Impossible, right?

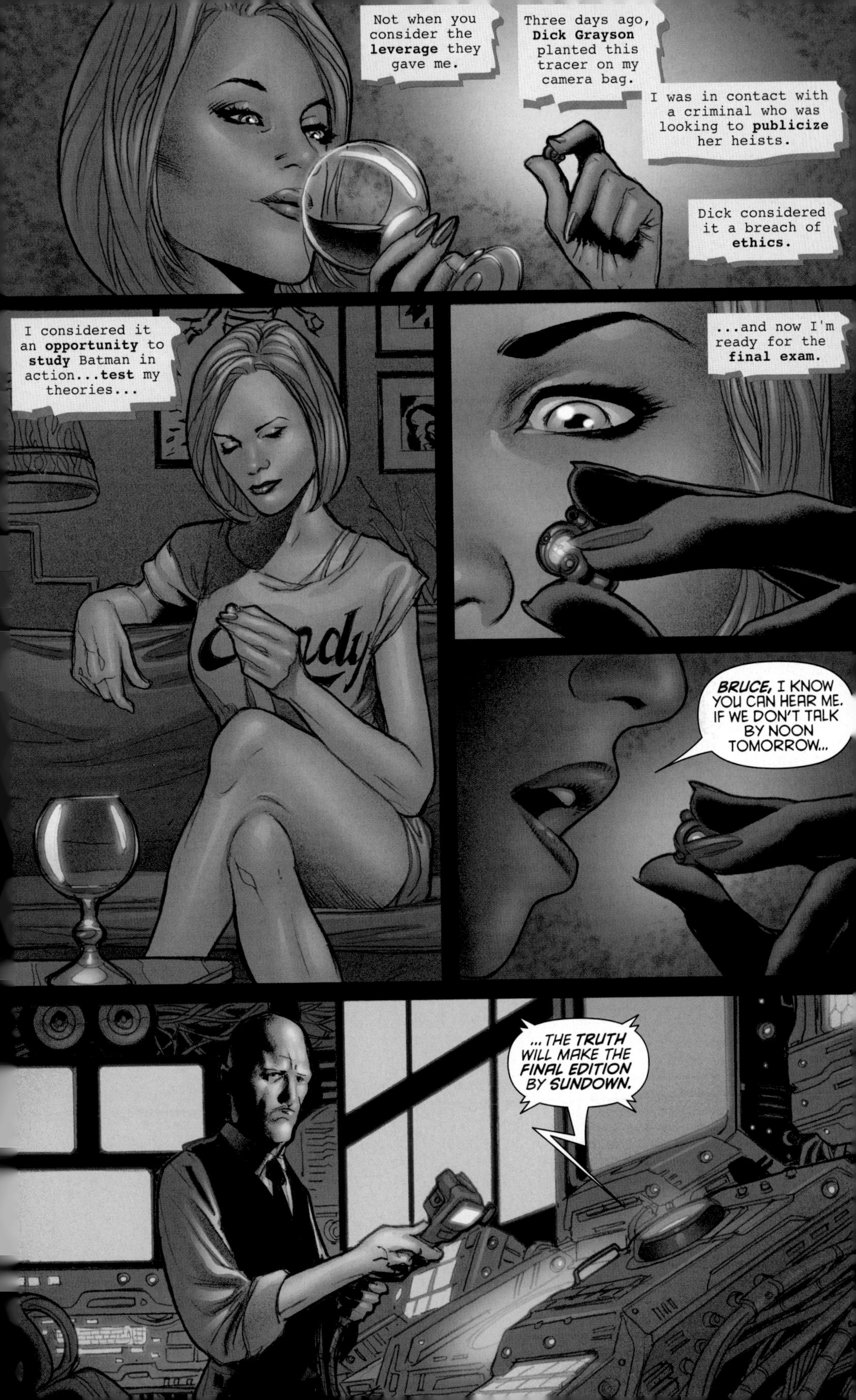
Not when you consider the leverage they gave me.
Three days ago, Dick Grayson planted this tracer on my camera bag.
I was in contact with a criminal who was looking to publicize her heists.
Dick considered it a breach of ethics.
I considered it an opportunity to study Batman in action...test my theories...
...and now I'm ready for the final exam.
BRUCE, I KNOW YOU CAN HEAR ME. IF WE DON'T TALK BY NOON TOMORROW...
...THE TRUTH WILL MAKE THE FINAL EDITION BY SUNDOWN.

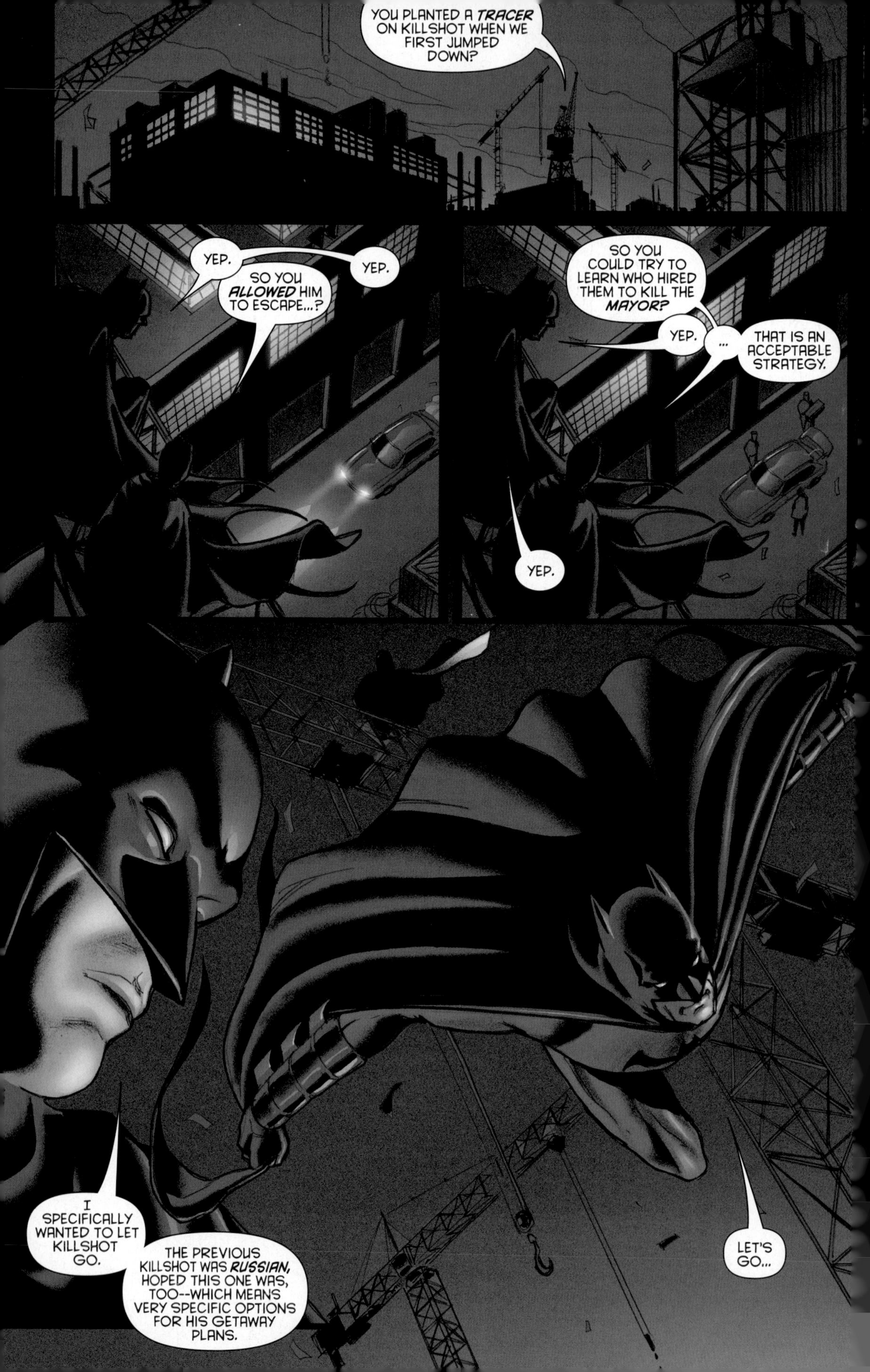

YOU PLANTED A *TRACER* ON KILLSHOT WHEN WE FIRST JUMPED DOWN?
YEP.
YEP.
SO YOU *ALLOWED* HIM TO ESCAPE...?
YEP.
SO YOU COULD TRY TO LEARN WHO HIRED THEM TO KILL THE *MAYOR?*
YEP.
...
THAT IS AN ACCEPTABLE STRATEGY.
YEP.
I SPECIFICALLY WANTED TO LET KILLSHOT GO.
THE PREVIOUS KILLSHOT WAS *RUSSIAN,* HOPED THIS ONE WAS, TOO--WHICH MEANS VERY SPECIFIC OPTIONS FOR HIS GETAWAY PLANS.
LET'S GO...

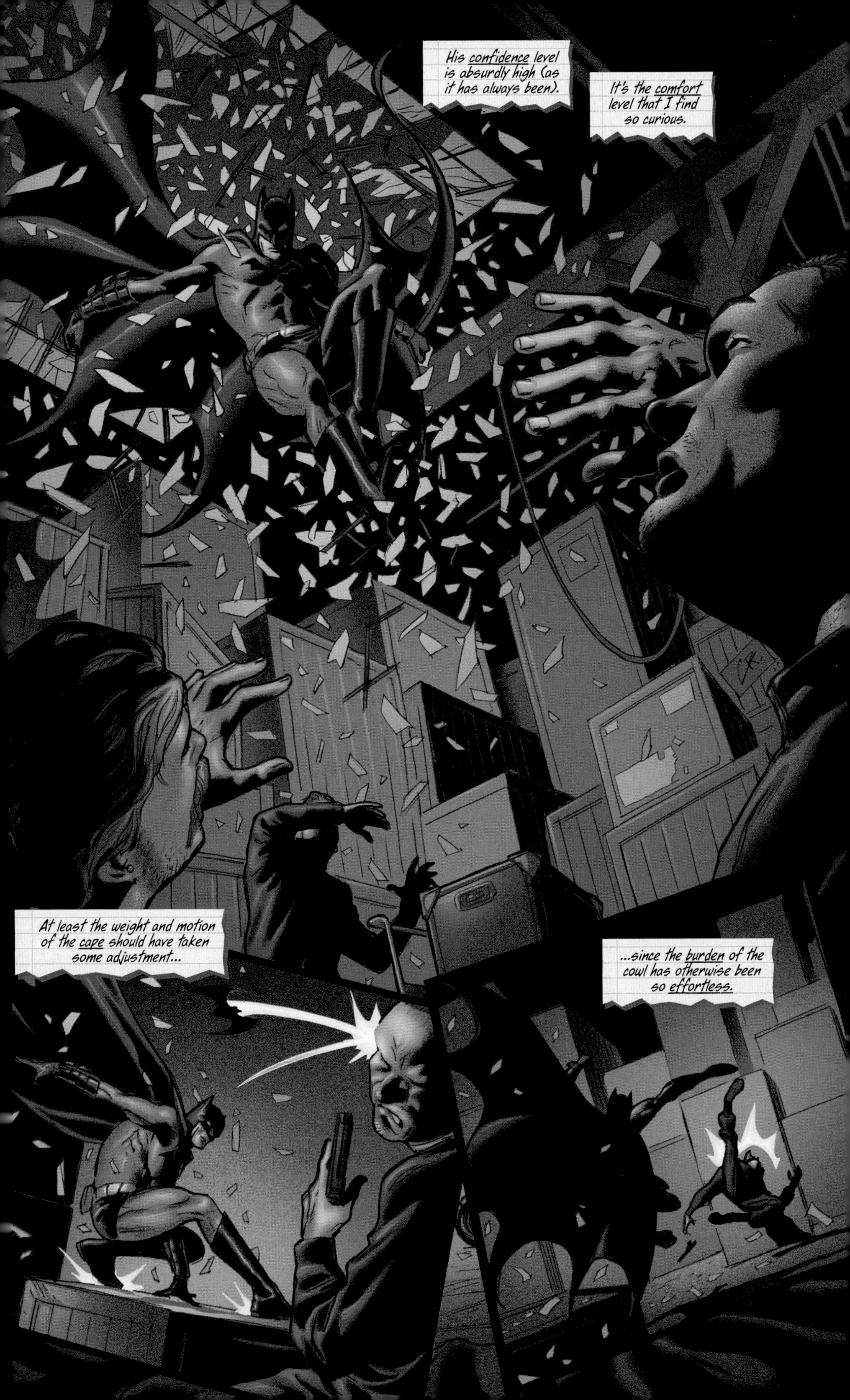
His confidence level is absurdly high (as it has always been).
It's the comfort level that I find so curious.
At least the weight and motion of the cape should have taken some adjustment...
...since the burden of the cowl has otherwise been so effortless.

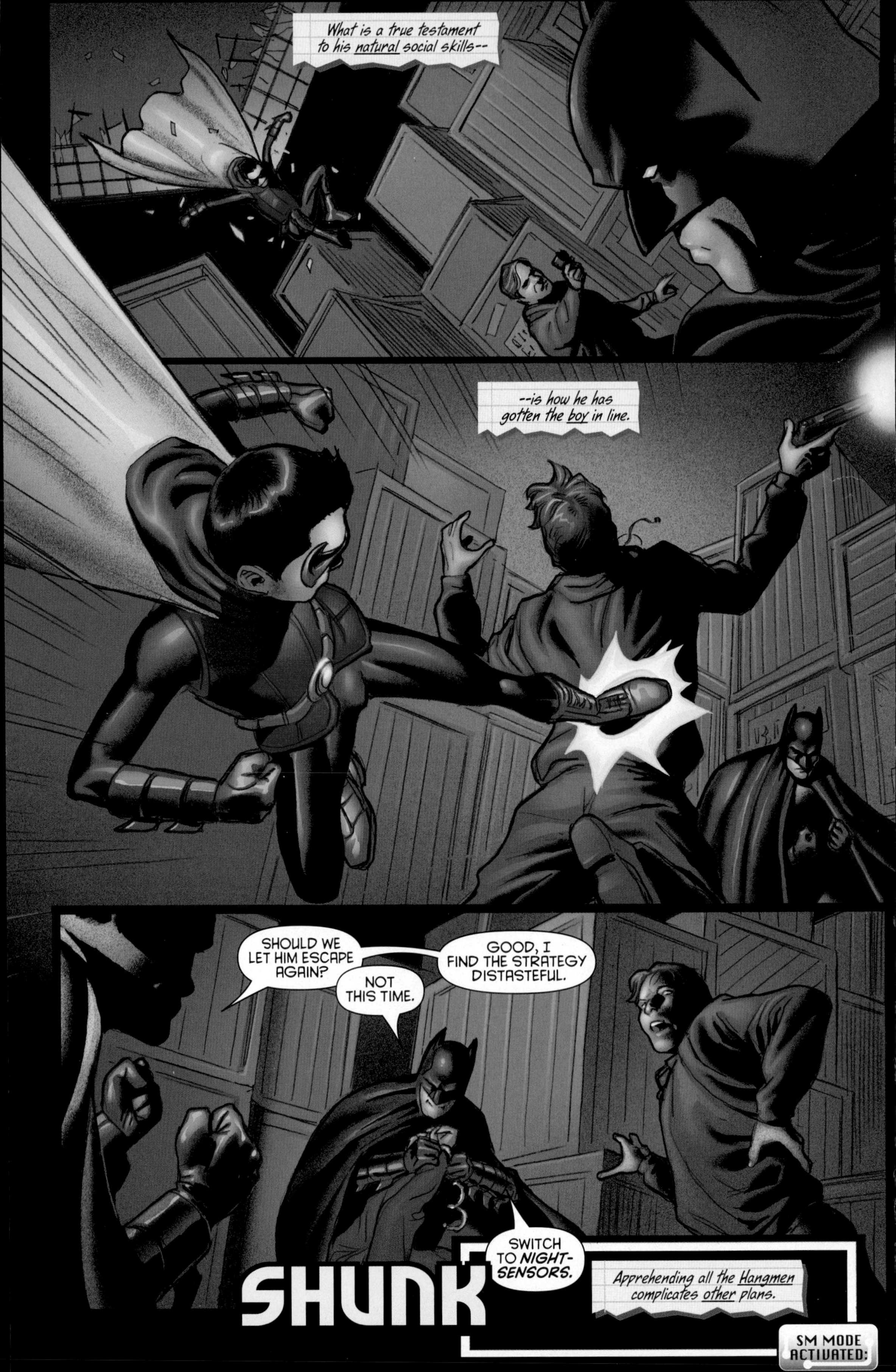
What is a true testament to his natural social skills--
--is how he has gotten the boy in line.
SHOULD WE LET HIM ESCAPE AGAIN?
NOT THIS TIME.
GOOD, I FIND THE STRATEGY DISTASTEFUL.
SWITCH TO NIGHT-SENSORS.
SHUNK
Apprehending all the Hangmen complicates other plans.
SM MODE ACTIVATED:

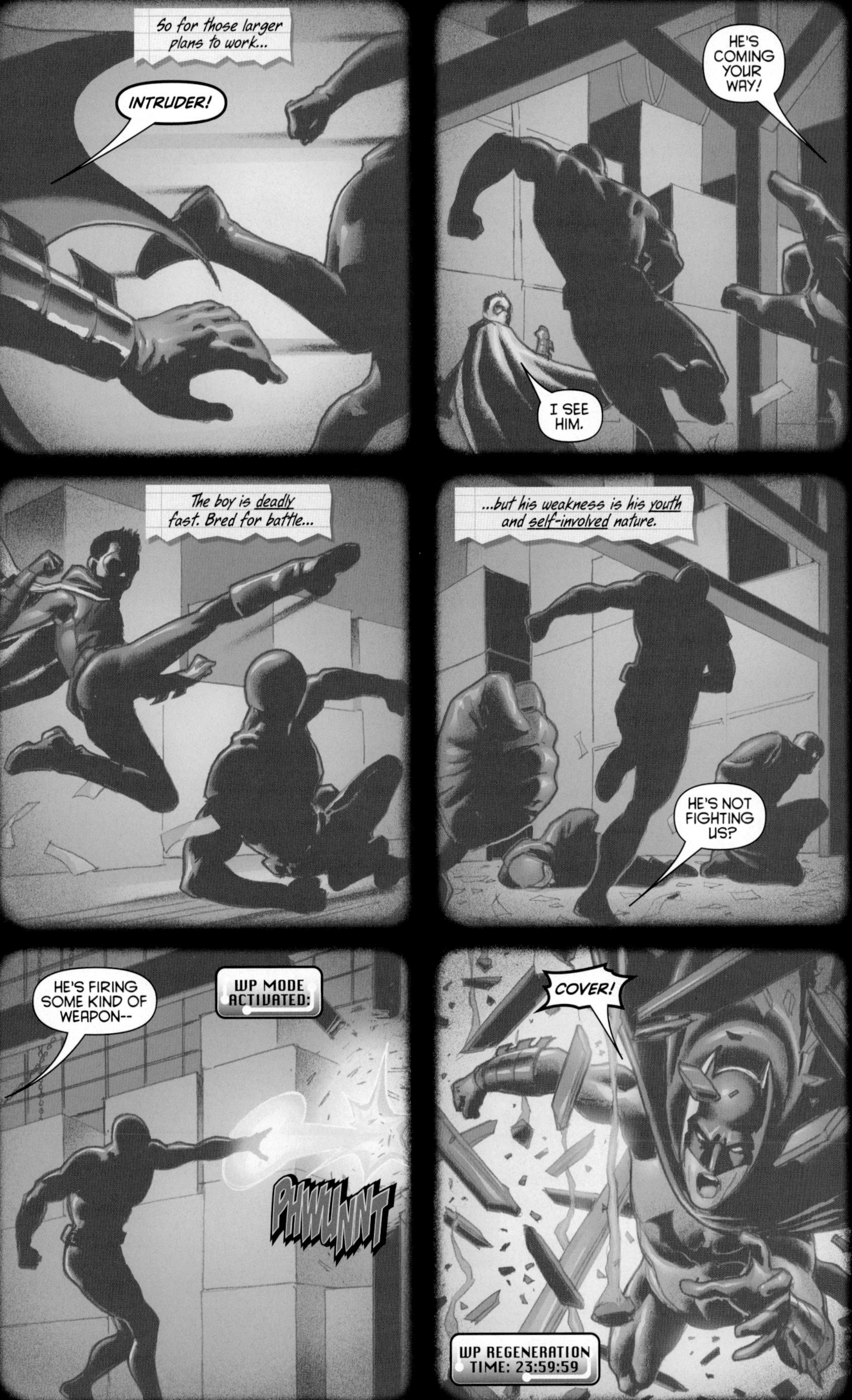
So for those larger plans to work...
INTRUDER!
HE'S COMING YOUR WAY!
I SEE HIM.
The boy is deadly fast. Bred for battle...
...but his weakness is his youth and self-involved nature.
HE'S NOT FIGHTING US?
HE'S FIRING SOME KIND OF WEAPON--
WP MODE ACTIVATED:
PHWUNNT
COVER!
WP REGENERATION TIME: 23:59:59

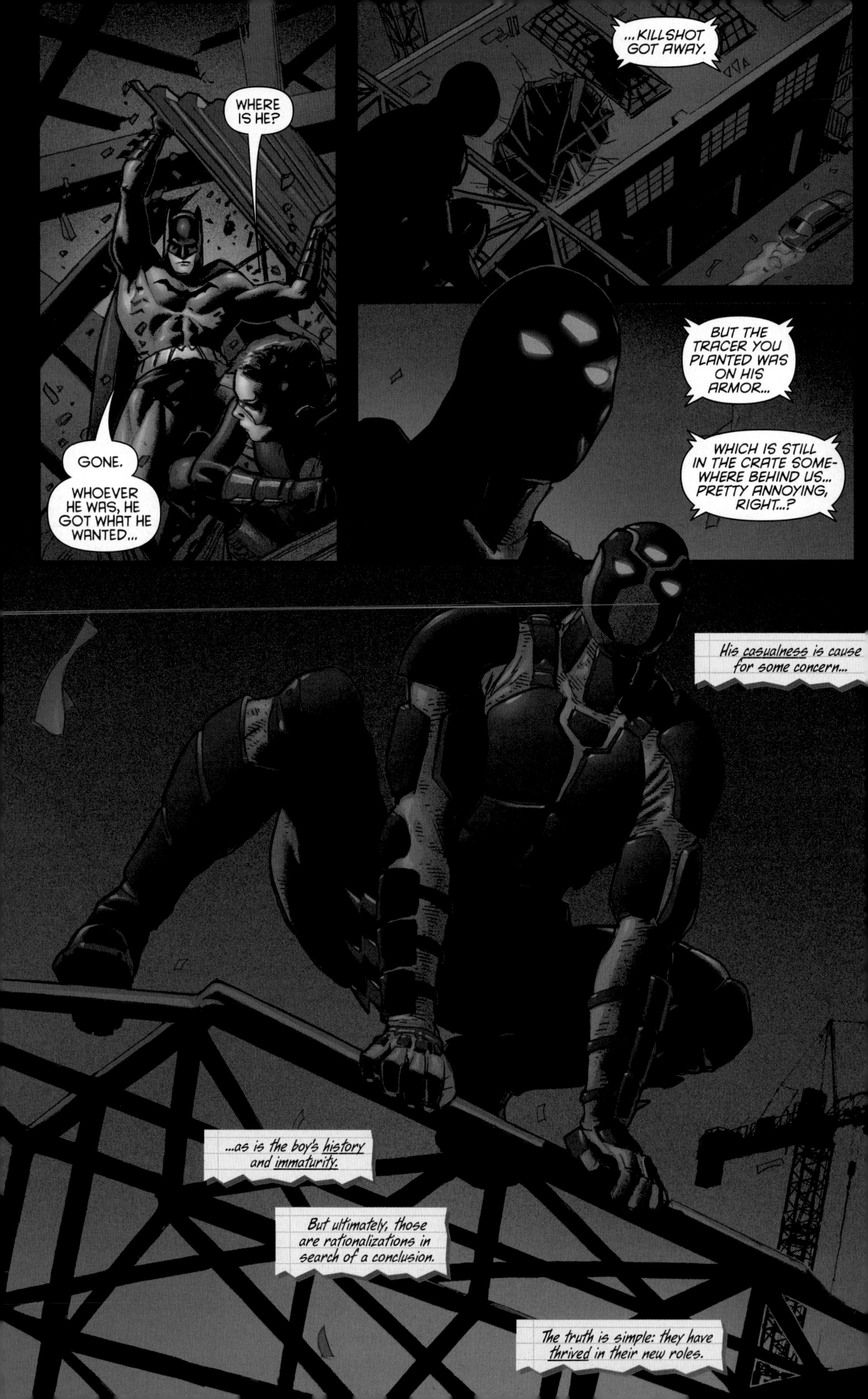
WHERE IS HE?
GONE.
WHOEVER HE WAS, HE GOT WHAT HE WANTED...
...KILLSHOT GOT AWAY.
BUT THE TRACER YOU PLANTED WAS ON HIS ARMOR...
WHICH IS STILL IN THE CRATE SOME-WHERE BEHIND US... PRETTY ANNOYING, RIGHT...?
His casualness is cause for some concern...
...as is the boy's history and immaturity.
But ultimately, those are rationalizations in search of a conclusion.
The truth is simple: they have thrived in their new roles.

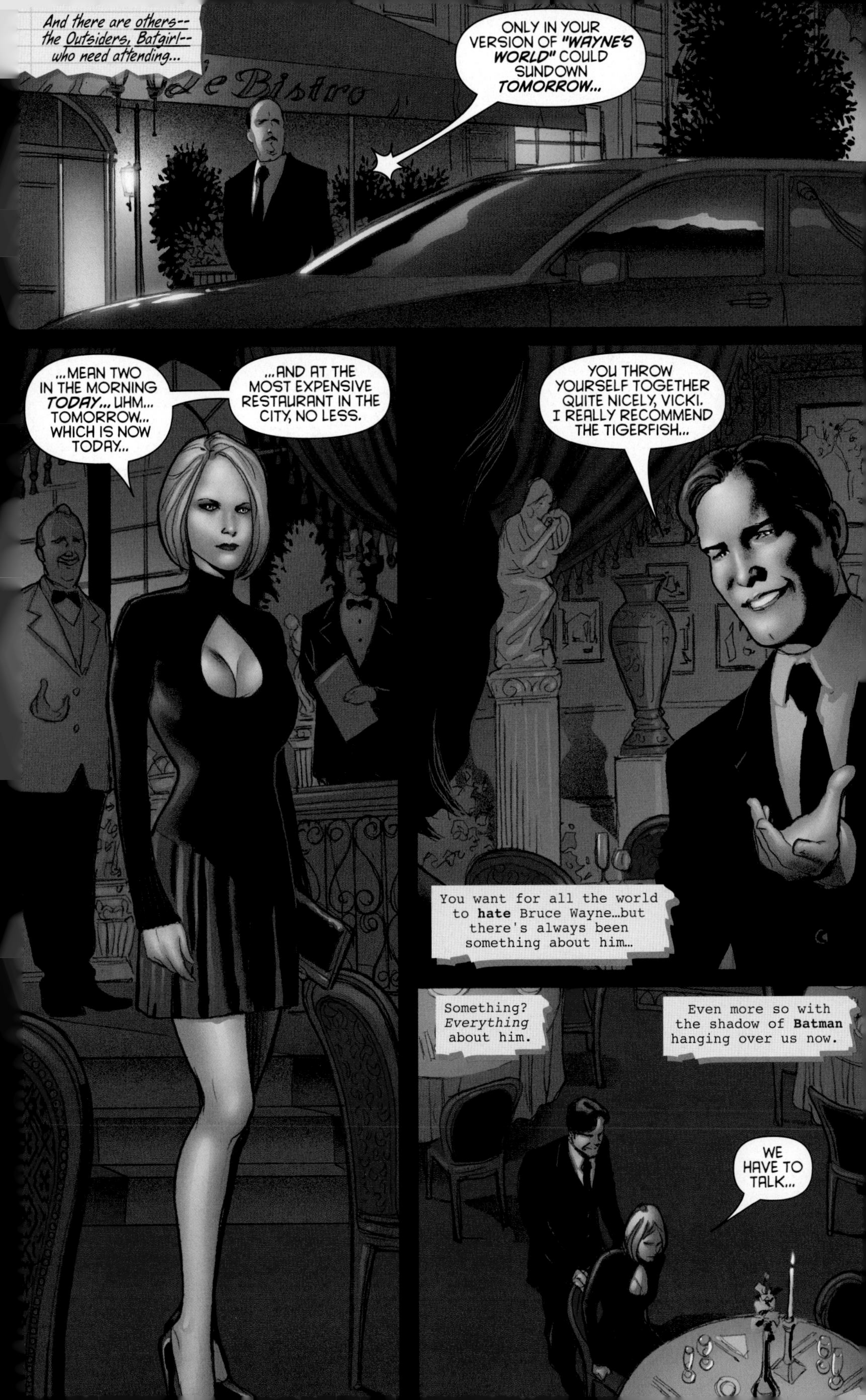
And there are others-- the Outsiders, Batgirl-- who need attending...
ONLY IN YOUR VERSION OF "WAYNE'S WORLD" COULD SUNDOWN TOMORROW...
Le Bistro
...MEAN TWO IN THE MORNING TODAY... UHM... TOMORROW... WHICH IS NOW TODAY...
...AND AT THE MOST EXPENSIVE RESTAURANT IN THE CITY, NO LESS.
YOU THROW YOURSELF TOGETHER QUITE NICELY, VICKI. I REALLY RECOMMEND THE TIGERFISH...
You want for all the world to hate Bruce Wayne...but there's always been something about him...
Something? Everything about him.
Even more so with the shadow of Batman hanging over us now.
WE HAVE TO TALK...

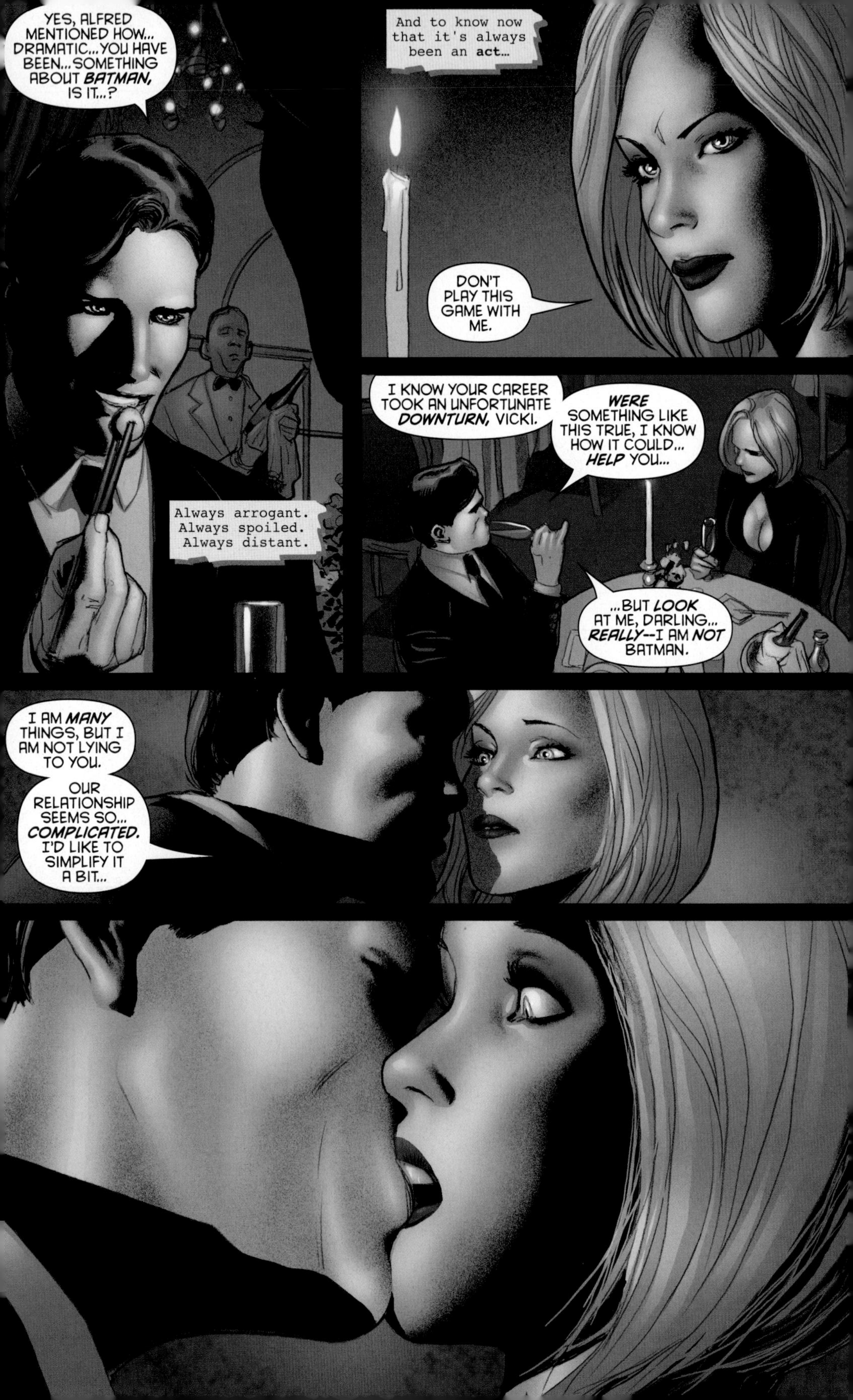
YES, ALFRED MENTIONED HOW... DRAMATIC... YOU HAVE BEEN... SOMETHING ABOUT BATMAN, IS IT...?
And to know now that it's always been an act...
DON'T PLAY THIS GAME WITH ME.
Always arrogant. Always spoiled. Always distant.
I KNOW YOUR CAREER TOOK AN UNFORTUNATE DOWNTURN, VICKI.
WERE SOMETHING LIKE THIS TRUE, I KNOW HOW IT COULD... HELP YOU...
...BUT LOOK AT ME, DARLING... REALLY--I AM NOT BATMAN.
I AM MANY THINGS, BUT I AM NOT LYING TO YOU.
OUR RELATIONSHIP SEEMS SO... COMPLICATED. I'D LIKE TO SIMPLIFY IT A BIT...

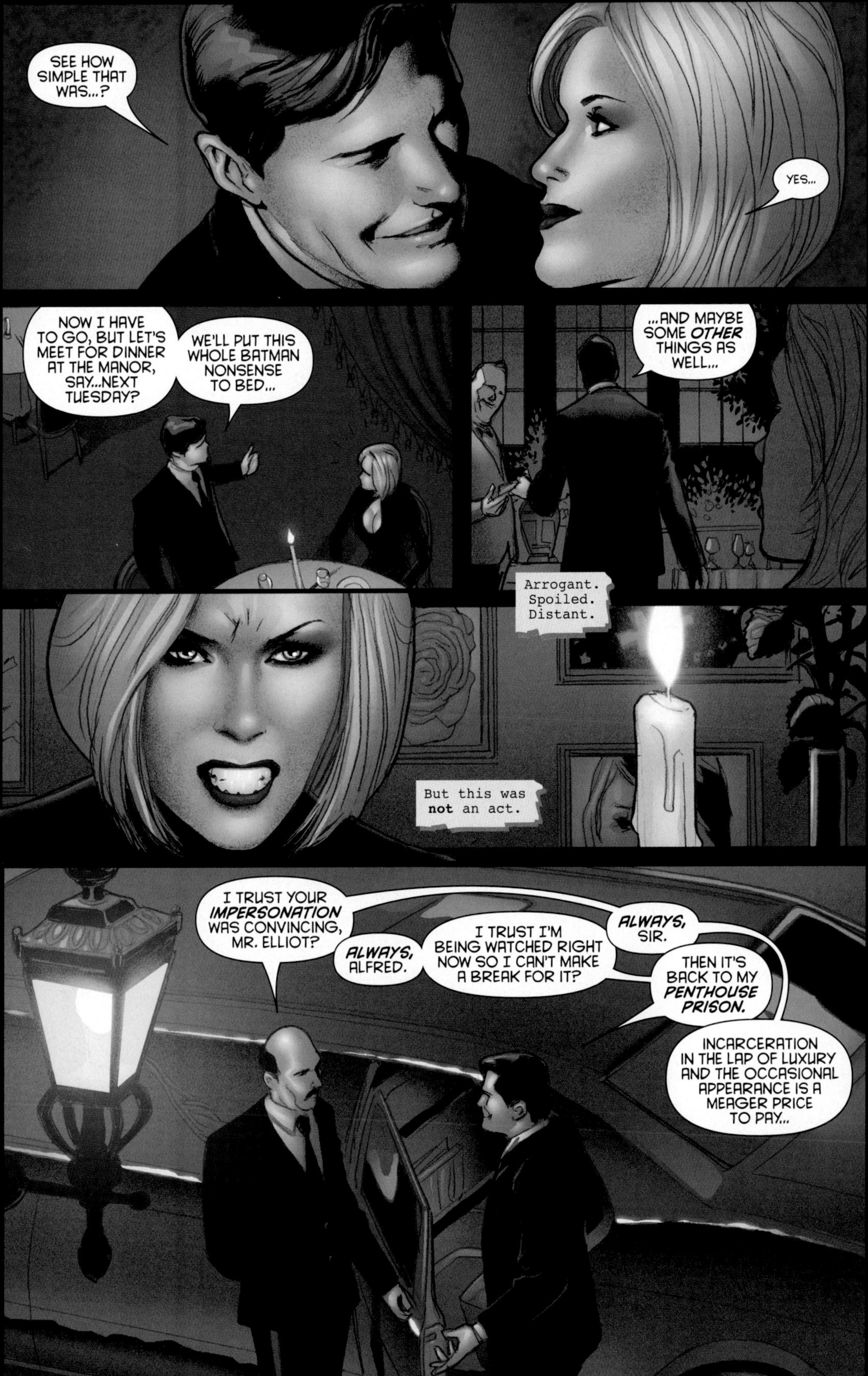

SEE HOW SIMPLE THAT WAS...?
YES...
NOW I HAVE TO GO, BUT LET'S MEET FOR DINNER AT THE MANOR, SAY...NEXT TUESDAY?
WE'LL PUT THIS WHOLE BATMAN NONSENSE TO BED...
...AND MAYBE SOME OTHER THINGS AS WELL...
Arrogant. Spoiled. Distant.
But this was not an act.
I TRUST YOUR IMPERSONATION WAS CONVINCING, MR. ELLIOT?
ALWAYS, ALFRED.
I TRUST I'M BEING WATCHED RIGHT NOW SO I CAN'T MAKE A BREAK FOR IT?
ALWAYS, SIR.
THEN IT'S BACK TO MY PENTHOUSE PRISON.
INCARCERATION IN THE LAP OF LUXURY AND THE OCCASIONAL APPEARANCE IS A MEAGER PRICE TO PAY...

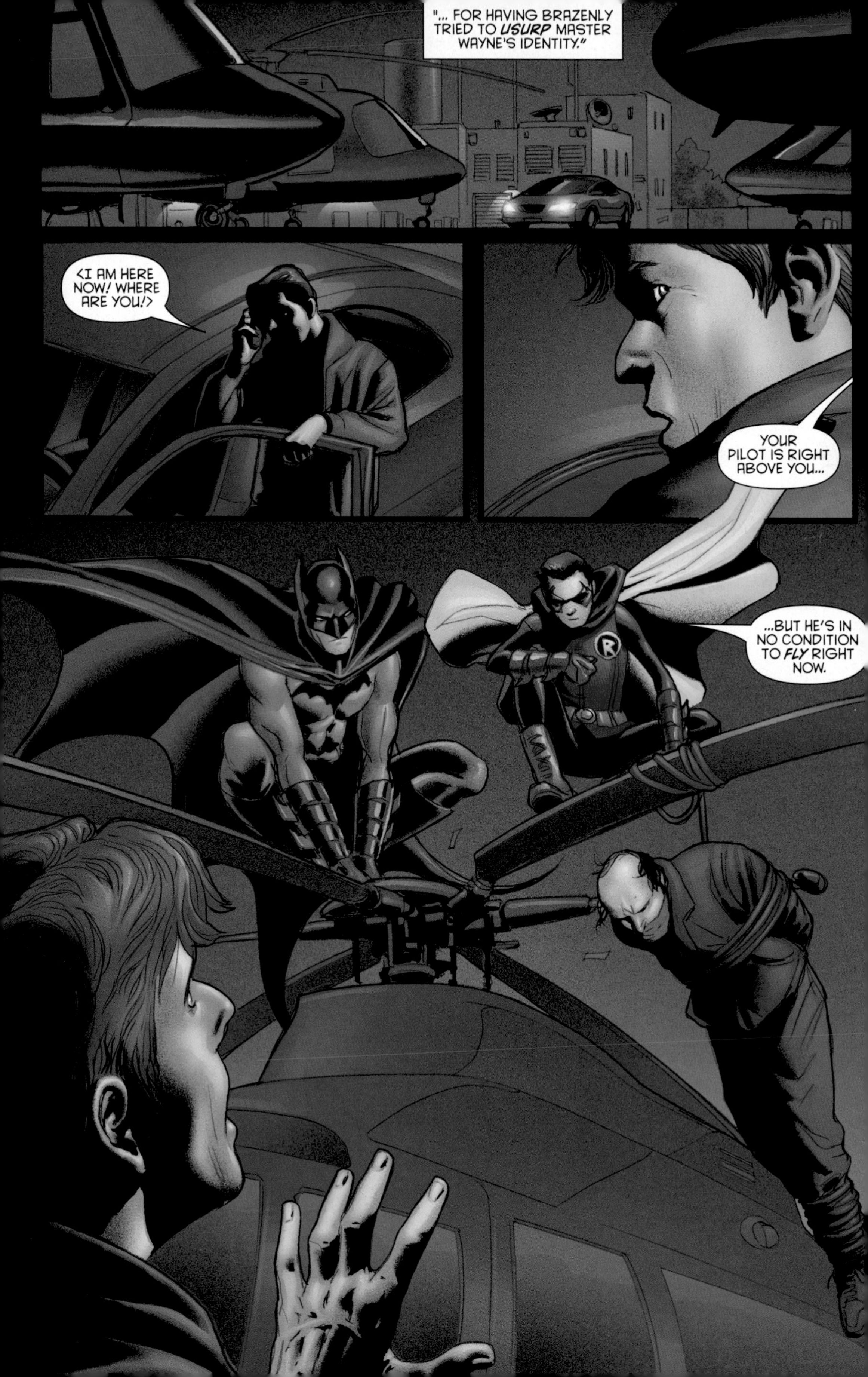
"... FOR HAVING BRAZENLY TRIED TO *USURP* MASTER WAYNE'S IDENTITY."
<I AM HERE NOW! WHERE ARE YOU!>
YOUR PILOT IS RIGHT ABOVE YOU...
...BUT HE'S IN NO CONDITION TO *FLY* RIGHT NOW.

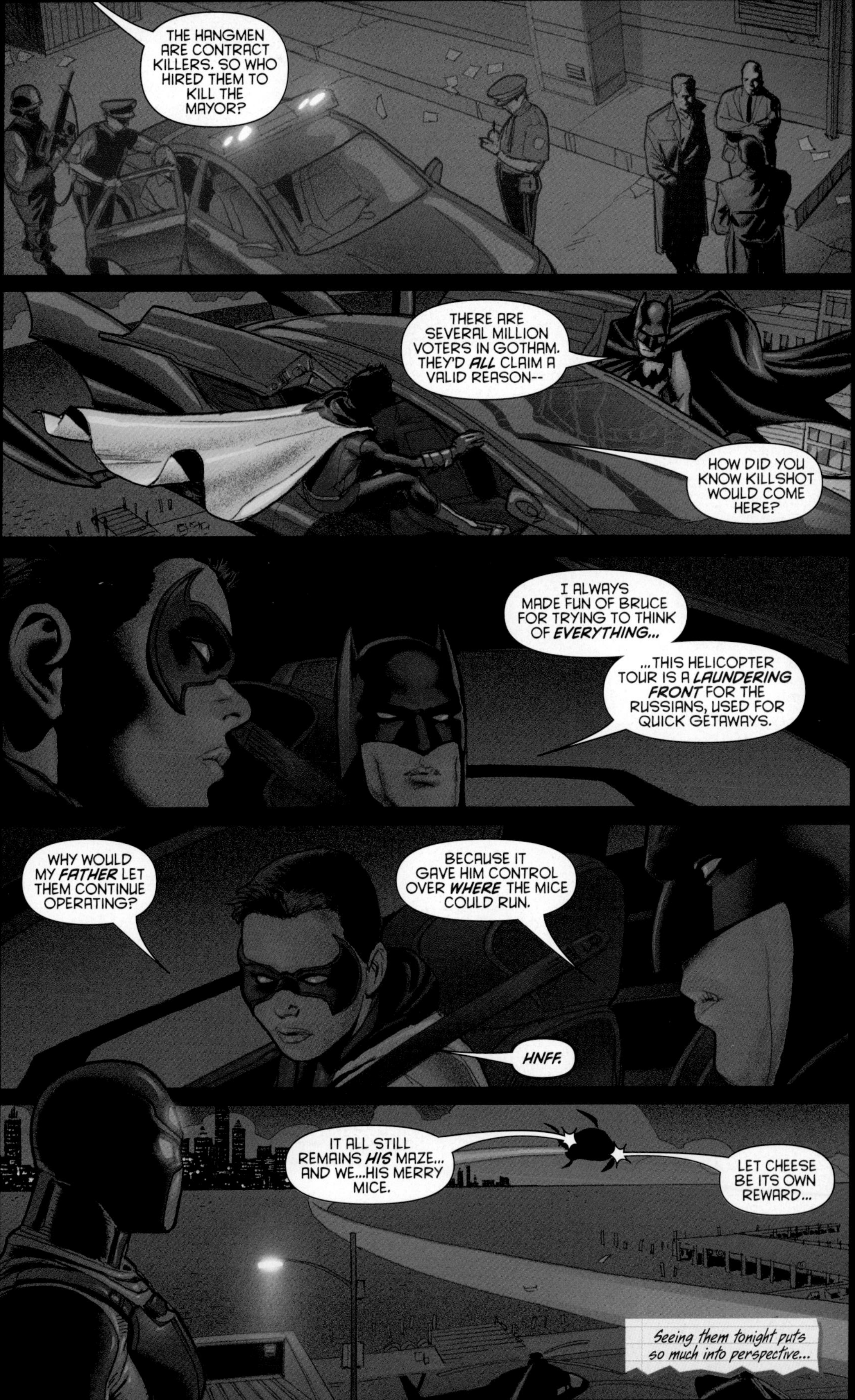
THE HANGMEN ARE CONTRACT KILLERS. SO WHO HIRED THEM TO KILL THE MAYOR?
THERE ARE SEVERAL MILLION VOTERS IN GOTHAM. THEY'D ALL CLAIM A VALID REASON--
HOW DID YOU KNOW KILLSHOT WOULD COME HERE?
I ALWAYS MADE FUN OF BRUCE FOR TRYING TO THINK OF EVERYTHING...
...THIS HELICOPTER TOUR IS A LAUNDERING FRONT FOR THE RUSSIANS, USED FOR QUICK GETAWAYS.
WHY WOULD MY FATHER LET THEM CONTINUE OPERATING?
BECAUSE IT GAVE HIM CONTROL OVER WHERE THE MICE COULD RUN.
HNFF.
IT ALL STILL REMAINS HIS MAZE... AND WE...HIS MERRY MICE.
LET CHEESE BE ITS OWN REWARD...
Seeing them tonight puts so much into perspective...

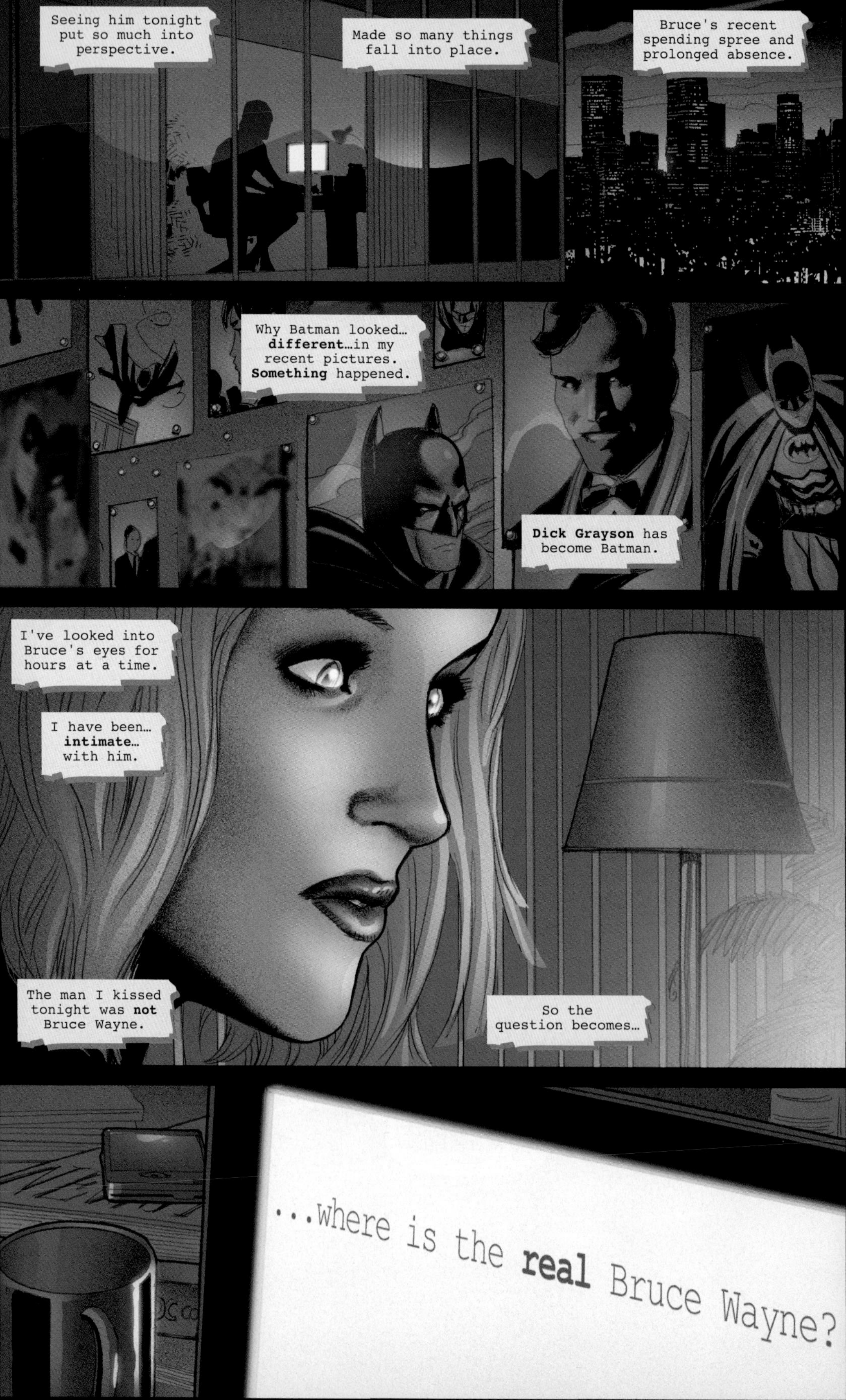
Seeing him tonight put so much into perspective.
Made so many things fall into place.
Bruce's recent spending spree and prolonged absence.
Why Batman looked... **different**...in my recent pictures. **Something** happened.
Dick Grayson has become Batman.
I've looked into Bruce's eyes for hours at a time.
I have been... **intimate**... with him.
The man I kissed tonight was **not** Bruce Wayne.
So the question becomes...
...where is the **real** Bruce Wayne?

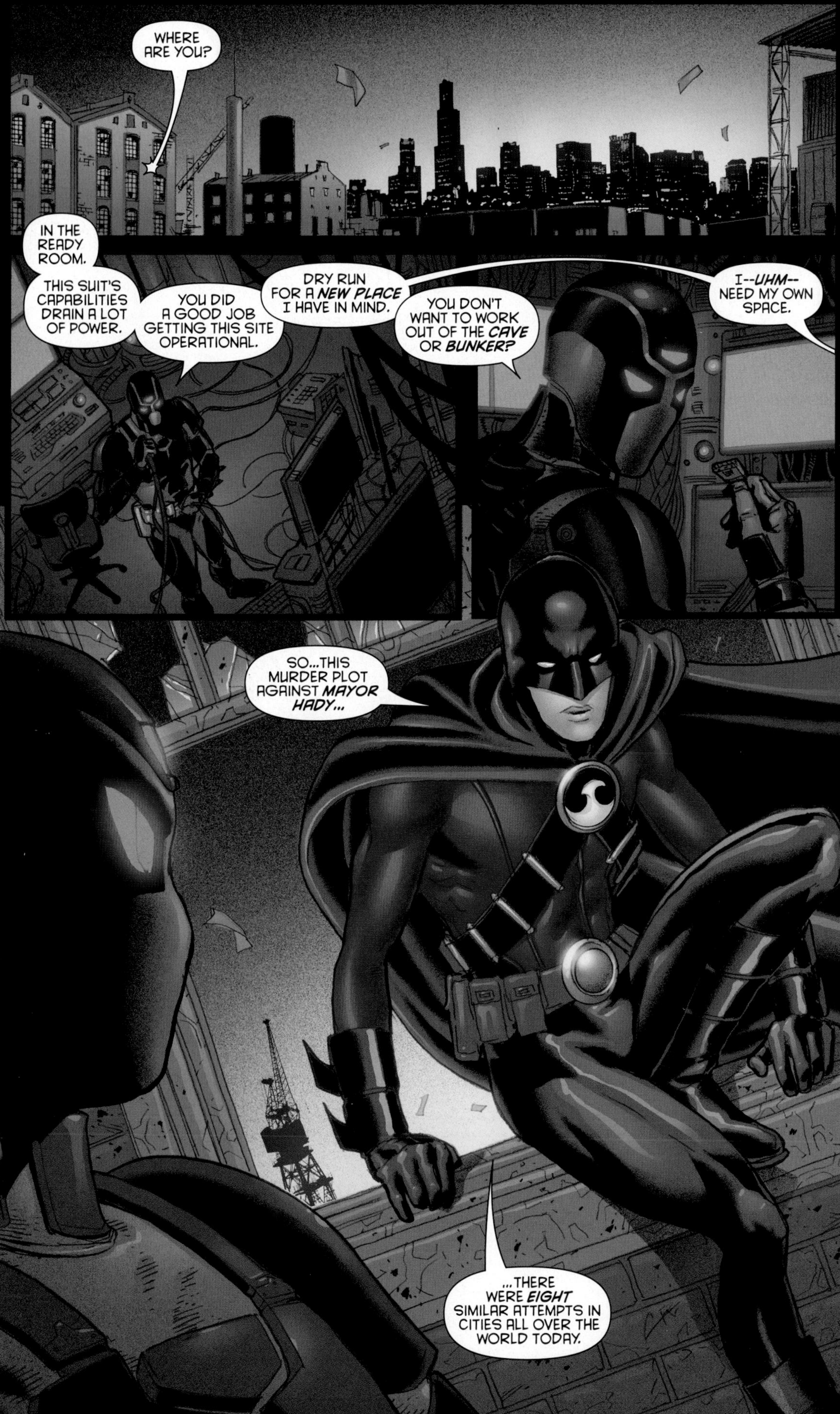
WHERE ARE YOU?
IN THE READY ROOM.
THIS SUIT'S CAPABILITIES DRAIN A LOT OF POWER.
YOU DID A GOOD JOB GETTING THIS SITE OPERATIONAL.
DRY RUN FOR A *NEW PLACE* I HAVE IN MIND.
YOU DON'T WANT TO WORK OUT OF THE *CAVE* OR *BUNKER?*
I--*UHM*-- NEED MY OWN SPACE.
SO...THIS MURDER PLOT AGAINST *MAYOR HADY*...
...THERE WERE *EIGHT* SIMILAR ATTEMPTS IN CITIES ALL OVER THE WORLD TODAY.

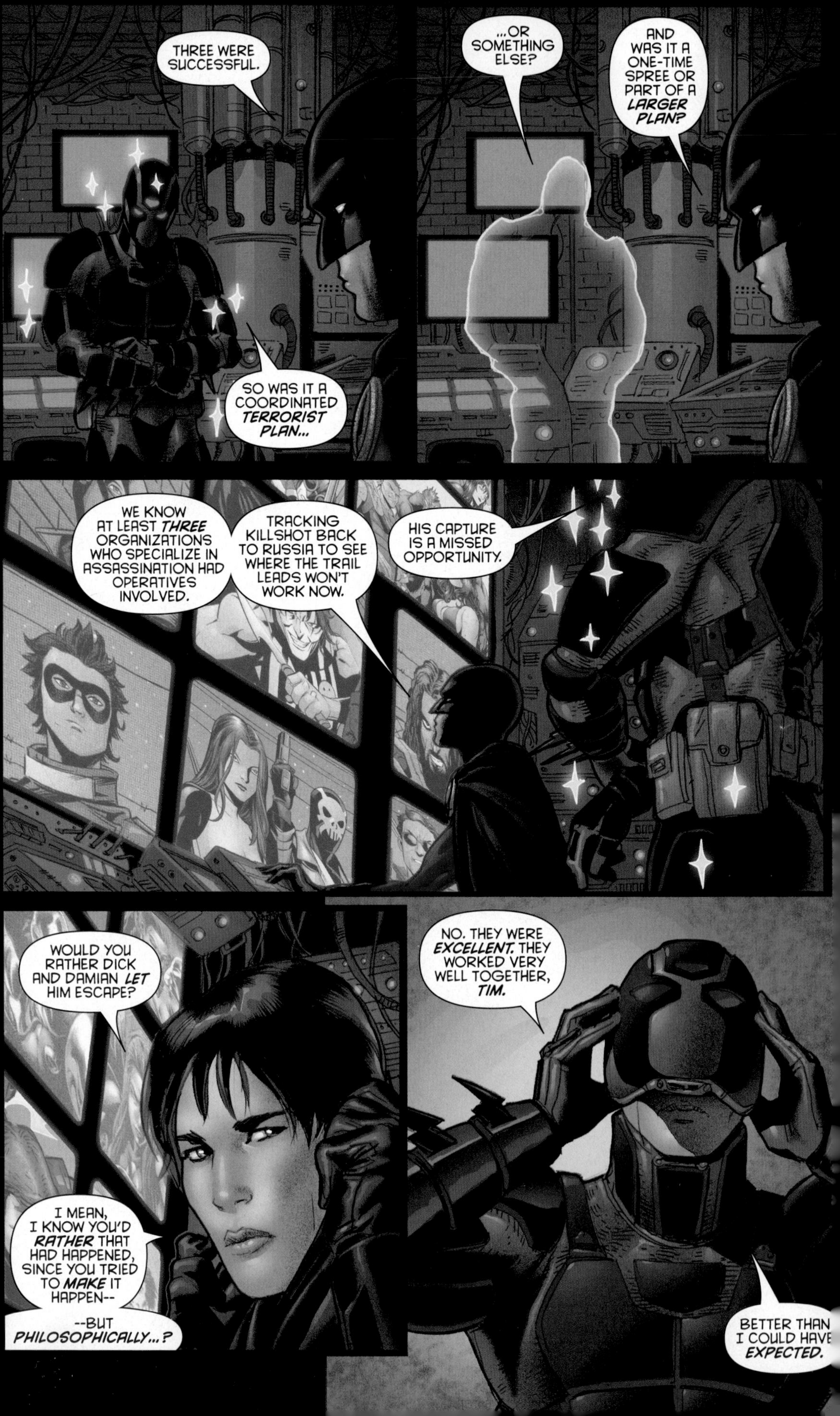
THREE WERE SUCCESSFUL.
SO WAS IT A COORDINATED *TERRORIST PLAN...*
...OR SOMETHING ELSE?
AND WAS IT A ONE-TIME SPREE OR PART OF A *LARGER PLAN?*
WE KNOW AT LEAST *THREE* ORGANIZATIONS WHO SPECIALIZE IN ASSASSINATION HAD OPERATIVES INVOLVED.
TRACKING KILLSHOT BACK TO RUSSIA TO SEE WHERE THE TRAIL LEADS WON'T WORK NOW.
HIS CAPTURE IS A MISSED OPPORTUNITY.
WOULD YOU RATHER DICK AND DAMIAN *LET* HIM ESCAPE?
I MEAN, I KNOW YOU'D *RATHER* THAT HAD HAPPENED, SINCE YOU TRIED TO *MAKE* IT HAPPEN--
--BUT *PHILOSOPHICALLY...?*
NO. THEY WERE *EXCELLENT.* THEY WORKED VERY WELL TOGETHER, *TIM.*
BETTER THAN I COULD HAVE *EXPECTED.*